FORENSIC PSYCHOLOGY

FORENSIC PSYCHOLOGY

From Classroom to Courtroom

Edited by

Brent Van Dorsten

University of Colorado Health Sciences Center
Aurora, Colorado

KLUWER ACADEMIC / PLENUM PUBLISHERS
New York/Boston/Dordrecht/London/Moscow

Library of Congress Cataloging-in-Publication Data

Forensic psychology: from classroom to courtroom/edited by Brent van Dorsten.
   p.   cm.
   Includes bibliographical references and index.
   ISBN 0-306-47270-8
    1. Psychology, Forensic.–   I. Van Dorsten, Brent.

RA1148 .F558 2002
614′.1—dc21

2002028657

ISBN 0-306-47270-8

©2002 Kluwer Academic / Plenum Publishers, New York
233 Spring Street, New York, New York 10013

http://www.wkap.nl/

10 9 8 7 6 5 4 3 2 1

A C.I.P. record for this book is available from the Library of Congress

Printed in the United States of America

Contributors

Alan A. Abrams, M.D., J.D.
San Diego, CA

Stanley L. Brodsky, Ph.D.
Department of Psychology
University of Alabama, Tuscaloosa, AL

James N. Butcher, Ph.D.
Department of Psychology
University of Minnesota, Minneapolis, MN

Alicia A. Caputo, Ph.D.
Department of Psychology
University of Alabama, Tuscaloosa, AL

Mary Alice Conroy, Ph.D.
Department of Psychology
Sam Houston State University, Huntsville, TX

Marla L. Domino, Ph.D.
Department of Psychology
University of Alabama, Tuscaloosa, AL

Brian Goodyear, Ph.D.
Private Practice, Aiea, HI

Laurence B. James, Ph.D., J.D.
Ewing & Ewing, P.C., Englewood, CO

Seth C. Kalichman, Ph.D.
Department of Psychology
University of Connecticut, Storrs, CT

Richard Rogers, Ph.D., ABPP
Department of Psychology
University of North Texas, Denton, TX

David L. Shapiro, Ph.D.
Center for Psychological Studies
Nova SE University, Ft. Lauderdale, FL

Kathleen Powers Stafford, Ph.D., ABPP
Psycho-Diagnostic Clinic, Akron, OH

Philip M. Stahl, Ph.D.
Private Practice, Danville, CA

Douglas A. Umetsu, Ph.D., ABPP
Tripler Army MC, Honolulu, HI

Brent Van Dorsten, Ph.D.
Department of Rehabilitation Medicine
University of Colorado Health Sciences, Denver, CO

Michael J. Vitacco, M.S.
Department of Psychology
University of North Texas, Denton, TX

Preface

Like many current forensic practitioners, I have never particularly aspired to be involved in legal proceedings, but have had this involvement gradually thrust upon me via my clinical assessments of patients with medical complaints. Throughout the years, my clinical activities have primarily entailed providing behavioral assessments and treatments for thousands of patients with work-related, motor vehicle accident, and the occasional physical assault injuries. Given the composition of this clinical caseload, the demand unavoidably rose for my non-expert legal opinions regarding diagnosis, prognosis, factors affecting treatment outcome, and disability issues associated with the sequelae of personal injury. As I continued to be involvement in clinical, teaching, and research activities, I began to be requested to provide forensic assessments for patients who were not familiar to me, but possessed many of the same diagnostic and prognostic issues. My role as an independent psychological evaluator frequently involved cases in which a person's verbal complaints and clinical presentation of disability were considered greatly in excess their physical findings, and suspicions of intentional production of symptoms for an identifiable goal were inevitably raised. Interestingly, other cases involved individual's who displayed generally normal patterns of physical and emotional recovery, yet were still perceived as "exaggerators" or "malingerers" by others. These brief scenarios exemplify a sample of the challenges routinely faced by forensic examiners. The gradual incorporation of my particular clinical expertise within the forensic arena was made possible by the thorough clinical psychology training I was fortunate to receive from my mentors at West Virginia University and the University of Mississippi Medical Center. This scientist-practitioner model training allowed me to enter the realm of expert witness testimony from an empirical perspective, supplemented by considerable self-education via readings, professional continuing education, and persistent involvement with teaching and research activities. I now sometimes consider myself more an "academic clinician" than a forensic specialist. For today's practitioners and students who desire instruction in forensic psychology, many professional educational opportunities, specialized training seminars, and formal academic training programs exist. Further, multiple national organizations, with accompanying scientific journals, have been formed to facilitate professional communication, and to stimulate research in the applications of psychology in law.

The proliferating interest in forensic psychology suggests that this field is likely to continue to expand and play an increasingly integral part of psychology's future. The steady development of reliable and valid assessment methods, and a maturing literature base have added to the value of psychological testimony. Psychologists have become central investigators in many areas of both criminal and civil law. Experienced forensic psychologists accept the significant responsibility of maintaining professional impartiality, and must avoid the tendency of others to equate "expert" with "she or he who can knows the answer to all the questions." In fact, the more knowledgeable some become in a specialized area, and the more aware they become of the limitations in the existing scientific methods and literature base, the more they might resist the label of "expert." It is perhaps their healthy respect for the yet unconfirmed knowledge that increases their value in the forensic field. Repeated necessity should make us comfortable with admitting what we do not know. Forensic psychology is a multidisciplinary venture, and maintaining a contemporary "expert-level" grasp of the professional literature in more than one area of specialization is a very daunting task. No single professional could be expected to adequately maintain expert knowledge of all areas, and it is for this reason that no single author could authoritatively report on all of the various areas addressed in this book. A multidisciplinary venture calls for multidisciplinary collaboration, as is reflected by the various Ph.D., M.D., and J.D. credentials of the authorship group.

Over the past decade, several books addressing the interaction between psychology and law have been written. This book is intended to expand upon the available literature by providing empirically supported insights regarding the current challenges faced by forensic psychologists. The chapters identify reasonable limitations of the current forensic data, and provide practical recommendations and caveats for those seeking to pursue practice in any of the specialty areas. The list of contributing authors is most impressive in terms of national and international reputation and, in fact, several have authored top selling books in their respective fields. It is hoped that this book will launch new insights and create new questions to stir the development of forensic psychology. It is apparent that no book can be fully inclusive of all specialty areas of forensic psychology, and there is no specific intent for any particular areas that have not been included in this effort.

Acknowledgements

I wish to express my thanks to my colleagues in the Department of Rehabilitation Medicine for their support and encouragement throughout the production of this book. I am specifically indebted to Jamie Santistevan, Vy Malcik, and Erin Parks whose professionalism and technical expertise have been invaluable, and allowed me to complete a project that would have been otherwise impossible.

I would also like to offer my heartfelt thanks to an unrivaled group of nationally and internationally known contributing authors. At project end, I remain in awe of your professional commitment and accomplishments, as do your peers. Sincere thanks for your generous sharing.

To my wonderful family and friends, I thank you for your love, friendship and encouragement to achieve things beyond what I might have had the courage to attempt. Thank you for your lessons of humility in success, objectivity to distinguish between failing and being a failure, and of the importance of maintaining an identity and zest for life well away from one's work.

To my wife Susie with whom I have the privilege of sharing a wonderful life. Thank you for your patience and support when my projects take away from our time together. You grace me with your presence, brighten my every day, and invariably make me a better person. My undying love and gratitude.

And finally, to the loving memory of my brother and best friend, Dr. Lee Van Dorsten, whose passion for learning and intellectual sharing has inspired me to pursue dreams which might have gone unfulfilled. His fire will burn within me until I finally rest.

Brent Van Dorsten

Denver, Colorado

Contents

Chapter 1

Forensic Psychology
Decades of Progress and Controversy

Brent Van Dorsten, Ph.D.
Department of Rehabilitation Medicine, University of Colorado Health Sciences Center, Denver, CO

1.   INTRODUCTION

Public awareness of psychological contributions in forensic affairs has greatly expanded in the past several years. From the release of Thomas Harris' *Silence of the Lambs* (1989), to John Douglas and Mark Olshaker's *Mind Hunter* (1995) and *Journey Into Darkness* (1997), the term "forensic" has taken on an exciting and dramatic aura of a "who-done-it," and the intricacies of criminal behavioral profiling. Public viewing of several outlandish "celebrity" criminal trials has further popularized the notion that it can be readily determined as to whether a given individual meets a certain "behavioral profile," or was in a given "frame of mind" at the time an event occurred. The public's voracious interest in the incredible capacity of certain forensic disciplines to "recreate" a given chain of events, often utilizing only the most minute pieces of evidence, has led to the current production of several popular television series featuring forensic investigation. However, this popularity has not come without cost, as most emerging disciplines in science quickly fall under close professional scrutiny. Many authors have expressed outrage at the apparent willingness of some forensic "experts" to provide projective testimony on topics that are, at best, empirically under-developed, and at worst, ripe for self-aggrandizing speculation (Bugliosi, 1996; Dawes, 1994; Hagan, 1997). As such, it seems fair to suggest that the remarkable technological advances observed in forensic medicine, pathology, and law enforcement have not been paralleled by similar advances in the field of forensic psychology. Nonetheless, the field of forensic psychology continues steady development as the specialized chapters in this book will reveal.

Mental health testimony in court has long been controversial in part due to the inherent limitations in the social sciences to specifically define, label, and predict human behavior. Many excellent works authored by mental health and law specialists have cautioned practitioners to maintain objectivity in assessments, remain within the bounds of scientific findings in reports and testimony, and to openly acknowledge the limitations of the social sciences (Ewing, 1985; Hess & Weiner, 1999; Melton, Petrila, Poythress, & Slobogin, 1997). These reasonable cautions form a solid foundation upon which a science can maintain its integrity while its database matures. The involvement of psychologists in forensic activities might appear less dramatic than the circumstances above, yet their input does not pale in importance considering the potential human impact. Psychologists and other mental health professionals frequently provide testimony upon which courts render decisions on critical issues including whether someone will be incarcerated or set free, whether parents may continue to house and raise children, or whether a given individual will be liable for compensating the injuries of another. This testimony is most commonly based upon a necessarily finite set of interactions with the individual in question, and upon a compilation of multiple sources of information. A common dictionary definition of the term "forensic" identifies these issues as "belonging to courts of law; used in courts or legal proceedings; or pertaining to or fitted for legal or public argumentation." (Webster's New Universal Unabridged Dictionary, 2nd Edition, 1983, pp. 718). Thus by definition, forensic examinations are conducted for the specific purpose of formulating a scientific opinion which will assist the trier of fact (i.e., judge or jury) in rendering a final decision. Along with the sense of recognition that many may feel when chosen to provide expert witness evaluation and testimony, comes a significant responsibility to maintain scientific rigor and provide the most objective opinion possible. In this book, several chapters are devoted to the specialized skills required of forensic experts, and the specialized guidelines under which these experts work. Additional chapters investigate several forensic areas in which psychologists are making important contributions including neuropsychology, civil commitment, sexual offenses, child abuse, child custody, competency to stand trial, civil commitment and personal injury.

2. HISTORY

The remarkable resurgence of popularity in the forensic sciences does not obscure the fact that psychological testimony in courts has a long and contentious history. In an impressively comprehensive review of the history of psychological involvement in legal settings, Bartol & Bartol (1997) suggest that field of forensic psychology dawned with research on issues related to testimony in the early twentieth century. This topic typifies the challenges of applying psychological research in legal matters as the specification of factors affecting testimony remains controversial after decades of further investigation. These authors identified other historical areas of psychological involvement in law including correctional and criminal psychology. During the early 1900's, while psychological researchers contributed to our understanding of human behavior, psychologists were not accepted as experts for the purpose of expert testimony. An American psychologist was first admitted to testify as an expert in 1921 (*State v. Driver*, 1921; cited from Johnson, Schopp, & Shigaki, 2000). While the psychologist was admitted as an expert on the topic of juvenile delinquency in this case, the court rejected his testimony since his conclusions were based upon psychological testing data which the court deemed insufficient to reliably detect deception. As such, although a non-physician had been admitted as an expert witness in court, the methods of psychological science were determined insufficient to assist the trier of fact at that time. This complex issue of lie detection in the courts contributed to a refined definition of expert testimony in the case of *Frye v. United States* (1923; cited from Hess, 1999). In *Frye*, the court held that in considering the limitations of any scientific discipline, an expert must formulate opinions on standards which were sufficiently established to have gained "general acceptance" in one's specific professional field. This *Frye* standard remained as the guiding criteria for years thereafter.

A decided preference for physician over non-physician experts dominated the witness selection process for decades in the early 1900's. By the 1940's and 50's, several court rulings challenged the subjective standard for an expert witness as having a medical degree, and found that psychologists could be recognized as experts to testify regarding select mental conditions and mental "responsibility" (Bartol and Bartol, 1997). Psychiatric groups organized opposition to these rulings, stating that only medical professionals should be allowed as experts since sanity was conceptualized as a disease. In 1962, the District of Columbia Court of Appeals offered a conditional, yet influential ruling that a lower court had erred in excluding psychological testimony and that psychologists could qualify as expert witnesses in cases regarding criminal responsibility (*Jenkins v. United States*, 1962). The *Jenkins* case, with its ruling that a specific title or type of training did not automatically include or exclude one from being admitted as an expert, profoundly increased the utilization of psychologists as experts in both civil and criminal cases. Specifically, the *Jenkins* ruling offered that a psychologist could be admitted as an expert to the extent that they possessed knowledge of a certain issue in excess of that which a layperson might possess, and that this knowledge would *probably* aid the trier of fact in making a determination.

In the years following the *Jenkins* ruling, the Federal Rules of Evidence (FRE, 1975) were legislated and many state courts have adopted these rules to date. In short, five primary Federal Rules of Evidence govern the admissibility and standards of expert testimony. While Rule 701 generally limits the testimony of laypersons to the description of events directly observed, Rules 702-706 are those which govern the admissibility of expert testimony. A thorough discussion of the intricacies of each of the legal rulings which have shaped the history of expert testimony in the United States is certainly beyond the scope of this chapter, but brief mention of selected portions will be attempted here. Comprehensive discussions are available by Brodsky in Chapter Two of this book, Hess (1999), and Melton, Petrilla, Poythress, & Slobogin (1997).

The most visible of the Federal Rules of Evidence is 702 which established the responsibility of the judge to serve as gatekeeper regarding the admissibility of expert testimony. Under Rule 702, a court may admit an expert's testimony to the extent that it is deemed that this expert may assist the trier of fact to understand the relevant aspects of scientific information. The individual may be qualified as an expert based upon specialized degrees or training, experience or other specific knowledge. Rules 703 and 704 address the bases upon which experts are expected to form their testimony and the circumstance of experts providing testimony on ultimate issue, and Rule 705 is that which suggests that experts might be required (typically upon cross-examination) to disclose the specific facts or data upon which their opinions are founded. Finally, Rule 706 allows the court to appoint its own experts if deemed necessary.

Loh (1981) reported that professional interest and forensic-related research increased ten-fold from the 1960's to mid-1970's, and the liberation of courts to admit different professions to provide expert testimony has been accompanied by continued refinement of rulings regarding the scientific nature of testimony. The *Daubert v. Merrill Dow* (1993) case provided the next highly influential federal ruling, and suggested that the basis of scientific testimony provided to assist the trier of fact must meet certain standards of both reliability and case-specific relevance. In short, this ruling specified that the methodology employed by an expert in formulating an opinion must be shown to be sufficiently valid by any of several measures including the capacity for empirical testing, peer publication, whether a reasonable error rate of the method has been established, or whether protocols exist regarding standardized implementation. While not intended to supercede the *Frye* standard, the *Daubert* rule provided somewhat more specific consideration regarding the methodology utilized by experts. Two additional recent rulings continue to exemplify what appears to be an increase in the scientific rigor desired of expert testimony by courts. In *Joiner v. United States* (1997), the Supreme Court extended the *Daubert* ruling regarding the reliability of the methods an expert might use to formulate an opinion. The *Joiner* ruling asserted that conclusions derived from the use of certain methods would need be reasonably limited in accordance with the limitations of those method. The *Joiner* ruling further concluded that even reliable and relevant scientific evidence could be excluded if it was determined that its value to the court did not exceed its potential to mislead or confuse the judge or jury. As such, these rulings have progressively required testimony to be reliably supported by established methods in an expert's given scientific community, and to have relevant bearing on the specific question at hand in order to meet the ultimate mission of increasing the court's understanding of the scientific issues. A more recent extension of the *Daubert* ruling was provided in the case of *Kumho Tire Co. v. Carmichael* (1999). In the *Kumho* case, the Supreme Court ruled that the admissibility standard which was applied to scientific testimony in the *Daubert* case was also applicable to "technical" and other types of "specialized" knowledge. Thus, "non-scientist" experts who testify (e.g., on the basis of multiple years of practical experience), can be held to the admissibility standard of reliability and acceptance by one's specific professional community as would scientifically based testimony. Stevenson (1999) concludes that challenges to the foundation of all types of expert testimony are likely to become more common, and that legal parties retaining an expert might wish to confirm the principles underlying the expert's opinions prior to seeking admission.

In summary, some of the more notable historic rulings affecting forensic psychology testimony suggest the greatest points of contention in the acceptance of psychologists as expert witnesses entailed debates over preferences for certain professional credentials and training (e.g., physician versus non-physician), and concerns regarding the limitations of social science methods. Interestingly, a brief review of the current forensic psychology literature suggests that these topics remain issues of debate. For example, a preference for physician experts was again identified in a recent survey published by Redding, Floyd, & Hawk (2001). These authors reported that a sizeable cohort of trial judges and attorneys subjectively favored psychiatrists as expert evaluators by over a two-to-one margin. Also, as per the discussions to follow, vocal skeptics remain regarding whether the methodology of social sciences and practice of clinical mental health allows sufficiently valid conclusions to be admissible in court (Dawes, 1994; Faust & Ziskin, 1988; Hagan, 1997). Many authors have cautioned that the scientific evidence base is insufficient to allow psychologists to offer testimony on ultimate court issues such as sanity, competence, or guilt (Fulero & Finkel, 1991; Melton, Petrila, Poythress, & Slobogin, 1997). Current forensic literature recommends that psychological experts have a professional and ethical responsibility to assist courts in decision-making by providing opinions based upon actuarial data summaries rather than clinical inferences whenever possible (Grove & Meehl, 1996; Otero-Zeno & O'Meara, 1991). However, available surveys of judges regarding the ultimate utility of data based testimony have not always supported this empirical inclination. For example, thirty judges were surveyed by Poythress (1981; cited from Redding, Floyd, & Hawk, 2001) regarding the most probative aspects of mental health testimony. To the chagrin of the scientist, this survey revealed that subjective clinical description and diagnosis were rated as more valuable than statistical data. Redding, Floyd, & Hawk (2001) attempted a modified replication of this study by surveying 59 trial judges, 46 prosecutors and 26 defense attorneys regarding their opinions of the utility of mental health testimony. The authors reported similar findings to Poythress in that respondents identified a clear preference for subjective testimony regarding clinical diagnosis over research or statistical data presentations.

While the legal restrictions regarding the admissibility of expert testimony may seem overly constrictive to some, they are important and may be inherently necessary to avoid the misrepresentation of psychological data. From a clinical practice perspective, most of the standards regarding admissibility of scientific testimony appear generally consistent with the standards for professional practice delineated within the current *Specialty Guidelines for Forensic Psychologists* (1991) and Ethical Principles of Psychologists authored by the American Psychological Association (APA, 1992). Among the various ethical principals for psychologists are mandates that professionals practice within their area of competence and acknowledge the limits of their expertise, attempt to prevent misuse or misinterpretation of psychological information, avoid unfounded public statements regarding psychological services, and maintain the highest scientific integrity by relying on founded scientific knowledge in formulating professional opinions. One might contend that principles similar to the legal requirements should be regularly used for most patient care activities.

Certainly, modern psychology training programs would be advised to maintain these philosophies in meeting their considerable responsibilities in training future scientists and practitioners.

The primary objective of expert witness testimony is to educate about both a specific area of science, and its relevant application to a specific circumstance. The act of being admitted as an expert witness suggests that one has professional education and specialized knowledge that will assist the trier of fact in their decision making duties beyond that which the average layperson might provide. Simply being retained by an attorney in no way qualifies one as an expert. A law firm does not retain a specific opinion, but rather a professional's ability to objectively derive one. The fundamental difference between a psychological expert and a layperson with a "common sense" notion of psychology, is the expert's ability to critically analyze the existing literature, employ valid and reliable assessment strategies, interpret a single person's data in the context of normative group data, identify the limitations in the available technology and literature, and empirically account for deviations in a given case from normative comparison data. In court, an expert is not intended to advocate for or against a plaintiff or defendant, but rather to advocate for the methods upon which they have formed their opinion, understanding that the utility of their conclusions may fall along different lines at different times. The potential influence of the retaining party on an expert's opinion emphasizes the need for professionals to remain cognizant of the factors influencing their assumptions. For example, if one's opinion is consistently applicable only to the defense or plaintiff's side of cases, it should reasonably prompt this expert to review their procedures, assumptions, and interpretations for potential bias. Otero-Zeno & O'Meara (1991) reported that even experienced expert witnesses may be subjectively influenced in their investigations by the specific side or "agency" which retains them. These authors further suggest that experts routinely engage in self-assessment of their personal impartiality, and adopt the perspective that they are working for the non-descript "court" to attempt to enhance objectivity.

3.   PSYCHOLOGY'S LIMITS AND THE LAW'S RESPONSIBILITY

Part of the controversy surrounding the application of psychological testimony in court may be attributable to the philosophical underpinnings which drive each profession. As discussed by Melton, Petrila, Poythress, &

Slobogin (1997), considerable philosophical differences exist between behavioral science and law regarding the certainty of conclusions which might be reached when combining information from multiple sources - each with inherent scientific limitations. When formulating forensic opinions, behavioral scientists are obligated to maintain the objectivity of science and stay within the bounds of empirical support, while courts have the considerable obligation of summarizing all sources of input into a firm and final dichotomous determination. Empirical behavioral findings are most commonly expressed with multiple qualifiers including limitations of the research design, limited populations for whom the findings may be applicable, and the specific conditions under which the findings may hold true to a scientific level of probability (i.e., $p > .05$). Conversely, legal proceedings are usually determined to a "reasonable degree of psychological probability" which is something analogous to "more than 50 percent of the time." Consequently, a natural conflict appears when the legal profession attempts to mold a series of logically imperfect psychological probability estimates into a succinct decision. While behavioral science ponders the conditions under which a certain result may hold true for a certain person or group, law requires that a dichotomous decision be rendered. Fair or unfair, psychological sciences have long been considered inferior to the natural sciences which possess the technology to arrive at conclusions with a definitive sense of certainty. In a widely quoted article by Faust & Ziskin (1988), a variety of factors were discussed relative to the purported inabilities of behavioral scientists to derive objective conclusions concerning human behavior, beginning with the relative paucity of reliable and valid scientific data concerning many aspects of behavior. Initial complexities relate to the relative heterogeneity of the phenomenon under observation (i.e., factors influencing the production of a specific human behavior) compounded by the heterogeneity of mental health observers themselves. For example, a wide range of emotional and behavioral responses are routinely observed in the general public following civil disaster. The specific characteristics that might predict which members of a population might develop an emotional or stress-mediated physical disorder as a result of exposure are unknown. What is known is that the majority of those exposed would be expected to show little long-term emotional damage, while a subset of others may be considerably impaired. Any of a variety of factors including extent of exposure to the crisis event, prior trauma exposure, personal relevance of the event, personal learning history, physiological predisposition, cognitive repertoire, available social resources, and intrinsic motivations might all vastly influence a given person's physical, emotional, and behavioral response to such an event. Hence, it seems inevitable that the "normal" range of human responses to any precipitating event would be difficult to succinctly predict.

The process of rendering psychological diagnoses is heavily weighted to verbal reports of symptoms. While clinical observation and professional "inference" may provide a component of diagnostic information, the majority of diagnostic criteria constitutes summations of a person's verbal description of symptoms and is not otherwise empirically verifiable. Thus considerable variation in the presentation, interpretation, and ultimate diagnosis of similar symptoms is possible. To make things more difficult, many subsets of symptoms reported by patients are not diagnostically specific and may satisfy at least a component of several different diagnoses - some with different treatments - some with different prognoses. As discussed by Van Dorsten and James in Chapter 11 of this book, this phenomenon of verbal report weighing heavily in diagnosis is more commonly shared with the medical sciences than may be apparent at first glance. To the extent that history or progression of reported symptoms is important in making diagnostic decisions (e.g., depressive episode versus history of dysthymia), we remain heavily dependent upon the individual's historical recall. Unfortunately, as is shown in many avenues of science, human beings may be notoriously unreliable observers of their own behavior; even for recent, high frequency events such as the number of minutes we exercise, what we eat, or how consistently we take prescribed medications. Finally, many emotional diagnoses can be feigned and research suggests that mental health professionals are often inaccurate in differentiating actual from feigned symptoms (Faust, Hart, Guilmette, 1988; Faust, Hart, Guilmette, & Arkes, 1988; Faust, Ziskin, & Hiers, 1991).

The inherent heterogeneity in mental health professionals begins with the decided lack of a unanimously accepted theory of human behavior that supports the accurate prediction of behavior. Multiple theories and philosophical frameworks exist - many of them conflicting - to describe and explain the properties of an identical behavior or emotion. For example, consider the relative difference in psychodynamic and cognitive-behavioral interpretations of depressive symptoms following a given event. Each viewpoint may be considered equally valid from a theoretical viewpoint, but considerable differences might appear in explanations of causation for the symptoms, treatment conceptualization and perhaps even timeframe and prognosis for symptom resolution. Faust and Ziskin (1988) concluded that the diagnostic agreement and predictive accuracy (i.e., prediction of future behavior) of mental health professionals is quite low and not markedly improved with clinical experience - in fact, perhaps not better than laypeople's impressions. Others have gone so far as to opine that the majority of psychological testimony is without merit in legal proceedings;

even constituting "total fraud" (Dawes, 1999; Hagen, 1997). As the number of psychology trainees grows, differences in training philosophies are likely to increase the divergent vantage points from which human behavior is viewed and explained.

4.   DIFFERENTIATING CLINICIAN AND FORENSIC EXPERT ROLES

Most practitioners are attracted to the mental health professions out of an intrinsic desire to help others by acknowledging and validating concerns, offering support and encouragement, and minimizing or eradicating suffering. As per the discussions by previous authors, the roles and responsibilities of clinicians and forensic examiners can differ in several important ways (Butcher & Miller, 1999; Hess, 1999; Melton, Petrilla, Poythress, & Slobogin, 1997).

Typically, clinical practitioners are inclined to accept a client's perceptions as valid, and to create an environment which provides support and empathic understanding, encourages exploration of issues, and offers professional insights to assist the client in making desired changes. Since patients most commonly self-refer for treatment, their report is considered an honest and frank representation of their symptoms and issues. The individual is presumed to be invested in symptom resolution and without specific motives for intentional misreporting. Challenging the validity of the client's perspective may not be routinely conducted. While similar intrapersonal tendencies cannot be forbidden of forensic psychologists, a clear distinction exists in that assisting the court with the provision of objective evidence takes ultimate precedence. Thus, the *court* need ultimately be perceived as the forensic examiner's "client." Courts, law firms, or insurance companies are the parties most commonly requesting evaluations, and an important departure from clinical practice is thus immediately apparent. In forensic circumstances, the individual does not choose the assessor and there is little emphasis placed upon establishing therapeutic rapport. Advocating for a patient's "best interests" is not a primary issue, having been replaced by a goal to obtain a fair and accurate compilation of information which addresses the specific legal question at hand. In only certain instances may there be an emphasis on treatment or symptom resolution, and in those cases in which treatment issues are addressed, the specific forensic assessor is nearly always excluded as a potential provider for the examinee. The unusual circumstances of the forensic assessment may naturally produce suspiciousness of the motives of the examiner, and realistic concern that one's report might somehow be used against them in a legal judgment. The simple process of reviewing the limits of confidentiality prior to beginning a forensic examination can instigate this concern, and may potentially have an adverse affect on cooperation with the assessment. Assuming this possibility, a forensic evaluator has the obligation of substantiating the validity of verbal report and assessing the capacity for deception in every case.

A forensic psychologist's objective is to assess and quantify a given person's symptoms or abilities in a larger comparative context. Many of the methods of data collection (i.e., clinical interview, record review, psychological testing) might seem similar in both clinical and forensic endeavors, yet the stringency of the standards for use of the findings differs. For example, clinical practitioners may favor exploratory projective tests for the subjective insights they might provide about an individual. Forensic examiners, however, may be expected to forgo most projective measures in favor of the normative, replicable, and relevant findings associated with standardized, objective psychometric measures. Forensic specialists accept the challenge of objective evaluation, interpretation of available data, assessing validity of responses, and checking for inconsistencies between report and behavioral performance. At times, the data obtained may seem to work against the examinee's case, but yet overall benefit the court in making a just ruling. This formidable assessment task must be accomplished as fairly to all parties as possible, and must include objective support for all methods used and opinions formed. Forensic specialists must maintain a comprehensive knowledge of the relevant literature, norms for all evaluation measures, and limits of the literature and one's expertise. While having a thorough knowledge of the literature may seem an obvious professional standard without regard for one's job, it is certainly not a given. In fact, Dawes (1994) suggested that less than one third of APA members regularly read one or more scholarly journals. Comprehensive, contemporary knowledge of the existing literature is not optional for forensic examiners.

Finally, the inherently adversarial nature of court proceedings stands in sharp contrast to the supportive, respectful and cooperative environment of mental health treatment. Mental health professionals have increasingly gained professional acceptance and respect, and may be unaccustomed to the confrontational nature of legal debate. Opposing attorneys may attempt to portray a psychological expert as biased, careless, or even incompetent. Of course, this depiction is contrasted to the expert of their choice who would be deemed as caring, respected, and professional. The familiar label "hired gun" may be used in a pejorative effort to cast doubt upon an expert's credibility by insinuating that their opinion is impacted by factors outside of professional reason (e.g., money, notoriety). Further, efforts may be made to cast doubt upon an expert's credentials or training, relevant experiences, academic productivity, or methods of assessment. This level of confrontation is well beyond what a psychologist may routinely encounter in their employment, and those accepting forensic responsibilities might expect to have credentials, relevant experience, and conclusions frequently challenged.

Considering the discomfort associated with controversy, many mental health practitioners may wish to avoid any "legalization" of their psychology practice and resist any exposure to legal issues. However, this distinct separation appears increasingly difficult to maintain, as even the most resistive practitioners may find themselves episodically involved with legal issues if they provide care to individuals with issues of criminal charges, competence, child custody, abuse, or emotional or cognitive injury claims following automobile or work-related injuries. To be certain, it seems increasingly difficult for practitioners to maintain clinical caseloads composed only of patients without legal issues. Hess (1999) discussed the increasingly reciprocal effect of psychology on courts and influence of law on the practice of clinical psychology. One may aspire to avoid legal contact, yet have episodic involvement via clinical patients involved in litigation, legal applications of one's research, professional affiliations or presentations, or scientific publication. Further, many professional practice circumstances may involve specific legal mandates including the duty to act in instances of threat of self-harm or intended harm to others, employment hiring and firing issues, patient termination or abandonment, supervision of trainees, verifying validity of opinions expressed in professional lectures, and the protection of research subject confidentiality. As such, at least a modicum of understanding of the interaction of psychology and law appears warranted for contemporary mental health professionals.

5.   FUTURE GROWTH OF FORENSIC PSYCHOLOGY

Throughout this chapter, the increasing interaction of psychological practice and law has been discussed. Whether by desire or necessity, mental health professionals and students alike are increasingly seeking forensic training. Individuals wishing to add or transition areas of clinical expertise can pursue continuing educational opportunities, workshop training, collegial supervision, and selected readings to enhance their knowledge of forensic activities. Others are pursuing formal degree training in any of a variety of academic training programs now available in the United States. The various types of formal academic training formats include combined JD/PhD programs, PhD programs with specialized program emphasis in forensic examination, and specialty master's degree programs such as master's in legal studies (MLS). As with most doctoral training, one may acquire additional concentrated exposure to forensic work in either pre-doctoral or post-doctoral internships. Each type of academic training format possesses inherent benefits and disadvantages included costs, length of training, relative professional autonomy, and level of entry into the work force. For example, the most extensive of the available training models might be the joint JD/PhD programs which essentially require students to enroll for both law school and graduate psychology courses, supplemented in advanced training years with supervised teaching, research, and practicum activities. However, Melton, Huss, & Tomkins (1999) suggest that thorough integration of the two degrees is difficult and that entry into professional employment may be more challenging than expected. Specifically, the diversity offered by the training format in combined programs may necessarily sacrifice some of the rigorous fundamental training of either discipline independently. As such, joint program graduates may be considered by some to be dual-discipline "generalists" rather than "specialists" in either. These authors suggest that joint degree graduates often must prioritize one portion of their combined training in which to enter the work force and establish solid professional credentials. The act of concurrently establishing oneself as a promising professional in both law and academic/forensic psychology may seem nearly impossible.

Programs which offer the PhD or PsyD degree with specialized emphasis in forensic work may sacrifice much of the law instruction of a combined program, but offer increased training in the application of forensic psychology skills in a clinical or research setting. A considerable time investment is again required, and this training may again be supplemented with pre- or post-doctoral work targeted to the interaction of law and psychology. Other professionals may elect to pursue specialized master's training, such as the master's in legal studies, to increase their abilities to apply specialized knowledge in their field of practice. Accepting the advantages and disadvantages of each type of training format, matching the type of training to one's professional goal for application need be a deciding factor. Attempts to standardize a core curriculum for forensic psychology training remain in their infancy. No definitive curriculum has been established, but published recommendations from the Villanova conference addressing psychology and law training included several different training models that programs could adopt to adequately meet professional consensus standards for forensic psychology training (Bersoff, Goodman-Delahunty, Gisso, Hans, Poythress, & Roesch, 1997). Continuing education opportunities are available to interested practitioners via a variety of advanced professional workshops at professional meetings and national training seminars. To adequately function in the field of forensic psychology, it is not required that psychologists become "junior attorneys," much as it is not necessary for psychologists to become physicians to make meaningful contributions in the rapidly expanding field of behavioral medicine. In fact, maintaining some academic autonomy may allow differing professions to make unique contributions to this multi-disciplinary endeavor. Without doubt, a forensic psychology expert must be a competently trained psychologist, with a working knowledge of a court's goals and responsibilities so that they might provide useful testimony to assist the trier of fact.

A cursory review of professional organization websites reveals several university based forensic psychology training programs. Several professional organizations have been established specifically to increase professional dialogue regarding forensic interests and activities, and other organizations now offer specialized sub-divisions to provide a forum for forensic psychology interactions. For example, the American Psychological Association (APA) Division 41 Psychology and Law Society currently boasts over 2,000 members, and the American College of Forensic Examiners (ACFE) lists 15,000 total members across several professional divisions including forensic psychology, medicine, nursing, law enforcement, engineering, accounting, and crisis intervention to name a few. The largest single division of the ACFE is the Board of Psychology Specialties, which is further divided into the multiple sub-specializations in which psychologists provide expert testimony. Finally, the American Board of Forensic Psychology provides certification in multiple psychology and law sub-specialized areas. This growth of training programs and professional forensic organizations in the United States over the past two decades has been matched with growing interest in Europe (Blackburn, 1996) and Australia. In fact, a sample of this year's international professional meetings include the 11th European Conference on Psychology and Law, the first Australian Psychological Society Forensic Psychology Conference, and the 22nd Meeting of the Australian and New Zealand Association of Psychiatry, Psychology, and Law. Consonant with the growth of professional organizations, the number of professional journals publishing relevant clinical, scientific and professional practice issues in the area of forensic psychology has expanded. A mere sample of available specialized journals discussing both criminal and civil involvement of psychologists includes *The Forensic Examiner, Law and Human Behavior, Behavioral Science and the*

Law, Law and Psychology Review, Psychology, Crime, and Law, Legal and Criminological Psychology, Psychiatry, Psychology and Law, and The Australian Journal of Forensic Psychology.

The involvement of psychological practitioners in court has a complicated and controversial history, and while growth has occurred slowly, the momentum in forensic psychology interest is unlikely to be blunted. This field must necessarily continue efforts to refine academic training standards so that those professionals in this specialized area have sufficient legal knowledge to provide a targeted, objective, and ethical scientific service to the public and the courts. The ultimate responsibility of improving the application of psychological sciences to any novel circumstance remains with the individual practitioners and scientists who strive to refine the validity of assessment measures, and maintain modesty in their utilization of current findings until the existing database may grow.

6.   REFERENCES

American Psychological Association (1992, December). Ethical Principle of Psychologists and Code of Conduct, *American Psychologist, 47*, 1597-1611.

Bartol, C.R., & Bartol, A.M. (1999). History of forensic psychology. In A.K. Hess & I.B. Weiner, (Eds.), *Handbook of Forensic Psychology*, 3-23.

Bersoff, D.N., Goodman-Delahunty, J., Gisso, T., Hans, V.P., Poythress, N.G. & Roesch, R.G. (1997). Training in law and psychology: Models from the Villanova conference. *American Psychologist, 52,* 1301-1310.

Blackburn, R. (1996). What *is* forensic psychology? *Legal and Criminological Psychology*, 1, 3-16.

Bugliosi, V. (1996). *Outrage: The Five Reasons O.J. Simpson Got Away With Murder.* Dell Publishing: New York.

Butcher, J.N. & Miller, K.B. (1999). Personality assessment in personal injury litigation. In A.K. Hess & I.B. Weiner (Eds.), *Handbook of Forensic Psychology.* John Wiley & Sons, Inc.: New York (pp. 104-126).

Daubert v. Merrell Dow Pharmaceuticals, Inc. 113 S. Ct. 2786 (1993).

Dawes, R.M. (1994). *House of Cards: Psychology and Psychotherapy Built on Myth.* The Free Press: New York.

Douglas, J., & Olshaker, M. (1997). *Journey Into Darkness.* Pocket Star Books: New York.

Douglas, J., & Olshaker, M. (1995). *Mind Hunter: Inside the FBI's Elite Serial Crime Unit.* Pocket Star Books:New York.

Ewing, C.P. (1985). *Psychology, Psychiatry, and the Law: A Clinical and Forensic Handbook.* Professional Resource Exchange, Inc.: Sarasota, FL.

Faust, D., Hart, T.J., & Guilmette, J. (1988). Pediatric malingering: The capacity of children to fake believable deficits on neuropsychological testing. *Journal of Consulting and Clinical Psychology, 56,* 578-582.

Faust, D., Hart, T.J., & Guilmette, J., & Arkes, H.R. (1988). Neuropsychologists capacity to detect adolescent malingerers. *Professional Psychology - Research and Practice, 19*, 432-438.

Faust, D. & Ziskin, J. (1988). The expert witness in psychology and psychiatry. *Science, 241*, 31-34.

Faust, D. & Ziskin, J., & Hiers J.B. (1991). *Brain Damage Claims: Coping with Neuropsychological Evidence*. Law and Psychology Press: Los Angeles.

Frye v. United State, 293 Fed. 1013 (D.C. CIR. 1923).

Fulero, S.M., & Finkel, N.J. (1991). Barring ultimate issue testimony. *Law and Human Behavior, 15*, 5, 495-507.

General Electric v. Joiner, 522 U.S. 136 (1997).

Grove, W.M., & Meehl, P.E. (1996). Comparative efficiency of informal (subjective, impressionistic) and formal (mechanical, algorithmic) prediction procedures: The clinical-statistical controversy. *Psychology, Public Policy, and Law, 2*, 293-323.

Hagan, M.A. (1997). *Whores of the Court: The Fraud of Psychiatric Testimony and the Rape of American Justice*. HarperCollins Publishers, Inc.: New York.

Harris, T. (1989). *The Silence of the Lambs*. St. Martin's Press: New York.

Hess, A.K. (1999) Serving as an expert witness. In A.K. Hess & I.B. Weiner (Eds.), *Handbook of Forensic Psychology*. John Wiley & Sons, Inc.: New York (pp.521-555).

Hess, A.K. (1999) Defining forensic psychology. In A.K. Hess & I.B. Weiner (Eds.), *Handbook of Forensic Psychology*. John Wiley & Sons, Inc.: New York (pp.521-555).

Hess A.K., & Weiner, I.B. (1999). *The Handbook of Forensic Psychology* (2nd ed.). John Wiley & Sons, Inc.: New York.

Jenkins v United States, 113 U.S. App. D.C. 300, 307F.2d 637 (1962).

Johnson, B., Schopp, L.H., & Shigaki, C.L. (2000). Forensic psychological evaluation. In R.G. Frank & Elliott, T.R. (Eds.), *Handbook of Rehabilitation Psychology*. American Psychological Association: Washington DC.

Kumho Tire Co. v. Carmichael, No. 97-1709. (U.S., March 23, 1999).

Loh, W.D. (1981). Perspectives on psychology and law. *Journal of Applied Social Psychology, 11*, 314-355.

Melton, G. B., Huss, M.T. & Tomkins, A.J. (1997). Training in forensic psychology and the law. In A.K. Hess & I.B. Weiner (Eds.), *Handbook of Forensic Psychology*. John Wiley & Sons, Inc.: New York (pp. 700-720).

Melton, G.B., Petrilla, J., Poythress, N.G., & Slobogin, C. (1997). Law and the mental health professions: An uneasy alliance. *Psychological Evaluations for the Courts*. The Guilford Press: New York. (pp.3-25).

Ogloff, J.R.P., Tomkins, A.J., & Bersoff, D.N. (1996). Education and training in psychology and law/criminal justice. *Criminal Justice and Behavior, 23*, 200-235.

Otero-Zeno, T.M. & O'Meara, D.P. (1991). Mental injury litigation: The roles of the lawyer and the psychologist. *Medical Psychotherapy, 4*, 17-26.

Redding, R.E., Floyd, M.Y., & Hawk, G.L. (2001). What judges and lawyers think about the testimony of mental health experts: A survey of the courts and bar. *Behavioral Sciences and the Law, 19*, 583-594.

Specialty Guidelines for Forensic Psychologists (1991). *Law and Human Behavior, 15*, 6, 655-665.

Webster's New Universal Unabridged Dictionary (2nd ed.). (1983). New York: Simon & Schuster, Inc.

Stevenson, E.E. (1999). Admissibility of expert testimony after *Kumho tire*. *The Colorado Lawyer, 28, 7*, 73-76.

Chapter 2

The Mental Health Professional in Court
Legal Issues, Research Foundations, and Effective Testimony

Stanley L. Brodsky, Ph.D., Alicia A. Caputo, Ph.D., and Marla L. Domino, Ph.D.
The University of Alabama, Tuscaloosa, AL

1.   INTRODUCTION

Along with graduate school qualification examinations, suicidal clients, and the occasional malpractice litigation, testifying in court may be among the most anxiety arousing events in the professional lives of mental health workers. The several factors that contribute to the concerns associated with testifying in court may be grouped under the general headings of context, exposure, and challenge.

First, let us address context. Most psychological professionals conduct their business in a cooperative and congenial setting. In these cooperative settings, the professionals are identified as helpers, their expertise is respected and unquestioned, and the target clients are generally appreciative and receptive. In the court setting, each of these elements is different. The opposing sides are competitive, seeking to win at the expense of the other side. Expertise is not automatically treated with respect. The target persons are not the recipients of helping services.

The second issue is exposure. Most mental health work is conducted in relatively protected and private settings. Psychological services are offered either one-to-one or in small groups, and usually behind closed doors. The work of some professionals may be subject to review or supervision, but by congenial and constructive colleagues, for whom the feedback is intended to improve performance. In the court setting, the professional is, literally,

17

exposed to view and to criticism. Greenberg (1997) has quipped that "when you are on the stand, you stand alone."

The third difference is in challenge. The courtroom context is often unfamiliar, the professional may feel exposed as a result, expert testimony can be a challenging role with unsettling consequences. In contested trials, hearings, or depositions, serious challenges may be directed toward the professionals' training, knowledge, methodology, results, and opinions.

In this chapter, we begin with the legal foundations on which testimony rests. It is a compelling professional responsibility to know the legal context in which ones testimony is seated. Next we move to research on effectiveness of court testimony. The foundations are modest, indeed, but they do present results mostly from court and trial simulation studies that address witness credibility. Finally, we conclude with practical considerations for the expert witness. We start with legal aspects.

2.   DAUBERT AND RULES OF EVIDENCE GOVERNING EXPERT TESTIMONY

Prior to the establishment of the Federal Rules of Evidence, courts looked to the *Frye* test (*Frye v. United States*, 54 App. D. C. 46, 47, 293 F. 1013, 1014) to determine the admissibility and utility of expert testimony. The test was "general acceptance" which required expert scientific evidence to be based on methodology accepted in the expert's professional field: "...the thing from which the deduction is made must be sufficiently established to have gained general acceptance in the particular field in which it belongs"

In the 1993 case of *Daubert v. Merrell Dow Pharmaceuticals, Inc.*, 509 U.S. 579, the admissibility of expert testimony was revisited. Evidence presented by eight medical experts was ruled inadmissible because the experts' methodology was not "generally accepted" within the medical field and the methodology was not stringently peer-reviewed. The Supreme Court asserted that, under Rule 402, the Federal Rules of Evidence (FRE) superceded *Frye* standards and that *Frye* and *Daubert* together are best utilized more as guidelines within the context of the FRE, rather than as independent determinants of admissibility. Under the *Daubert* test, expert testimony should be assessed via the "reliability" standard (that the information presented be grounded in scientific standards and methodology over time) and a "relevancy" standard (that the testimony offered be relevant to the legal issues at hand and assist the trier of fact in resolving the legal question). Trial judges should make this assessment not on the basis of the conclusions drawn, but rather on the "soundness" of the data and the methodology.

In a special 1999 issue of *Psychology, Public Policy, and Law*, experts in psychology and law commented on the impact of *Daubert* on social science evidence and expert testimony. Shuman and Sales (1999), concluded that *Daubert* has had little quantifiable influence on the type of testimony admitted into court. Nevertheless, *Daubert* has highlighted concerns about judges' mastery of scientific methodology and resulting data, about judges' ability to determine the reliability and validity of testimony, about expert testimony based on clinical experience, about experts who formulate legal conclusions, and about experts who extend their testimony beyond their professional competency. The definition of reliability and validity not only varies between the legal and social science fields, but within the social sciences themselves (Saxe & Ben-Shakhar, 1999). It has been argued that social scientists select research and published articles that support their point of view, much like the adversarial nature of criminal trials. Because theories are not considered proof and may only be endorsed or discounted, the court must assess, instead, the soundness of the empirical testimony presented (Saxe & Ben-Shakhar, 1999).

In part because it is a guideline and not a mandate, *Daubert* has been applied inconsistently to different forms of testimony and social scientific evidence (Shuman & Sales, 1999). Strictly speaking, the criteria outlined in *Daubert* should prohibit any expert clinical or forensic testimony not based on sound scientific methodology (Grove & Barden, 1999; Slobogin, 1999). However, to perform the function that the law desires, *Daubert* must flexibly allow testimony that is impossible to demonstrate "scientifically," such as an offender's mental status during a previous event (Slobogin, 1999).

It has been suggested that *Daubert's* emphasis on scientifically-based data can prevent experts from utilizing "junk" science, and that, in turn, social science experts should refuse to offer testimony that falls short of the *Daubert* standard (Grove & Barden, 1999). Tenopyr (1999), notes these difficulties; no standard batteries of tests exist to assess any given diagnosis or circumstance, that psychometric properties are not available for many tests, and those available are often interpreted subjectively. Most research assessing the effectiveness and utility of social scientific surveys is conducted within a political-cultural milieu. Furthermore statistical power and effect size in empirical endeavors have been neglected. This series of critiques provides reason to scrutinize further the admissibility of expert testimony from the specific perspectives of the Federal Rules of Evidence.

3.   **FEDERAL RULES OF EVIDENCE: EXPERT TESTIMONY AND OPINIONS**

Five Federal Rules of Evidence address expert testimony. They are excerpted with a commentary on each rule.

3.1   Rule 702. Testimony by Experts

If scientific, technical, or other specialized knowledge will assist the trier of fact to understand the evidence or to determine a fact in issue, a witness qualified as an expert by knowledge, skill, experience, training, or education, may testify thereto in the form of an opinion or otherwise.

The role of the expert is to assist the trier of fact in understanding the legally relevant aspects of the case within that expert's realm of expertise. The admissibility of an expert's testimony is a judgment made by the court and is not mandated by or restricted to academic or educational credentials. In conjunction with lists of witnesses and exhibits, experts' opinions to be presented at trial must be revealed at or before the time of disclosure, which is typically 30 days or more before the trial date.

The expert must be able to substantiate her/his methodology through published corroborations by other experts within the field or scientific community. Like *Daubert*, Rule 702 departs from the *Frye* "generally accepted" standard and involves a more restrictive score of permissible expert testimony. The admissibility of expert testimony is determined by the trial judge who acts as a gatekeeper as set forth in *Daubert*.

Rule 702 and *Daubert* work hand-in-hand. *Daubert* suggested that judges assess the reliability of expert testimony on the basis of four factors: testability of the theory on which the data or methodology is based, the extent of peer review of the theory, error rates of the methodology, and acceptability within the relevant field. Rule 702 does not exclude opinions based in relevant and professional knowledge and experience. In addition, the criteria for assessing admissibility generalizes to all testimony offered by an expert (e.g., "technical" and "other specialized" knowledge), as determined in *Kumho Tire Co., Ltd., v. Carmichael* (1999); that is, to be admissible, expert testimony must address the specific legal issue at hand.

The gatekeeping guidelines of the trial judge are not legally required and should be applied on a case-by-case basis; moreover, the judge should assess the reliability of expertise through "reasonable" standards.

3.2 Rule 703. Bases of Opinion Testimony by Experts

The facts or data in the particular case upon which an expert bases an opinion or inference may be those perceived by or made known to the expert at or before the hearing. If of a type reasonably relied upon by experts in the particular field in forming opinions or inferences upon the subject, the facts or data need not be admissible in evidence.

The phrase "reasonably relied upon" is central to Rule 703. This rule departs from *Frye* standards of "general acceptability" to data "reasonably" utilized by similar experts in the field. The focus is on the "reasonability" of testimony within the specific legal issue at trial, as opposed to determining whether or not the technique or information presented is widely practiced and acknowledged. Rule 703 has also been interpreted to allow an explanation of the information presented by the expert; courts are permitted to allow data not independently admissible under, for example, hearsay rules, and social scientists (e.g., Melton et al., 1997), have cautioned against offering testimony that cannot be explained to the trier of fact.

According to Rule 703, experts may derive information from three sources: 1) observation of the evaluee, 2) "presentation at the trial," (e.g., via hypothetical questioning or basing expert opinion on trial testimony that establishes case facts), or 3) outside sources (e.g., published journal articles, mental health records, testing results). Melton et al. (1997), suggest that forensic testimony should be based on a variety of information sources. Clinicians should be thoroughly prepared to defend in court the use of such sources and to consult closely with the attorney as to the laws governing the admissibility of such evidence.

Expert testimony is, of course, open to scrutiny by the opposing side and challenges to presented testimony may be based not only on guidelines offered in the FRE and *Daubert*, but also on possible violations of the defendant's Fifth Amendment rights, illegal seizure of evidence, inapplicability of the results of current psychological testing to past actions or mental states, or inadmissibility of "hearsay" evidence (Melton et al., 1997). As Lubet (1998), has indicated, expert testimony may utilize inadmissible evidence but whether or not this evidence may be verbally recounted during a trial is questionable.

3.3   Rule 704. Opinion on Ultimate Issue

(a) Except as provided in subdivision (b), testimony in the form of an opinion or inference otherwise admissible is not objectionable because it embraces an ultimate issue to be decided by the trier of act.

(b) No expert witness testifying with respect to the mental state or condition of a defendant in a criminal case may state an opinion or inference as to whether the defendant did or did not have the mental state or condition constituting an element of the crime charged or of a defense thereto. Such ultimate issues are matters for the trier of fact alone.

Rule 704 asserts that experts are prohibited from offering ultimate legal conclusions regarding the mental status of an offender at the time of the offense, a task assigned to the court or jury. Other expert opinions that address an ultimate issue are allowed.

Some observers contend that the testimony of mental health professionals should provide data useful to the trier of fact but should never offer any conclusions or opinions as to the ultimate legal issue. However, clinicians' resistance to occasional instructions from the court to answer the ultimate legal issue may be the cause of tension: mental health professionals often avoid offering such a conclusive statement as legal actors press for exactly that (Brodsky, 1999). In contrast to Rule 704, some legislative statutes allow or demand the clinician to render an opinion on ultimate legal issues.

Court pressures to offer opinions on ultimate legal issues often synergize with a mental health professional's desire to influence the outcome. But this is not the only problem for clinical testimony. Mental health professionals sometimes offer testimony beyond their boundaries and level of expertise. Clinicians should testify only to issues of mental health that will impact the immediate legal issue and to state the limits of their expertise.

3.4   Rule 705. Disclosure of Facts or Data Underlying
Expert Opinion

The expert may testify in terms of opinion or inference and give reasons therefore without first testifying to the underlying facts or data, unless the court requires otherwise.   The expert may in any event be required to disclose the underlying facts or data on cross-examination.

Unless asked to explain, experts may offer opinions or testimony without first explaining the information base from which these opinions came. Rule 705 puts the responsibility on the opposing attorney during cross-examination of uncovering essential facts or data on which the expert's opinion has been based. This rule stems from a desire to limit hypothetical questions to experts, which were historically used to subvert trial protocol by advocating for support of an argument, expending excessive court time, and allowing for summation of trial arguments part way through trial proceedings.

3.5   Rule 706. Court Appointed Experts

The court may on its own motion, or on the motion of any party, enter an order to show cause why expert witnesses should not be appointed, and may request the parties to submit nominations. The court may appoint any expert witnesses agreed upon by the parties, and may appoint expert witnesses of its own selection. The court shall not appoint an expert witness unless the witness consents to act... A witness so appointed shall advise the parties of the witness' findings, if any; the witness' deposition may be taken by any party; and the witness may be called to testify by the court or any party. The witness shall be subject to cross-examinations by each party, including a party calling the witness.

The court, on its own accord or on motion from either party (defense or prosecution), may offer an opinion as to why an expert witness should not be appointed. The court may appoint its own expert witness, with or without input from either party, but, of course, the witness has to agree. Although the use of court-appointed experts is infrequent, it is, nonetheless, a viable practice. The court may exercise its right to withhold or disclose to the jury that the expert was court-appointed. The experts must share their findings with both parties, and either party (or the court) can call the witness to testify. Both parties may take the expert's deposition, and both parties will have the opportunity to cross-examine the expert, should the expert be called to testify.

4.   RESEARCH INTO EXPERT TESTIMONY

The proper role of expert witness testimony has been characterized as primarily educative in nature (Kovera, Gresham, Borgida, Gray, & Regan, 1997; Miller & Allen, 1998). Indeed, the purpose of expert testimony is to assist the fact finder in the pursuit of more valid conclusions than would be possible in the absence of such testimony (Kovera et al., 1997). For example, experts have been useful at explaining the factors that influence accuracy of eyewitness identification (Cutler, Dexter, & Penrod, 1989; Cutler, Penrod, & Dexter, 1989); such explanations have increased mock jurors' understanding of how to evaluate eyewitness reports (Kovera et al, 1997).

Investigations into aspects of the efficacy of expert testimony have especially addressed the potential adversarial affiliation of the expert (Griffith, Libkuman, & Poole, 1998; Sugarman & Boney-McCoy, 1997), and the content of the testimony itself (Brekke & Borgida, 1988; Kovera et al., 1997). Verdict outcome and believability have served as typical indicators of expert testimony effectiveness.

4.1   Believability of Key Witnesses

The effect of the adversarial affiliation of the expert (that is, being called by the prosecution versus by the defense) on the believability of such key witnesses as victims and defendants has been assessed (Griffith et al., 1998; Sugarman & Boney-McCoy, 1997). Undergraduate mock jurors in one study (Griffith et al., 1998), read vignettes of a civil trial involving repressed memories of sexual abuse by an adult plaintiff's father. Subjects read one of four testimony conditions: no testimony; testimony for the plaintiff, testimony for the defense, and testimony for both parties. Results indicated that participants who read expert testimony for the plaintiff, both by itself and in conjunction with testimony for the defense, rated the plaintiff's case as stronger and the defendant as more likely to have committed the sexual abuse than participants in the no testimony condition. Furthermore, participants exposed to testimony for the plaintiff rated the defendant's case as weaker than participants in the other three conditions. Testimony for the defense did not negatively impact evidence for the plaintiff, however, as indicated by similar ratings in the plaintiff and both experts conditions.

A study of child sexual abuse testimony (Sugarman & Boney-McCoy, 1997), utilized a vignette methodology similar to that of Griffith and colleagues (1998). Undergraduate participants rated the defendant as more believable and the abuse victim as less believable when the expert testified about the fallibility of repressed memories. The testimony of a prosecution expert witness, however, did not significantly predict the believability of either defendant or victim.

Content of expert testimony and its influence on the believability of witnesses has also been addressed. Distinctions have been made between standard and concrete expert testimony (Brekke & Borgida, 1988; Kovera et al., 1997; Schuller, 1992). Standard expert testimony involves empirically based explanations of the relevant psychological issues (e.g., misconceptions regarding the behavior of rape victims), without linking the research to the case at hand. Such testimony may be thought of being provided by "pure" experts, for whom testimony is unattached to the case. Concrete expert testimony provides both the explanations and the links to the case at hand through the use of hypothetical examples. Brekke and Borgida (1988), investigated the differential credibility of a rape victim as a function of whether mock jurors were exposed to standard or concrete expert testimony regarding rape myths and the behavior of rape victims. Participants who heard concrete testimony were more likely to consider the victim credible than those who heard standard testimony.

Kovera and colleagues (1997), also investigated repetitive testimony, which involves initial standard testimony with a summary of relevant research later in the trial, in the absence of a link to the case at hand. The goal was to examine the underlying mechanisms contributing to the effectiveness of concrete testimony. Results indicated that repetitive testimony was related to increased ratings of credibility of the child witness in the mock trial of sexual abuse, whereas concrete and standard testimony had no effects. Interactions were also found between type of testimony and the degree of child witness preparedness for trial. Subjects rated the child's mother and a prosecution witness as more credible and the defendant less favorably when a prepared child witness was presented in conjunction with standard or repetitive testimony. On the other hand, more favorable ratings were found with the combination of concrete expert testimony and unprepared child witnesses. These findings support the contention that concrete testimony more successfully achieves the educative goal of expert testimony.

4.2   Verdicts

The impact of various aspects of expert testimony content on verdict decisions also has been examined. Two studies investigated the effect of an expert's affiliation on juror verdicts (Griffith et al., 1998; Sugarman & Boney-McCoy, 1997). An expert's affiliation with the plaintiffs or defense did not influence the plaintiff's monetary compensations awarded to plaintiffs in a mock civil sexual abuse trial (Griffith et al., 1998), or conviction rate in a mock criminal sexual abuse trial (Sugarman & Boney-McCoy, 1997). The same study reported a significant relation between guilty verdicts and expert testimony on repressed memories, as opposed to testimony on memories never repressed, in sexual abuse trial simulations (Sugarman & Boney-McCoy, 1997). The authors hypothesized that the presence of repressed memories may be suggestive of a more severe assault, which therefore might result in more guilty verdicts.

Relations between verdict choice and testimony type (standard, repetitive, and concrete) have also been addressed. Concrete expert testimony, in comparison to standard or an absence of testimony, was associated with harsher adjudication decisions in mock rape trials (Brekke & Borgida, 1988) and with less severe verdicts in mock domestic violence trials (Schuller, 1992).

Subsequent studies revealed that a prepared child witness presented with standard or repetitive testimony or an unprepared child witness presented with concrete testimony, led to increases in convictions in mock child sexual abuse trials (Kovera et al, 1997).

Several factors limit the generalizability of the research on expert witness effectiveness. One is the reliance on undergraduate samples, to the exclusion of other populations. A second is the use of simulated trials and case examples, as opposed to conducting research with actual jurors. Third, the most common focus of the trials has been charges of sexual offenses. Such crimes are more emotionally charged than many other types of offenses (e.g., burglary, auto theft, drug possession), and, therefore, may lead to differential efficacies of expert testimony. These limitations should be rectified in future research.

5.   CREDIBILITY OF EXPERT WITNESSES

The adversarial nature of the USA justice system renders the expert witness open to attack by opposing counsel. Indeed, this antagonistic bent is evident in the number of published works offering advice both on the most effective presentations of expert testimony (e.g., Blau, 1998; Brodsky, 1991, 1999; Melton, Petrila, Poythress, & Slobogin, 1997), and on the most effective means of discrediting that testimony (e.g., Azevedo, 1996; Ziskin, 1995).

Several factors have been hypothesized to increase the credibility of an expert witness. These factors have been reviewed at length elsewhere (Brodsky, 1991, 1999; Melton et al., 1997), and only will be listed briefly here. They include professional, conservative clothing (Blau, 1998; Melton et al., 1997); good eye contact with the jury and judge (Melton et al., 1997);

the maintenance of composure in the face of harassment by opposing attorneys (Brodsky, 1991; Melton et al., 1997); and positive narrative techniques (Brodsky, 1991; Melton et al., 1997). Several factors threaten the credibility of an expert witness in the eyes of a jury. One is the perception of expert witnesses as "bought," as "hired guns," or, more scathingly, as "whores," (Azevedo, 1996; Brodsky, 1991; Mossman, 1999). This perception arises from the fact that expert witnesses typically are paid for their testimony by one side of the adversarial system. Indeed, expert witnesses may destroy their own credibility by charging fees that are deemed "outrageous" by juries, such as occurred in the case of a medical expert who earned over $1 million in a four year span from reviewing cases and testifying on a part-time basis (Azevedo, 1996). The view of expert witnesses as "hired guns" and "whores" is so pervasive that such references even appear in case law (Mossman, 1999).

Other factors also threaten expert witness credibility. Azevedo (1996), outlined several of these factors. One is excessive time spent testifying, at the expense of time devoted to the practice of the profession in which one professes to be expert. Second, some experts are tempted to exaggerate their credentials or testify on issues about which their knowledge is marginal. These professional "stretches" render experts vulnerable to rigorous cross-examination exposing the true limits of their training and knowledge. A third factor is ignorance of the facts of the specific case about which an expert is testifying. Fourth, exposed inconsistencies between current testimony and testimony in previous cases may be damaging. A fifth threat to credibility is inconsistency between experts' testimonies and their actual professional practices, whereby they profess one practice and perform another (Azevedo, 1996). Finally, the use of unreliable or invalid scientific methods appropriately threatens credibility, as does insufficient knowledge of the methods used as a framework for the testimony (Blau,1998; Rotgers & Barrett,1996). Obviously, honesty, consistency, and professional competency are the best policies when serving as an expert witness.

6. TOWARD BEING AN EFFECTIVE WITNESS

6.1   Exceptional Levels of Preparation

If a single theme cuts across the literature about testimony, it is that the sine qua non of good testimony is exceptionally careful preparation (Brodsky, 1991, 1999; Lubet, 1999). In contrast, much of the applied work undertaken by clinical psychologists may be thought of as following the knowledge already in hand, and from which treatment or assessment comes. They rarely engage in deep and broad literature reviews, unless they are confronted with an unusual syndrome. For court testimony, the effective witness reviews the current scholarly foundations of the immediate issues and methodology. These practices are not only important, but in many jurisdictions are consistent with the demands of the law, as noted already in the FRE and Daubert criteria.

This need to prepare may be best understood by reviewing the essential questions asked of experts in court as falling into two categories:

1. What do you know?
2. How do you know what you know?
3. The latter question is often posed in ways that require a reply in terms of reliable and valid methods, standardized procedures, meaningful norms, and generalizable research in peer reviewed journals. Thus, suppose an attorney demands,
4. "Doctor, can you identify even one statistical study in one peer reviewed journal in the past five years that supports your interesting notion of young boys being able to develop appropriate gender identities when mothers are the primary parents?"
5. The witness should be in a position to cite more than one study. If the witness can state the number of subjects, the results, the authors, and the journals in which the articles appeared, the response helps to insulate the witness from further attacks on knowledge.
6. How to prepare? No one solution exists, but the common methods are to check the major search engines and databases, newly published reviews and books, to check with colleagues, and to gather information from continuing education experiences.

6.2   Anxiety About Testifying

In workshops on expert testimony, the one concern most often expressed is that unmanageable anxiety will interfere. Typical comments made by new or infrequent witnesses are they are afraid they will freeze, fearful their minds will go blank, or worried that their highly visible anxiety will be detrimental. Expert witnesses should know, first, that anxiety is normative. Even experienced experts feel butterflies in their stomachs, have episodes of diarrhea, or may be tense and shaky prior to testimony. However, there are methods for coping with such situational anxiety. They include:

1. Habituation to the courtroom milieu. Sitting in the witness box in an empty courtroom for a while allows anxiety to dissipate. Instead of being in an unfamiliar room, witnesses learn what they will see, how their voices will project, what the witness chair feels like (sometimes awkward and uncomfortable) and where to walk when called in a live trial.
2. Watching other witnesses. If the rule forbidding witnesses to watch other testimony is waived, and the rule sometimes is waived on request, the witness can see the mundane aspects of many proceedings, the style of the attorneys, and become accustomed to the trial's events.
3. Using what you know. Many mental health experts are already skilled at helping others in diminishing anxiety. Yet many witnesses fail to use the relaxation techniques they already know for themselves. Deep breathing, progressive muscle relaxation, standardized meditation, guided imagery, and other methods from the usual treatment repertoire can make a difference.

6.3   The Direct Examination as a Segue To Masterful Testimony

Most witnesses fear cross-examinations. Yet the direct examination provides a potential framework and segue to the cross-examination for easy and masterful presentation of self. The key is knowing the questions to be asked. In order for that knowledge to be gained, one has to meet with the retaining attorney, and to go over a tentative list of questions to be asked. If they are known, that opening aspect of testimony can be understood as answers are thought out articulately, and one can develop a rolling momentum of comfort and expertise.

Not all attorneys are willing to develop questions in advance -- although wise attorneys take the time and make the effort to "prepare" their witnesses.

We encourage witnesses to be insistent about having the questions written for their approval, their answers given in advance so attorneys know what the replies will be, and for the attorney and witnesses to have a clear understanding of the nature of the direct examination.

6.4   Cross-Examinations

More than any other aspect of the legal process, witnesses fear the cross-examination. We have come to think of the cross-examination as a battle for power and control between the witness and attorney, in which the battlefield is made up of a mixture of straightforward queries and responses and of professional and personal challenges, all seated within a context of adversarial process and nonverbal messages (Brodsky, 1991, 1999).

6.5   Nondefensiveness

If any single issue harms credibility of witnesses, it is the appearance of compromise of objectivity. The triers of facts scrutinize witnesses for hints of partiality. This perception of compromise arises especially when witnesses engage in defensive responding to cross examination questions. The defensiveness communicates that the witness is so committed to a point of view that he or she is unwilling to acknowledge even routine and obvious contradictory information. Good witnesses give opposing counsel what they have the right to expect: answers that may contradict the direct examination statements in some ways. However, one's opinions should always be based on the evaluation or other professional knowledge and never on court questions.

6.6   Discovery and Depositions

Experts identified prior to trial are subject to rules of "discovery," in which each side is legally obligated to share any information relevant to the legal issue (reports, documents, identities of potential witnesses, evidence). Almost all data or work products of the testifying expert are open to "discovery." Lubet (1998), suggests that experts also assist the retaining lawyer in determining the appropriate and essential documents they in turn should request for discovery. In addition, experts may be required to answer interrogatories and participate in depositions, in which questions are asked regarding credentials and content of the expert's testimony.

Testifying in depositions occupies a major role of evaluating experts in civil litigations. Considerable information that influences decisions about settlements emerges during questioning in depositions. Questions in depositions are mostly asked by opposing counsel without the leavening presence of judge and jury. Depositions, therefore, often tend to be wide-ranging, and sometimes exceptionally abrasive and intrusive.

Witnesses in depositions are obligated to report fully and accurately the nature of their credentials, bases of knowledge, information used, methodology, and results. Problems may arise when attorneys become rude or excessively personal, or demanding answers beyond the scope of the expert's opinion.

The very same reasons that attorneys can ask such questions are the reasons that witnesses can decline to answer. That is, the customary controls and rules of trial court have been supplanted by a degree of informality as the deposing attorney seeks out information. Two principles can serve to guide expert witnesses if they are confronted by demanding and insulting attorneys.

First, do not make any statements in depositions that you are not prepared to make in open court. If you have not yet formulated an opinion on some aspect of the case, say so and resolutely decline to offer an opinion. Never extrapolate further than your data allow. Do not volunteer information unless you have a good professional reason to do so.

Second, do not allow yourself to be insulted or attacked personally. Consider, for example, a case in which alcohol abuse by the defendant is an issue. Experts might be asked if they drink, if they have ever been drunk, if they have ever been falling down drunk, and whether they have ever done things while drunk that they wish they had not done. It is acceptable to respond that you are neither prepared nor willing to talk about any aspect of your alcohol use (regardless of whether you have ever had any alcoholic drinks). At this point attorneys may bluster and state that they will get the judge to order you to answer such questions. Assuming that the retaining attorney has not intervened, you should consider replying that you would indeed follow orders of the court, if the court so rules.

Similar attorney threats are bluffs that should be called. After all, many attorneys use depositions as fishing expeditions for weaknesses and as tests of how tough witnesses are likely to be in the trial. Know the governing statutory and case law in your jurisdiction about depositions, and comply with the limits of your knowledge. Beyond that, it may be up to you to set limits and boundaries of what you answer.

7.   SUMMARY

This chapter discussed the legal context and research foundations of expert testimony, as well as providing introductory practical guidelines to increase efficacy of witnesses. Expert testimony can be an unsettling and frightening experience for many clinical professionals. We advise a committed understanding of the legal roles of experts, coupled with ethical and competent professional conduct as the best pathway to constructive experiences on the stand. At its best effective delivery of findings and opinions can be professionally rewarding and personally satisfying.

8.   REFERENCES

Azevedo, D. (1996). Disarming hired guns. *Medical Economics, 73*, 174-183.

Blau, T. H. (1998). *The psychologist as expert witness* (2nd ed.). New York: John Wiley & Sons, Inc.

Brekke, N., & Borgida, E. (1988). Expert psychological testimony in rape trials: A social-cognitive analysis. *Journal of Personality and Social Psychology, 55*, 372-386.

Brodsky, S. L. (1991). *Testifying in court: Guidelines and maxims for the expert witness.* Washington, DC: American Psychological Association.

Brodsky, S. (1999). *The expert witness: More maxims and guidelines for testifying in court.* Washington, DC: American Psychological Association.

Cutler, B. L., Dexter, H. R., & Penrod, S. D. (1989). Expert testimony and jury decision making: An empirical analysis. *Behavioral Sciences and the Law, 7*, 215-225.

Cutler, B. L., Penrod, S. D., & Dexter, H. R. (1989). The eyewitness, the expert psychologist, and the jury. *Law and Human Behavior, 13*, 311-322.

Greenberg, S. A. (1997). The civil practice of forensic psychology. Seattle: American Academy of Forensic Psychology (Workshop Handout).

Griffith, J. D., Libkuman, T. M., & Poole, D. A. (1998). Repressed memories: The effects of expert testimony on mock jurors' decision making. *American Journal of Forensic Psychology, 16*, 5-23.

Grove, W., & Barden, R.C. (1999). Protecting the integrity of the legal system: The Admissibility of testimony from mental health experts under Daubert/Kumho analyses. *Psychology, Public Policy, and Law, 5*, 224-242.

Kovera, M. B., Gresham, A. W., Borgida, E., Gray, E., & Regan, P. C. (1997). Does expert psychological testimony inform or influence juror decision making? A social cognitive analysis. *Journal of Applied Psychology, 82*, 178-191.

Lubet, S. (1998). *Expert Testimony: A Guide for Expert Witnesses and the Lawyers Who Examine Them.* National Institute for Trail Advocacy: Notre Dame, Indiana.

Melton, G. B., Petrila, J., Poythress, N. G., & Slobogin, C. (1997). *Psychological evaluations for the courts: A handbook for mental health professionals and lawyers* (2nd ed.). New York: The Guilford Press.

Miller, J. S., & Allen, R. J. (1998). The expert as educator. In S. J. Ceci & H. Hembrooke (Eds.), *Expert witnesses in child abuse cases: What can and should be said in court* (pp.137-155). Washington, DC: American Psychological Association.

Mossman, D. (1999). "Hired guns," "whores," and "prostitutes": Case law references to clinicians of ill repute. *Journal of the American Academy of Psychiatry and the Law, 27*, 414-425.

Rotgers, F., & Barrett, D. (1996). Daubert v. Merrell Dow and expert testimony by clinical psychologists: Implications and recommendations for practice. *Professional Psychology: Research and Practice, 27*, 467-474.

Saxe, L., & Ben-Shakhar, G. (1999). Admissibility of polygraph tests: The application of scientific standards post-Daubert. *Psychology, Public Policy, and Law, 5*, 203-223.

Schuller, R. A. (1992). The impact of battered woman syndrome evidence on jury decision processes. *Law and Human Behavior, 16*, 597-620.

Shuman, D., & Sales, B. (1999). The impact of Daubert and its progeny on the admissibility of behavioral and social science evidence. *Psychology, Public Policy, and Law, 5*, 3 - 15.

Slobogin, C. (1999). The admissibility of behavioral science information in criminal trials: From primitivism to Daubert to voice. *Psychology, Public Policy, and Law, 5*, 100 - 119.

Sugarman, D. B., & Boney-McCoy, S. (1997). Impact of expert testimony on the believability of repressed memories. *Violence and Victims, 12*, 115-126.

Tenopyr, M. (1999). A scientist-practitioner's viewpoint on the admissibility of behavioral and social science information. *Psychology, Public Policy, and Law, 5*, 194 - 202.

Chapter 3

Ethical Issues in Forensic Psychological Evaluation

David Shapiro, Ph.D.
Center for Psychological Studies, Nova SE University, Ft. Lauderdale, FL

1.   INTRODUCTION

Prior to the 1992 Code of Ethics of the American Psychological Association (A.P.A.), there was little in the Code that specifically dealt with forensic practice. In fact, one of the problems with the 1981 and 1989 Codes was the fact that many of the difficulties and ethical pitfalls encountered by forensic practitioners were not well delineated in those Codes. The current, 1992 Code of Ethics, not only has a section dedicated to forensic issues, but also contains a number of other standards, which have clear implications for forensic practice. In addition, a joint committee of the American Psychology Law Society and the American Academy of Forensic Psychology wrote what are now called the *Specialty Guidelines for Forensic Psychologists*, published in the journal *Law and Human Behavior* in December of 1991. *The Specialty Guidelines* were designed to provide more detailed discussion of certain areas that were still vaguely defined by the Code of Ethics of the American Psychological Association. Nevertheless, the wording of several of the Guidelines had, in fact, been incorporated almost verbatim into the current Ethics Code, reflecting the strong influence that these guidelines had on the current Code. Of course, specialty guidelines are not enforceable as part of the Ethics Code but they serve, nevertheless, as background material that could help one more fully define the various parts of the Ethics Code.

As noted above, while there is a specific section dealing with forensic issues, one can see very clearly the application of the current Ethics Code in a variety of forensic assessment procedures. For example, General Principle A, Competence, speaks of psychologists "recognizing the boundaries of their particular competencies and the limits of their expertise." Within a forensic setting, with the so-called "battle of the experts," there is always a temptation to "over-represent oneself" and this general principle, as well as specific standards, alert psychologists to the necessity to avoid doing this. The general principle dealing with professional and scientific responsibility requires the avoidance of improper and potentially harmful dual relationships, urging the psychologist to "clarify professional roles and obligations." Very often in forensic settings, these role boundaries become blurred and fact witnesses find themselves testifying as expert witnesses. Under General Principle F, Social Responsibility," the statement appears that "Psychologists try to avoid misuse of their work." This represents an ongoing ethical dilemma in forensic practice since attorneys, in an adversarial setting, will attempt to use the data from psychological tests and interviews for the furtherance of their case, and psychologists are in a constant quandary regarding the appropriate release of certain materials.

In the following chapter, various parts of the Ethical Principles of Psychologists and Code of Conduct will be discussed in terms of their relationship to forensic practice. Attempts will also be made to correlate these with applicable parts of the *Specialty Guidelines for Forensic Psychologists* and finally deal with those parts of the *Specialty Guidelines* that are unique to that document, in other words, not covered in the Ethical Standards.

2.   APPLICABILITY OF THE ETHICS CODE

Standard 1.01 indicates that a psychologist's activities may be reviewed under the ethical standards "only if the activity is part of his or her work-related functions or the activity is psychological in nature." This was intended to prevent an Ethics Committee intruding into a psychologist's private life. What becomes somewhat ambiguous, of course, is when a psychologist, as private citizen, makes some comment regarding, for instance, a forensic matter in which she or he has not been professionally involved. There will be a tendency on the part of the media, of course, to present this as a professional opinion. Psychologists need to exercise great caution in responding to such requests. At the same time, psychologists should not engage in behavior that would be questionable ethically were it a part of their professional activities and expect to avoid responsibility for the effects by claiming that it was done as part of their private and personal, rather than professional lives.

2.1   Example

A psychologist assisted a police department in interrogating a suspect by hypnotizing him. The defendant underwent some psychological deterioration and there was ultimately a complaint filed against the psychologist. The psychologist claimed that he was not working as a psychologist, nor did he have a professional relationship with the defendant, but was rather consulting with the police department and that therefore his activities were out of the scope of the current Ethics Code.

While the psychologist may be technically correct, this behavior is highly questionable in terms of its impact on the defendant and the assertion that it has nothing to do with the psychologist's work-related activities.

3.   ETHICS AND THE LAW

For many years, there has been a perception in the mental health community that the legal system and codes of professional ethics are light years apart. In fact, when one surveys many legal decisions, the similarities are often greater than the discrepancies. The discrepancies tend to be overly dramatized and polarize members of the mental health and legal communities. Nevertheless, there are certain times that ethical responsibilities do conflict with the law. Standard 1.02 discusses this and requires psychologists to make known to the relevant legal authorities (that is, judges and attorneys) their commitment to the Ethics Code and "take steps to resolve the conflict in a responsible manner." An area in which this occurs most frequently is a demand for discovery of a psychologist's records. While a psychologist's concern is to preserve the confidentiality of the records, under certain circumstances, as for example, when a client puts her or his mental state into litigation, the privilege attached to those records has been waived. The Ethics Code does not require the psychologist to break the law. The taking of reasonable steps to resolve the conflict would, however, require the psychologist to notify the legal authority in question about the ethical dilemma involved and attempt to work the matter out informally, for example, with appropriate consent, providing the records to another mental health professional. Generally, this strategy is effective. On those occasions when it is not effective, the psychologist may have to file a "Motion to Quash" or "Motion for a Protective Order" explaining in a more formal manner the same issues that were previously discussed informally. Once this Motion has been filed, an evidentiary hearing will be convened by the judge to hear arguments on the merits of the two positions, namely to disclose or withhold the records. If the Court orders the psychologist to reveal the records, then the psychologist can do so, making appropriate documentation of the Court Order. The psychologist described in this example would certainly be taking reasonable steps to resolve the conflict, both informally and formally. There is no ethical conflict, however, in following the lawful Court Order.

Guideline IV G of the *Specialty Guidelines* discusses this issue in a bit more detail. This Guideline gives examples of the "reasonable steps, including obtaining consultation from fellow forensic professionals, obtaining the advice of independent counsel, or arranging for a direct conference with the legal representatives involved."

4.   BOUNDARIES OF COMPETENCE

Standard 1.04 requires psychologists to practice only within the boundaries of their competence, and further defines this as "based on their education, training, supervised experience or appropriate professional experience." This particular standard is important for a number of reasons. First, as noted earlier, there is always a temptation within an adversarial system to misrepresent or to over-represent one's credentials in order to more effectively present one's conclusions and opinions. This standard requires a psychologist, within a forensic setting, to exercise some self-restraint and "policing of oneself," asking oneself exactly what education, training, supervised experience or professional experience are relevant to the issue at hand. In addition, it is somewhat interesting that the definition of competence, according to this Code of Ethics, is very close to the definition of expert as provided in the Federal Rules of Evidence. Federal Rule of Evidence 702 defines an expert as someone who has knowledge, skill, education, experience, and training such that they can render an opinion that would be of assistance to the trier of fact. Especially since we are dealing with the ethical standards and their relationship to forensic activities, this parallel becomes quite striking and should serve to remind psychologists to ask themselves, prior to undertaking an assessment and/or prior to testifying, exactly what expertise they have in a particular area. The Standard then goes on to discuss a psychologist's entering a new area or an area involving new techniques and cautions them to only do so only after studying the area, training, being supervised in or receiving consultation in the area from people competent to do so. Section C of the same Standard further expands on emerging areas in which the generally recognized standards for preparatory training do not yet exist. Again, this highlights the need for self-examination, competence, and taking careful steps to avoid harming an individual as a result of the lack of well-defined knowledge in such areas. For instance, psychologists who are working in the area of recovered memories in which there is so much controversy at present, would do well to review all of the current literature, undertake supervision with people who have written in the area or done research in the area, and be exceedingly cautious in the application of their learning in an area such as this.

Section III of the *Specialty Guidelines for Forensic Psychologists* discusses the area of competence in a great deal of detail. In addition to what has already been noted in terms of the Ethics Code, the *Specialty Guidelines*, discussing competence within a forensic context, imposes on the psychologist an affirmative obligation not mentioned in the Ethics Code. That is, psychologists presenting forensic work in Court must present to the Court "specific matters to which they will testify, the boundaries of their competence, the factual bases for their qualifications as an expert, and the relevance of those factual bases to their qualifications as an expert on the specific matters at issue." That is, a forensic psychologist must be prepared to present to the court the reasons why her/his training is relevant to the specific matters being decided in a specific courtroom case. In addition, a psychologist representing herself/himself as a forensic expert must, in addition to psychological knowledge, have a "reasonable level of knowledge and understanding of the legal and professional standards" governing their participation as experts in legal proceedings. In other words, a psychologist would be obligated to know which Standard, for instance, regarding admissibility of expert testimony would be applicable in a particular courtroom setting. There are, in fact, several such standards regarding admissibility and a psychologist would have to know whether in a given case the Standard is the "general acceptability rule" or some variation of the Federal Rules of Evidence or the "relevant and reliable rule."

Guideline III of the *Specialty Guidelines* also refers to an understanding of the civil rights of parties in legal proceedings, managing one's conduct so as not to diminish or threaten those rights and withdrawing from a legal proceeding when personal or professional relationships or personal values or moral beliefs may interfere with the ability to practice competently. A psychologist in a forensic setting must understand the legal basis, for instance, of a defendant's refusal to participate in an examination and avoid any coercive techniques that might threaten those "civil rights."

5.   MAINTAINING EXPERTISE

Standard 1.05 requires psychologists essentially to participate in continuing education in order to maintain competence in the skills they use and to maintain a level of awareness of current scientific and professional information. In other words, current developments in forensic assessment instruments, normative data regarding the applications of psychological testing within forensic settings, and the manners in which a competent forensic assessment is performed should be pursued by psychologists doing forensic work. A psychologist, for instance, who is unaware of certain forensic assessment instruments regarding the assessment of competency to stand trial or criminal responsibility, who fails to utilize any instruments that assess the potential for malingering or who fails to look at the new normative standards for using psychological testing in forensic settings could be seen as violating this particular standard.

Guideline VI A of the *Specialty Guidelines* amplifies this requirement even further. In addition to repeating the statement regarding the necessity to maintain current knowledge, this Guideline speaks of an obligation to use current knowledge in "selecting data collection methods or procedures for an evaluation, treatment, consultation, or scholarly empirical investigation." In other words, the maintenance of up-to-date, current knowledge dictates the kinds of assessment instruments that one would use. For example, there has been a profusion of research and writing in the field of neuropsychological assessment. A psychologist who is asked to address a neuropsychological issue and fails to utilize current assessment instruments, relying instead on outmoded screening instruments, would clearly be in violation of this Standard.

In a similar manner, a psychologist who does an "intuitive" interpretation of the Rorschach test without using the well-validated studies that have emerged in the past 15 years would also be in violation of this Standard. Psychologists who utilize the MMPI and rely on a clinical normative database, rather than utilizing current databases validated in forensic populations, would also have difficulty indicating that they have adhered to this Standard. Standard 1.06, regarding the basis for scientific and professional judgments, logically derives this previous discussion in that psychologists need to be aware of and utilize the most recent data.

6.   THE ISSUE OF INFORMED CONSENT

The necessity for informed consent in forensic evaluations has a lengthy judicial history going back at least 20 years. One of the deficiencies of the current Code of Ethics is the fact that while there is an informed consent section in the therapy area, it is notably lacking both from the discussion of assessment and from the discussion of forensic activities. What the current Code of Ethics does is to "compress" these concerns about informed consent into Standard 1.07, having to do with describing the nature and results of psychological services. This Standard speaks about the need to provide "appropriate information before-hand about the nature of such services and appropriate information later about results and conclusions." This statement goes to the entire issue of informed consent in forensic evaluations, especially criminal responsibility evaluations. The necessity, in a criminal responsibility evaluation, to inform the defendant of the nature of the evaluation, the lack of confidentiality in the evaluation, and to whom the results of the evaluation will be disclosed, are all important aspects of the informed consent to the evaluative process. There are some states in which if a defense attorney retains an expert and that expert reaches a conclusion that is not beneficial to that defense attorney, the negative opinion is protected by attorney-client privilege and need not be revealed to the government (e.g., *United States vs. Alvarez*, 1975, *State vs. Pratt*). On the other hand, there have been rulings in several states that once the defense raises a psychiatric issue or a mental state defense, the defendant has essentially waived attorney-client privilege and the results of the evaluation are available to the government (e.g., *Edney vs. State*, *Noggle vs. Marshall*). What could conceivably happen under these circumstances is that an expert, originally retained by the defense, may reach a conclusion not helpful to the defense and could potentially then be subpoenaed and compelled to testify as a government witness. If the government has retained the expert, any material that would be of assistance to the defense must be revealed. Finally, if the evaluation is Court Ordered, there is no privilege at all and the results of the evaluation need to be turned over to all concerned parties (including the prosecutor, defense attorney, and judge). Clearly, then, this is a complex issue and a clinician performing a forensic assessment must be knowledgeable about the law in the state or Federal jurisdiction in which she or he is practicing. Once this legal knowledge is obtained, the psychologist can then incorporate it into an appropriate informed consent document. For instance, the defendant being examined by an expert retained by the defense in a state in which attorney-client privilege doctrine prevails would be told something along the following lines: "You need to be aware of the fact that unlike the traditional doctor-patient relationship in which what you tell me is confidential, the results of this evaluation will be shared with your defense attorney. This will not go beyond your attorney unless you and your attorney choose to use it in court. Under those circumstances, the report will be revealed to the government."

On the other hand, if one is working in a state in which there is disclosure to the government, in addition to the non-confidential nature of the relationship, one would need to state to the defendant: "Your defense attorney has requested that this evaluation be conducted. Once this evaluation is complete, it will be revealed both to your attorney and to the district attorney."

If retained by the prosecution, the informed consent statement would again contain the disclosure of non-confidentiality, that the government has retained one and that the results of the evaluation will be provided to the government attorney and to the defense attorney.

Finally, if the evaluation is Court Ordered, the defendant must be informed of that fact and also of the fact that all parties will receive copies of the report, namely, the judge, the prosecutor, and the defense attorney.

In addition, of course, one also needs to assess the defendant's capacity to render informed consent. While, in a Court Ordered evaluation, consent technically is not required (though it would be advisable), any evaluation on behalf of either a defense attorney or a prosecutor demands that the defendant be competent to render an informed consent to the procedure. If this consent cannot be obtained, then under no circumstances should the evaluation proceed. It is possible for a defense attorney to give substitute judgment for the conduct of an evaluation but a prosecutor is not allowed to do so. If faced with such a circumstance, the clinician should let the Court know that the defendant is incompetent to render informed consent to the evaluation.

It is also important to note that incompetence to render informed consent does not necessarily refer to incompetence to participate in other decisions or to not be criminally responsible. Each of these functional capacities (see Grisso, 1986) must be examined in its own right. Grisso has extensively discussed this concept of functional legal capacities, cautioning that one cannot infer them directly from clinical assessments. One of the most common errors made by practitioners who are attempting to transition from a traditional clinical to a forensic practice is making such inferences. Grisso outlines, the reasons for regarding each functional capacity as unique and distinct from all of the others. A defendant, for instance, who may be incompetent to stand trial may, in fact, be competent to participate in or reject a particular form of treatment. An individual competent to stand trial may not be competent to represent herself or himself in Court or waive counsel.

Whether or not written informed consent is necessary or essential is a question that often arises. While it is certainly an ideal, one frequently encounters defendants who, either because of paranoia or lack of cooperation, refuse to sign such a document. The discussion of the consent issues in such cases should be included in the body of the report, including observations of why the examiner was of the opinion that the defendant was competent to render informed consent despite the refusal to sign the form.

Standard 1.07 of the Ethics Code requires that the psychologist provide "appropriate information beforehand about the nature of such services and appropriate information later about results and consultations." This material is supposed to be conveyed in "language that is reasonably understandable to the recipient of the services." The Standard does provide for the fact that, in certain settings, psychologists may be precluded by law or by organizational roles from providing the information. Under such circumstances, they need to inform the individuals or groups with whom they are working.

6.1   Example

A psychologist who was performing evaluations of fitness for duty for a police department evaluated a police officer who had been referred to him by his commanding officer. The psychologist made no mention of the nature of the referral to the police officer being evaluated, performed an evaluation, sent the report to the commanding officer, and ultimately the officer was removed from active duty. The officer filed a complaint alleging not only lack of confidentiality but also the fact that he was never informed that the results of the evaluation would be forwarded to his commanding officer. The psychologist responded that it should have been clear to the complainant that a report would go to the commanding officer and that this was not a confidential doctor-patient relationship. The psychologist was urged to be far more careful in his informed consent procedures, making sure that a client did not assume the confidentiality of their relationship and making sure that the parties to whom the material would be disclosed are fully explained.

In summary, this Standard would require a psychologist to explain to the person being evaluated who she or he is, who it is that retained her or him, what the nature of the evaluation will be, that it is not a confidential doctor-patient communication, and to whom the results will be disclosed.

Section IV of the *Specialty Guidelines* deal with the same issue, once again, in more detail than the Ethics Code. This Section of the Guidelines talks about postponing an evaluation if a client is unwilling to proceed with the evaluation until such time as that individual can be placed in contact with her/his attorney. When the client or defendant or party is not competent to render informed consent, legal counsel is notified and the Court is notified, with the psychologist awaiting direction from the Court. A very important point, which is not contained within the Ethics Code, but is discussed in the *Specialty Guidelines*, is that once the subject of the evaluation is informed of the intended use of the evaluation, and its work product, "The psychologist may not use the evaluation work product for other purposes without explicit waiver to do so by the client or the client's legal representative." This addresses an all too common dilemma encountered in forensic practice. A psychologist will perform an evaluation addressing one forensic issue and will then be asked to extrapolate from those findings to another issue regarding which the defendant or client had not been evaluated. Generally, these questions cannot be answered based on the limited information that has been obtained in the first evaluation. The psychologist must make it very clear to the referring source that these other questions cannot be answered based on the available data. In addition, if the psychologist plans to use the results of the clinical evaluation in some other context, the psychologist must clarify this anticipated further use and obtain whatever consent or agreement is required by law from either the defendant (client) or legal representative.

7.   AVOIDANCE OF HARM AND MISUSE OF INFLUENCE

Standards 1.14, 1.15 and 1.16 of the A.P.A. Ethics Code may be taken conceptually together as a unit. Standard 1.14 requires psychologists to "take reasonable steps to avoid harming" patients, clients and others with whom they work and to try to minimize harm where it is foreseeable and unavoidable.

While this certainly appears to be a very straightforward statement, many psychologists do not perceive or think through the potential harm in their forensic activities.

For example, psychologists may be asked to perform evaluations regarding whether an individual is competent to be executed. A psychologist needs to carefully think through just what the implications of a finding of competency for execution might be. In addition, if an individual is found not competent to be executed, a psychologist would need to come to grips with whether or not she or he would want to participate in the treatment program to restore that individual to competency for execution.

In a similar manner, many psychologists are now being called upon to perform so-called "sexual predator evaluations," whether or not an individual is prone to act in a violent, sexually-predatory manner in the future. Before undertaking such an evaluation, a psychologist would need to familiarize herself/himself with the available literature regarding prediction of sexual recidivism and only if that psychologist is comfortable with making predictive statements under the circumstances of rather limited research should the psychologist proceed with such evaluations.

In a similar manner, Standard 1.15 requires that a psychologist be on the alert to a variety of factors that could conceivably result in misuse of that psychologist's influence. All too often, requests will come to a psychologist to render an "expert" opinion on an area in which there is, in fact, very little scientific or professional expertise, but rather the person making the request of the psychologist is attempting to lend an aura of scientific credibility to an area in which there is, in fact, no empirical or scientific research. For example, psychologists have frequently been asked their opinions on whether someone "fits the profile" of a serial killer, of a murderer, or of a child molester. Since there is, in fact, no empirical or scientific literature that addresses such issues, the psychologist should be very clear that any statements made by the psychologist are not utilized in a manner to convey something that, in fact, can have no basis in psychological science.

Standard 1.16 is essentially an extension of 1.15. Here, if a psychologist learns of misuse or misrepresentation of her/his work, she/he should take reasonable steps to correct or minimize the misuse or misrepresentation. If a psychologist finds out that an attorney has misrepresented her/his data, that attorney will need to be contacted in order to bring to the attorney's attention the inappropriate use of the data. Documentation of this contact should be maintained within the psychologist's files. Informally, this may serve to put the attorney on notice that if the psychologist testifies, she/he may qualify certain conclusions that will make evident the attempted misuse of the data. Under these circumstances, it is unlikely that the attorney will call that psychologist as a witness.

An extension of this concept within Section VI of the *Specialty Guidelines* talks about the expert having an affirmative obligation to "maintain professional integrity by examining the issue at hand from all reasonable perspectives, actively seeking information that will differentially test plausible rival hypotheses." In other words, the psychologist must maintain "an open mind," gathering all available data before reaching a conclusion.

Section II B of the *Specialty Guidelines* also speaks about psychologists making a "reasonable effort" to ensure that their services are used in a responsible and forthright manner. Sometimes, of course, the psychologist is constrained by various rules of evidence that would not allow her/him to make known to certain people the fact that there is a misuse of their data or influence occurring. Under such circumstances, as noted above, at the very least, the psychologist needs to document an effort to contact the attorney who has been misusing the data.

8.   MULTIPLE RELATIONSHIPS

Standard 1.17 of the Ethics Code speaks about the need to avoid, whenever possible, multiple relationships. It notes, of course, that there may be situations where it is not feasible or reasonable to avoid these relationships, but under all circumstances psychologists have to be sensitive to the potential harmful effects of such multiple relationships. The Ethics Code essentially uses as a "filter" or "screen" for such relationships "impairment of objectivity, effective performance of the psychological function or harm or exploitation to the other party." If a pre-existing relationship would create a risk of harm, the psychologist then attempts to avoid taking on certain professional or scientific obligations. If the multiple relationship arises due to unforeseen factors, the psychologist attempts to resolve it, keeping in mind the obligation to "the affected person." The *Specialty Guidelines*, Guideline IV D, speaks about the forensic psychologist "taking reasonable steps to minimize the potential negative effects of these circumstances (that is, the multiple relationship) on the rights of the party, confidentiality, and the process of treatment and evaluation."

Generally, most clinicians understand the reasons for the avoidance of multiple relationships in a clinical setting, but this principle is often poorly understood within a forensic domain. Quite simply stated, one cannot be an effective therapist in terms of assisting a client or patient to deal with her or his difficulties if one has also been involved in doing a comprehensive forensic evaluation of that individual. A comprehensive assessment, which includes interviewing of witnesses, reviewing of outside reports, assessing the possibility of malingering or secondary gain, essentially gives the forensic clinician "too much" knowledge to be of assistance to the patient, and to maintain the free-flowing attention necessary to truly help the patient unravel personal difficulties. A therapist should also make every effort to avoid becoming involved in any litigation as an expert witness.

Unfortunately, therapists frequently believe that because they know the patient so well, they are capable of answering relevant legal questions. Given a comprehensive model of forensic assessment in which multiple data sources are integrated, it is virtually impossible to address these issues because psychotherapy is not directed toward such issues as the obtaining of external verification of a patient's perceptions. If the therapist, through no advance intention on her or his part, does become involved in litigation, the therapist must scrupulously avoid rendering any opinions relevant to the legal matters at hand. The therapist, rather, must simply describe the course of psychotherapy and how the patient may have changed. The treating therapist then is testifying not as an expert witness but as a lay or fact witness. Attorneys often fail to recognize this crucial distinction. Attorneys will customarily refer a patient to a physician for examination and treatment "if deemed necessary." Indeed, when the examination is solely for the purpose of diagnosis in order to render appropriate treatment, the mixing of roles is permissible. Forensic psychologists need to inform attorneys, however, that a diagnosis made as part of a treatment program is not the same as rendering an expert opinion in a legal proceeding. A treating therapist should never be called as an expert witness. Greenberg and Schuman comprehensively outline these role differences. Greenberg and Schuman outline 10 reasons why the roles should not be mixed, including who the client is, the relational privilege, the cognitive set of the expert, the nature of the relationship, the differing areas of competency, the nature of the hypotheses tested, the degree of structure in the relationship, the scrutiny applied to the information, the goal of the professional, and the impact on the relationship of critical judgment by the psychologist.

9.   THIRD PARTY REQUESTS FOR SERVICES

When a psychologist agrees to provide services at the request of a third party, for instance, an attorney, there must be, at the outset of the services, a clarification of the nature of the relationship which each party, such that the defendant does not come to perceive the psychologist as a therapist. This has, in part, been described earlier in the discussion of Standard 1.07 having to do with informed consent. As noted earlier, the psychologist cannot merely assume that the person being evaluated understands the lack of confidentiality or understands to whom the material will be disclosed. This needs to be made very explicit. The Standard goes on to describe the situation in which a foreseeable risk may arise of the psychologist being called upon to perform conflicting roles. Under such circumstances, there must be a further clarification of the nature and direction of responsibilities. The clarification must include exactly what role the psychologist will play, how the material will be obtained, and the limits on confidentiality, consistent with what was described in the informed consent section.

The *Specialty Guidelines* again discuss this material in a fair amount of detail in order to amplify on the Code of Ethics. Prior to even accepting the referral, a psychologist has an affirmative obligation to inform the party seeking services of a number of factors, including the fee. Attorneys will frequently enlist the aid of a psychologist in a forensic case and instruct the psychologist to obtain payment from the plaintiff (or defendant) or from a health insurance company. The psychologist must clearly indicate that this cannot be done for at least two reasons. First, the attorney, not the plaintiff or the defendant, is the client and the attorney is therefore responsible for the payment of the fee. Secondly, such charges cannot be passed on to an insurance company because insurance companies will not pay for forensic evaluations and to bill them as any other form of service would be tantamount to insurance fraud.

The psychologist must clarify activities, obligations, and relationships in their past that might produce a conflict of interest. For instance, had there been a professional conflict between two psychologists or a business venture which did not succeed, one of those psychologists should not assume a role of expert in a case in which the other psychologist is involved. As noted above, the psychologist needs to clearly indicate to an attorney or other referral source what the limits of her/his competence are, indicating whether or not she/he has specific training in a specific area. This is unfortunately frequently not observed and one sees forensic "jacks of all trades" testifying in Court. The psychologist must also know enough about scientific and professional literature to turn down a referral which asks for an opinion on which there is no empirical scientific or professional literature, such as, as noted above, the request for testimony about certain "profiles."

10.   SUPERVISION

Standard 1.22 of the A.P.A. Ethics Code, as well as Section II A of the forensic *Specialty Guidelines*, speak about the necessity of making sure that people acting under one's supervision have the training to act competently, that these psychologists provide proper training and supervision to the people they supervise, and that they assume responsibility for the behavior not only of themselves, but also of their supervisees, trainees, and employees.

One of the areas in which this becomes quite problematic is that of neuropsychological assessment in which it is standard practice for a psychologist to utilize psychometricians in order to administer the actual test batteries. The supervisory psychologist then interprets the batteries and will write a report. Very close supervision must be exercised because such areas as fatigue, lack of cooperation and deliberate attempts at deception can clearly skew the results of the neuropsychological assessment. Supervisors, under such circumstances, would have an ethical obligation to provide training to their supervisees regarding observation of these crucial elements and the need to include material related to these issues in their reports and documentation.

11.   DOCUMENTATION

This Section of the A.P.A. Code not only talks about documentation in general, but also specifically addresses the documentation necessary in legal proceedings. The language in this is borrowed directly from the *Specialty Guidelines* and it therefore becomes enforceable as part of the Ethics Code. Essentially, this Standard deals with the issue of when there is a reasonable anticipation that professional services will be used in legal proceedings the psychologist has a responsibility to maintain records in the kind of detail that is even higher than that expected for normative clinical standards. Such records are in "a detail and quality that would be consistent with reasonable scrutiny in an adjudicative forum." That is, if a psychologist undertakes Court-related work, by so doing, with her/his advanced understanding that the material will be used in Court, the psychologist must maintain very carefully documented records. The reason for this is that, when undertaking a forensic assessment, subject to Court Order or Rules of Evidence, the data that formed the basis for the evidence or services is legally discoverable. The *Specialty Guidelines* talk about the standard being higher than that for general clinical practice. The distinction between a clinical and a forensic record is the "definable foreknowledge" that the services will be used within "an adjudicative forum" (in other words, a Court or Administrative Hearing). Psychologists working within forensic settings must be aware of the rules of confidentiality and privilege and these duties and obligations regarding documentation come into place "from the moment they know or have a reasonable basis for knowing that their data and evidence derived from it are likely to enter into legally relevant decisions."

11.1   Example

A psychologist was appointed by a Court to supervise visitation. This is clearly a situation in which the psychologist would have a "reasonable basis" for knowing that the material would be used in legally relevant decisions, since the psychologist made a recommendation, based on the supervised visitation, for unsupervised visitation. However, when asked to justify the relatively sketchy nature of his notes, the psychologist contended that this was a clinical, rather than a forensic function. There is little doubt that undertaking Court-ordered supervision and writing reports to the Court regarding the appropriateness of supervised or unsupervised visitation is, in fact, a forensic function and requires the additional careful documentation required by this Standard.

Since these records may well be reviewed by a Court, by attorneys or by opposing expert witnesses, the documentation must be quite extensive and the nature of the derivation of conclusions from the data very clearly specified.

12.   ADEQUACY OF ASSESSMENT

A very important part of the Ethical Standards appears in Section 2.01. It is particularly important because previous versions of the Ethics Code did not address this issue, namely, the adequacy of the data to support conclusions. This is always highly relevant in a forensic setting. Prior versions of the Ethics Code essentially had no sections that allowed the disciplining of a psychologist who would reach conclusions without adequate data. Under the old Ethics Code, conceivably, one could indicate that the psychologist misused assessment techniques but there was little that dealt with the need for an adequate basis and adequate documentation in order to support certain conclusions. This, in fact, appears in two different parts of the current Ethics Code, Section 2.01 and Section 7.02(a). It essentially requires psychologists to not only have the data to support their conclusions, but also requires that whatever conclusion, recommendation or diagnosis a psychologist makes, that psychologist is responsible for providing the data upon which the conclusion is based. This requires that a psychologist have more than "an intuitive feel" in order to make a certain diagnosis. It requires adherence to standard procedures in administering and interpreting psychological testing rather than the use of an idiosyncratic approach to the assessment. Certainly, no one wants to interfere with the creativity of psychologists, but important decisions regarding a patient or client based on more than just hunches or intuitions are now required.

12.1   Example

A patient who had suffered a closed head injury and was undergoing cognitive rehabilitation was referred to a psychologist for an IME (independent medical evaluation). That psychologist failed to review any records and failed to administer any psychological tests, instead concluding, based on a brief clinical interview, that the patient was malingering. He contended that he could not have used any of these other sources of data because they would have "biased" his conclusions.

This is clearly an inadequate basis for a conclusion of this magnitude since, of course, we are dealing with an apparent neuropsychological impairment and this psychologist did no neuropsychological assessment. In addition, there are many well-validated tests for malingering, none of which this psychologist relied upon in rendering his conclusion that this patient was malingering.

In addition, it is essentially a "standard of care" in the forensic area to utilize and integrate multiple sources of data. Were a psychologist to reach an opinion in a forensic evaluation based only on clinical interview and did not utilize multiple sources of data, one could clearly state that there was a violation of Standard 2.01(b) due to the insufficient information relied upon. This would, of course, also provide excellent ammunition for cross-examination of that expert.

13.   USE OF ASSESSMENTS AND INTERVENTIONS

This Standard in the Ethics Code has two very important sections. Section 2.02(a) deals with the use of assessment techniques "in a manner and for purposes appropriate in light of the research on or evidence of the usefulness and proper application of the technique." Unfortunately, an all too common occurrence is that psychologists will make "wild" interpretations of certain psychological tests or utilize tests in forensic settings for purposes for which the tests have not been validated or for norm groups on whom the test has not been normed or standardized. This can clearly lead not only to frank distortions but to misapplication and misunderstanding of the significance of a test score.

13.1   Example

A psychologist, in testifying, described the Minnesota Multiphasic Personality Inventory as "an emotional x-ray" and further stated that the test could reveal what was going on in the defendant's mind at the time of the offense. This is clearly a statement that goes beyond the bounds of any available research and therefore represents a violation of this Standard.

13.2   Example

A psychologist performed an evaluation of an inmate who was scheduled to appear in front of the parole board. The psychologist administered an MMPI-2 and obtained a profile with elevations on Scales 4 and 8. The psychologist recalled that some articles that had been published about Charles Manson described him as having elevations on Scales 4 and 8 of his MMPI. The psychologist therefore wrote in his report that since this inmate had a "Charles Manson profile," he should be turned down for parole.

This is clearly a misuse of the test, for it implies that everyone who obtains elevations on Scales 4 and 8 of the MMPI are like Charles Manson, a conclusion for which there is no research to document this finding, nor is it a proper application of the technique.

13.3   Example

A psychologist was asked to evaluate a fifteen-year-old boy regarding whether or not his case could be returned to a juvenile court since he had been charged as an adult. The psychologist took a test, which had been validated on adult male forensic populations (that is, prison and maximum security inmates) and administered it to this fifteen year old who had never been arrested previously. The psychologist merely eliminated the items that did not apply, prorated the test results and reached the conclusion that this young man was "well on his way to becoming a psychopath" and therefore should not be returned to juvenile court. This again is clearly an inappropriate application and an inappropriate use of this particular test.

The second part of this Standard has to do with a dilemma frequently encountered by psychologists performing forensic assessments. This is the release of raw psychological test data to persons not qualified to interpret it. It is important to note that this Standard does not prohibit psychologists from releasing data to non-psychologists but rather requires that the person receiving the data be qualified to use the information. There have been extensive discussions in the literature what this phrase "qualified" really means. If a psychologist has reached a conclusion within a forensic setting based partly or wholly on the results of psychological testing, and the plaintiff or defendant in the case has introduced their mental state into litigation, then opposing counsel under the Rules of Discovery is entitled to see that data. However, the Ethical Standard requires that only people "qualified" to use the data receive it. This appears to be a conflict between the Ethics Code and the law, but, as noted earlier, the psychologist is required only to take "reasonable steps" to document adherence to the Ethics Code and the communication of this documentation to other sources. Parenthetically, this statement represents a dramatic improvement over the earlier Ethics Codes, which did not address this point at all. In 1987, the *General Guidelines for Providers of Psychological Services* did discuss the issue. Psychologists have generally recognized the conflict and have attempted to resolve it by inviting the party demanding the records to provide the name of the licensed professional competent to interpret the data to the holder of the records and then either send the records to that licensed professional or arrange a meeting where the records are mutually reviewed. As noted earlier, this informal approach is usually successful and most frequently an attorney who has issued a subpoena will merely provide the name of the licensed psychologist who has been retained to review the records.

If counsel persists in demanding the records, and will not provide the name of the opposing expert, it is then the clinician's responsibility to file either a Motion to Quash the subpoena or a Motion for Protective Order. Once this is done, the Court will review the matter and the judge will issue an opinion detailing whether or not the psychologist is obligated to reveal the records to the opposing attorney. As noted earlier, as long as the psychologist attempts to adhere to the Ethical Code and documents that adherence, following a lawful Court Order would not be regarded as a violation of the Code of Ethics.

On occasion, due to the specific Rules of Discovery, an attorney might not be willing to disclose the name of the expert who has been retained. Under such circumstances, a psychologist may write to the attorney who has issued the subpoena and obtain a notarized statement that the records will be revealed only to the psychologist retained by opposing counsel and will not be re-disclosed. A suggested format to responding to the initial request for raw data follows below:

Re: Subpoena to (Doctor) In The Case Of (Client)

Dear (Attorney):

This response is to your letter of (Date) requesting that I comply with the subpoena issued from (Court).

That subpoena requests the production of the results of psychological tests conducted on (Name of Plaintiff or Defendant). The Ethical Principles of Psychologists and Code of Conduct (A.P.A. 1992) require that I sent that data only to someone qualified to utilize the information.

If you will consider providing me with the name of the licensed psychologist qualified to interpret the data that you have retained to review the material, I will be glad to provide the data directly to that psychologist.

Very truly yours,

It is important that the clinician utilize this approach for several reasons. First, of course, is what is noted above, that the Ethical Standards require disclosure only to another qualified professional. Secondly, the Courts have essentially recognized the legitimacy of the demand to reveal raw data only to another licensed psychologist. The Courts, according to several recent decisions, do not recognize other grounds for withholding test data. For instance, Courts have ruled that withholding of the raw data cannot be justified under a Fifth Amendment argument.

The *Specialty Guidelines* speak about the need to maintain test security and that access to the information is "restricted to individuals with a legitimate and professional interest in the data." When providing records and raw data, "The forensic psychologist takes reasonable steps to ensure that the receiving party is informed that raw scores must be interpreted by a qualified professional in order to provide reliable and valid information."

14. ASSESSMENT IN GENERAL AND SPECIAL POPULATIONS

The Ethics Code requires that psychologists be aware of the proper applications and uses of the techniques that they use and are sensitive to situations in which particular techniques or norms may not be applicable, for instance, in a forensic setting. Given the recognition that scores may mean different things in forensic settings than in clinical settings, psychologists must make qualifying statements about the degree of certainty with which diagnoses, judgments or predictions can be made about individuals.

As noted above, certain tests now do have normative data based on forensic and correctional populations. The clinician doing a forensic assessment should attempt, whenever possible, to utilize these forensic, rather than clinical, norms. If using a test, which does not have such norms, then the clinician must speak to the limitations of the validity and reliability of the conclusions or recommendations, since the population being tested is different from the population on which the test was normed. This would not, however, allow what was described earlier as essentially the "making up" of a new test in the description of the use of the Psychopathy Checklist with a fifteen-year-old boy.

14.1 Example

A psychologist within a correctional facility was asked to evaluate inmates regarding the appropriateness of their transfer to a less secure facility. The psychologist utilized a clinically normed MMPI and concluded, based on the test results, that the defendant was defensive, therefore out of touch with his underlying hostility, and therefore should not be transferred to a less secure facility.

Clearly, this psychologist failed to factor in the crucial effect of the setting or context, namely that any inmate being evaluated for a less secure environment would appear defensive when the norms were based on a clinical setting.

14.2   Example

A psychologist was asked to evaluate a police officer in a fitness for duty examination. The police officer was administered the Rorschach psychodiagnostic technique and rejected six out of the 10 Rorschach cards. The psychologist concluded from this that the police officer was very defensive, was most likely repressing great amounts of rage and for that reason would not be safe to be carrying a firearm.

This psychologist clearly failed to factor in the context or the situation in which the officer was being evaluated, namely that he was aware that the results would be used to determine his fitness for duty and he would, of course, under those circumstances, be rather defensive. At no point were any reservations about the accuracy or limitation of the interpretations made. This need is reflected in Standard 2.05, which indicates that psychologists must take into account the various test factors and characteristics of the person being assessed "that might affect psychologist's judgments or reduce the accuracy of their interpretations." The need to utilize test scoring and interpretive services that are attuned to the specific population being assessed is described in Standard 2.08 of the Ethics Code.

15.   ADVERTISING AND OTHER PUBLIC STATEMENTS

Section 3 of the Ethics Code deals with advertising and public statements. As noted earlier, the "public statement" in which a forensic psychologist often finds herself or himself is one made in Court in which there is an attempt to make the psychologist "more qualified" than she or he, in fact, is. A psychologist can generally be counted on to not blatantly misrepresent her/his credentials. However, Sections 3.02(b) and (c) deal with the situation encountered when someone else makes deceptive statements about the psychologist's practice, professional, or scientific activities. The statement recognizes that these are frequently out of the psychologist's control but still requires the psychologist to make reasonable efforts to correct the misimpression. For example, in a recent case, a psychologist was retained to provide expertise regarding individuals who commit domestic violence. The opening statement by the defense attorney misrepresented the nature of this expert's opinion and indicated that the psychologist would render testimony that the defendant did not "fit the profile of a murderer," though he had, in fact, been convicted on several occasions of domestic violence. Not only would this statement be inaccurate, it would also violate several of the ethical standards already discussed regarding the proper use of assessment techniques and not making a statement out of the bounds of one's competence. The psychologist notified the attorney that this was an improper and inappropriate characterization of the testimony and the attorney subsequently did not utilize this psychologist's testimony.

This is also reflected in the *Specialty Guidelines*, Guideline VII A 1, which requires that "forensic psychologists take reasonable steps to correct misuse or misrepresentation of their professional products, evidence, and testimony."

Standard 3.03 speaks to the need to avoid false, deceptive, misleading, or fraudulent statements "either because of what they state, convey or suggest, or because of what they omit." For example, until recently, when the American Board of Professional Psychology issued a statement prohibiting the practice, a number of experts listed as part of their qualifications that they were "Board eligible" for the American Board of Forensic Psychology. This sounds like a very impressive credential except that in reality it does not exist at all. One is either Board certified or not, with no intermediate qualification described as Board eligible. Certainly Board eligible means that they are eligible to take the examination, but this is clearly an example of something that is suggested, "because of what they omit," namely, that such a credential does not exist. In addition, psychologists doing forensic work will be deceptive regarding their credentials again because of what they omit.

15.1 Example

In a recent case, a psychologist described himself on his letterhead as a Diplomate of the American Board of Professional Psychology but failed to indicate in what area his Diploma was. He then proceeded to title his report, Forensic Psychological Evaluation.

Clearly the implication of this, through omission, was the fact that he was Diplomated in forensic psychology. In fact, his Diplomate was in industrial organizational psychology and had nothing to do with the forensic context. Such deceptive practices should be avoided.

16.   PRIVACY AND CONFIDENTIALITY

Standard 5.01 restates the need to discuss, at the outset of a relationship, "and thereafter as new circumstances may warrant," limitations on confidentiality and the foreseeable uses of the information generated through their services. This, of course, restates several of the issues that were discussed previously under the heading of Informed Consent.

17.   FORENSIC ACTIVITIES

As noted earlier, the current version of the Ethics Code is the first to have a section exclusively concerned with forensic activities.

As noted earlier, Standard 7.02(a) is a re-statement of Section 2.01(b) dealing with the basing of recommendations on techniques that are sufficient to provide appropriate substantiation for findings. Section (b) of this Standard requires that, with certain very narrow exceptions, the individual about whom conclusions are being rendered must be personally interviewed. One cannot provide written or oral forensic reports or testimony about the psychological characteristics of an individual in most circumstances unless the psychologist has conducted an examination of the individual "adequate to support the statements or conclusions." The proper application of this Ethical Standard should serve to put the curbs on certain professionals who misuse what is called "behavioral science profiling." While these techniques are well-documented in many publications from the Behavioral Sciences Unit of the Federal Bureau of Investigation, they are used to identify classes of individuals rather than specific people. Many psychologists have, in fact, misused such behavioral science profiling in order to suggest that a given individual is the perpetrator of a particular crime, based on an analysis of the crime scene and supporting documentation, without ever having seen the individual. This is, in essence, the "flip side" of the ethical dilemma noted earlier in which psychologists are asked to indicate that a particular defendant does not fit the "profile" of someone who committed a particular act, and therefore should not be prosecuted. Either extreme represents an ethical violation. Nevertheless, Section (c) of Standard 7.02 recognizes that in certain forensic contexts an attorney may wish to block the examination for various legal reasons. This happens on occasion when one is conducting an assessment of criminal responsibility. Recognizing that this occurs, this Section of the Ethics Code states that "when, despite reasonable efforts, such an examination is not feasible (that is, a personal interview of the individual), psychologists clarify the impact of the limited information on the reliability and validity of their reports and testimony and they appropriately limit the nature and extent of their conclusions or recommendations." In other words, in many circumstances, an attorney may refuse to make a particular defendant available for interview. Under those circumstances, the psychologist cannot render any conclusions regarding that person's mental state. At other times, certain witnesses, family, or friends may refuse to be interviewed or may be informed by an attorney to refuse participation in the evaluation. Under these circumstances, the Ethics Code is very clear, "The conclusions need to be qualified in light of the missing data." These exact observations are also found in the *Specialty Guidelines*, Section VI H, from which the language in the Ethics Code was derived.

However, there are certain circumstances in which a psychologist will be called upon not to examine an individual, but rather to evaluate the work of another professional in a particular situation. The expert may be given, for instance, a copy of that expert's raw data, as well as their report. Under such circumstances, the forensic psychologist must be scrupulous about not rendering any opinions about the individual who has not been examined. Rather, the only statements that can be made are whether or not the conclusions contained in the report can be derived from or are consistent with the raw data presented. Alternative hypotheses may be suggested based on the data, but again, it must be made clear that, not having interviewed the individual, the forensic psychologist is not making any conclusions, recommendations, or diagnoses.

Section VII B of the *Specialty Guidelines* comments on a problem often encountered when a forensic psychologist is commenting upon another's work. Occasionally, one recognizes that the work is very poorly assembled and very poorly documented. However, any inflammatory or derogatory statements about the opposing expert must be avoided. "When evaluating or commenting upon the professional work product or qualifications of another expert or party to a legal proceeding, forensic psychologists represent their professional disagreements with reference to a fair and accurate evaluation of the data, theories, standards, and opinions of the other expert or party." This caution should be observed both in written materials and in courtroom/ deposition testimony.

Standard 7.03 dealing with clarification of role restates what has already been discussed in the section on multiple relationships.

A standard entitled "Truthfulness and Candor" requires the psychologist once again to "describe fairly the bases for testimony and conclusions" reflecting, once again, what was stated in Section 2.01, namely that a psychologist needs to be prepared to deal very explicitly with the specific data upon which a particular statement, conclusion, recommendation, or diagnosis is based. Consistent with the limitations on validity and reliability noted in the Assessment Section (Standard 2.05), the forensic section again talks about the necessity to acknowledge limits of data or conclusion in order to avoid misleading.

Standard 7.05, dealing with prior relationships, again restates what has already been documented in Standard 1.17, dealing with multiple relationships.

18.   RESOLUTION OF ETHICAL ISSUES

Standards 8.04 and 8.05 deal with the psychologist's obligations, first to attempt to informally resolve an ethical violation and secondly, if the informal resolution fails, to report that ethical violation to an Ethics Committee or Licensing Board. A particular exception to this appears to occur in forensic assessments in which an expert cannot communicate with an opposing expert regarding these issues. Such would be seen, within a forensic context, as attempting to influence another witness or attempting to intimidate them with fears of an ethical violation. While in a non-forensic context it is certainly appropriate to handle concerns about ethical violations in this manner, when one is an opposing expert witness, one cannot follow the same guidelines. Under such circumstances, the most one can do is to communicate one's concerns to the retaining attorney who may choose to utilize this information in cross-examination. Of course, if the case has been concluded, the above constraints would not apply, provided the Court matter is not ongoing and subject to change or revision such as custody determination.

19.   SPECIALTY GUIDELINES FOR FORENSIC
PSYCHOLOGISTS

Certain aspects of the *Forensic Specialty Guidelines* do not have parallels in the A.P.A. Code of Ethics. While they do not therefore represent enforceable Standards, they are important in that they set a standard of practice for anyone who represents herself/himself to the Court or judicial system as a forensic psychologist.

This definition of forensic psychologist and forensic psychology is delineated in the introductory section, which again talks about the "definable foreknowledge" that one's work, data, and conclusions will be used in a forensic setting. If a psychologist undertakes an evaluation with this understanding, she or he is then bound by the Guidelines delineated herein. Other psychologists, who are performing primarily clinical functions, who may become involved in a forensic setting, for example, as a result of having been subpoenaed, but have not entered into the situation as a "forensic psychologist" are not bound by the Guidelines but may consult them for assistance.

A section of the *Specialty Guidelines*, which requires an understanding of case law and legal precedents, is found in Section VI D, which speaks of forensic psychologists not providing forensic services prior to an individual's representation by counsel. The purpose of this Guideline is derived from a large number of early cases in which psychologists would interview and examine defendants immediately upon their arrest and would obtain statements that may, in fact, have been incriminating prior to their being represented by counsel, who most likely would have warned them not to make such statements. The only exception to this is when the forensic services are pursuant to a Court Order and even then the forensic psychologist needs to inform the Court prior to providing the services. If a psychologist is required to provide emergency mental health services, such as in a therapeutic role, the psychologist should attempt to refrain from any other kind of participation in the case, consistent with the concerns about not entering multiple relationships.

20.   FORENSIC METHODOLOGY

A series of provisions in the *Specialty Guidelines* deal with the process of the forensic evaluation. There is, within forensic assessment, a standard of practice, which requires the seeking of "third party data." Such seeking of third party data can only be done with either approval of the relevant legal party (an attorney) or as a consequence of a Court Order. Forensic opinions should not be based exclusively on such third party data, but rather on an integration of data, such that the third party data is corroborated by personal examination and observation. This data needs to be gathered in a manner that is "standard for the profession."

Several sections of the *Specialty Guidelines* deal with the potential for misuse of the data gathered within the forensic assessment. The ethical aspects of this misuse have been detailed previously, but the psychologist doing forensic work must be aware of the legal strictures as well. For that reason, "a psychologist doing a forensic assessment must avoid offering information from the investigation or evaluation that does not bear directly upon the legal purpose of the professional service." This is an expansion of a point noted earlier that there may be efforts to derive opinions regarding unrelated matters from a psychologist's investigation. Therefore, for example, if a psychologist has conducted a criminal responsibility evaluation, she/he should not venture, on the basis of that evaluation, to render an opinion on potential for violence. In a similar manner, if one has evaluated competency to stand trial, one should not address a variety of other competencies without further investigation. A related point is that no statements made by a defendant in the course of a forensic examination can be admitted into evidence in any criminal proceeding except on an issue with respect to mental condition, which the defendant has herself or himself introduced. Forensic psychologists have an affirmative obligation to protect the records such that such statements cannot be misused. In other words, for example, if a psychologist is evaluating a defendant on a murder charge and during the course of the evaluation the defendant indicates to the psychologist that he has, in fact, murdered 10 other people, the psychologist should not include that information in the report. The only rare circumstance under which this may be included is if it is within the context of a professional opinion that perhaps the individual tends, because of his or her own psychopathology, to confess to crimes which he or she has not committed. Generally, however, it is wise to avoid including any such statements.

Under the heading of Public and Professional Communications, generally, forensic psychologists should avoid making public statements about legal proceedings in which they are involved. The only circumstance in which such public statements would be generally acceptable is when there has been some misuse or misrepresentation of the testimony and again, pursuant to other parts of the Ethics Code, the psychologist has a responsibility to correct the misimpression.

The principle noted earlier of investigating a forensic problem from all reasonable perspectives in order to maintain professional integrity does not preclude forceful presentation of an opinion once all of the data has been analyzed and integrated. A forensic psychologist is prohibited from participating in a misrepresentation of the evidence through either inclusion or omission. They, in fact, are required to disclose all sources of information obtained and from which source certain written products or testimony were derived.

Finally, there has been an ongoing debate for many years regarding ultimate legal issues. An ultimate issue can best be described as that which the Court or jury decides: e.g., did a defendant commit a crime or not; was a defendant "legally insane" at the time of the offense; is the father or the mother the better custodial parent. The *Specialty Guidelines* do not prohibit testimony on ultimate issues but rather emphasize that a psychologist's essential role as expert to the Court is to assist the trier of fact and that the expert's observations, inferences and conclusions must be distinguished from legal facts, opinions and conclusions. In other words, while a psychologist should not go out of her or his way to address an ultimate issue, if called upon to do so by a Court, the psychologist is "prepared to explain the relationship between the expert testimony and the legal issues and facts of an instant case."

Looking further at this problem, few psychologists would disagree with the fact that one's report should not state that a client is or is not sane or does or does not have diminished capacity, for these are legal issues. The difficulty generally arises when one goes to the level of behavioral description just below these issues. There are some psychologists who contend that even addressing the criteria for these issues (sometimes described as penultimate) is going beyond the bounds of our expertise. Some psychologists, in fact, regard such statements as actually unethical. Some scholars have observed that mental health professionals involved in forensic work should do no more than describe the human behavior observed, leaving such issues as whether or not the defendant "lacked substantial capacity" to the trier of fact. This position is flawed for a variety of reasons. First, if an individual has performed a careful and comprehensive forensic evaluation, with all of the empirical referents needed, in a description of behavior, it becomes little more than a semantic point to describe that behavior in a great deal of detail or to state that the behavior constituted "a lack of substantial capacity to appreciate wrongfulness." If an individual is grossly psychotic and commits a crime due to her/his misperception of reality, is there any reason that a forensic examiner cannot opine that the defendant "lacked substantial capacity to appreciate the wrongfulness" of the behavior?

While this may be merely a semantic issue, the more troubling issue is what actually happens in a Court of law when a mental health professional refuses to address an ultimate issue, stating that it is either unethical to do so or goes beyond the bounds of their competence. What, unfortunately, happens is Courts turn to less well-trained, less competent, less ethical individuals who are more than willing to give an opinion on any topic without adequate empirical verification. Perhaps in the best of all possible worlds, mental health professionals may not have to address ultimate legal issues. This should be made clear to Courts, to attorneys and to various judicial bodies, perhaps through a process of ongoing continuing education. However, to prevent Courts turning to experts who are willing to give opinions based on no data, we may very well need to address ultimate issues, but be sure we are doing so by providing enough empirical basis for our opinions.

In summary, we need to look carefully at the Code of Ethics and the *Specialty Guidelines* in order not only to maintain the integrity of our forensic work but also to present the material in a manner that is meaningful to decision makers in the judicial system.

21.   REFERENCES

American Psychological Association (1992, December), *American Psychologist 47*:1597-1611.

American Psychological Association (1981), Ethical Principles of Psychologists, *American Psychologist 36*:633-638.

American Psychological Association (1990), Ethical Principles of Psychologists (Amended June 2, 1989), *American Psychologist 45*:390-395.

American Psychological Association (1987), *General Guidelines for Provision of Psychological Services*, Washington, D.C.

Edney vs. State, 556 F.2nd, 556 (Second Circuit, 1977).

Specialty Guidelines for Forensic Psychologists (1991), *Law and Human Behavior 15(6)*:655-665.

Greenberg, S. and Schuman, D. (1997), Irreconcilable Conflict Between Therapeutic and Forensic Roles. *J Prof Psychol Res Pract 28*(1):50-57.

Grisso, T. (1986), *Evaluating Competencies*. New York, Plenum pp 15-29.

Noggle vs. Marshall, 706 F.2nd 1408 (Sixth Circuit, 1983).

State v. Pratt, 398 NE.2nd, 421 (Maryland Court of Appeals, 1979).

U.S. v. Alvarez, 519 F.2nd, 1036 (Third Circuit), 1975.

Chapter 4

Assessment in Forensic Practice
An Objective Approach

James N. Butcher, Ph.D.
Department of Psychology, University of Minnesota, Minneapolis, MN

1.   INTRODUCTION

Psychologists have been welcomed in the courtroom as expert witnesses with greater frequency in recent years, in large part through the reputation and scientific information that can be provided by psychological tests (Boccacini & Brodsky, 1999). The science of psychological assessment can add a great deal to the understanding of the psychological and mental health status of individuals who are caught up in the legal process.

One major value of using standard psychological tests in forensic assessment is that subjectivity in evaluating persons can be eliminated or substantially reduced. Psychological tests can be of value in forensic assessment only insofar as their results are objective and provide valid information that are beyond that of impressionistic judgment.   The interpretations are more credible than other avenues of information gathering such as interview or witness reports. Objective testing can provide information on psychological characteristics that is less influenced by extraneous factors (Meehl, 1997; Grove & Meehl, 1996). For example, in family custody determinations, which are often colored by acrimony and mutual blaming, an objective perspective on the adjustment (or lack thereof) of the parties involved is often valuable for courts to use to make decisions about custody. Procedures that require subjective judgment for interpreting can lead to biased assessment because they can be influenced by the situation itself or by the psychologists own opinions. Interpretations can be more easily manipulated or channeled into a favored direction with subjective techniques than when more objective measures, with well-defined interpretive procedures, are used.

2.   PROBLEMS FACING PSYCHOLOGISTS IN FORENSIC EVALUATIONS

Many forensic practitioners were originally trained in clinical or counseling psychology where psychological assessments are conducted in order to help clients. The focus is much different in forensic work; the client being assessed may *not* be helped by the evaluation. Clinical assessment practice may be a somewhat smoother and less adversarial career path than forensic assessment work even with the recent turmoil created by managed care. Conducting forensic exams (whether in family custody, personal injury, or criminal court evaluations) can be controversial and charged with tension and acrimony.

Although the practice of forensic psychology differs substantially from clinical and counseling psychology, it can be a very rewarding career, both professionally and financially. See the discussion provided by Hess (1999), on serving as an expert witness. Forensic psychological opportunities have expanded substantially in recent years and many clinical and counseling practitioners have changed from clinical to forensic practice.

Many individuals working in the forensic assessment field have had little or no formal training in conducting forensic evaluations or experience in court testimony. Recently, I received a telephone call from a psychotherapist who lamented the fact that his therapy practice had "dried up" because of managed care limitations on payment and he had decided to re-channel his professional efforts into forensic work, particularly psychological evaluations. He wanted to know "what the F scale of the MMPI-2 was all about" because he had heard that this was an important measure in conducting forensic examinations. Mid-career shifts in activity require substantially more retraining than was apparent from this practitioner's questions.

The aspiring forensic practitioner should be aware that evaluations in forensic settings and his or her credentials and expertise might be vigorously challenged in court. Forensic evaluations need to be crafted in a careful and defensible manner.

Pope, Butcher, and Seelen (2000), recently pointed out 10 potential problem areas or pitfalls that await the unprepared forensic assessment psychologist:

1. Using psychological tests without having well-grounded expertise, up-to-date training in instruments, and area at issue.
2. Administering tests without appropriate informed consent.
3. Using any modified form of administration that has not been adequately and objectively verified.
4. Using obsolete forms of a test as though they are the current standard.
5. Failing to assess factors that might reasonably affect the validity of the testing (e.g. medications taken by the client, client's vision problems, client's familiarity with English, disruptions occurring during testing).
6. Administering a test without close and continuous monitoring (i.e., sending tests home with the client).
7. Interpreting or otherwise making inferences about the clinical scales on an invalid profile.
8. Building a psychological test interpretation to fit a legal theory developed by the legal team.
9. Failing to distinguish clearly and explicitly among unsubstantiated hypotheses, probabilistic statements based on actuarial data, and reasonable or absolute certainties.
10. Using non-standard interpretations of scales, patterns, or profiles (i.e. idiosyncratic interpretations that are not a part of standard interpretive information available in texts, articles, and so forth).

This article focuses upon several issues pertinent to conducting quality forensic evaluations, which include psychological tests with the goal of meeting the highest standards of practice that can withstand close scrutiny in the adversarial system and avoid problems that can emanate from flawed evaluations.

3. COMMONLY USED TESTS IN FORENSIC EVALUATIONS

When it comes to choosing the psychological tests to be incorporated into a particular forensic test battery, practitioners tend to be conservative and choose from a "short list" of well-established instruments whose results can be depended upon in court.

The most widely used instruments are the MMPI-2 for personality assessment and the Wechsler scales for intellectual measurement. In a recent survey of licensed mental health professionals, the MMPI-2 was ranked as being the most frequently administered test (Frauenhoffer, Ross, Gfeller, Searight, & Piotrowski, 1998). Other surveys have reported similar conclusions (Lees-Haley, 1992; Lees-Haley, Smith, Williams, & Dunn, 1996; and Borum & Grisso, 1995). In fact, 100 percent of frequent assessors surveyed used the MMPI or MMPI-2 in personal injury cases (Boccaccini & Brodsky, 1999). They also reported that the MMPI was the only instrument used by the majority of psychologists conducting emotional injury assessments. Piotrowski (1998), reported that the MMPI/MMPI-2 was the most frequent instrument for assessing pain with 76% of respondents reporting that they "almost always" use the instrument for pain assessment.

The most frequently used instruments such as the WAIS-III and the MMPI-2 typically do not have problems meeting the requirements of the federal guidelines for expert testimony as established by the *Daubert* ruling, (to be discussed below), as a means of establishing expertise. Newer instruments might be considered "experimental" because they have been less extensively researched and are not as widely used in practice. Consequently, they are more likely to be challenged as not being "standard of care" instruments.

3.1   The Need for Strict Adherence to Standard Administration, Scoring and Interpretive Procedures

Some of the most flawed psychological assessments encountered in forensic practice involve situations in which the psychologist has deviated from standard testing procedures, as this practice tends to produce results that are uninterpretable. Most psychological tests are published with manuals that detail procedures for the various stages in the testing process: including arranging the test situation, presenting standard test stimuli, collecting standard information, systematic recording of responses, standard test processing and scoring, and using appropriate interpretations. Deviations from these standardized testing procedures can result in a "spoiled test" and in interpretations that do not withstand external scrutiny. Although a plethora of examples of such deviations from standard operating procedures can be found; three will be provided below:

- A few years ago a psychologist in a high visibility court case testified that he had administered only a nine card Rorschach to assess the client. He further explained that he *only* gives a 9 card Rorschach, deleting Card V from the administration, because everyone knows that it is a bat anyway!
- One of the most frequent administration flaws in testing involves deviating from recommended procedures by giving the client a paper-pencil test booklet and answer sheet and allowing them to take the test home to complete. In one such situation, when a man was being tested in a personal injury case he "became tired," and thinking the test "too long," asked his wife to finish the last portion of the items by answering them as though she were him.
- Some of the most extreme deviations from standard practice occur in the interpretation realm, with psychologists providing idiosyncratic even bizarre interpretations of test results. One recent example occurred in a personal injury case in which the litigant was claiming to have had trauma to his inner ear (following a situation in which his "ears popped" on a commercial airline flight). Neither the medical tests or the psychological tests supported the litigant's claim of damages, however, the psychologist interpreted the MMPI-2 profile pattern as being "consistent with the inner ear trauma syndrome," a condition that, as a literature review unearthed, has never been empirically studied with the MMPI-2.

4. TRAINING IN THE ADMINISTERING, SCORING, AND INTERPRETING FORENSIC ASSESSMENT PROCEDURES

Psychologists need to have demonstrated competence in the administration, scoring, and interpretation of the procedures or tests they are using in the forensic evaluation. Yet, it is typically difficult for a person to obtain extensive training in the specified types of evaluation. There are three primary avenues through which psychologists pursue expertise on a particular psychological test: formal graduate and post-graduate training programs, professional continuing education programs, and self-study.

Graduate training programs tend to focus upon providing general exposure to a few of the major assessment instruments such as the Wechsler scales or MMPI-2, with little attention paid to lesser used instruments. Belter and Piotrowski (1999), surveyed training directors of 33 terminal masters degree programs and reported a developing trend away from teaching projective techniques. Objective assessment methods such as the MMPI-2, Wechsler scales, and Millon Clinical Multiaxial Inventory (Millon, 1994), were the tests most frequently endorsed as "essential" for practice.

Formal training programs typically offer limited individual practical experience in particular settings such as forensic evaluations. It is difficult, in the context of a graduate-training program, to obtain sufficient "real world" experience in conducting child custody examinations or assessing litigants in personal injury cases for students to become expert. This is often left for postgraduate work. Few clinical, health psychology or counseling programs are geared to provide in-depth experience in such evaluations. One exception is in the psychological assessment of persons in correctional-based forensic programs. There are a number of programs that have specific training placements in correctional psychology settings (Melton, 1999)

It is possible to gain further experience (or in some cases obtain initial training experience) on various assessment techniques through professional educational programs dedicated to assessment training such as the Rorschach Workshops or MMPI-2 Workshops. Several professional organizations such as the American Psychological Association (APA), and some APA divisions such as Divisions 12 and 41, occasionally provide professional education programs oriented toward test interpretation, as do the Society for Personality Assessment (SPA), and the Southeastern Psychological Association (SEPA). As with graduate training programs, such continuing education[JS1] programs are more likely to offer programs on widely used instruments.

Relying upon self-study (e.g. through reading test manuals, textbooks, and research articles), as the only means of developing skills in a particular psychological assessment technique can be problematic. Clearly, some instruments are easier to learn through self-study than others because of their more structured format, their generally agreed upon interpretive strategies, and the wealth of information available on them. Self-study does not usually incorporate the all-important practical supervision on test interpretation that is usually required to hone the learner's skills. The greatest problem with relying upon self-study to gain or update expertise in an instrument is that the "self-study" background is difficult to document or certify in order to address questions about the expert's credentials from opposing attorneys.

A possible consequence of an expert witness's failure to obtain rigorous training in forensic assessment, or failure to appropriately document this expertise is the fact that this is often fertile ground for attorneys to address in cross-examination questions that are designed to cast doubts on the expert's credibility. Many persons practicing in the area of forensic psychological assessment have limited training in the procedures they are using, a situation that offers a good opportunity for opposing attorneys to raise doubts about credibility. See possible cross-examination questions concerning background and training that are presented in the handbook by Pope et al. (2000.)

4.1   Assure that there is a Supporting Research Base for the Instrument or Instruments Used

What criteria should govern the incorporation of a particular test in a forensic test battery? The legal system has provided some guidance for courts in this matter through the *Daubert* Ruling. The court decision in *Daubert vs Merrell* Dow Pharmaceuticals (Goodman-Delahunty, 1995; Reed, 1996; Schopp, & Quattrocchi, 1995; Zonana, 1994), has provided important standards for expert witness testimony concerning admissibility of evidence. Under these rulings, expert testimony is evaluated on its basis in the methods and procedures of science. Emphasis is placed upon such factors as falsifiability, error rates, acceptance by peer review, published findings, and broad professional acceptance of the procedures. Expert testimony needs to be comprised of conclusions that are based upon procedures and methods that are accepted by the field (Goodman-Delahunty, 1997; Penrod, Solomon, Fulero, & Cutler, 1995; Rotgers & Barrett, 1996).

Psychological research available on test instruments provides further guidelines for test selection. Before becoming involved in a forensic evaluation, it is essential that the psychologist become familiar with the psychological test literature pertinent to the case. A literature search of pertinent factors should be conducted before the evaluation is undertaken in order to determine if there are special problems or issues to consider. For example, if your opinion is being sought about likely or expected "psychological disability" that might result from experiencing chronic pain, then it is necessary to conduct a literature search of the particular instruments that you plan to use in order to determine their "experience base" in evaluating chronic pain patients. Conducting an Internet literature search is a relatively quick and easy matter today. The psychological literature on an assessment technique or problem area can be obtained free of charge through *PsychInfo* for members of the American Psychological Association (APA) at the website. Though perhaps less relevant to the psychologist, the legal precedents in the case can also be found through several legal case search sites on the Internet. For further information about obtaining literature to guide forensic assessments see Piotrowski (1993). (See findlaw.com for free legal research, or lexus.com and Westlaw.com for fee based legal research).

4.2   Assure that the tests being used are appropriate for the questions being addressed

Be aware of the limitations of a particular test or procedure that is being considered for use in the assessment. A particular psychological test might have a "normative" sample that is too limited for the comparison being made or may have been developed in a way that limits its utility for forensic evaluation where high testing standards are required. For example, the MCMI instruments do not use a normative reference group with which to compare a client's score but instead use psychiatric "base rate" scores to compare a particular test result to those produced by a group of psychiatric patients. Thus specific client's scores are meaningful only in the context of the client being viewed as a psychiatric patient. If the evaluation is conducted to determine *whether* or not a person is responding like a psychiatric patient (i.e. do they have psychological problems) or are they free of psychological symptoms, then the MCMI cannot provide an appropriate answer. For example, if the test were being used in a personnel screening context, then virtually no applicants would be recommended for employment because they would all be shown to have some psychological problems. In addition, Rogers et al. (1999), question whether the MCMI-III meets *Daubert* criteria given the low validity and high error rates that have been reported.

An instrument may have limitations because the norms were collected on an unusual sample or in non-standard ways, which might not be defensible in forensic assessment. For example, the Basic Personality Inventory (BPI), (See Jackson, 1989), was normed using data collection procedures that raise doubts as to the adequacy of the reference population. These investigators collected data in an uncontrolled manner-test booklets were mailed to potential subjects who were asked to complete the inventory. In addition, most of the normative population responded to only a portion of the items (1/3) rather than to the whole test-a procedure that limits the use of item statistics that require full response to items on a scale. Finally, since the test developers did not attempt to balance the sample for ethnicity, the vast majority of the subjects in the normative population were white. The norms of the BPI are not sufficiently representative of the general population to serve as a general norm for comparing forensic cases.

4.3   Forensic Evaluations Usually Involve Clients Who Have a Motivation to Present a Particular Test Pattern

Virtually all people being evaluated in the context of a forensic assessment may have motivation to make a particular impression or be viewed in a particular way on the psychological evaluation. It behooves the psychologist to carefully evaluate the client's cooperation, particularly the extent to which their testing is open, frank, and credible. Many psychological tests do not have a means of detecting "managed impressions" or exaggerated responding so prominent in forensic evaluations, and there is no way of the psychologist knowing whether the client has accurately presented a true picture of his or her psychological make-up. For example, on the WAIS-III, a person wishing to appear intellectually impaired might do so simply by not giving the correct answers or not answering in the time allotted. There are no validity scales on the Wechsler, scales or on most of the projective techniques, to guide the practitioner in assessing the credibility of the persons responding.

The MMPI-2 contains many more ways of assessing invalidating response patterns than any other psychological measuring instruments do. The validity indexes assess a range of invalidating conditions. Several measures address general "patterns" of deviant responding such as answering randomly, responding "all true" or "all false," some item omissions and there are measures to assess response inconsistency (VRIN and TRIN). A number of scales have been developed for the MMPI-2 that are sensitive to the content of the items; for example, to assess test defensiveness (Scales K and S), extreme virtue claiming (scale L), and exaggerated or faked responding (F, F(B), and F(p). See the discussion on validity scales on the MMPI-2 in Graham (2000), an Pope, et al., (2000).

The fact that a test does not contain validity indices does not mean that all responses to it are open and honest; it only means that the test fails to detect invalidating conditions. However, response patterns to psychological test items tend to be constant across instruments in a battery. Deviant response patterns on the MMPI-2 are likely to be present on other instruments in the test battery. It is likely that persons who are defensive on one test in a battery would also be defensive on other measures in the battery, whether specific or not those instruments possessed validity indices to detect invalidating conditions (see the discussion by Butcher, in press, a). Several specific validity scales have been developed, such as the SIRS (Rogers, Salekin, & Sewell, 1999), to assess malingered test responding in forensic cases.

4.4   Deciding upon Test Interpretations Once Protocol Validity is Established

Because forensic evaluations are so vulnerable to motivations to distort or to present a particular pattern, test interpretations need to be provided cautiously unless sufficient cooperation is assured.   Clients producing invalid records can be retested if the practitioner can be assured that the reason for the initial invalidation can be eliminated. If it can be assured that the client has approached the testing in a manner that has not invalidated the record then interpretation can proceed. It is important to use instruments that have an established validity for the population being studied.   With a sound research base (including information on any limitations or adjustments on the conclusions drawn), appropriate conclusions can be incorporated in the interpretation.

4.5   Using Computer-based Interpretations in a Forensic Study

One way of increasing the objectivity of test interpretation in forensic assessments is to incorporate a computer-based test interpretation in the evaluation. Some forensic psychologists are hesitant to use computer-based reports in their evaluation because of concerns that statements will be provided in the report that cannot be defended in court. For the most part, however, the computer report represents the most likely and most generalizing interpretation for the protocol in question. Such interpretations are provided "unselectively" for data that have been associated with the particular test performance. Whether or not the reluctant psychologist chooses to use computer-based evaluation of the case those interpretations may find themselves into the case proceedings from an opposing expert psychologist. Consequently, the hesitant psychologist will likely have to deal with the information contained in the report on cross-examination in either case.   Those interested in procedures for incorporating computer-based interpretations into their evaluation are referred to Pope, et al., (2000), and Butcher (in press b).

Computer-based interpretations are widely accepted in contemporary applied psychology. McMinn et al. (1999), recently studied the reluctance of practicing psychologists to incorporate new technology, such as fax machines, answering machines, the internet, computers, and so forth, into their practice and concluded that "monumental technological innovations appear to be having little impact on clinical practice." However, practitioners appear to be more willing to incorporate technological aids in their practice in the area of test scoring and interpretations. McMinn et al., concluded that "Computerized software has become widely accepted as a way to administer, score, and interpret psychological tests" (p. 171). In two recent surveys the rate of acceptance of computer-based test processing has been shown to be strong. Ball, Archer, and Imhof (1994), reported that 2/3 of respondents surveyed, incorporated computer-based evaluations into their assessment; and Downey, Sinnett, and Seeberger (1998), found the same percentage of the sample they surveyed used computer scoring, and 43.8% used computerized interpretive reports in their practice.

4.6   Avoid the Trap of Going Beyond The Data When Shaping Test Conclusions to Support a Legal Point

As noted earlier, one of the pitfalls that forensic psychologists face is that of the perceived need to "tailor" the psychological evaluation to fit the legal theory of the case, even though the results might be ambiguous or might not specifically support the point being addressed. The psychological study that has been developed and tailored to language needed for a specific legal theory might not hold up against careful expert testimony to the contrary. It is natural for the consulting psychologist to want to help those who employ them as a consultant, however, in the forensic area or for a particular case or a particular point this goal might be difficult to accomplish. An attorney who wants to win a case might (subtly or not so), try to get the consultant to testify to a particular point or slant the report in the case to address factors that will make their case stronger, even though the data do not support those particular conclusions. In one recent case, for example, the litigant was claiming (and may well have had), severe pain after an unsuccessful medical procedure. Her MMPI-2 profile did *not* resemble known patterns of people in high stress cases, but was essentially an invalid profile because of an extremely high L scale score; the profile showed little else but somatization on the clinical scales. An objective MMPI-2 interpretation of her profile would not provide support for her claims that she was feeling, depressed, tense, and anxious as a result of her "trauma." When the plaintiff's attorney was informed that the most likely interpretation of the profile did not suggest these post-traumatic psychological symptoms, he attempted to "shape" the psychologist's testimony by requesting (or encouraging) the psychologist to distort the findings in ways that would be apparent to any MMPI-2 expert (and contrary to the consultant's own writings).

The case described earlier in which the psychologist wrote in his report that the MMPI-2 matched cases of "inner ear trauma" is another example in which the conclusions offered could not be supported by the test data or the research literature.

It is best for the psychologist to formulate the psychological impressions independent of the specific needs of counsel in order to identify areas where their testimony would likely conflict with the theories of the case and to determine any limitations to the test interpretations. The psychologist who must sit alone on the witness stand and explain the findings in response to probing questions about what the testing "actually shows." Psychologists should be aware that attorneys might try to shape the testimony of experts and be careful not to incorporate interpretations that cannot be defended by the actual test data.

The "active role" that some attorneys take in shaping testimony on psychological evaluations has been studied. Wetter and Corrigan (1995), surveyed 70 attorneys and 150 law students with respect to whether they thought it appropriate to brief their clients before they took psychological tests. The majority of lawyers and law students thought it was the responsibility of the attorney to brief their clients on the testing beforehand. Interestingly, the role of "training" expert witnesses by American attorneys recently became the subject of a high visibility case in Britain. The case involved a prominent litigant who was immersed in a libel suit against a British politician. The litigant apparently employed an American attorney to "prep" his witnesses for trial-a situation that created a great deal of discussion in the legal community as to the differences in witness preparation strategies between the American and British legal systems (London Times, December 3, 1999). The American attorney was cross-examined by the British solicitor with respect to the alleged differences in witness training in the United States versus Britain, all of which he denied. Nevertheless, many attorneys in the UK hold the view that there is more "polishing" of testimony of witnesses (including expert testimony), during trial preparation in the United States than in Britain.

4.7 Same data, Different Conclusions: Staged Battles of Experts

The adversarial legal system fosters the development of the "strongest case scenarios" from both sides of a legal dispute. This often means that both sides will have their professional consultants providing expert testimony and in many cases providing opposing and contradictory interpretations of the same measures!

Even objective personality assessment instruments, such as the MMPI-2, where there is substantial agreement on the meaning of particular test scores on scales, can be the subject of opposing views. One can readily identify areas where "experts" might disagree. For example, one set of variables, which used the original MMPI items that are referred to, as the "subtle-obvious" keys are a case in point. The controversial Weiner-Harmon scales (Weiner, 1948), were alleged to assess client's motives without their being aware that they had disclosed them. These measures have not proven to be valid or useful measures in clinical assessment (Nelson, Pham, & Uchiyama, 1996; Weed, Ben-Porath, & Butcher, 1990). Several widely used textbooks on the MMPI-2 (Butcher & Williams, 1992; Graham, 2000; and Pope et al. 2000), recommend against their use. Yet, one textbook on MMPI-2 (Greene, 1991), devotes considerable space to the interpretation of these measures, essentially championing their use to assess clients. Most researchers have argued against their use, and the test publisher has discontinued these scales from official test materials following a survey of researchers into their utility and validity. Such theoretical disagreements can become a focal point in cases where a practitioner might want to use those measures to fit into a theory of the case.

How do these battles play out in front of the triers of fact? The outcome often hinges upon which expert is seen as more knowledgeable and credible. In many situations, however, jurors are not capable of determining which expert's view is most accurate, and the experts may serve only to cancel each other out or to confuse the case issues further.

5.   COMMUNICATING RESULTS OF A FORENSIC EVALUATION

In the majority of cases, an official written report describing the client will be requested and will likely become an exhibit if the case goes to trial. However, in some situations, the attorney will not want a written report in order to avoid disclosing fully and in advance the expert's opinions to the other side. It is important to determine what specific questions or issues need to be addressed in the report so that the test results can be targeted accordingly.

Space limitations in this article do not allow more than a brief discussion of some pertinent factors in developing a forensic report. Several points that bear on communicating the findings in a forensic evaluation will be described. Interested readers can find several sources that describe the major elements of a forensic report more fully (Butcher, 1999; Pope, et al., 2000; Weiner, 1999).

It is important for the psychologist evaluator to include a description of the testing conditions to assure that the reader of the report has a clear idea of any important situational factors that could have influenced the testing. Test conclusions need to be limited to areas the instrument was designed for and not stretched to answer improper questions. Psychological tests are not devised for, nor are they specific enough, to answer legal questions such as whether a person fits the profile of a sexual predator. They also cannot be used to answer generic questions such as whether a person is guilty or innocent.

Psychological reports should not be slanted simply to match the particular legal theory of the case. Regardless of who hires the psychologist, the evaluation should be conducted objectively and the report written for the court. The view that the psychologist-expert has a duty to the court in conducting objective evaluations, without regard for who retained them has been formalized in a recent ruling in the United Kingdom. The Civil Procedure Rules of 4/99 govern the action of psychologists and others who serve as expert witnesses in court (*The Psychologist*, 1999). Central to the new procedures is the mandate that psychologists address their reports to the court itself and not to the retaining party. Moreover, reports must comply with certain requirements in structure and content in order to demonstrate that they are unbiased and comprehensive in form. The reports need to contain several features including: details of the expert's qualifications, a signed "statement of truth" with respect to the facts and opinions included, and a summary of any "range of opinions." One new power that the court possesses is that there could be a single expert assigned to serve for both sides in a dispute rather than having experts on each side. The courts in Britain, of course, operate differently than those in the United States and the rule would not likely be acceptable to US courts and trial attorneys.

6.   SUMMARY

This article explores the role of objective psychological tests in forensic evaluation. A number of problems that face psychologists who conduct forensic evaluations were discussed and methods of increasing the credibility of the forensic psychological evaluation were noted. The need for strict adherence to standard administration, scoring, and interpretive procedures was underscored because many forensic evaluations are flawed by deviation from standard procedures.

The need for psychologists to acquire appropriate training in the administration, scoring, and interpretation of the procedures was discussed and the selective use of assessment procedures that have a supporting research base was recommended in order to satisfy the legal criteria of scientific acceptability.

The fact that forensic evaluations frequently involve clients who have a motivation to deceive was described and the importance of assessing validity of response patterns was noted. Psychological tests should only be interpreted if the protocol validity is established in order for the results to represent a valid characterization of the client's behavior and problems. The psychologist must assure that the assessment instruments used in a test battery are the most appropriate and valid procedures for the particular situation.

The forensic psychologist was also advised to be aware of the trap of being seduced into going beyond the test data and shaping test conclusions to support a legal point. Having conservative and data oriented conclusions in the psychological evaluation will go a long way toward presenting a problem-free testimony. The "battle of experts" that almost always occur in forensic cases can be a problem to both sides in a case. The difficult and embarrassing circumstance of having extremely different case conclusions for the same test data that occurs in the staged battles of experts can be reduced if the psychologist's involved stick to a data based interpretation of their results. The use of computer-based interpretations for psychological tests was described as one way in which the practitioner could obtain the most objective interpretation of a particular test. Finally, the chapter focused upon the importance of clear communication of the results of a forensic evaluation.

7.   REFERENCES

Ball, J. D., Archer, R.P., Imhof, E. A. (1994). Time requirements of psychological testing: A survey of practitioners. *Journal of Personality Assessment, 63*, 239-249.

Belter, R. W. & Piotrowski, C. (1999). Current status of Master's level training in psychological assessment. *Journal of Psychological Practice, 5* (1), 1-5.

Boccaccini, M. T. & Brodsky, S. L. (1999). Diagnostic test use by forensic psychologists in emotional injury cases. *Professional psychology: Research and Practice, 31*, (1), 251-259.

Borum, R. & Grisso, T.(1995). Psychological test use in criminal forensic evaluations. *Professional Psychology, 26*, 465-473.

Butcher, J. N. & Williams, C. L. (1992). *MMPI-2 and MMPI-A: Essentials of clinical interpretation*. Minneapolis, MN: University of Minnesota Press.

Butcher, J. N. (1999). *A beginner's guide to the MMPI-2*. Washington, D. C.: American Psychological Association.

Butcher, J. N. (2000). Dynamics of personality test responses: The empiricist's manifesto revisited. *Journal of Clinical Psychology. 56 (3)*, 1-12.

Butcher, J. N. (in press). Computer-based assessment strategies for clinical decision making. In J. R. Graham & J. A. Naglieri (Eds.). *Handbook of assessment psychology.*

Daubert v. Merrell Dow Pharmaceuticals. 113S. Ct 2786 (1993).

Downey, R. B., Sinnett, E. R. & Seeberger, W. (1998). *The changing face of MMPI practice. Psychological Reports, 83* (3, Pt 2), 1267-1272.

Frauenhoffer, D., Ross, M. J., Gfeller, J., Searight, H. R., & Piotrowski, C. (1998). Psychological test usage among licensed mental health practitioners: A multidisciplinary survey. *Journal of Psychological Practice, 4* (1), 28-33.

Goodman-Delahunty, J. & W. E. (1995). Compensation for pain and suffering and other psychological injuries: The impact of Daubert on employment discrimination claims. *Behavioral Sciences and the Law, 13*, 183-206.

Goodman-Delahunty, J. (1997). Forensic psychological expertise in the wake of Daubert. *Law and Human Behavior, 21*(2), 121-140.

Graham, J. R. (2000). MMPI-2: *Assessing personality and psychopathology*. Third Edition. New York: Oxford University Press.

Greene, R. L. (1991). *MMPI-2/MMPI: An interpretive manual*. Boston: Allyn & Bacon.

Grove, W. M. & Meehl, P. E. (1996). Comparative efficiency of informal (subjective, impressionistic) and formal (mechanical, algorithmic) prediction procedures: The clinical-statistical controversy. *Psychology, Public Policy, and Law, 2*, 293-323.

Hess, A. K. (1999). Serving as an expert witness. In A. Hess & I. Wiener (Eds.) *Handbook of forensic psychology* (Second edition). (Pp. 521-555). New York: Wiley.

Lees-Haley, P. R. (1992). Psychodiagnostic test usage by forensic psychologists. *Amerian Journal of Forensic Psychology, 10*, 25-30.

Lees-Haley, P. R., Smith, H. W., Williams, C. W. & Dunn, J. T. (1996). Forensic neuropsychological test usage: An empirical survey. *Archives of Clinical Neuropsychology, 11*, 45-51.

London Times (1999, December 3). *U. S. lawyer in clash with QC over Al Fayad* (p.6).

McMinn, M. R., Buchanan, T., Ellens, B. M., & Ryan, M. (1999). Technology, professional practice, and ethics: Survey of findings and implications. *Professional Psychology: Research and Practice, 30* (2), 165-172.

Meehl, P. E. (1997). Credentialed persons, credentialed knowledge. *Clinical Psychology: Science and Practice, 4*, 91-98.

Melton, G. et al. (1999). Training in forensic psychology and the law. In A. K. Hess & I. I. Weiner (Eds). *The handbook of forensic psychology*. (Pp. +++). New York: Wiley.

Millon, T. F. (1994). *MCMI-III: Manual*. Minneapolis, MN: National Computer Systems.

Nelson, L. D., Pham, D., & Uchiyama, C. (1996). Subtlety of the MMPI-2 Depression Scale: A subject laid to rest? *Psychological Assessment, 8*, 331-333.

News Release (1999). Expert witnesses and the new civil procedure rules. *The Psychologist, 12*, (12), p. 582.

Penrod, S. D., Solomon, M., Fulero, J. D., and Cutler, B. (1995). Expert testimony on eyewitness reliability before and after Daubert: The state of the law and the science. *Behavioral Sciences and the Law, 13,* 229-259.

Piotrowski, C. (1993). Legal issues in the inpatient setting: A framework for literature retrieval strategies. In M. B. Squire, et al. (Eds.) *Current advances in inpatient psychiatric care: A handbook.* Westport, CT: Greenwood Publishing Group, Inc.

Piotrowski, C. (1998). Assessment of pain: A survey of practicing clinicians. *Perceptual and Motor Skills, 86,* 181-182.

Pope, K. S., Butcher, J. N., & Seelen, J. (2000). *MMPI/MMPI-2/MMPI-A in court: Assessment, testimony, and cross-examination for expert witnesses and attorneys.* (Second edition) Washington, D.C.: American Psychological Association

Reed, J. E. (1995). Fixed vs. flexible neuropsychological test batteries under the Daubert Standard for the admissibility of evidence. *Behavioral Sciences and the Law, 13,* 315-322.

Rogers, R., Gillis, J. R., Dickens, S. E. & Bagby, M. (1991). Standardized assessment of malingering: Validation of the Structured Interview of Reported Symptoms. *Psychological Assessment, 3*(1), 89-96.

Rogers, R., Salekin, R. T. & Sewell, K. W. (1999). Validation of the Millon Clinical Multiaxial Inventory for Axis II disorders: Does it meet Daubert standard? *Law & Human Behavior, 23,* (4), 425-443.

Rorschach Workshops, *"MMPI-2 Workshops,"* Department of Psychology, University of Minnesota, Asheville, Minneapolis, Minnesota.

Rorschach Workshops, *"MMPI-2 Workshops,"* Department of Psychology, University of Minnesota, Asheville, North Carolina.

Rotgers, F. & Barrett, D. (1996). Daubert v Merrell Dow and expert testimony by clinical psychologists: Implications and recommendations. *Professional Psychology: Research and Practice, 27* (5), 467-474.

Schopp, R. F. & Quattrocchi, M. R. (1995). Predicting the present: Expert testimony and civil commitment. *Behavioral Sciences and the Law, 13,* 159-181.

Weed, N. C., Ben-Porath, Y. S., & Butcher, J. N. (1990). Failure of the Weiner-Harmon MMPI subtle scales as predictors of psychopathology and as validity indicators. Psychological Assessment: *A Journal of Consulting and Clinical Psychology, 2,* 281-283.

Wiener, D. N. (1948). Subtle and obvious keys for the Minnesota Multiphasic Personality Inventory/ *Journal of Consulting Psychology, 12,*164-170.

Weiner, I. (1999). Writing forensic reports. In A. K. Hess & I. I. Weiner (Eds). *The handbook of forensic psychology.* (Pp. +++). New York: Wiley.

Wetter, M. W. & Corrigan, S. K. (1995). Providing information to clients about psychological tests: A survey of attorney's and law student's attitudes. *Professional Psychology, 26,* 495-474.

Zonana, H. (1994). Daubert v. Merrell Dow Pharmaceuticals: A new standard for scientific evidence in the courts. *Bulletin of the American Academy of Psychiatry and Law, 22* (2), 309-325.

(I would like to express my appreciation to Steve Glickman, of Glickman & Glickman law firm, Beverly Hills, CA. for his helpful comments on an earlier draft of this manuscript.)

Chapter 5

Forensic Assessment of Malingering and Related Response Styles

Richard Rogers, Ph.D., ABPP and Michael J. Vitacco, M.S.
Department of Psychology, University of North Texas, Denton, TX

1.   INTRODUCTION

A cursory review of DSM-IV (American Psychiatric Association, 1994, p. 683), suggests that malingering "should be strongly suspected" in forensic evaluations when the evaluatee is uncooperative with the evaluation and treatment, warrants the diagnosis of antisocial personality disorder, or reports a disability discrepant with clinical findings.   An incautious application of DSM-IV is likely to lead forensic psychologists to commit grievous errors in diagnosis and classification.   Indeed, many psychologists are surprised to learn that the DSM-IV model completely lacks scientific foundation.

As illustrated by the first paragraph, an important objective of this chapter is to correct the missteps and mistakes that are often observed in evaluations of malingering.   Current risk models of malingering remain unsubstantiated. When standardized methods are not employed, traditional evaluations are likely susceptible to examiner bias.   A second important objective of the chapter is the selective application of empirically validated methods for the evaluation of malingering.   Clinical methods are best understood in terms of their detection strategies.   A major focus of this chapter will be an examination of specific detection strategies in light of feigned presentations. As a way of introduction, the chapter will begin with a synopsis of malingering and related response styles.

2.   MALINGERING AND RELATED RESPONSE STYLES

The terminology to describe response styles has become standardized during the last decade (Rogers, 1988, 1997). As a brief review, these terms are discussed:

1. *Malingering* refers to the "intentional production of false or grossly exaggerated physical or psychological symptoms" (American Psychiatric Association, 1994, p. 683) in the service of an external goal. The production of symptoms must be voluntary; otherwise, somatoform disorders should be considered. The motivation must be assessed as "external," otherwise the diagnosis of factitious disorder must be entertained. Motivations include financial gain, increased attention and support from others, and avoidance of adverse circumstances.

2. *Somatoform disorders* are a grouping of diagnoses based on the unintentional production of physical symptoms. They are differentiated from malingering in that symptoms are (a) typically limited to physical symptoms that "suggest a medical condition" (American Psychiatric Association, 1994, p. 445), and (b) not subjected to the patient's control. As a result of the latter, external objectives are not observed. Finally, somatoform disorders are held to an unwieldy standard: their symptoms are not "fully explained" by a medical condition, mental disorder, or the direct effects of substance abuse. Examples include hypochondriasis, unexplained pain, and conversion symptoms.

3. *Factitious disorders* refer to the intentional production of physical or psychological symptoms solely for the purposes of becoming a patient and adopting a sick role. Rogers, Bagby, and Rector (1989), questioned the conceptual and practical implications of this diagnosis. Practitioners must be able to assess the intentional production (presumably voluntary) of symptoms to satisfy psychic needs (presumably involuntary). The exclusion of external incentives becomes problematic in that environmental changes often result from patient status: (a) compensation, (b) removal from stressful work, and (c) diminished family responsibilities.

4. *Secondary gain* is a clinical construct that posits either unintentional (psychodynamic and behavioral perspectives) or intentional (forensic

perspective) rewarding and perpetuation of a patient's disability (see Rogers & Reinhardt, 1998). Given its controversies, the use of secondary gain in forensic settings to describe a response style is strongly questioned (see subsection entitled "Utilization of Quasiconstructs").

5. *Irrelevant responding* refers to a response style whereby the patient does not become involved in the assessment process. Most often, replies are unrelated to the content of the clinical inquiries. In completing a multiscale inventory, some evaluatees answer test items without reading them. Reasons for irrelevant responding are manifold; they include (a) lack of motivation, (b) illiteracy, (c) psychotic interference, (d) oppositionality, and (e) malingered confusion. An important caveat is that irrelevant responding often produces a highly inconsistent response pattern. Unless systematically addressed, these inconsistencies may be mistaken for malingering. For example, a randomly completed MMPI-2 will have extreme elevations on F and Fb scales.

6. *Defensiveness* refers to a response style that is the polar opposite of malingering. Defensiveness occurs when the patient intentionally denies or grossly minimizes physical or psychological symptoms in order to meet an external goal.

7. *Hybrid responding* refers to a combination of response styles. The prototypical example of hybrid responding is the male sex offender who may exaggerate his childhood history of abuse, be self-disclosing about current psychological problems, and deny paraphilic urges and behavior.

8. *Feigning* refers to the deliberate fabrication or gross exaggeration of psychological or physical symptoms. The term does not specify the patient's motivation. Because psychological testing cannot infer patient motivation, feigning is often preferred to malingering in describing the results of standardized measures.

3. IMPORTANCE OF MALINGERING TO FORENSIC EVALUATIONS

The determination of malingering is a preeminent issue in forensic evaluations. Its determination is likely to play a decisive role in (a) the interpretation of reported psychopathology and apparent cognitive impairment and (b) the rendering of conclusions on the relevant legal issues. Once malingering has been established, the typical practice is to assume imprudently that all symptoms are bogus. A malingerer's genuine symptoms are likely to be suspected if not categorically discounted. The challenge for forensic psychologists is how to establish legitimate disorders in the face of malingering.

The motivation of individuals involved in legal proceedings is frequently suspect. Especially in a criminal context, legal professionals and the lay public are apt to believe that litigants are attempting to "beat the system" (Perlin, 1994). When testimony about malingering is introduced, this testimony may overshadow all other evidence. Suspicions are confirmed; the litigant's motivations are exposed. The determination of fraud and deceit, implicit in malingering testimony, may play a preponderant role in the legal outcome. It is our assumption that any testimony about malingering, however weak, may be a preemptive strike in determining the verdict in a particular case. This assumption places an onerous burden on forensic psychologists when providing testimony on issues of malingering.

4.   MISSTEPS AND MISTAKES IN MALINGERING EVALUATIONS

A major objective of this chapter is to correct common errors made in the course of malingering evaluations. Errors occur because of examiner biases, adoption of unsubstantiated risk models, and the utilization of ill-defined constructs. Each of these issues will be considered separately.

4.1   Examiner Bias

A common criticism (Colbach, 1997), of forensic evaluations is that impartiality is not achievable. However, the current discussion is far more circumscribed; it addresses potential biases among forensic mental health professionals regarding their views of malingering.

Psychologists, who differ markedly from their colleagues in finding most or very few forensic cases to be malingering, must consider the possibility of systematic bias in conducting these evaluations. Survey data from more than 500 forensic psychologists suggest that the prevalence of malingering in forensic cases averages about 15.7% (Rogers, Sewell, & Goldstein, 1994), to 17.4% (Rogers, Salekin, Sewell, Goldstein, & Leonard, 1998). Because of differences in settings and psychologists' expertise, considerable variability is expected (*SD* = 14.4%). Therefore, only extremes should be construed as evidence of potential bias.

- In conducting post-doctoral forensic workshops, we occasionally meet seasoned psychologists who have never seen a malingering case. We are convinced that the operative principle is embodied in the statement, "If you don't look for it, you won't find it." Differential diagnosis is not an intuitive process. If forensic psychologists do not systematically evaluate malingering, then their reports are likely to be predetermined (i.e., biased against this classification).

- Statistically, the likelihood is very small (1.2%) that a forensic psychologist would evaluate the majority of forensic cases (≥ 50%) as malingering. We hypothesize that the operative principle for over classification of malingering is encapsulated in the following statement, "I know it's there, I just have to find it." If forensic psychologists have a very low threshold for the ascertainment of malingering, then their reports are likely to be predetermined (i.e., biased toward this classification).

Preliminary data (Rogers et al., 1994) yielded non-significant trends that raised several hypotheses about the relationship between theoretical positions and the classification of malingering. Experts who favored the criminological model, implicit in DSM-IV, had a greater trend than others to see malingerers as warranting the diagnosis of antisocial personality disorder and being unlikely to respond to treatment. A reasonable assumption is that forensic psychologists who embrace the DSM-IV perspective will (a) overemphasize malingering in forensic cases and (b) underemphasize malingering in non-forensic cases. Despite very limited data on theoretical positions, forensic psychologists are cautioned to review their own positions and its relevance to the assessment of malingering.

Rogers and Shuman (2000), counseled forensic experts to explore how their general emotions (e.g., like or dislike) and overall attitudes (e.g., empathetic or non -empathetic) toward the evaluatee. Occasionally, forensic psychologists develop countertransference feelings toward the evaluatee. These feelings, positive or negative, can influence the expert's perceptions of the evaluatee, including the appraisal of his or her motivation (Dembe, 1998). In such cases, forensic psychologists may fall victim to the *ad hominem fallacy*. With the *ad hominem fallacy* (Dauer, 1989), the expert improperly generalizes from a specific set of attributes (e.g., deceitful in business transactions) to another, possibly related issue (e.g., malingering). It becomes immediately apparent that deceptive business practices offer no definitive information about malingering. We have observed the *ad hominem fallacy* most often on inpatient units when an obviously manipulative patient is subsequently mischaracterized as a malingerer.

5.   UTILIZATION OF QUASI-CONSTRUCTS FOR MALINGERING

Forensic psychologists sometimes sidestep the explicit classification of malingering and invoke constructs that are often open to misinterpretation. Especially in the civil arena, psychologists may employ such constructs as "secondary gain" and "symptom magnification." As discussed below, these constructs differ substantially from malingering on two grounds: (a) imprecision in their conceptualization and (b) their lack of validation.

5.1   Secondary Gain

Secondary gain was originally a psychodynamic construct; it was conceived as an unconscious defense in the service of intrapsychic needs. Subsequently, psychologists from a behavioral perspective have employed the construct of secondary gain to understand how patients' illness behavior was perpetuated. Behavioral psychologists consider secondary gain as selective reinforcements of a patient's disability by health care professionals and family members. From a behavioral perspective, the patient does not exercise choice; his or her illness behavior is shaped behavioral contingencies imposed by significant others and the health care system. Contrasted with the psychodynamic and behavioral perspective, forensic psychology has utilized the concept of secondary gain as a convenient but simplistic explanation for a patient's continued impairment. Within a forensic perspective, the concept of secondary gain is based on unsubstantiated inferences about the patient's motivation to exaggerate impairment in order to achieve external incentives.

As described by Rogers and Reinhardt (1998), psychologists may confuse the *potential* for secondary gain with the *determination* of secondary gain. For example, a patient may receive substantial compensation while avoiding a stressful work environment. The same patient may express a continued interest in receiving compensation. Is this secondary gain? Not necessarily. With diminished income, a patient's concern about his or her future financial status is completely understandable. The same patient may also openly express relief about not having to cope with a stressful career or a troublesome supervisor. Is this secondary gain? Not necessarily. The patient is self-disclosing a common, almost universal, desire to reduce stress and conflict. Any considered attempt to manipulate the disability for continued gain would not logically include this self-disclosure. Therefore, facile inferences about a patient's willingness to receive undeserved benefits (secondary gain) lack foundation in psychological knowledge and should be excluded from the courtroom.

A further problem with secondary gain relates to inferences based on the magnitude of the expected reward. Psychologists may erroneously equate higher levels of reward with higher likelihood for secondary gain. Although the opposite corollary is likely true (no incentives, no secondary gain), we have no evidence of increased likelihood of secondary gain with increased rewards. We are concerned that psychologists project their own temptations onto their evaluatees. As an informal observation, we find the construct of secondary gain is more likely to be invoked when the compensation is substantial (e.g., more than $10,000 per month) than subsistent (e.g., less than $500 per month).

5.2   Symptom Magnification

The concept of "symptom magnification" is sometimes employed in forensic cases to circumvent the classification of malingering. Symptom magnification is an ill-defined term used to describe the exaggeration of symptoms with the implication that this exaggeration is deliberate and goal-oriented. Several observations are germane. First, its implied meaning largely parallels malingering, but lacks its explicit definition. Second, the level of exaggeration remains unspecified. Mild to moderate levels of exaggeration are difficult to operationalize, given the subjectivity in reporting symptoms, and the role of mental disorders in distorting the accuracy of symptom recall. As an example of the latter, depressed patients tend to "overreport" Axis II symptoms (see Rogers, in press). In light of its conceptual vagueness and unwarranted connotation, the term "symptom magnification" should not be utilized in forensic evaluations or testimony.

6.   DSM-IV AND IMPLICIT RISK MODELS

For the last two decades, DSM (i.e., DSM-III; American Psychiatric Association, 1980; DSM-III-R; American Psychiatric Association, 1987; and DSM-IV; American Psychiatric Association, 1994) has posited an implicit risk model for malingering. It is considered a risk model because it does not classify malingering but merely provides an unspecified likelihood that malingering is strongly suspected. This risk model is based on one static (antisocial personality disorder) and three fluid (medicolegal evaluation, uncooperativeness, and discrepant findings) risk factors. In many criminal cases, defendants will automatically meet at least two factors (i.e., antisocial personality disorder plus medicolegal evaluation). As a result, malingering would be "strongly suspected" in large numbers of criminal forensic cases where actual evidence of feigning is non-existent. From the civil arena, most parents in child custody cases do not cooperate with the forensic evaluations because they deny both their own psychological problems and limitations in parenting. If the DSM-IV indices were applied rigorously, the majority of child-custody parents would be strongly suspected of malingering because they meet at least two indices: medicolegal evaluation and uncooperativeness. Ironically, the error rate would approximate 100%. These parents are not malingering, but are engaged in a diametrically opposite response style, namely defensiveness.

Rogers (1990), tested the DSM risk model of malingering in a criminal forensic sample. He found that the criterion of two or more indices had an alarming false positive rate of approximately 80%. No other studies have addressed this issue. Forensic psychologists place themselves in an untenable position if they utilize the DSM risk model of malingering. Not only has the model not been rigorously tested, but the available data indicate that it is likely to be wrong four out of five times in identifying malingerers.

7.   MODELS FOR THE ASSESSMENT OF MALINGERING

Some forensic psychologists appear to rely upon the MMPI-2 as a general screen for possible malingering. We suspect that this reliance is based on a misunderstanding of malingering. When examined closely, the MMPI-2 is ill equipped to examine certain domains of malingering. The purpose of this section is twofold. First, the different domains of malingering are explored. Second, detection strategies for each domain are reviewed.

Rogers et al. (1998), asked 221 forensic experts to identify their most prototypical malingering cases in a forensic context. The results were examined for three separate domains: (a) psychopathology and mental disorders, (b) intellectual or neuropsychological impairment (hereinafter referred to as "cognitive"), and (c) medical syndromes. Several salient findings emerged. First, relatively few cases (25 or 11.3%) qualified for multiple domains; therefore, these domains may be useful as discrete categories. Second, both cognitive impairment (43 or 19.5%) and medical syndromes (35 or 15.8%) were well represented. Psychologists need to consider multiple domains in conducting forensic evaluations.

In the following subsections, we explore what is required (tasks and decisions) of malingerers when feigning mental disorders or cognitive impairment, Psychologists are in a better position to understand malingering if they appreciate the basic challenges and dilemmas that malingerers must confront. We have chosen not to examine feigned medical syndromes in depth ·because empirical studies are generally lacking or emphasize the factorial rather than malingering perspective of feigned physical illness (Cunnien, 1997).

7.1   Feigned Mental Disorders

Feigned mental disorders differ from other forms of malingering in their requirements. First and foremost, the malingerer must have a convincing production of psychopathology, symptoms, and associated features. For example, an individual feigning schizophrenia must be able to produce a believable set of symptoms that follow the natural course of a schizophrenic disorder. In this case, the individual must create a credible progression from prodromal symptoms (e.g., deficits in interpersonal functioning) to the active phase of the disorder (e.g., hallucinations and delusions). A typical progression is also sometimes observed with specific symptoms. Psychotic patients rarely begin with florid delusions. More typically, overvalued ideas become increasingly intense until they represent fixed beliefs in spite of incontrovertible evidence to the contrary (i.e., delusions).

A second requirement of feigned mental disorders extends beyond the fabrication of psychopathology. Malingerers of mental disorders must be able to also generate plausible responses and reactions to their purported symptoms. In the case of feigned schizophrenia, a malingerer would need to create a plausible response to hearing auditory hallucinations. Does he or she treat the hallucinations as an ordinary voice? If not, what differences can be reported or observed? In some cases, a malingerer does not plan sufficiently for questions about emotional reactions or behavioral responses. In these instances, malingerers may appear baffled by questions and may respond (honestly) with "I don't know." In other instances, malingerers mask their bafflement with either sudden confusion or unexpected anger. While sudden changes sometime occur with genuine disorders, the highly selective timing of these changes may be significant.

A third requirement is the malingerer's presentation to the examiner. In simulating a mental disorder, the malingerer must decide about how impaired he or she should appear. A difficult challenge is matching the content (e.g., hopelessness) with the process (e.g., depressed voice and tearfulness) of communication. In contrast, persons feigning schizophrenia must decide what type of incongruity between content (e.g., paranoid ideation) and emotion (e.g., flat or inappropriate affect) might be expected.

7.2   Feigned Cognitive Impairment

Unlike feigned mental disorders, malingerers of cognitive impairment do not need to develop an elaborate and believable set of symptoms and associated features. Rather, their primary requirements are "effortful failures." Although some malingerers attempt to fail without appearing to try (e.g., blurting out obviously wrong answers), this approach is unlikely to be successful for two reasons. First, this approach to malingering is likely to result in indiscriminant failures. Such failures are likely to produce improbably low scores on cognitive measures that are discrepant with indices of functioning. Second, the obvious lack of effort is likely to be associated with a motivation for failure.

In feigning cognitive impairment, a difficult requirement is that malingerers sidestep the competitive desire to appear intelligent and intact. In some instances, individuals claim gross inabilities to perform memory and other cognitive functions. When confronted with challenging intellectual tasks, however, they become invested in succeeding at the test. A challenge for persons feigning cognitive impairment is to appear involved in the testing while not becoming invested in their own success. In our clinical experience, the desire to appear intelligent can outweigh all other considerations. Several empirical studies (Heaton, Smith, Lehman, & Vogt, 1978; Mittenberg, Theroux-Fichera, Zielinski, & Heilbronner, 1995), offer indirect support for this observation. When asked to feign marked cognitive impairment, research participants still tend score in the average range of intellectual abilities.

In feigning cognitive impairment, malingerers must appreciate differences in cognitive complexity. Failure at a relatively simple task (e.g., recall of over learned material, such as the alphabet) is unlikely to occur in persons who are successful at more complex tasks (e.g., verbal analogies or short term memory). On this point, Mittenberg, Azrin, Millsaps, and Heilbronner (1993), found on the Wechsler Memory Scale-Revised (WMS-

R; Wechsler, 1987), that simulators performed more poorly than expected on relatively simple cognitive tasks in comparison to their overall performance.

Most persons referred for psychological evaluations are not compromised in all spheres of their cognitive functioning. Therefore, a second requirement for feigned cognitive impairment is deciding which abilities are impaired and which remain intact. As a specific example, an individual feigning amnesia must decide what memories and abilities are compromised. Because amnestic syndromes are relatively specific, memory deficits for dissociative amnesia (e.g., loss of personal memories) must be differentiated from organic amnesia (e.g., anterograde amnesia). Indeed, malingered amnesia is frequently detected by the indiscriminant reporting of pervasive memory loss. With selective memory "losses" (both personal and non-personal), the malingerer faces a very different challenge. Ironically, he or she must be able to remember the "lost" memories in order to make a plausible presentation. In summary, malingerers must decide which cognitive deficits to portray and remain consistent in this portrayal.

A third requirement of persons feigning cognitive impairment is to make decisions about their awareness of, and reaction to, their simulated impairment. Depending on the type of brain injury, genuine patients may be unaware of their deficits. In fact, Lopez et al. (1994), found a significant negative relationship between the awareness of loss and the severity of cognitive deficits. In simulating cognitive deficits, malingerers must make decisions about their awareness of these apparent impairments. In addition, malingerers must anticipate questions about their daily functioning with direct implications for their claimed deficits. If "aware" of impairments, the malingerer must gauge how to present his or her emotional reaction to the purported impairment.

7.3 Conclusions about Feigning

Many malingerers simply fail to take into account the numerous critical decision points in their efforts at feigning. As a result, malingerers lose credibility when they report preposterous symptoms or unbelievable cognitive deficits. Marked incongruities (e.g., an erudite discussion of diminished concentration) also mar the malingerer's credibility. Often preoccupied with the presentation of bogus symptoms and deficits, malingerers neglect their responses and reactions to these difficulties. To the skilled psychologist, this failure to consider critical issues may contribute to the clinical detection of their malingering attempts.

Forensic psychologists may fail to take into account atypical and incongruous presentations. We are not suggesting that these experts fail to utilize standardized indices for the detection of malingering. Rather, we are concerned that the current focus on quantified cut scores, while very appropriate, has not detracted from more integrative determinations regarding an evaluatee's response styles. As an egregious example, we recently reviewed a forensic report that focused for pages on individual test results but overlooked extreme between-test incongruities. While these incongruities did not necessarily suggest malingering, they indicated the need for a systematic appraisal of response styles.

The clinical assessment of malingering relies predominantly on established detection strategies that are empirically tested and validated with specific measures. In light of the challenges that malingerers face, forensic psychologists may wish to also consider the following:

1. The emergence and sequencing of symptoms. Examples include (a) the sudden appearance of symptom(s) (e.g., reliving a combat-related PTSD experience) to explain an antisocial act, or (b) no history of unwarranted suspiciousness or hypervigilance preceding florid paranoid delusions.
2. Surprised confusion and speculations about symptoms. Examples include (a) surprise when asked to describe the physical characteristics of a visual hallucination or (b) apparent guessing about symptoms associated with a panic attack.
3. Marked incongruities in clinical presentation of symptoms. Examples include (a) animated description of severe depression or (b) demonstrating an ability to recall earlier questions from the clinical interview verbatim, while failing simple verbal memory tasks. Several cautions are in order. First, many genuine patients are inconsistent in their presentation of symptoms and abilities. Second, bona fide patients often lack insight and accurate self-appraisal about their functioning.
4. Marked discrepancies in reported versus observed impairment. Examples include (a) complaints of overwhelming generalized anxiety, but collateral data about active involvement in social events, or (b) reports of a chronic incapacity to relate to others that are incompatible with observed interpersonal functioning.

8. DETECTION METHODS FOR FEIGNED PSYCHOPATHOLOGY AND FEIGNED COGNITIVE IMPAIRMENT

This section provides a synopsis of detection strategies and psychometric measures for the classification of malingering. This synopsis is not intended as a substitute for the development of a sophisticated understanding of malingering and other response styles. The standard reference is Rogers (1997), *Clinical Assessment of Malingering and Deception*. For cases of feigned cognitive impairment, we also recommend Reynolds (1998), *Detection of Malingering During Head Injury Litigation*.

The previous section underscored the key distinction between feigned mental disorders and feigned cognitive impairment. Feigned mental disorders require the plausible creation of symptoms and associated features. Feigned cognitive impairment requires a plausible selection of intellectual and neuropsychological deficits. For feigned cognitive impairment, these deficits are simply failures on standardized measures; they do not require the fabrication of bogus psychopathology. Strategies for the detection of malingering generally follow this key distinction: Detection strategies for feigned mental disorders focus on clinical presentation while detection strategies for feigned cognitive impairment address abilities and capacities.

8.1 Detection Strategies for Feigned Mental Disorders

We examine eight detection strategies for the evaluation of feigned mental disorders. For each strategy, we present a description of the strategy and representative examples of the strategy (i.e., specific scales of standardized measures). Because of the extensive training and experience necessary to conduct forensic evaluations, this discussion assumes that readers have a thorough background in diagnostic measures. Finally, key references are provided for each of the measures.

1. *Rare Symptoms*. Rare symptoms are one of the most robust strategies for the detection of malingering. Rare symptoms are characterized by their sheer infrequency among populations of mentally disordered persons. The most common examples of rare symptoms are found in psychotic symptomatology (e.g., neologisms and thought insertion), although examples can be found with anxiety (e.g., atypical phobias) and mood symptoms (e.g., sustained buying sprees). Evaluatees, who endorse a

disproportionate number of rare symptoms, are suspected of malingering.
Representative examples of scales include the following:
- Structured Interview of Reported Symptoms (SIRS; Rogers, Bagby, &
  Dickens, 1992), Rare Symptom (RS) scale
- MMPI-2 Fp scale[1]
- Personality Assessment Inventory (PAI) Negative Impression (NIM)
  scale

2. *Symptom Combinations.* Symptom combinations are a detection strategy
   based on symptom pairs that rarely occur together. Among relatively
   common symptoms, a malingerer must decide which symptom pairs are
   unlikely to co-occur. As a clinical example, paranoid ideation is unlikely
   to be associated with histrionic symptoms of sexually seductive behavior.
   As a matter of convention, items of opposite content (i.e., contradictory
   symptoms, such as insomnia and hypersomnia) are excluded, because
   such items can be foiled. This strategy is highly sophisticated in its
   consideration of unlikely symptom pairs, which are not likely to be
   obvious to most malingerers. Examples include the following scales:
   - SIRS Symptom Combinations (SC) scale
   - Schedule of Affective Disorders and Schizophrenia (SADS; Spitzer &
     Endicott, 1978) specialized Symptom Combinations (SC; see Rogers,
     1997) scale

3. *Atypical Profiles.* Atypical profiles can be assessed on multi-scale
   inventories when certain relationships among clinical and validity scales
   are observed that rarely occur among genuine patients. Given the
   polythetic nature of these scales, the meaning of these unexpected scale
   patterns is likely to be obscured. Therefore, this strategy is not
   recommended for inventories with substantial item overlap. The
   following is an example of this strategy:
   - Morey's (1996) PAI Malingering Index

4. *Stereotypical Misconceptions.* As discovered by Gough (1954), both
   professional and nonprofessionals have stereotypical misconceptions
   about how patients respond to multi-scale inventories. Stereotypical
   misconceptions represent those items (e.g., frequent nightmares)
   mistakenly believed to occur in the majority of patients with mental
   disorders. In the only example (MMPI-2 Ds Scale; Gough, 1954),
   simulators typically endorsed more than 60% of these stereotypical items
   while genuine patients endorsed substantially fewer (rough estimates in

---

[1] The MMPI-2 F scale is often categorized as a rare-symptom strategy. Technically, the F
scale is composed of test items that were very infrequent among *non-disordered* normative
sample. Its items do not appear to be especially infrequent in clinical samples. For
example, Greene (1997) found patients endorsed items on the F scale at approximately a
13% rate.

the 29 to 36% range). Although often overlooked, stereotypical misconceptions and rare symptoms provide complementary detection strategies based on unexpected endorsement rates. The primary example of this detection strategy is the following:

− MMPI-2 Ds Scale and its condensed version, the Dsr Scale

5. *Indiscriminant Symptom Endorsement.* As its name implies, this strategy is based on a non-selective reporting of symptoms, which represents a greater breadth and range than typically found in genuine patients. When given a broad array of symptoms, most genuine patients do not endorse the majority of these items in the pathological direction. This strategy is the most effective when a wide range of symptomatology is represented. Examples include the following:

− SIRS Symptom Selectivity (SEL) scale
− MMPI-2 Lachar-Wrobel (LW) critical item list
− SADS Indiscriminant Symptom Endorsement

6. *Symptom Severity.* Symptom severity is a detection strategy based on the proportion of symptoms endorsed by the evaluatee at a severe, extreme, or unbearable level. An unexplored variant of symptom severity would be identification of specific symptoms that are almost never reported at extreme levels. Examples of symptom severity include the following:

− SIRS Symptom Severity (SEV) Scale
− SADS Symptom Severity Scale

7. *Blatant and Subtle Symptoms.* To clarify, blatant symptoms are obvious indicators of a serious mental disorder while subtle symptoms are often viewed as everyday problems. As a clinical example from major depression, a suicide attempt would be characterized as a blatant symptom, while early morning awakening is likely to be construed as a subtle symptom. Seasoned forensic psychologists are likely to recognize this blatant-subtle distinction with the MMPI-2 O-S (i.e., total T score difference between Weiner-Harmon "obvious" and "subtle" subscales). Marked differences in O-S can be indicative of malingering (Greene, 1997). Contrary to general perceptions, malingerers do *not* necessarily report more blatant than subtle symptoms; the observed differences are accounted for by T score transformation (i.e., fewer "obvious" symptoms are needed on the MMPI-2 to achieve the same T score as "subtle" symptoms). Rogers et al. (1992), found that simulators tended to score higher on both blatant and subtle symptoms. Examples of blatant and subtle symptoms include:

− MMPI-2 Obvious-Subtle (O-S) difference and total score for Obvious-only subscales
− SIRS individual Blatant (BL) and Subtle (SU) scales

8. *Reported versus Observed Symptoms.* This strategy is based on marked discrepancies between what the evaluatee reports and what is clinically observed. By its nature, this detection strategy focuses on verbal and nonverbal behavior that is clearly observable.   An example is the following:
   – SIRS Reported versus Observed (RO) scale
   As previously noted, psychologists will need to consult readily available references in using the above strategies. For convenience, key references for feigned mental disorders are organized by specific measures:
   – SIRS: see Rogers et al. (1992) and Rogers (1997)
   – MMPI-2: see Berry (1995), Greene (1997), and Rogers, Sewell, and Salekin (1994).
   – PAI: see Morey (1991, 1996); Rogers, Sewell, Cruise, Wang, and Ustad (1998); and Rogers, Sewell, Morey, and Ustad (1996).
   – SADS: see Rogers (1997).

8.2   Detection Strategies for Feigned Cognitive Impairment

   A parallel structure is used for feigned cognitive impairment.   We describe nine detection strategies and provide representative examples. For more extensive coverage of detection strategies, see Rogers, Harrell, and Liff (1993).
1. *Floor Effect.* The floor effect strategy relies on very basic cognitive abilities.   Among neuropsychological referrals that are deemed testable, these items should be passed by nearly everyone. As a clinical example, nearly every neuropsychological patient is able to identify his or her gender.   Because genuine patients rarely fail, the floor-effect strategy appears superficially analogous to the rare-symptom strategy for feigned mental disorders. However, floor-effect items have two important limitations: (a) the items are so simple that their purpose may be transparent, and (b) malingerers may not be tempted to fail them, because they do not need or desire to appear so grossly impaired. Representative examples include the following:
   – Rey 15-Item (see Lezak, 1995)
   – Test of Malingered Memory (TOMM; Tombaugh, 1997)[2]

---

[2] Although the TOMM includes other detection strategies, its classification is based essentially on the floor effect.

- Word Memory Test (Green, Astner, & Allen, 1996)
2. *Performance Curve.* This strategy is built on the simple but elegant principle that the "level of success should be proportionate to item difficulty." When the full spectrum of item difficulty is represented, patients with genuine intellectual or neuropsychological impairment demonstrate a predictable decline (curve) from comparatively easy items (high level of success) to very difficult items (i.e., "no" success on open-ended responses and "chance" success on multiple-choice answers). Malingerers often fail disproportionately on items of easy to average difficulty; inspection of their performance curves may reveal more gradual declines than found with genuine patients. Representative examples include the following:
- Validity Indicator Profile (VIP; Frederick, 1997)
- Specialized scoring the Ravens Progressive Matrices (see Gudjonsson & Shackleton, 1986)
3. *Symptom Validity Testing.* Symptom validity testing (SVT) is a detection strategy based on an improbable failure rate. With a forced-choice paradigm, genuine patients with gross impairments will not fail all items. Depending on the number of choices, the highest proportion of failed items can be calculated for an "honest" effort. Given two choices, for example, any genuine effort should not substantially exceed 50% (i.e., pure guessing or chance). Malingerers can be detected if failure rates significantly exceed chance. The SVT strategy is based on an important assumption, namely that the alternatives are equiprobable.[3] Its effectiveness is likely dependent on item difficulty: Very easy items may not be missed for the same reasons as floor effect; very difficult items are likely to produce chance probabilities in both genuine patients and malingerers. The best items for SVT are those that range from moderately low to moderately high in item difficulty. Representative examples include the following:
- Portland Digit Recognition Test (Binder, 1990)
- Computerized Assessment of Response Bias (Allen, Conder, Green, & Cox, 1997)
4. *Forced Choice Testing.* Forced choice testing (FCT) is based on "poorer than expected" performance (Pankratz & Binder, 1997). Unlike SVT, which is based on specific probabilities, FCT is a general estimate based on group comparisons between genuine patients and simulators. Any decision (e.g., "likely to be a malingerer") is highly dependent on the criterion groups. As an example, if severe dementias were not

---

[3] This assumption is not inviolable. As long as the specific likelihood for each alternative is known, the overall probabilities could be calculated.

represented in the clinical samples, then a demented person may be misclassified by FCT as a malingerer. Representative examples include the following:
  – Portland Digit Recognition Test (Binder, 1990)
  – 21 Item Memory Test (Iverson, Franzen, & McCracken, 1991)
5. *Magnitude of Error.* On most psychological tests, the emphasis is on correct responses (i.e., none, partial, or full credit). The magnitude-of-error strategy focuses on the opposite issue, namely how "wrong" was the incorrect response. Rogers et al. (1993), posited that malingerers might be detectable by either near misses (e.g., 15 ounces to a pound) or gross errors (e.g., 5 miles between planets). While preliminary research is promising (Martin, Franzen, & Orey, 1998), no representative measures are yet available.
6. *Atypical Presentation.* Test results that do not make "neuropsychological sense" are sometimes considered indicative of feigning. The atypical presentation strategy is based on the premise that test results for genuine patients follow a predictable pattern. Patterns of test scores that markedly deviated from this pattern are suspected of malingering. This assumption is very open to question, given (a) the heterogeneity of test scores among normal, clinical, and brain-injured populations; and (b) the issue of comorbidity (i.e., substance abuse and other Axis I disorders) and its largely unexplored independent and interactional effects on test patterns. A representative example includes the following:
  – Comparison of Attention/Concentration Index on the WMS-R to General Memory Index (see Mittenberg et al.,1993)
7. *Psychological Sequelae.* Psychological sequelae refer to symptoms and associated features that often accompany neuropsychological impairment. The strategy posits systematic differences in psychological sequelae for those feigning cognitive impairment. This strategy remains largely unexplored. However, research suggests that unimpaired persons can make reasonable inferences about the psychological sequelae for concussion syndromes (Mittenberg, DiGiulio, Perrin, & Bass, 1989). Whether inferences about these sequelae translate into convincing portrayals remains an unexplored question. No standardized measures are available to evaluate psychological sequelae.
8. *Violation of Learning Principles.* Persons with and without memory impairment should correspond to basic learning principles when faced with standardized tasks. For example, memory retention should be superior for recognition (e.g., a multiple-choice format) than recall (e.g., responses without any cues). Some research has shown that simulators appear unaware of this learning principle (for a discussion, see Cercy, Schretlen, & Brandt, 1997). In general, the detection strategies that

incorporate learning principles yield group differences, but have not yet offered sufficient discriminability to identify potential malingerers. An example includes the following:
- Dot Counting Test (Lezak, 1995)
9. *Compound Strategies.* Rogers and Sewell (1997), have proposed that single strategies be combined into single composite scores for the identification of feigned cognitive impairment. For example, performance curve could be combined with reaction time. An inverse relationship is expected with item difficulty; difficult items should have a low success rate but require more time. As a further example, magnitude of error could be combined with probabilities derived from SVT. In a forced-choice paradigm, the likelihood of gross errors could be calculated to see whether the proportion exceeds chance probability.

Compound strategies may also assist in addressing the enduring problem of coached malingerers. The vulnerability of detection strategies to coaching is well known. The possibility of simple instructions (e.g., "Do better than chance.") foiling time-intensive tests is very concerning. Because of this vulnerability, psychologists sometimes go to considerable lengths to obscure the true purpose of the testing. However, obfuscating the purpose of testing appears inconsonant with professional practice. As an alternative, Rogers and Sewell (1997), have suggested the development of measures with compound strategies for detecting poor effort and feigning. Rather than relying on a single parameter, such measures could examine multiple indices and compound strategies. Preliminary data (Bender & Rogers, 2000), suggest that evaluatees can even be informed about the purpose of testing (e.g., rule-out malingering) and not jeopardize their usefulness for feigned cognitive impairment.

9.   SUMMARY

Determinations of malingering are likely to play a pre-emptive role in forensic evaluations. When malingering issues are raised, both the validity of the evaluatee's claim and the merits of the psycholegal issue are called into question. As a result, forensic psychologists have a heightened responsibility to ensure that their evaluations of malingering meet the highest standards of practice. Misclassifications of malingering carry a heavy toll in forensic evaluations that cannot be underestimated.

The assessment of malingering is complicated by the introduction of controversial constructs (e.g., secondary gain and symptom magnification) and unreliable risk factors (i.e., DSM-IV indices). Biases (e.g., ad hominem fallacy) are likely to distort the assessment process and introduce unknown error into the conclusions. A major objective of this chapter is to highlight potential missteps in the evaluation of malingering. Invoking the ethical principle of non-malificence (Gillon, 1986), it is imperative that forensic psychologists "cause not harm" because of potential bias or misconceptualization of malingering.

The chapter also underscored the complexity of malingering determinations. Rather than simply rely on validity indicators, it is essential that forensic psychologists understand the underlying detection strategies. Moreover, malingering should not be viewed monolithically. By focusing separately on feigned mental disorders and feigned cognitive impairment, differences in malingered presentation and its detection become immediately obvious. The synopsis of detection strategies is intended as a starting point. In achieving specialized knowledge on malingering, forensic psychologists should avail themselves of standard references and specialized measures. Appropriate training and supervision are vital components of forensic consultations, which assume a paramount role with complex assessments of response styles.

10.   REFERENCES

Allen, L. M.,III, Conder, R. L., Jr., Green, P., & Cox, D. R. (1997*). CARB '97 Computerized Assessment of Response Bias.* Durham, NC: CogniSyst Inc.

American Psychiatric Association. (1980). *Diagnostic and statistical manual of mental disorders.* (3rd Ed.), Washington, DC: Author.

American Psychiatric Association. (1987). *Diagnostic and statistical manual of mental disorders.* (3rd Revised), Washington, DC: Author.

American Psychiatric Association. (1994). *Diagnostic and statistical manual of mental disorders* (4th Ed.). Washington, DC: Author.

Bender, S., & Rogers, R. (2000). [Neuropsychological test data on malingering]. Unpublished data, University of North Texas, Denton, TX.

Berry, D. T. R. (1995). Detecting distortion in forensic evaluations with the MMPI-2. In Y. S. Ben-Porath, J. R. Graham, G. C. N. Hall, R. D. Hirschman, & M. S. Zaragoza (Eds.), Forensic applications of the MMPI-2 (pp.82-102). Newbury Park, CA: Sage.

Binder, L. M. (1990). Malingering following minor head trauma. *The Clinical Neuropsychologist, 4,* 25-36.

Cercey, S. P., Schretlen, D. J., & Brandt, J. (1997). Simulated amnesia and the pseudo-memory phenomena. In R. Rogers (Ed.), *Clinical assessment of malingering and deception.* (2nd ed.; pp. 85-107). New York: Guilford.

Colbach, E. M. (1997). The trouble with American forensic psychiatry. *International Journal of Offender Therapy and Comparative Criminology, 41,* 160-167.

Cunnien, A. J. (1997). Psychiatric and medical syndromes associated with deception. In R. Rogers (Ed.), *Clinical assessment of malingering and deception* (2nd ed.; pp. 23-46). New York: Guilford.

Dauer, F. W. (1989). *Critical thinking: An introduction to reasoning*. New York: Barnes and Noble.

Dembe, A. E. (1998). The medical detection of simulated occupational injuries: A historical and social analysis. *International Journal of Health Services, 28*, 227-239.

Frederick, R. I. (1997). *Manual for the Validity Indicator Profile* (VIP). Minneapolis: National Computer Systems.

Gillon, R. (1986). *Philosophical medical ethics*. New York: Wiley.

Gough, H. G. (1954). Some common misconceptions about neuroticism. *Journal of Consulting Psychology, 18*, 287-292.

Green, P., Astner, K., & Allen, L. M., III. (1996). *The Word Memory Test: A manual for oral and computer-administered forms*. Durham, NC: CogniSyst Inc.

Greene, R. L. (1997). Assessment of malingering and defensiveness on multiscale inventories. In R. Rogers (Ed.), *Clinical assessment of malingering and deception* (2nd ed.; pp. 169-207). New York: Guilford.

Gudjonsson, G. H., & Shackleton, H. (1986). The pattern of scores on Raven's matrices during "faking bad" and "non faking" performance. *British Journal of Clinical Psychology,. 25*, 35-41.

Heaton, R. K., Smith, H. H., Lehman, R. A. W., & Vogt, A. T. (1978). Prospects for faking believable deficits on neuropsychological testing. *Journal of Consulting and Clinical Psychology, 46*, 892-900.

Iverson, G. L., Franzen, M. D., & McCracken, L. M. (1991). Evaluation of an objective assessment technique for the detection of malingered memory deficits. *Law and Human Behavior, 15*, 667-676.

Lezak, M. D. (1995). *Neuropsychological assessment*. (3rd ed.). New York: Oxford University Press.

Lopez, O. L., Becker, J. T., Somsak, D., & Dew, M. A. (1994). Awareness of cognitive deficits and anosognosia in probable Alzheimer's disease. *European Neurology, 34*, 277-282.

Martin, R. C., Franzen, M. D., & Orey, S. (1998). Magnitude of error as a strategy to detect feigned memory impairment. *The Clinical Neuropsychologist, 12*, 84-91.

Mittenberg, W., Azrin, R., Millsaps, C., & Heilbronner, R. (1993). Identification of malingered head injury on the Wechsler Memory Scale-Revised. *Psychological Assessment, 5,* 34-40.

Mittenberg, W., DiGiulio, D. V., Perrin, S., & Bass, A. E. (1989). Symptoms following mild head injury: Expectations as etiology. *The Clinical Neuropsychologist, 3*, 297.

Mittenberg, W. Theroux-Fichera, S., Zielinski, R. E., & Heilbronner, R. L. (1995). Identification of malingered head injury on the Wechsler Adult Intelligence Scale-Revised. *Professional Psychology: Research and Practice, 26*, 491-498.

Morey, L. C. (1991). *Personality Assessment Inventory: Professional manual*. Tampa: Psychological Assessment Resources, Inc.

Morey, L. C. (1996). *An interpretive guide to the Personality Assessment Inventory (PAI)*. Tampa: Psychological Assessment Resources, Inc.

Pankratz, L., & Binder, L. M. (1997). In R. Rogers (Ed.), *Clinical assessment of malingering and deception* (pp. 223-236). New York: Guilford.

Perlin, M. L. (1994). *The jurisprudence of the insanity defense*. Durham, NC: Carolina Academic Press.

Reynolds, C. R. (Ed.) (1998). *Detection of malingering during head injury litigation.* New York: Plenum.

Rogers, R. (Ed.) (1988). *Clinical assessment of malingering and deception.* New York: Guilford.

Rogers, R. (1990). Models of feigned mental illness. *Professional Psychology, 21,* 182-188.

Rogers, R. (in press). *Diagnostic and structured interviewing: A handbook for clinical practice* (2nd ed.). New York: Guilford Publications.

Rogers, R. (Ed.) (1997). *Clinical assessment of malingering and deception* (2nd ed.). New York: Guilford.

Rogers, R., Bagby, R. M., & Dickens, S. E. (1992). *Structured Interview of Reported Symptoms (SIRS) and professional manual.* Odessa, FL: Psychological Assessment Resources, Inc.

Rogers, R., Bagby R. M., & Rector, N. (1989). Diagnostic legitimacy of factitious disorder with psychological symptoms. *American Journal of Psychiatry, 146,* 1312-1314.

Rogers, R., Harrell, E. H., & Liff. C. D. (1993). Feigning neuropsychological impairment: A critical review of methodological and clinical considerations. *Clinical Psychology Review, 13,* 255-274.

Rogers, R. & Reinhardt, V. (1998). Conceptualization and assessment of secondary gain. In G. P. Koocher, J. C., Norcross, & S. S. Hill, III (Eds.), *Psychologist's desk reference* (pp. 57-62). New York: Oxford University Press.

Rogers, R., Salekin, R. T., Sewell, K. W., Goldstein, A., & Leonard, K. (1998). A comparison of forensic and nonforensic malingerers: A prototypical analysis of explanatory models. *Law and Human Behavior, 22,* 353-367.

Rogers, R., & Sewell, K. W. (1997). *Manual for the Test of Cognitive Abilities* (TOCA). Unpublished measure, University of North Texas, Denton, TX.

Rogers, R., Sewell, K. W., Cruise, K. R., Wang, E. W., & Ustad, K. L. (1998). The PAI and feigning: A cautionary note on its use in forensic-correctional settings. *Assessment, 5,* 399-405.

Rogers, R., Sewell, K. W., Morey, L. C., & Ustad, K. L. (1996). Detection of feigned mental disorders on the Personality Assessment Inventory: A discriminant analysis. *Journal of Personality Assessment, 67,* 629-640.

Rogers, R., Sewell, K. W., & Goldstein, A. (1994). Explanatory models of malingering: A prototypical analysis. *Law and Human Behavior, 18,* 543-552.

Rogers, R., Sewell, K. W., & Salekin, R. (1994). A meta-analysis of malingering on the *MMPI-2. Assessment, 1,* 227-237.

Rogers, R., & Shuman, D. W. (2000). *Conducting insanity evaluations.* New York: Guilford Publications.

Spitzer, R. L., & Endicott, J. (1978). *Schedule of Affective Disorders and Schizophrenia* (3rd ed.). New York: Biometrics Research.

Tombaugh, T. N. (1997). The Test of Memory Malingering (TOMM): Normative data from cognitively intact and cognitively impaired individuals. *Psychological Assessment, 9,* 260-268.

Weschsler, D. (1987). *Wechsler Memory Scale--Revised manual.* San Antonio: Psychological Corporation.

Chapter 6

Assessing Competency in Criminal Proceedings

Alan A. Abrams, M.D., J.D.[4]
San Diego, CA

1.   INTRODUCTION

The standards for competency in criminal proceedings[5] are, at first glance, among the most uniform and least controversial in the law. A defendant may not be put to trial unless he "has sufficient present ability to consult with his lawyer with a reasonable degree of rational understanding... [and] a rational as well as factual understanding of the proceedings against him."[6] This is referred to as the *Dusky* standard in the forensic literature after the case in which the Supreme Court summarized the Federal standard for competency to stand trial.[7] In *Pate v. Robinson* (1966), the Supreme Court

---

[4] The author wishes to acknowledge the very valuable assistance of his wife, Karen Gurneck, his colleague, Christine Taylor, Ph.D. and Professor Grant Morris.

[5] Competency to stand trial is frequently referred to as fitness to stand trial, and so the terms "competency" and "fitness" are used interchangeably in both psychological and legal writing.

[6] *Dusky v. United States*, 362 U.S. 402, 402 (1960).

[7] In fact, the then Federal statute, 18 U. S. C. § 4244 explicitly mandated this standard. The Supreme Court decided that the trial record did not contain sufficient evidence to demonstrate that this was the actual standard used by the district court at trial. Milton Dusky, the defendant, was charged with kidnapping, rape, and transportation across state lines. He was tried in Federal court. Mr. Dusky was extensively evaluated at the United States Medical Center for Federal Prisoners at Springfield, Missouri. The evaluations and

held that the failure to observe procedures adequate to protect a defendant's right not to be tried or convicted while incompetent to stand trial deprives him of his due process right to a fair trial.

The present chapter proposes that this apparent uniformity belies many problem areas of law, social policy, morality, philosophy, and psychology. Examples of these concerns include: the extent to which a defendant with a severe Axis II disorder, particularly psychopaths, can cooperate rationally with their attorney; the degree to which an impulsive defendant can make reasoned choices among alternatives, whether a despondent defendant who fires his attorney and refuses to put on a defense in order to insure a death sentence should be tried while in that mental state, how juvenile immaturity should be reconciled with the *Dusky* standard, and whether a paranoid who wishes to appear *in pro se* to use the court as a forum for his preoccupations instead of an effective defense should be allowed to do so. While the clinician's evaluation can point out the social and moral questions involved in a particular case, the primary focus must be an accurate assessment of the defendant's functional abilities and limitations. Just how the abilities and limitations fit into the legal standard is ultimately a question for the trier of facts.

The vast body of legal decisions on competency to stand trial provide only hints at what specific content, what level of rationality, reason, cooperation or understanding fills the generalized requirements.[8] A number

---

testimony by the psychiatrists were that Mr. Dusky was not competent. However at his competency hearing, the district judge found that "the defendant [is] oriented to time and place and [has] some recollection of events." On appeal the Circuit Court noted: "How much mental capacity or alertness a defendant must have to be able to assist his counsel in a case where the defense is insanity, is, we think, a question of fact for the trial court." *Dusky v. U.S.*, 271 F.2d 385, 397 (8th Cir. 1959). On remand, Mr. Dusky was found competent and then guilty. This was upheld on appeal. *Dusky v. U.S.*, 295 F.2d 743 (8th Cir. 1961).

[8] Prior to the decision in *Godinez v. Moran*, 509 U.S. 389 (1993), competency was considered fundamental to, but distinct from, the exercise of other procedures that promote fair trials. "Competence to stand trial is rudimentary, for upon it depends the main part of those rights deemed essential to a fair trial, including the right to effective assistance of counsel, the rights to summon, to confront, and to cross-examine witnesses, and the right to testify on one's own behalf or to remain silent without penalty for doing so." *Riggins v. Nevada*, 504 U.S. 127, 139-140 (1992) (opinion concurring in judgment). The Court's decision in Godinez blurs the distinctions. See e.g. Justice Kennedy's concurrence in Godinez: "Although the Dusky standard refers to 'ability to consult with [a] lawyer,' the crucial component of the inquiry is the defendant's possession of 'a reasonable degree of rational understanding.' In other words, the focus of the Dusky formulation is on a particular level of mental functioning, which the ability to consult counsel helps identify." c.f. *Weiter v. Settle*, 193 F. Supp. 318 (W.D. Mo. 1961) (proposing eight required functions for competency).

of mental health commentators have attempted to provide concrete or operational substance to the level of mental functioning described by the *Dusky* standard. Professor Bonnie (1992, 1993), has proposed considering two separate constructs: competence to assist counsel and decisional competence. These would then include: (1) the capacity to understand the basic elements of the adversary system; (2) the capacity to relate pertinent information to counsel concerning the facts of the case; (3) the capacity to appreciate one's situation as a defendant in a criminal prosecution; (4) the capacity to understand information relevant to the specific decision at issue; (5) the capacity to think rationally about alternative courses of action; (6) the capacity to appreciate one's situation as a defendant confronted with a specific legal decision; and (7) the capacity to express a choice among alternatives. However, there is little to quantify these elaborations in the law, and many cases cannot be reconciled with the proposed psycho-legal requirements for competency.[9] Florida, in their Rules of Criminal Procedure, suggests six factors for the examiner to consider.[10] In the statutory or constitutional language, there appears to be two fundamental components: (1) an informational, reasoning, and cognitive component; and (2) a communicative component. Others have found a requirement for specific legal knowledge, a capacity to function effectively in the legal environment, and to use information appropriately in one's own defense (Miller, 1994). Others take a more limited view of what is required to be competent.[11] Roesch and Golding (1980), reject any reductionist approach to competency.

---

[9] See generally Freckelton, I. (1996) Rationality and flexibility in assessment of fitness to stand trial. *International Journal of Law and Psychiatry, 19*, 39-59.

[10] Florida Rules of Criminal Procedure, section 3.211(a). Lexis Law Publishing, 2000. "(l) The experts shall first consider factors related to the issue of whether the defendant meets the criteria for competence to proceed; that is, whether the defendant has sufficient present ability to consult with counsel with a reasonable degree of rational understanding and whether the defendant has a rational, as well as factual, understanding of the pending proceedings. . . 2(2) In considering the issue of competence to proceed, the examining experts shall consider and include in their report: (A) the defendant's capacity to: (i) appreciate the charges or allegations against the defendant; (ii) appreciate the range and nature of possible penalties, if applicable, that may be imposed in the proceedings against the defendant; (iii) understand the adversary nature of the legal process; (iv) disclose to counsel facts pertinent to the proceedings at issue; (v) manifest appropriate courtroom behavior; (vi) testify relevantly; and (B) any other factors deemed relevant by the experts."

[11] See e.g the Canadian case *R. v. Taylor*, 11 OR (3d) 323 (1992) cited by Freckelton, I. (1996). Rationality and flexibility in assessment of fitness to stand trial. International Journal of Law and Psychiatry, 19, 39-59: "[The test is] whether an accused can recount to his/her counsel the necessary facts relating to the offence in such a way that counsel can then properly present a defense. It is not relevant to the fitness determination to consider whether the accused and counsel have an amicable and trusting relationship, whether the

There are both contextual and moral components in competency decisions based on the judge or jury's notion of "fairness," "justice," or "mercy" that may trump clinical findings. This is also true in many other areas of forensic mental health. Abstract inferences of mental capacity or incapacities may be compared with the facts of the defendant's charges, prior history and the decision maker's feelings about evidence of guilt, responsibility, and awareness of the effect of a finding on incompetency to stand trial. These non-clinical factors must be considered when trying to harmonize the case summaries of highly publicized cases or court decisions, with the scientific writings calling for more exact standards. Other non-clinical issues, such as offense characteristics, even appear to affect, which defendants are considered or referred for competency to stand trial evaluations.[12]

Nonetheless, the evaluating clinician's fundamental role is to provide the trier of facts with thorough data regarding the defendant's present functioning, an assessment as to the validity of the defendant's presentation, and clear reasoning relating present functioning to the statutory requirements.[13] The clinician needs to address multiple areas of psychological functioning with sufficient data to support the opinion about the level of ability in that area. While clinicians typically provide an ultimate opinion regarding the defendant's competency, the clinician should also alert the court or retaining attorney regarding problems in reaching that opinion. The factors that were balanced, both for and against the finding, should be made explicit. This is particularly important with those special case defendants discussed below.

---

accused has been cooperating with counsel, or whether the accused ultimately makes decisions that are in his/her best interests."

[12] Warren, J. I., Rosenfeld, B., Fitch, W. L., & Hawk, G. (1997). Forensic mental health clinical evaluation: An analysis of interstate and intersystemic differences. *Law and Human Behavior, 21*, 377-390; Poythress, N. , Bonnie, R. J., Hoge, S. K., Monahan, J., & Oberlander, L. B. (1994). Client abilities to assist counsel and make decisions in criminal cases. *Law and Human Behavior, 18*, 437-452; Nicholson, R. A., & Johnson W.G. (1991). Prediction of competency to stand trial: contribution of demographics, type of offence, clinical characteristics and psycholegal ability. *International Journal of Law and Psychiatry, 14*, 267-97; Berman, L. M., & Osborne, Y.H.. (1987) Attorney's referrals for competency to stand trial evaluations: comparisons of referred and nonreferred clients. *Behavioural Sciences and the Law, 5*, 373-80.

[13] In fact, the clinician may be asked to provide an opinion on a defendant's competency at some time in the past. This may occur if the case is remanded on appeal because there was no competency evaluation at the time of the original trial, or if there is a claim that the defendant was incompetent to waive a fundamental right at an earlier time in the process. The clinician's task is to provide a retrospective assessment of the defendant's "present" functioning at that earlier point.

2. HISTORY OF THE CONCEPT

The early common law alternately used the phrases "non compos mentis," "absolutely mad," "in a frenzy," "nonsane mind and memory," or "present insanity," rather than incompetence to stand trial. The often quoted rationale for this prohibition was summarized by Blackstone in the Eighteenth Century as: "Also if a man in his sound memory commits a capital offense, and before arraignment for it he becomes mad, he ought not to be arraigned for it, because he is not able to plead to it with that advice and caution that he ought. And if after he has pleaded the prisoner becomes mad, he shall not be tried; for how can he make his defense?"[14] Concern about trial in absentia when an accused is "mentally absent" or incapacitated provided the rationale for prohibiting criminal process against the insane.[15] Presumably the same historical underpinnings for incompetency in the civil law also formed part of the basis for criminal incompetence. Civil competencies typically question one's understanding of one's circumstances, and the nature and consequences of one's actions. The right to not be tried while insane could not be waived at common law. Though a judge had discretion to appoint a jury to determine present sanity, there was no right to a jury trial at common law. The defendant was either kept in prison or committed to a hospital for the insane. Trial could resume when the defendant "recovered his understanding."[16] Incompetency was not limited to psychiatric conditions. There are also cases in the common law of; for example, a deaf mute not being tried because "[he] cannot understand the proceedings."[17] A more specific standard evolved in the Nineteenth Century. Pre-*Dusky* court opinions stated the test for competency, as "whether the accused was in truth incapable of understanding the proceedings, and intelligently advising with his counsel as to his defense."[18] History of the

---

[14] 4 Blackstone Commentaries 24 (1765).

[15] In re Dennis, 51 Cal.2d 666, 672 (1959) ("Mere physical presence without mental realization of what was going on would obviously be of no value to the accused."; Foote, C. (1960). A comment on pre-trial commitment of criminal defendants. *University of Pennsylvania .Law Review, 108*, 832-846.

[16] 1 Hale Pleas of the Crown 35 (1874).

[17] Cited in *Youtsey v. U.S.*, 97 F. 937, 941 (1899).

[18] Youtsey at 946; see also *People v. McElvaine*, 26 N.E.929, 932 (1891) ("incapable of understanding this proceeding, or of making his defense, or of instructing his counsel as to his defense, if he has one."); Webber v. Commonwealth, 119 Pa. St. 223 (1888). This articulation of the meaning of "unsound mind" began to appear in English cases in the mid 19th century. See e.g. *King v. Pritchard*, 7 Car. & P. 303, 304, 173 Eng. Rep. 135 (1836) ("whether the prisoner has sufficient understanding to comprehend the nature of this trial, so as to make a proper defence to the charge.")

concept of competency to stand trial implies several core values of our legal system: adversarial trials with reasonable participation by the defendant; dignified proceedings; and accurate outcomes. The requirement of competency is also responsive to the belief that a fair trial cannot occur in the absence of sound defendant judgment and understanding of defense choices. However, as the Supreme Court frequently asserts: "the law does not require that a defendant receive a perfect trial, only a fair one."[19] Thus the question, "How fair is fair?" is reframed in the competency assessment as, "How rational, how reasonable, how competent is competent?". Justice Kennedy's formulation that competency addresses the defendant's possession of "a reasonable degree of rational understanding"[20] leaves the specific content of the constituent elements quite variable.

3.   SCOPE OF COMPETENCY APPLICATIONS

Though the concept under discussion is traditionally stated as competency to stand trial, it in fact begins with arraignment, and ends at the pronouncement of sentence. Questions of competency may be raised at any time within these bounds, and may be raised multiple times. It may be raised by either the prosecution, the defense, or by the court. Competency may also be an issue at a probation or parole revocation hearing.[21] Some authors have suggested that the concept should be labeled "adjudicative competency" because it is applied throughout the initial criminal proceedings (Hoge et al., 1997). There is no generally recognized concept of competency to file an appeal, or competency to be fined or imprisoned (i.e. you can be sent to prison or appeal even if you become "incompetent" after sentencing.) Competency, however, is required to waive the right to an appeal, just as with the waiver of any other right. There is the additional concept of competency to be executed for those sentenced to capital punishment.

At each step in a criminal proceeding, the defendant is faced with choices: whether to give a statement to police; to obtain representation; to attempt self-representation; to accept a plea bargain; or whether to testify at trial. These choices involve asserting or waiving constitutional rights. In

---

[19] *Michigan v. Tucker*, 417 U.S. 433 (1974).

[20] *Godinez v. Moran*, 509 U.S. 389 (1993).

[21] *U.S. v. Baker*, 807 F.2d 1315 (6th Cir 1986); *U.S. v. McCarty*, 747 F. Supp. 311 (ED NC 1990).

Godinez v. Moran[22] the Supreme Court collapsed all of these other aspects of criminal competency into competency to stand trial. Thus competency to confess, to waive representation by an attorney, to waive presence at trial, to waive a jury trial, to waive the right to appeal, or to plead guilty became measured by *Dusky* standards.[23] The language in *Godinez* did not simplify the determination of competency, and may have expanded its content. The Court in *Godinez* pronounced that "the capacity for `reasoned choice' among the alternatives available to him." was identical to the *Dusky* "rational understanding of the proceedings."[24] However the Court added the requirements that valid waivers of constitutional rights must also be knowing, intelligent and voluntary, in addition to the *Dusky* requirements for competency to stand trial. The knowing and voluntary inquiry for waiver of rights is to determine if the defendant actually understands the significance and consequences of the decision, and whether it is coerced. If the *Godinez* standard is meant to apply only to external coercion, the mental health

---

[22] *Godinez v. Moran*, 509 U.S. 389 (1993). The Supreme Court rejected the argument that waiving criminal constitutional rights required a higher level of competency. "While psychiatrists and scholars may find it useful to classify the various kinds and degrees of competence, and while States are free to adopt competency standards that are more elaborate than the Dusky formulation, the Due Process Clause does not impose these additional requirements." See also *Faretta v. California*, 422 U.S. 806 (1975) assuring a constitutional right to self-representation if the waiver of assistance of counsel is voluntary, knowing and intelligent. Knowing and intelligent are used as synonyms in the decisions. Prior to the decision in Godinez many states and the Ninth Circuit imposed higher standards for competency for a defendant waiving a fundamental right such as assistance of counsel. For example, prior to the decision in Godinez, California required this added level of competency. See e.g. *People v. Burnett*, 188 Cal. App. 3d 1314 (1987). Following Godinez, California equated competence to waive counsel with competence to stand trial. *People v. Hightower*, 41 Cal. App. 4th 1108 (1996). It is possible that the decision in Godinez will serve to expand the skills which a defendant must possess to be competent, particularly relating to abilities to make decisions affecting their defense.

[23] *Godinez v. Moran*, 509 U.S. 389 (1993). Godinez thus imposes an enhanced Dusky standard for the waiver of constitutional rights of the criminal defendant. The defendant must have both the Dusky capacity to understand consult, and in addition the actual knowledge of the implications of the waiver. Id. footnote 12. The application for example to the severely intoxicated suspect who is arrested and then questioned after a Miranda warning will be problematic because the determination of competency will be retrospective and speculative. Such a defendant will most likely be competent when examined weeks later in a state of sobriety.

[24] The Court's rejection of a two step competency process, a lower threshold first step, and a higher threshold second step as more critical skills and rights are involved, suggests that this is foreclosed as a solution to the competency issue. Interpreting whether the decision means competency to stand trial standards should be higher is not possible.

clinician has no further role to play.[25] A court may consider the role mental illness plays in restricting voluntary choices, and thus reopen the issue of clinical input at the second prong of the waiver inquiry. The level of understanding for a choice to be intelligent and knowing remains undecided. A minority of states require mental competency for extradition proceedings.[26]

4.   LEGAL PROCEDURE

The clinician is strongly advised to review the penal code or code of criminal procedure for the specific jurisdiction where the examination is performed. While the substantive statutory test varies little, the procedure is quite variable. Typically, the defense attorney informs the court that their client does not appear to understand, or cannot cooperate. A declaration from a clinician may be added to support the claim in order to meet the sufficient, reasonable, or good faith doubt threshold for a competency examination and hearing. The prosecution or the court can also raise the question of the defendant's competency. There are no specific guidelines as to when sufficient or bona fide doubt exists.[27] Defense counsel has an obligation as an officer of the court to raise concerns over competency, even if the defendant objects (George, 1989).[28] A defendant who is not represented by counsel must have an attorney appointed until a finding of competency is made. Some states provide for additional protections for defendants who oppose a competency examination.[29] The criminal proceedings are suspended until there is a ruling that the defendant is competent.

---

[25] See e.g. *Colorado v. Connelly*, 479 U.S. 157 (1986) (confession of severely mentally ill defendant compelled by command hallucinations is admissible so long as no state coercion involved). The Court did not address whether Connelly was competent to waive his 5th Amendment right, only that he was not coerced. Initially Connelly was found incompetent to stand trial. Thus a different outcome may have occurred if the Godinez ruling had been in effect.

[26] Comment (1999). In re Hinnant: The relevance of competence in interstate extradition proceedings. *Criminal and Civil Confinement, 25*, 469-494.

[27] See *Pate v. Robinson*, 383 U.S. 375 (1966); *Drope v. Missouri*, 420 U.S. 162 (1975); *Branscomb v. Norris*, 47 F.3d 258 (8th Cir. 1995).

[28] George Jr., B. J. (reporter) (1989). *ABA Criminal Justice Mental Health Standards* (Standard 7-4.2(c), pp. 176-183). Washington, D.C.: American Bar Association.

[29] See e.g. Cal. Penal Code section 1369(a) (West, 1999).

In the past, most competency evaluations were performed at in-patient units in state hospitals. Presently, requests for competency evaluations are most often addressed from the court to a forensic unit organized by the county. The referral may either request information to help a judge decide if there is a basis for doubt regarding the defendant's ability to stand trial, or to provide an opinion on the question of present competency. In some cases, if doubt is raised regarding the defendant's competency, the court permits the prosecutor and defender to each submit a name of a clinician for the actual evaluation. Courts can order a competency evaluation over the defendant's objections.[30] The courts may use a competency report as the only basis for their opinion. Courts can use a single report against multiple reports if the findings are well supported. Courts can even disregard the unanimous opinions of experts if they find other evidence more convincing.[31] Because a verdict can be reversed on appeal if the appellate court believed that a competency investigation was required, judges tend to be liberal in referring defendants for evaluations. Similarly, some judges consider it better to err on the side of over-inclusion when a fundamental right is involved, and rule some "close calls" as incompetent, and order the defendant to the state hospital for further study. At the time of the hearing, the burden of proof can be on either party[32], but if placed on the defendant, cannot be more than preponderance of the evidence.[33] A finding of incompetency most often results in confinement in a locked state hospital. Some states allow for community treatment, or even outpatient treatment. When the treatment facility believes the defendant has been restored to competency, the court is notified and a restoration hearing is held.

Though the methods of decision used at trial are far from uniform, there is typically little explication of the court's reasoning, with only the mere conclusion in conformity with *Dusky* being stated. The published appellate opinions on the topic of competency to stand trial primarily address whether a trial judge abused discretion by failing to order a formal evaluation or whether the trial court's determination of competency was "clearly erroneous" (a heightened standard of review), when the defendant alleges

---

[30] *U.S. v. Huguenin*, 950 F.2d 23 (1st Cir. 1991).

[31] *People v. Marshall*, 15 Cal. 4th 1 (1997) ("the jury is not required to accept at face value a unanimity of expert opinion.")

[32] *Medina v. California*, 505 U.S. 437 (1992) (a state may presume criminal defendant is competent to stand trial, and place the burden of proving incompetency on the defendant, if the burden of proof required is mere preponderance of evidence.)

[33] *Cooper v. Oklahoma*, 517 U.S. 348 (1996) (a state cannot require criminal defendant to prove incompetency by clear and convincing standard of proof because then some defendants would stand trial who were more likely than not incompetent.)

they were not fit to be tried on appeal of their conviction.[34] A state court's findings are given a presumption of correctness in federal habeas review.[35] These high standards for appellate reversal inhibit the evolution of more specific substantive legal criteria for determining incompetency to stand trial.

5.   SYMPTOMS, DIAGNOSES AND INCOMPETENCE

The Constitution clearly does not prohibit the trial of the mentally ill, only those who lack the ability to meaningfully participate in their trial.[36] No single fact, symptom, score, diagnosis, or behavior can be considered as determinative of competency.[37] The mere presence of mental illness, no matter how severe, does not necessarily result in a finding of incompetency. Because competency to stand trial is a global concept in which mental illness is only one factor, it has been difficult to establish clear clinical or empirical parameters. Nonetheless, because symptom severity, cognitive deficits, and poor contact with reality are major contributing factors in incompetency to stand trial, it is not surprising that studies show the majority of defendants identified as incompetent either have some combination of low I.Q., psychotic symptoms, or affective disorder.[38] The presence of a psychotic

---

[34] See *Drope v. Missouri*, 420 U.S. 162 (1975); *Vickers v. Stewart*, 144 F.3d 613 (9th Cir. 1998) ; *U.S. v. Morrison*, 153 F.3d 34 (2d Cir. 1998) ; *U.S. v. Williams*, 998 F.2d 258 (5th Cir. 1993); *People v. Marshall*, 15 Cal. 4th 1 (1997) ("In reviewing a jury verdict that a defendant is mentally competent to stand trial, an appellate court must view the record in the light most favorable to the verdict and uphold the verdict if it is supported by substantial evidence. Evidence is substantial if it is reasonable, credible, and of solid value.")

[35] See *Oats v. Singletary*, 141 F.3d 1018 (11th Cir. 1998); *Boag v. Raines*, 769 F.2d 1341 (9th Cir. 1985).

[36] *Eddmonds v. Peters*, 93 F.3d 1307 (7th Cir. 1996).

[37] *Vogt v. U.S.*, 88 F.3d 587 (8th Cir. 1996); see also Drope "There are, of course, no fixed or immutable signs which invariably indicate the need for further inquiry to determine fitness to proceed".

[38] Nicholson, R. A. & Kugler, K. E. (1991). Competent and incompetent criminal defendants: A quantitative review of comparative research. *Psychological Bulletin, 109*, 355-370; Hart, S. D. & Hare, R. D. (1992). Predicting fitness to stand trial: The relative power of demographic, criminal, and clinical variables. Special Issue: Psychopathology and crime. *Forensic Reports, 5*, 53-65; Ustad, K. L., Rogers, R., Sewell, K. W. & Guarnaccia, C. A. (1996). Restoration of competency to stand trial: Assessment with the Georgia Court Competency Test and the Competency Screening Test. *Law and Human Behavior, 20*,

disorder or mental retardation alone is not sufficient for a finding of incompetency (Ohayon, Crocker, St-Onge & Caulet, 1998). Courts tend to make findings in agreement with clinicians (Reich & Tookey, 1986). However clinicians may use legally irrelevant facts, such as a past history of hospitalizations, or the nature of the crime, in making a decision (Plotnick, Porter & Bagby, 1998). Obviously many severely mentally ill persons are found competent to stand trial and then proceed to a trial on the issue of whether they are guilty or not guilty by reason of insanity.

6.   EVALUATION PRACTICE

A competency evaluation has more similarity to a disability evaluation, than to an insanity evaluation.[39] It is entirely oriented to present functioning, and tries to unify a multitude of separate functional capacities into a global dichotomous decision. The clinician's goal is to collect sufficient information about current functioning and limitations to provide a basis for an appropriate decision by the trier of fact. There is no simple checklist methodology that will fit all cases. A general, comprehensive methodology incorporates a clinical interview, psychological testing, and substantiating collateral information obtained from third parties. As Justice Frankfurter stated, "the task of judging the competence of a particular accused cannot be escaped by announcing delusively simple rules..."[40]

Both the defense attorney and the prosecuting attorney should be contacted prior to examining the defendant, to obtain their views on the defendant's behavior in court, responses in court, and ability to communicate. Both parties should be informed that you would review any documents they wish to submit relevant to the issue. The defense attorney must be informed of the evaluation. The clinician should ask counsel for permission to tape record the examination. The clinician should also inform counsel that they will be asking the defendant to sign release of information forms. The defense attorney should also be asked about the problems working with the defendant, and asked about specific circumstances of

---

131-146; Reich, J., Wells, J. (1985). Psychiatric diagnosis and competency to stand trial. *Comprehensive Psychiatry, 26*, 421-550.

[39] As in disability evaluations, the important data to be provided to the decision maker are the functional limitations of the person being evaluated in multiple areas. See e.g. Abrams, A. A., Taylor, C., & Levy, C. (in press). Deception in disability benefit programs. *American Journal of Forensic Psychiatry.*

[40] *Adams v. United States* ex rel. McCann, 317 U.S. 269, 277 (1942).

impaired understanding or cooperation. There is no legal right for the defense attorney to be present during the evaluation,[41] but often inviting both the prosecutor and the defense attorney to be present will allow the clinician to address their concerns at the end of the exam by inquiring into matters not previously covered during the interview in sufficient detail. The clinician can also obtain more meaningful information on problems of cooperation by observing the defendant interact with their attorney.

Very close attention must be paid to the earliest moments of the interview; how the defendant arrives at the interview, their gait and grooming, the defendant's interactions with the transporting deputy, the defendant's first reactions, and first responses, because these are the least structured moments of the evaluation. The purpose of the examination should be explained in a brief statement. (e.g. "Mr. X, I'm Dr. Y. The court has asked me to talk with you to find out your ability to understand what is going on with your case. I will prepare a written report on our meetings for the court.") Asking the defendant to then put this back into their own words can give the clinician a preview of the issues that will need exploration. Practical considerations of informed consent should be addressed at the beginning of the examination. The clinician should not guarantee any degree of confidentiality of the interview or the report, and should make this clear to the defendant. The defendant should be told that his cooperation is voluntary. Whether material from the competency evaluation can be used in the criminal trial differs from jurisdiction to jurisdiction, and depends on the proposed use.[42] If material can be introduced, then the clinician should provide a Fifth Amendment warning that the material discussed might be introduced into their criminal trial and used against them. Again the defendant should be questioned about their understanding of the meaning of these warnings. The defendant should be asked if there are any special problems that would affect their cooperation or ability at present, such as taking medications, illness, recent bad news, or a recent head injury. If the defendant is obviously severely impaired, the clinician must be especially conscientious to avoid compromising the defendant's rights.

---

[41] *Buchanan v. Kentucky*, 483 U.S. 402 (1987).

[42] See *Estelle v. Smith*, 451 U.S. 454 (1981); *Wise v. Bowersox*, 136 F.3d 1197 (8th Cir. 1998); *U.S. v. Santos*, 131 F.3d 16 (1st Cir. 1997); *People v. Stanfill*, 184 Cal.App. 3d 577 (1986) (defendant's choice to testify during his trial waived privilege and allowed statements from competency evaluation to be introduced for impeachment.) See also White, W.S. (1995). Government psychiatric examinations and the death penalty. *Arizona Law Review*, 37, 869-894.

The general approach of moving from unstructured questions to a more structured inquiry into competency issues is best. The clinician's primary role is to provide details and examples to the court, not mere conclusions. Throughout the evaluation the clinician should be probing and documenting the defendant's ability to cooperate, to communicate in a rational manner, to apply rational thinking to specific problems, to understand the legal proceedings and to comprehend the material that is discussed. At the same time, it is standard practice to provide the court with a more general psychological evaluation and diagnostic formulation. Initial use of open-ended questions such as asking the defendant to talk generally about themselves, or to indicate why they think their attorney asked the court for a mental health doctor to talk with them, can provide much information while avoiding concerns about biasing the responses. The defendant should be asked later in the interview specifically about current symptoms, problems being in custody, a history of the present symptoms, current activities, and how the defendant spent the prior day, current treatment and medications, their biography, past psychiatric history, substance use history, education history, medical history, family history, criminal or legal history, employment history, and history of important relationships. This information will complete the general diagnostic evaluation, provide real time views of communication styles and cognitive functioning, and give historical data to compare the present findings against for consistency. The clinician should try to collect names and phone numbers of people who have recently visited, or whom the defendant called on the phone, and ask for signed consent to contact them regarding their observations and knowledge of the defendant's recent behavior. The clinician should make detailed notes on the defendant's demeanor and responses during the interview and ask further about areas where symptoms, understanding, or communication appear to be a problem. The clinician should then do a standard mental status exam, with emphasis on cognitive functioning. A Folstein mini-mental status is helpful.[43] The main purpose of the mental status exam is to assess the defendant's ability to engage in rational communication and information processing; to understand questions, provide relevant answers, accept correction when answers are tangential or loose, and make reasonable inferences about causes and effects in their life. The clinician must pay careful attention to contradictory behaviors, performance, or other data in assessing the validity of the defendant's presentation.

---

[43] Folstein, M. F., Folstein S. E., McHugh P. R. (1975). "Mini-Mental State ": A practical method for grading the cognitive state of patients for the clinician. *Journal of Psychiatric Research, 12*, 189 -198.

For the inquiry into more specific competency issues, the defendant should be advised not to discuss the specifics of their actions that led to their arrest, and also not to mention anything they spoke about in confidence with their attorney. The clinician should again ask the defendant to repeat back what they understood of these warnings. If the defendant starts to bring up this sensitive material, the clinician must consider whether to stop further discussion or repeat a warning. This can be decided on the clinician's estimation of the defendant's rational understanding of the warning. The clinician can then ask about the defendant's prior experience in court, either civil or criminal, what they were in court for, how they plead, who their attorney was, how they thought the attorney did, how they got along with their attorney, their involvement in the case, the roles of the other parties, how the case turned out, who decided the case, and how they felt about the outcome. Significant areas are asked about in more detail, for example the process of plea-bargaining, or the planning of a defense. This focus on a past case gives the defendant a chance to talk about legal proceedings in a less affectively charged arena and also avoid the problems of invading the attorney-client privilege or creating a Miranda violation. The ability to assist in one's own defense typically will require the defendant to have some basic grasp of the facts of the case and how to counter the prosecution's case. The inquiry about this must be carefully performed so as to not violate the defendant's right. The clinician can ask similar questions about the current case as were asked about prior court experiences: what they are presently charged with, what the charges mean, what plea they entered or plan to enter, what defenses they have considered, what are the possible sentences they face, what the district attorney (D.A.) is saying they did, what they would like the judge or jury to understand about them in their trial, what the most worrisome evidence against them is, whether anybody is wrong in what they told the police about them, whether they have been offered a plea bargain, what that is, what they think about it, and finally how the findings of the competency exam will affect their case. The clinician can also ask about their arrest, what warnings the police gave them when arrested, what those warnings meant, and how they proceeded. The examiner might consider also asking about the very most recent time the defendant was in court; what the reason for the appearance was, what they did, what preparation they did with their attorney for the appearance, who else was in court, what those other people did, what their roles are, and what will happen next. The clinician should then ask about their attorney and their relationship with their attorney; their attorney's name and a physical and emotional description, how often they talk, what they talk about in general, what is positive and negative in their talks, and whether they feel the attorney is interested in them. This will often provide important information about the defendant's ability to communicate with their attorney. Finally the clinician needs to ask the "rote" questions: what is the general function of the judge, jury, D.A., court reporter, witnesses, defense attorney, what is the meaning of a guilty plea or finding, what of an innocent plea or finding, what a plea bargain is, whether it would cause problems if they lied to their attorney, how that would cause problems, whether they have to testify in court if they do not want to, and what an appeal is.

Third party information can be useful, particularly the jail medical records, prior medical and mental health records, and prior prison files. If deceit is suspected, a full range of third party information should be obtained. If psychological testing is needed, a second session is typically scheduled.

The evaluating clinician cannot just be concerned with the individual defendant. The evaluating clinician who only has contact with the defendant is in a position similar to the marriage therapist, when only one partner is assessed. The clinician asked to perform the competency evaluation also has to evaluate whether and why the relationship between client and attorney is failing or failed. Much of this information may not be available. The attorney may have valid concerns that their information might compromise the defense for example if the attorney has strong evidence of guilt which the D.A. is likely to discover, and the attorney views the client's rejection of a favorable plea bargain and insistence on a trial as irrational. A related area of real conflict between attorneys and clients is the question of just who will control the defense. This is most problematic when the attorney believes a mental health defense will produce a better outcome or avoid a death sentence, and the defendant insists on a trial based on the defense of innocence or justification. If the defendant rejects the proposed use of a mental health defense, the attorney may feel compelled to raise the question of competency to avoid claims of attorney incompetence during appeals. There may be personal issues involved that the attorney does not want to confront, for example, the client does not trust the attorney and cannot obtain a new attorney, and, therefore, provides inadequate cooperation, there are racial or gender tensions, the attorney is uncomfortable with mentally ill clients, or too busy to spend the necessary time building a relationship. The clinician may suspect that the attorney is raising the issue of competency in a strategic manner, for example perhaps in discussing an unfavorable confession provided to the police, the attorney mentioned that it could be suppressed if the client were judged incompetent at the time of the confession. The information received from either side should be assessed for potential distortions or strategic maneuvering.

A separate problem can result from attorney requested competency evaluations, when the defense or prosecuting attorney also asks the clinician to comment on an insanity plea. This can lead to poorly differentiated reasoning on these two very different issues, or at worst a confusion of the two.[44]

Finally, whether to provide the "ultimate" conclusion would appear to be a matter of personal preference. There is no compelling reason not to state a conclusion in the written report. It is necessary to explicitly indicate the reasoning process that connects the facts reported in the findings to the conclusion reached. The court may not allow the examiner to testify regarding the conclusion during a hearing however.

7.   PSYCHOLOGICAL TESTING FOR COMPETENCY

The premise of any psychometric test for competency is that the measured variable is quantifiable, and a valid estimator of the inferred quality. Because competency to stand trial is a purely abstract legal concept, test developers steer a perilous course between substituting their values or beliefs regarding what abilities, in what quantity, are required for a finding of competency, and the lack of objective reality. Agreement by examiners is not a reliable measure of reality. Some thoughtful test developers have frankly stated that a purely objective test for competence determination is neither possible nor desirable (Hoge et al., 1997). None of the currently available tests have scales to correct for deceitful responding. Therefore the tests will produce excessive false positives (competent defendants mislabeled incompetent). Bagby et al. (1992), have criticized the factor analyses underlying several of the tests, and the uncertainty of the relevant domains that compose the competency construct. Nonetheless, they can be quite helpful as screening devices to supplement the clinical evaluation, and as a means of gathering additional data.[45] The following are a variety of inventories available to help in the assessment of competency in criminal proceedings.

The Competency Screening Test (CST). (Laboratory of Community Psychiatry, 1973). This instrument is a brief, 22-item, sentence completion test that is both cognitive and projective. The items are simply structured: for

---

[44] See *U.S. v. Williams*, 998 F.2d 258 (5th Cir. 1993).

[45] See generally Cooper, D. K., & Grisso, T., (1997). Five year research update (1991-1995): Evaluations for competence to stand trial, *Behavioral Sciences and the Law, 15,* 347-364; Grisso, T. (1986). Evaluating competencies. New York: Plenum.

example "When I go to court the lawyer will . . ." The answers are scored from 0 to 2, and a score of 20 or below is suggested as a cutoff for further evaluation. It can be used to quickly screen out the obviously competent, and to reveal problem areas, particularly in the attorney client relationship, that may require further more detailed exploration.[46] The CST produces an abundance of false positives, likely reflecting the defendant's control over the test outcome, and the failure of the test to distinguish antisocial attitudes from incompetency (Ustad, Rogers, Sewell & Guarnaccia, 1996).

The Competency Assessment Instrument (CAI). (Laboratory of Community Psychiatry, 1973). This instrument looks at 13 areas of actual and hypothetical relevance in the determination of competency, including ones such as capacity to cope with the stress of incarceration awaiting trial. The defendant is asked a series of questions from each area, for example "Is there anyone likely to tell lies about you in this case...Why?" It is dependent on self-report. Each of the 13 areas is rated from 1 (clearly incompetent) to 4 (clearly competent). The suggested cutoff is a substantial number of scores of 3 or below. The test is poorly normed, so the meaning of the cutoff score is in doubt. However, it can be useful as a reminder of topics to explore during the evaluation. It can lead to information that might not otherwise be brought out.

The Georgia Court Competency Test (GCCT) and the Mississippi State Hospital revision (GCCT-MSH). (Wildman, Batchelor et al., 1978; Nicholson, Briggs, and Robertson, 1988). These instruments are rapid screening devices that are designed to yield an abundance of false positives, i.e. to screen out the obviously competent. Low scores are indicative of a need for further evaluation. The defendant is shown a diagram of an empty courtroom and asked questions about locations and functions of court personnel, and then questions about charges, the attorney, and outcomes of adjudication. Three factors assessed are general legal knowledge, courtroom layout and specific legal knowledge (Bagby, Nicholson, Rogers & Nussbaum, 1992). Gothard et al. (1995, 1994), have suggested that results on the GCCT can imply a finding of malingering when scores are extremely low.

The MacArthur Competence Assessment Tool - Criminal Adjudication (MacCAT-CA) and the MacArthur Structured Assessment of the Competencies of Criminal Defendants (MacSAC-CD). (Hoge et al. 1999, Hoge et al. 1997). The MacCAT-CA is a refined and shortened version of

---

[46] Lipsett, P. D., Lelos, D., & McGarry, A. L. (1971). Competency for trial: A screening instrument. *American Journal of Psychiatry, 128*, 105-109; Randolph, J. J., Hicks, T., & Mason, D. (1981). The Competency Screening Test: A replication and extension. *Criminal Justice and Behavior, 8,* 471-481.

the MacSAC-CD, consisting of 22 items. These instruments provide hypothetical vignettes to the examinee, and then ask specific questions raised by the vignettes. The clinician then explores the defendant's reasons for a particular response. Examinees are also assessed on their ability to learn new information as the vignettes are expanded by additional facts. Scores are used to assess understanding of general trial issues, rational thinking ability, and appreciation of their own case. Observations are also encouraged regarding the defendant's ability to recognize and remember relevant information, ability to communicate in a coherent manner, and function in courtroom roles. The scoring protocol identifies a middle ground of mild impairment and a level of clinically significant impairment. The MacCAT-CA is somewhat weighted toward valuing cognitive abilities, and considers ability to learn as more than mere static knowledge. This emphasis on capacity is a significant advance over other measures, where merely saying, "I don't know" to enough questions places you in the incompetent range. This instrument also provides a more multidimensional assessment than do the other instruments.

More complex psychometric tools designed to assess competency also exist, such as the *Computer Assisted Competency Assessment Tool (CADCOMP)*[47] (Bernard et al. 1991), or the *Interdisciplinary Fitness Interview (IFI)*[48], (Golding, Roesch & Schreiber, 1984), but they require either the involvement of an attorney, or availability of a computer.

None of these tests should be taken at face value given the significant problems with truthful responding. The clinician should use cutoff scores only as general guidelines. Extreme scores should be considered as possibly deceitful. In the report to the court or the attorney, the clinician should consider dissecting the test or tests, and presenting and analyzing the data item by item. The clinician should also consider reviewing the answers with the defendant, providing correct information and retesting, and recording the new responses separately.

More general psychometric testing for neuropsychological functioning, symptom severity or personality structure remain very useful. One study looking at the WMS-R and the WAIS-R found significant differences between competent and incompetent defendants in measures of episodic memory and social intelligence (Nestor, Daggett, Haycock & Price, 1999).

---

[47] Barnard, G. W., Thompson, J. W., Freeman, W. C., Robbins, L., Gies, D., & Hankins, G.C. (1991). Competency to stand trial: Description and initial evaluation of a new computer-assisted assessment tool (CADCOMP). *Bulletin of the American Academy of Psychiatry and the Law, 19*, 367-381.

[48] Golding, S. S., Roesch, R., & Schreiber, J. (1984). Assessment and conceptualization of competency to stand trial: Preliminary data on the Interdisciplinary Fitness Interview. *Law and Human Behavior, 9*, 321-334.

Simple checklists of symptoms are not recommended because of the ease of deceitful and exaggerated reporting. The Rorschach has utility in the hands of an experienced tester because it requires more skill to produce acceptable deceitful responses.

7.1   Special Defendants

Often the examiner may believe they can make a rapid initial judgment about the defendant's competency, and then use the remainder of the exam to collect consistent data to confirm the impression. This occurs at both extremes; the defendant too withdrawn or psychotic to even make contact with, or the defendant conversant with every aspect of their case, but a poor fit with their attorney. These may seem like easy evaluations, but the clinician is advised to resist making such a decision before finishing the examination. In many cases the clinician will reach their decision with a high degree of confidence in their opinion. The next sections will discuss those more difficult cases and types of defendants, in which the examiner may not be able to make an ultimate decision with a reliable degree of certainty. The clinician may rather just present the court with an explication of the issues and the data, for example that the defendant is very likely to be disruptive and aggressive during any proceedings, and that this may significantly affect their actual participation in their own defense. In addition to requiring balancing degrees of psychological ability in the areas of relevance, these problem cases often also involve social value balancing that the clinician may not be ready to perform.

7.2   The Deceitful Defendant

A claim or finding of incompetency can have many potential benefits for a client and their attorney: it can provide a chance to test how mental health clinicians view the defendant prior to having to enter a plea, if a Not Guilty by Reason of Insanity (NGRI) plea is being considered; it can provide a later argument that the defendant was found severely mentally ill at the competency stage to support an NGRI plea or to aid in plea bargaining a lesser sentence; it can lead to suppressing evidence unfavorable to the defense if a confession or permission to search was given when the defendant was incompetent; it can delay trial so that witnesses or evidence become unavailable; or it can lead to a complete dropping of criminal charges.[49]

These benefits can lead to strategic behaviors to win a finding of incompetency, or to incorporate the process of an incompetency proceeding into the defense or prosecution plans. Matthew Hale, writing in the 17th century noted: "But because there may be great fraud in this matter, yet, if the crime be notorious...the judge may do well to impanel a jury to inquire...whether it be real or counterfeit."[50]

The case of Vincent "the Chin" Gigante is instructive on the remarkable ability of a defendant to exaggerate symptoms.[51] Mr. Gigante was indicted in 1990, and 1993, with various racketeering and murder charges related to his alleged control of the Genovese Organized Crime Family in New York City. Four prominent forensic psychiatrists evaluated Gigante to determine his competency to stand trial; two court appointed and two hired by the defense. One of the court appointed psychiatrists expressed a concern regarding malingering, but all four concluded Gigante was not competent to stand trial. They reported that Gigante was unable to do simple arithmetic, did not know the name of his attorney, the names of his children, thought God was his attorney, heard "bad" voices, had visions, and could not speak in complete sentences of more than four words. Further they considered that Gigante had a history of nearly 15 psychiatric hospitalizations, once yearly, with similar symptoms. Gigante was described as often wandering in his neighborhood in an old bathrobe and pajamas, babbling to himself, and urinating in the street. However, the Federal District Court Judge had extensive information from FBI surveillance and the testimony of former organized crime members that

---

[49] The prosecution may also seek benefits of an incompetency finding to possibly turn up more evidence while the defendant is being examined by clinicians at a state hospital or to effect incarceration in a hospital. For example, the poet Ezra Pound spent 13 years in St. Elizabeth's Hospital as incompetent to stand trial, and was never actually tried as a traitor. See Torrey, E. F. (1984). *The roots of treason: Ezra Pound and the secret of St. Elizabeth's.* New York, NY: McGraw-Hill.

[50] 1 Hale Pleas of the Crown 35. See *United States v. Chisolm*, 149 F. 284, 288 (SD Ala. 1906) ("it would be a reproach to justice if a guilty man . . . postponed his trial upon a feigned condition of mind, as to his inability to aid in his defense"). See also *U.S. v. Santos* 131 F.3d 16 (1st Cir. 1997); *U.S. v. Espinal*, 769 F. Supp. 116 (SD NY 1991); Wasyliw, O.E., Grossman, L.S., Haywood, T.W. & Cavanaugh, J.L. (1988). The detection of malingering in criminal forensic groups. *Journal of Personality Assessment, 52*, 321-333.

[51] See *U.S. v. Gigante* (2d Cir. 1999) 166 F.3d 75; *U.S. v. Gigante* (ED NY 1996) 925 F. Supp. 967; *U.S. v. Gigante* (ED NY 1998) 996 F. Supp. 194; Span, P. (1997, June 24). The Chin faces the judge at last; Vinnie Gigante has been acting a little crazy. Why not? Until now, it's kept him out of court. *The Washington Post* B1; Rashbaum, W. (1996, May 16). A mob of shrinks told to rethink The Chin. *The New York Daily News*, p. 17; Gigante verdict upheld; Next issue is sentencing. (1997, September 25). *The New York Times*, p.B4.

in between visits to the hospital, Gigante was directing the crime family, mediating disputes between crime families in his role on the mob "Commission," and visiting with his mistress, where he would read the paper and conduct business. The judge ordered the four psychiatrists to accept the extensive information on Gigante's activities as true, and report back to the court. The two court appointed psychiatrists then found him competent to stand trial. The judge ruled that Gigante: "deliberately feigned mental illness from the late 1960's...[and regarding his present symptoms] the reasonable inference...is not that his condition has deteriorated, but rather that the imminent threat of prosecution has increased his incentive to malinger." Gigante stayed out of custody for seven years on bail while his trial was pending. Gigante was tried and convicted in 1997. He then raised the objection that he was incompetent to be sentenced. An evaluation at the Federal Correctional Institution in Butner, North Carolina, reported that Gigante was possibly suffering from dementia, but that he also had shown signs of faking symptoms of mental illness.[52] Gigante's ability to deceive both his treating doctors and the forensic evaluators should serve as a caution for evaluators to do the extra work of contacting third parties and insisting on full records.

California has started an educational program for the courts and evaluators because of the large number of defendants who feign symptoms of a mental disorder to gain admission to the state hospitals in order to avoid criminal prosecution.[53] The full extent of this problem is likely not determinable because of the problems determining who is malingering or exaggerating symptoms. In a recent review of Utah Competency to stand trial evaluations, the issue was rarely addressed, but somewhere between 5 - 10 % of defendants were thought to be malingering (Skeem, Golding, Cohn & Berge, 1998). Other chapters of this text will address the issue of malingering more fully. This is a field that is still in the early stages of development.

In every competency evaluation, the clinician should provide the court with detailed examples to support the clinician's assessment regarding the defendant's truthfulness in presenting or reporting symptoms. The clinician needs to be aware that in many jails the prisoners share information about how to act in a psychiatric examination, such as for example to never look the doctor in the eye, always look at the floor or wall, take a long time before answering, tell the doctor Satan commands you to hurt yourself. Further,

---

[52] The occurrence of both actual and exaggerated disorders in the person being evaluated is common in all forensic settings. See e.g. Abrams, A. A., Taylor, C., & Levy, C. (in press). Deception in disability benefit programs. *American Journal of Forensic Psychiatry.*

[53] Testimony of Jon DeMorales, Executive Director, Atascadero Hospital to The Little Hoover Commission, October 28, 1999.

many defendants have some personal familiarity with time-limited substance induced psychoses, and can use those experiences as a basis for reporting current symptoms. The assessment of truthfulness is becoming the most essential, and also the most time consuming portion of the evaluation. Items that should be gathered and considered are reports from the deputy sheriffs who interact with the defendant on a daily basis, regarding hygiene, activities of daily living (ADL's) and communications, and whether the defendant acts differently when he knows he is being observed; review of current jail medical and mental health records; interviews with friends and family members, and particularly with those whom the defendant may have spoken with, either in person or on the phone while in custody; full review of prior medical and mental health records; review of prison records if available, particularly work, disciplinary and academic assessments; review of school records and employment records; detailed information about the defendant's activities in the prior two years; review of arrest records; a discussion with the defendant's present defense attorney regarding his or her observations of the defendant, and what problems have been encountered; and if possible, interviews with attorneys and judges regarding the defendant's behavior in prior legal proceedings. The clinician needs to consider what information is consistent with the defendant's presentation, what isn't, and make an assessment of reliability. Other indicators of deceitful presentation are evasions, for example "I don't know" responses to simple questions, approximate answers, preservative answers, only giving one word responses, ability to discuss more complex aspects of the proceedings, but not to know, for example, what the charges are or what a judge does. As indicated in other chapters, the easy cases of deceitful symptom reporting to detect are those that "overdo" it with very atypical symptoms or combinations of symptoms - catatonia, dementia, depression, global amnesia, and multisensory hallucinations. More subtle exaggeration of disability can require extended assessments. Cases involving neuropsychological disabilities can also be assessed with one of the newer tests for malingering that are well constructed and normed, such as the Test of Memory Malingering[54] (TOMM). The TOMM, a forced choice test, shows clear evidence of malingering when the subject scores significantly below chance, indicating conscious suppression of the accurate choice. Defendants found to be malingering neuropsychological deficits as part of their symptom presentation, should be carefully scrutinized regarding the remainder of their symptoms. Tests for psychological symptom malingering,

---

[54] Tombaugh, T. N. (1996). *Test of Memory Malingering*. New York, NY: Multi-Health Systems.

such as the Structured Interview of Reported Symptoms (SIRS)[55], Rorschach or MMPI-2, do not have the discriminative power of the neuropsychological tests, but can provide additional information.[56] A similar process of information gathering, separate from the clinical interview, is needed when the defendant refuses to cooperate, speak, or permit the examination.

Willful failure to disclose information or to cooperate with counsel will not usually lead to a finding of incompetency, even if the failure to cooperate is irrational.[57] Failure to cooperate as a result of mental illness may suggest an actual inability to cooperate. Failure to cooperate can sometimes occur along with malingered mental illness.[58] The *Dusky* standard looks at defendant's capacity to cooperate and assist counsel. Defendants do not have a duty to cooperate or to follow their attorney's advice.

7.3   The Amnestic Defendant

A defendant may become severely brain damaged or amnesic following an alleged crime, for example as a result of a suicide attempt, car accident during a high speed chase, being shot in the head during the crime, or being assaulted by other inmates while in custody. A defendant may have been extremely intoxicated at the time of the crime, and when sober cannot recall events or intentions.[59] Even though this would appear to significantly impair the defendant's ability to assist in their defense, courts have been reluctant to view this as an absolute barrier to trial, and will consider cases according to individual circumstances. Factors that a court will consider include the strength of the government's case, the ability to reconstruct the events of the alleged crime without the defendant's testimony, the nature and extent of

---

[55] Rogers, R., Bagby, R. M., & Dickens, S. E. (1992) *Structured Interview of Reported Symptoms* (SIRS). Odessa FL: Psychological Assessments Resources.

[56] Preliminary, but very interesting work addressing the problem of malingering in competency assessments has been done by Dr. Shayna Gothard. See Gothard, S., Viglione Jr., D.J., Meloy, J. R., & Sherman, M. (1995). Detection of malingering in competency to stand trial evaluations. *Law and Human Behavior, 19*, 493-505; Gothard, S., Rogers, R., & Sewell, K. W. (1995). Feigning incompetency to stand trial. *Law and Human Behavior, 19*, 363-373.

[57] *U.S. v. Velasquez*, 885 F.2d 1076 (3rd Cir. 1989).

[58] *U.S. v. Kokoski*, 865 F. Supp. 325 (SD W Va. 1994).

[59] See generally Koson, D. & Robey, A. (1973). Amnesia and competency to stand trial. *American Journal of Psychiatry, 130*, 588-591; Rubinsky, E. W., & Brandt, J. (1986). Amnesia and criminal law: A clinical overview. *Behavioral Sciences and the Law, 4*, 27-46.

impairment, and the impact on the defendant's ability to testify and participate in his defense.[60] This is the most concrete explication of factors in any area of competency to stand trial evaluation. The approach to the amnesic defendant provides the fullest glimpse into the non-clinical factors that may be considered in a court's competency determination. For example, the court may reason that the evidence is so detailed and compelling, and that there are such credible witnesses, that nothing the defendant could offer would make any difference, so there is no "unfairness" in continuing the trial. Though only the amnesia cases have articulated these factors, it is very likely that juries and judges make analogous judgments regarding the fairness of trying the particular defendant in all cases. The evaluation must focus on the defendant's mental abilities at the time of the examination separate from the amnesia at the time of the incident.

7.4   The Medically Ill Defendant

Medical conditions that affect cognitive functioning or behavioral control can be a basis for a finding of incompetency.[61] Though some statutes require incompetency to be the "result of mental disorder or developmental disability"[62], any medical condition that affects central nervous system (CNS) functioning would have a psychiatric diagnosis also, such as one of the dementia diagnoses or Mental Disorder Not Otherwise Specified (NOS) Due to General Medical Condition (DSM-IV 293.9). CNS impairments resulting from medications used to treat either medical or psychiatric illness can also give rise to a finding of incompetency. This could be coded as Other Substance-Related Disorder NOS (DSM-IV 292.9) or Adverse Effects of Medication NOS (DSM-IV 995.2). The use of a diagnosis of "Primitive Personality" has been suggested for some hearing impaired defendants (Vernon & Raifman, 1997).

---

[60] *U.S. v. Rinchack*, 820 F.2d 1557 (11th Cir. 1987); U.S. v. Villegas, 899 F.2d 1324 (2nd Cir. 1990) ; *U.S. v. Swanson*, 572 F.2d 523 (5th Cir. 1978); *U.S. v. Wilson*, 263 F. Supp 528 (D.C. 1966) (establishing a post as well as pretrial competency hearing, in order to determine whether the amnesia affected the right to a fair trial.)

[61] *Jackson v. Indiana*, 406 U.S. 715 (1972) (defendant both deaf and mute); *Featherston v. Mitchell*, 418 F.2d 582 (5th Cir. 1969) (defendant with blackouts); *U.S. v. Gambino*, 828 F. Supp. 191 (SD NY 1993) (defendant with heart condition).

[62] See e.g. Cal. Penal Code section 1367(a) (West 1999).

7.5   The Paranoid Defendant

The paranoid, manic, or paranoid schizophrenic defendant poses a particularly difficult problem to the criminal justice system, and these problems may begin with the competency determination. These defendants are often bright, articulate, hyper-verbal, and hyper-rational. Instead of problems with a mental "absence", they can be far too involved in their case. Frequently the severely ill paranoid views the trial, not as a criminal proceeding, but as a forum to express their delusions and preoccupations.[63] Since it is rare that a defense attorney shares a similar view, the paranoid defendant often refuses to cooperate with a competency evaluation, demands to be found competent and to represent himself, denies any mentally illness, and refuses to consider a psychiatric defense or accept psychiatric treatment. The competency evaluator is placed in the position of deciding to what extent the wish to not cooperate with their attorney or follow the attorney's advice is willful or significantly irrational. This dilemma then places the evaluator and the court in a Catch-22 position for which there are no satisfactory solutions.[64] The Supreme Court's decision in *Godinez*[65] requires a fitness determination before such a defendant can be allowed to waive the right to counsel, but if found competent to stand trial, the question then is whether the waiver of representation is voluntary and knowing. Either the court has to endure an undignified spectacle of *in pro se* ravings and a sense of an unfair trial or face depriving a defendant of fundamental rights or the possibility of never bringing the case to trial. The case of Colin Ferguson in New York represents the first prong. The case of the Unabomber, Theodore Kaczynski is illustrative of the second prong.[66] Kaczynski was evaluated at the Federal Correctional Institution in Butner, North Carolina, and was

---

[63] See *U.S. v. Veatch*, 842 F. Supp. 480 (WD Okla 1993); *Mass. v. Simpson*, 689 N.E.2d 824 (1998).

[64] See Morris, G. H. & Snyder, A.C. (1993). Mental disorder in the criminal process; Stan Stress and the Vietnam/sports conspiracy, Westport, Conn.: Greenwood Press. Justice Reinhardt of the Ninth Circuit Court of Appeals has recently written an opinion asking the Supreme Court to reconsider its decision in *Faretta v. California*, 422 U.S. 806 (1975) which granted all competent defendants the right to represent themselves, even at their own peril. Justice Reinhardt posed the question as whether a marginally competent criminal defendant has the right after *Godinez* to waive their right to a fair trial. *U.S. v. Farhad*, 190 F. 3d 1097 (9th Cir. 1999).

[65] *Godinez v. Moran*, 509 U.S. 389 (1993).

[66] See Mello, M. (1999). *The United States of America versus Theodore John Kaczynski: Ethics, power and the invention of the Unabomber.* New York, NY: Context Books; Booth, W. (1998, September 12). Gender confusion, sex change idea fueled Kaczynski's rage, report says. *The Washington Post*, p. A7; Court to hear request by Kaczynski for trial. (1999, October 24). *The New York Times*, p. 30.

diagnosed with paranoid schizophrenia, but felt to be competent to stand
trial. He had opposed the evaluation. The judge then refused to allow
Kaczynski to represent himself, to choose a lawyer who would present his
anti-technology views, or to make any changes in the plea bargain which his
attorneys had concluded with the prosecutors. The United States Court of
Appeals for the Ninth Circuit is now considering whether Mr. Kaczynski's
guilty plea was voluntary; whether he was properly denied the right to
represent himself, and whether a defendant, in a death penalty trial, has a
right to prevent his court-appointed lawyer from presenting evidence of
mental impairment as a defense.[67] In his appeals brief, Kaczynski wrote:
"From shortly after his arrest...Kaczynski made it clear to his attorneys that
if presented with a choice between life imprisonment and a death sentence,
he would just as soon have the death sentence, or would even prefer it to life
imprisonment... For months preceding the trial there was tension between
Kaczynski and his counsel concerning defense strategy... The tension
became acute on 11/25/97, when Kaczynski learned that his counsel
intended to portray him as suffering from major mental illness." Kaczynski's
struggles with his court appointed attorneys raises complex questions about
the scope of "decisional competency" and whether a defendant should be
allowed to make risky, ideological or political decisions about their
defense.[68]

The other prong of the legal systems' dilemma is seen in the case of Colin
Ferguson. On Dec. 7, 1993, Colin Ferguson went on a shooting spree on a
Long Island Railroad train. He killed 6 commuters and wounded 19 others
before he was stopped. Ferguson apparently was carrying letters claiming he
was the victim of a conspiracy. At trial he was initially represented by
renowned attorneys William Kunstler and Ronald Kuby, who planned to
argue an insanity defense. Both the defense and prosecution psychiatrists
diagnosed Ferguson as paranoid and delusional, but the prosecution
psychiatrist felt Ferguson was competent to stand trial. Ferguson, like
Kaczynski, was bright and articulate. After the judge ruled Ferguson
competent to stand trial, he then allowed Ferguson to fire his attorneys,
withdraw his insanity defense and represent himself at trial. Kunstler and
Kuby were appointed as advisers. During the trial, Ferguson mimicked legal
mannerisms, but with bizarre, irrational content. He tried to subpoena
President Clinton and Gov. Mario Cuomo as defense witnesses. He argued
that there were 93 counts to the indictment "because it was 1993. Had it been
1925 it would have been 25 counts." Despite the testimony of numerous

[67] A brief that's fit to print. (2000, February 1). *The Recorder*, p. 1.
[68] See Lloyd, J. (2000, June 6). Should the accused direct own trial strategy? *The Christian
Science Monitor*, p.2.

eyewitnesses, and victims, Ferguson presented his absurd defense: he was framed, and it was really a white man who went on the shooting spree. At sentencing, Ferguson compared himself to John the Baptist, discussed world hunger and the Irish Republican Army, rejected the significance of remorse in comparison to justice, and restated: "I continue to maintain that I was not the shooter on the train and that the shooter was a white person...John the Baptist lived in the wilderness, a humble man, and he was put into prison for no reason...He was beheaded by a criminal justice system similar to this." The judge imposed the maximum sentence of 200 years to life, commenting: "I have never presided over a trial with a more selfish and self-centered defendant."

Kunstler and Kuby later wrote: "He was operating under the delusion that he was perfectly sane and perfectly innocent, and any attempt to get him to accept an insanity defense was obvious proof of the widespread conspiracy against him. He was incapable of recognizing his best interests, let alone acting on them."[69]

On appeal, the appeals court found that the trial judge properly determined that Mr. Ferguson was competent to stand trial, and therefore competent to waive his right to counsel and proceed in his own defense, under the *Godinez* standard.[70]

Often the paranoid defendant will not tolerate a competency evaluation for very long. The defendant quickly understands that you will not assist in his agenda, and can become insistent that the evaluation end. These defendants may have extensive writings, threatening letters, or journals that the clinician can review, in addition to third party observations. The clinician should present the data, outline the problem of distinguishing willfulness from illness, and allow the court to make its determination. The paranoid defendant would likely score in the competent range on most of the formal psychometric tests. While paranoid defendants or paranoid schizophrenics may have a lower rate of response to treatment, the clinician should also outline this possibility, as well as his or her reasoning about the defendant's competency to make treatment decisions.

---

[69] Colin case can make law sane. (1995, March 7). *The New York Daily News*, p. 29 " (trial characterized as a: "bizarre and obscene spectacle, somewhere between bear-baiting and a patient takeover of a mental institution.")

[70] See Bid for retrial is denied In '93 L.I.R.R. slayings. (1998, December 3). *The New York Times*, p. B14; Column 5; Hester, J. (1998, December 11). Counsel for the defense. *The New York Daily News*, p. 113; Rail gunman to spend life behind bars. (1995, March 23). *The New York Times*, p. B1; Van Biema, D. (1995, February 6). A fool for a client: Accused L.I.R.R. killer Colin Ferguson is defending himself, and that may be something of a crime. Time, 145, p. 40. (describing case as "Jeckyll and Hyde visit Bleak House.")

7.6   The Suicidal Defendant

Closely related is the dilemma of the depressed, suicidal capital defendant who waives the right to an attorney and acts *in pro se* to prevent putting on a defense in order to be sentenced to die.[71] This "suicide by court" is analogous to the increasingly recognized "suicide by cop".

The facts underlying the case of *Godinez v. Moran*[72] presented this issue. Richard Moran had a severe drug addiction. In August 1984, he walked into the Red Pearl Saloon in Las Vegas, fatally shot the bartender and an off-duty cook, and took the cash register. He then set fire to the saloon in an attempt to burn it down. Nine days later, he shot his ex-wife to death, then shot himself in the abdomen and tried to slash his wrists. Two days after that, he called police to his hospital bed and confessed. Moran first pleaded innocent, but then told the judge in November 1984, that he wanted to fire his lawyers, plead guilty and prevent the presentation of any evidence against a death sentence. Moran later appealed claiming that his plea and waiver of counsel were not freely and voluntarily entered because he was heavily medicated at the time of his guilty plea, and thus he was incompetent to waive his rights. Moran was executed by lethal injection in Nevada, on March 30, 1996. In his dissent to the Supreme Court decision affirming the conviction, Justice Blackmun wrote: "Just a few months after he attempted to commit suicide, Moran essentially volunteered himself for execution: he sought to waive the right to counsel, to plead guilty to capital murder, and to prevent the presentation of any mitigating evidence on his behalf. The psychiatrists' reports supplied one explanation for Moran's self-destructive behavior: his deep depression." Some states have prohibited a defendant from representing himself to insure a death sentence.[73] Once convicted, and condemned, some prisoners will waive all appeals to insure they are killed. In *Rees v. Payton*[74] the Supreme Court required a hearing on competency (emphasizing rational choice) before a condemned prisoner could be allowed to refuse assistance of counsel and terminate legal appeals (Strafer, 1983).

---

[71] *Wilkins v. Bowersox*, 145 F.3d 1006 (8th Cir. 1998); Noland v. Dixon, 831 F. Supp. 490 (WD NC 1993); Ill. v. Kinkead, 695 N.E.2d 1255 (1998).

[72] *Godinez v. Moran*, 509 U.S. 389 (1993).

[73] *People v. Chadd*, 28 Cal. 3d 739 (1981).

[74] *Rees v. Payton*, 384 U.S. 312 (1966).

7.7   The Mentally Retarded Defendant

Attorneys or judges may not specifically identify the basis for the referral as due to mental retardation, but may notice impaired communication or understanding of proceedings. The diagnosis of mental retardation requires impaired adaptive functioning as well as a depressed cognitive or intellectual measurement. Reports that merely restate the result of IQ testing are of little value. Questioning the defendant about placement in special education, level of school completed, ability to hold jobs, interviews of family members, and review of school records, if available, will identify many defendants who may have a mental retardation diagnosis.[75] Non-forensic tests of adaptive functioning can provide information about the defendant's capacities (Jacobson & Mulick, 1996). A specific test for competency to stand trial has been developed for mentally retarded defendants, the CAST-MR. (Everington 1992). The CAST-MR provides useful information about the defendant's ability to comprehend their legal situation, separate from their I. Q.[76] Neither a diagnosis of mental retardation or a low IQ score, even one below 70, are sufficient for a finding of incompetency.[77] The clinician should not assume that a diagnosis of mental retardation will provide a basis for a finding of incompetency. Again an explicit presentation of deficits in competency related area is required. Restoration of competency should require more than rote repetition of over-trained answers.

7.8   The Juvenile Defendant

Some states have a minimum statutory age, below which children will not be considered capable of committing a crime "unless they knew its

---

[75] See generally Appelbaum, K .L. (1994). Assessment of criminal-justice-related competencies in defendants with mental retardation. *Journal of Psychiatry and Law, 22,* 311-327; Appelbaum, K .L. & Appelbaum,P. S. (1994). Criminal-justice-related competencies in defendants with mental retardation. *Journal of Psychiatry and Law, 22,* 483-503.

[76] Everington, C. & Dunn, C. (1995). A second validation study of the Competence Assessment for Standing Trial for Defendants with Mental Retardation. *Criminal Justice and Behavior, 22,* 44-59. See also Fulero, S. & Everington, C. (1995). Assessing competency to waive Miranda rights in defendants with mental retardation. *Law and Human Behavior, 19,* 533-543.

[77] See *People v. Johnson,* 700 N.E. 2d 996 (1998); M.D. v. State, 701 So. 2d 58 (1997); *State v. Jenkins,* 379 SE2d 156 (1989).

wrongfulness."[78] In the only study of very young juvenile offenders, fewer than half of the defendants, 13 year old or younger, were judged on clinical evaluation to be competent.[79] Those juveniles who are charged are likely protected by the same standards for competency to stand trial as adults, though state statutes may not explicitly provide for this.[80] A more lenient standard has not been enacted by any legislature.[81] The juvenile offenders' rational and factual understanding of the criminal process and their ability to cooperate with counsel is closely related to their social, emotional, and cognitive development. So, for example, it is typical for juveniles to view their attorney as an adult authority figure to whom they will then deny any wrong-doing to.[82] The ability of juveniles to waive constitutionally guaranteed rights, which requires a finding of competency to stand trial, suggests the crucial importance of further development in this area.[83]

Juvenile courts are based on the assumption that juvenile offenders are immature, and the task for the examiner is to identify that combination of immaturity, cognitive impairment, learning disability, and mental illness that distinguish the competent from the incompetent offender. There are no current guidelines on whether there should be a different standard of competency for juveniles tried in juvenile court or in adult court.[84] After a finding of incompetency, the proper disposition of the juvenile will be problematic. As more and younger juveniles are tried in adult court, these questions will require clearer development.[85]

---

[78] See e.g. Ca. Penal Code section 26 (West 1999).

[79] *Cowen, V. & McKee*, G. (1995). Competency to stand trial in juvenile delinquency proceedings: Cognitive maturity and the attorney-client relationship. *University of Louisville Journal of Family Law, 33*, 629-666.

[80] See James H. v. Superior Court, 77 Cal.App.3d 169 (1978); In re S.H.,, 469 S.E.2d 810 (1996); In re Welfare of S.W.T., 277 N.W.2d 507 (1979); Szymanski, L.(1998). *Juvenile competency to stand trial. National Center for Juvenile Justice Snapshot, 3*, 1.

[81] See *State v. E.C.*, 922 P.2d 152 (1996).

[82] See Buss, E.. (1996).You're my what? The problem of children's misperceptions of their lawyers' roles. *Fordham Law Review, 64* 1699.

[83] See. Feld, B. C. (1989). The right to counsel in juvenile court: empirical study of when lawyers appear and the difference they make. *Journal of Crime, Law & Criminology, 79*, 1185.

[84] See Heilbrun, K., Hawk, G., & Tate, D.C. (1996). Juvenile competence to stand trial: Research issues in practice. *Law and Human Behavior, 20*, 573-578.

[85] See generally Grisso, T. (1999). Juvenile competency to stand trial: Questions in an era of punitive reform ABA Criminal Justice Section, Juvenile Justice Center.

8. DISPOSITION AND RESTORATION

After a finding of incompetency, typically the defendant is committed for a discrete period of time for treatment and cure.[86] In *Jackson v. Indiana* (1972), the court was faced with the disposition of someone who would never likely be restored to competency. *Jackson* was a young man who was mentally retarded, deaf, and without speech or written language, who was unable to learn sign language. *Jackson* was arrested for two robberies, one of $4 and the other of $5. The Court held that an incompetent defendant could not be held for life if there was no possibility of restoring sanity, and after a reasonable amount of time would have to be released or committed under other statutes, and the charges dropped.[87] Some states have special statutes for the continuing civil commitment of those persons found incompetent to stand trial based on a dangerousness standard.[88]

Defendants found incompetent to stand trial are nearly always referred for in-patient treatment at a state hospital. Treatment includes interviews, observation, didactic sessions geared toward explaining the judicial process, the meaning of concepts and roles of relevance to a trial, counseling, and perhaps treatment with medication. Most state statutes specifically provide for treatment as a consequence of a finding of incompetency to stand trial.

The question of involuntary medication treatment to restore competency remains uncertain. There is no general constitutional right for an incompetent defendant to refuse psychiatric treatment, however the state must show a sufficiently strong justification for the treatment. Some jurisdictions require a separate judicial finding of incompetence to make medical decisions before the incompetent to stand trial defendant can be

---

[86] It has been estimated that there are approximately 15,000 criminal defendants in state hospitals at any one time judged incompetent to stand trial. Noffsinger, S. (2000). Restoration to competency. *AAPL Newsletter, 25*, 7-8.

[87] For example, 18 U.S.C. §4241(d) allows four months.

[88] See e.g. California Welfare and Institutions Code section 5008 (h)(1)(B) defining grave disability for defendants found incompetent to stand trial and not restored to competence within the statutory period: "A condition in which a person, has been found mentally incompetent under Section 1370 of the Penal Code and all of the following facts exist: (i) The indictment or information pending against the defendant at the time of commitment charges a felony involving death, great bodily harm, or a serious threat to the physical well-being of another person. (ii) The indictment or information has not been dismissed. (iii) As a result of mental disorder, the person is unable to understand the nature and purpose of the proceedings taken against him or her and to assist counsel in the conduct of his or her defense in a rational manner." (West 1999).

forceably medicated over the defendant's objections.[89] In federal cases, the court must also find that involuntary medication is in the best medical interests of the defendant or that the defendant would have chosen treatment if he were competent.[90] Some states view restoration of competency as more important than the individual liberty to refuse treatment.[91] Treatment refusal is not always irrational. Ladds and Convit (1994), found that treatment refusal might relate to a denial of illness, delusions, concerns about medication side effects, or no reason at all.

The Supreme Court nearly addressed the right to refuse medication that might restore competency in *Riggins v. Nevada* (1992). The court did not prohibit the use of involuntary medication to restore or maintain competency, but required a state showing of medical appropriateness and overriding justification. The Court avoided the more difficult issue saying: "The question whether a competent criminal defendant may refuse antipsychotic medication if cessation of medication would render him incompetent at trial is not before us."[92]

All of the same legal rights and procedures apply when a defendant has been treated, and the hospital reports to the court that they believe he is now fit. In practice, these findings are given great weight because of the extensive time for observation of the defendant at the hospital. A defendant's strategic motives may have changed after an initial finding of competency to stand trial, so that a restoration exam may be viewed differently by the defendant.[93] Defendants have a right to raise the issue of competency even after it is restored, but many states require new or greater evidence than in the original hearing.

---

[89] See *People v. Jones*, 15 Cal 4th 119 (1997); *Shabazz v. State*, 729 So. 2d 813 (1998)(no requirement for hearing if defendant does not object to medication).

[90] See *U.S. v. Brandon*, 158 F.3d 947 (6th Cir. 1998) (judicial hearing required); *U.S. v. Charters*, 863 F.2d 302 (4th Cir. 1988) (en banc) reversing *U.S. v. Charters*, 829 F.2d 479 (4th Cir. 1987) (restoring competency to stand trial is not sufficiently strong reason to allow involuntary medication).

[91] *State v. Laws*, 244 S.E. 2d 302 (1978).

[92] Id.

[93] See generally Ladds, B., Convit, A., Zito, J., & Vittrai, J. (1993). The disposition of criminal charges after involuntary medication to restore competency to stand trial. *Journal of Forensic Sciences, 38*, 1442-1459.

9.   COMPETENCY TO BE EXECUTED

One of the earliest Supreme Court decisions on a mental health question was *Nobles v. State of Georgia* (1897). Elizabeth Nobles was sentenced to death, and the question of her present insanity arose after sentencing. The Court quoted Blackstone's commentary that "if he [the condemned] appears to be insane, the judge, in his discretion, may, and ought to, reprieve him."[94] Though every state had a statute forbidding the execution of the "insane", no particular procedures or hearings were required. In 1950, the Supreme Court held that not executing the insane was an act of executive clemency, and not a constitutional mandate.[95] Pregnant women, children and the incompetent have traditionally been spared from execution by state statutes. Estimates of the level of severe mental illness among condemned prisoners have been estimated to be as high as 70%.

In 1986, the U.S. Supreme Court constitutionalized the prohibition against executing the insane through the Eighth Amendment's ban on cruel and unusual punishment.[96] The Court, however, could not agree on a constitutional standard for determining incompetence for execution. Justice Powell proposed, "that the Eighth Amendment forbids the execution only of those who are unaware of the punishment they are about to suffer and why they are to suffer it."[97] Each state's statute typically defines a standard similar to that articulated by Justice Powell, though a minority of states further require that the condemned be able to assist in his own defense.[98] The required and due procedures also vary between states, for example whether there is a right to a jury trial to determine competency or to a judicial hearing on restoration of sanity after an initial finding of incompetency.

The court in *Ford v. Wainwright* (1986), based its decision on both historical tradition, the possibility of new evidence being produced when the prisoner is returned to competency, and moral considerations of the humanity, or inhumanity, of executing a prisoner who may not be able to

---

[94] *id.*, citing 4 Blackstone Commentaries 396.

[95] *Solesbee v. Balkcom*, 339 U.S. 9, 14 (1950); see also dissent in Ford v. Wainwright, 477 US 399 (1986).

[96] *Ford v. Wainwright*, 477 US 399 (1986).

[97] *id.*, at 477 U.S. 422.

[98] See e.g. Justice Frankfurter's more expansive recommendation adopted in the American Bar Association's Criminal Justice Mental Health Standards 7-5.6(b): "A convict is incompetent to be executed if . . .[in addition] the convict lacks sufficient capacity to recognize or understand any fact which might exist which would make the punishment unjust or unlawful, or lacks the ability to convey such information to counsel or to the court". George Jr., B. J. (reporter) (1989). *ABA Criminal Justice Mental Health Standards* (Standard 7-5.6(b), pp. 290-293). Washington, D.C.: American Bar Association.

prepare spiritually for his or her impending death. Justice Traynor, in his concurrence in *Phyle v. Duffy* (1949), addressed the moral dilemma of applying humanitarian standards to executions: "If the possibility of a subsequently refreshed memory were enough to prevent the execution of an insane man, it would render unconstitutional any capital punishment, since it is possible to speculate endlessly about the possibilities that would rescue a condemned man from execution provided it were delayed long enough...Is it not an inverted humanitarianism that deplores as barbarous the capital punishment of those who have become insane after trial and conviction, but accepts the capital punishment of sane men."[99]

The test for death competency is primarily cognitive, though not simply a factual recitation of the sentence. Semantic memory is also required; along with some ability for abstract thought.[100] The motivation to exaggerate or malinger if this is the only means of avoiding execution is certainly strong. A claim of incompetency will provide materials for additional appeals and delay.[101]

In *Perry v. Louisiana* (1990), the Supreme Court remanded the case to the Louisiana courts to reconsider whether an inmate could be made competent to be executed by the use of forced medication. The Supreme Court did not decide the question, though it proposed considering the issue in terms of the opinion expressed in *Washington v. Harper* (1990). On remand, the Louisiana Supreme Court held that it violated the Louisiana Constitution to medicate a prisoner against his will to make him competent to be executed.[102]

There is considerable commentary on the ethics of execution competency evaluations and the constitutionality of forced treatment to restore competency to allow execution.[103]

---

[99] id., at 158-9.

[100] See generally Heilbrun, K. S. (1987). The assessment of competency for execution: An overview. *Behavioral Sciences and the Law, 5,* 383-396.

[101] See *Phyle v. Duffy,* 34 Cal. 2d 144, 150-51 (1949): "Dr. Rappaport explained that shortly after Phyle's commitment to the hospital, he [Phyle]'told me very frankly he had faked the whole thing and he was surprised [the prison psychiatrist] was fooled but not suprised that he fooled the warden. . . . He said other prisoners conducted examinations and that naturally if they are friendly and want to help you they would indicate to you what you should say and what the answer should be."

[102] *Louisiana v. Perry,* 610 So. 2d 746 (1992).

[103] Arriago, B. A. & Tasca, J. J. (1999). Right to refuse treatment, competency to be executed and therapeutic jurisprudence: Toward a systemic analysis. *Law & Psychology Review, 23,* 1-47; Jenkins, R .K. (1995). Fit to die: Drug-induced competency for the purpose of execution. *Southern Illinois University Law Journal, 20,* 149-179; Winick, B. J. (1992). Competency to be executed: A therapeutic jurisprudence perspective. *Behavioral Sciences and the Law, 10,* 317-337; Mossman, D. (1992). The psychiatrist and execution

10.   SUMMARY

The concerns about the fairness of subjecting a significantly impaired defendant to criminal process embody fundamental values of our society. The global, social principles, which most citizens agree with: fairness, equality, justice, do not provide any specific content for the forensic mental health evaluator. The development of more specific operational content for competency to stand trial has been inhibited by the nearly uniform statutes, the procedural focus of most appellate decisions, philosophical differences on how much cooperation between a defendant and their attorney is required, the level of rationality required, and the high standards of appellate review. Only in the cases concerning amnesic defendants has there been significant development beyond the *Dusky* formula. It has thus become the task of the mental health field to try to provide concrete or operational standards for the determination of competency to stand trial for the courts to accept or reject. Numerous discrete specific competency areas can be identified and rated, but the reduction of the full, complex assessment in a dichotomous decision, competent or not, remains problematic. The existence of particular classes of problem defendants will hopefully be addressed in the same detailed manner as the courts have done with the amnesic defendant. At present, the mental health clinician must address the issue of defendant's truthfulness, and the areas and likely degrees where defendant's cognitive impairments, thought disorder, or psychopathology limit their ability to participate in the adversarial process. Substantiation of limitations through psychological testing, and third party information, is the best practice. Detailed documentation of the evaluation process is essential.

Competency to be executed is a problematic concept, with tenuous moral or legal underpinning. The role of clinicians in providing opinions in this area is a matter of personal ethics and the need to comply with stated professional ethics.

Hopefully, the provision of specific content by mental health clinicians will become incorporated into appellate decisions and allow more congruence between the psychological evaluation and the legal decision. The process of maturation of legal principles is a feed-forward cycle, in which important new court decisions, scientific developments, and law review analyses of concepts in light of legal developments stimulate the refinement

---

competency: Fording murky ethical waters. *Case Western Reserve Law Review, 43,* 1-95; Bonnie, R. J. (1990). Dilemmas in administering the death penalty. *Law and Human Behavior, 14,* 67-97; Brodsky, S. L. (1990) Professional ethics and professional morality in the assessment of competence for execution. *Law and Human Behavior, 14,* 91-97.

of concepts. The clinician's role will continue to center on the provision of meaningful data and analysis of the defendant's functioning in court related tasks.

11.   REFERENCES

Bagby, R. M., Nicholson, R. A., Rogers, R., & Nussbaum, D. (1992). Domains of competency to stand trial: A factor analytic study. *Law and Human Behavior, 16*, 491-507.

Barnard, G. W., Thompson, J. W., Freeman, W. C., Robbins, L., Gies, D., & Hankins, G.C. (1991). Competency to stand trial: Description and initial evaluation of a new computer-assisted assessment tool (CADCOMP). *Bulletin of the American Academy of Psychiatry and the Law, 19*, 367-381.

Bonnie, R. J. (1993). The competence of criminal defendants: Beyond Dusky and Drope. *University of Miami Law Review, 47*, 539-601.

Bonnie, R. J. (1992). The competence of criminal defendants: A theoretical reformulation. *Behavioral Sciences and the Law, 10*, 291-316.

Dusky v. United States, 362 U.S. 402 (1960).

Everington, C. T. (1990). The competence for standing trial for defendants with mental retardation (CAST-MR): A validation study. *Criminal Justice and Behavior, 17*, 147-168.

Ford v. Wainwright, 477 US 399 (1986).

George Jr., B. J. (reporter) (1989*). ABA Criminal Justice Mental Health Standards.* Washington, D.C.: American Bar Association.

Godinez v. Moran, 509 U.S. 389 (1993).

Golding, S. S., Roesch, R., & Schreiber, J. (1984). Assessment and conceptualization of competency to stand trial: Preliminary data on the Interdisciplinary Fitness Interview. *Law and Human Behavior, 9*, 321-334.

Gothard, S., Viglione Jr., D. J., Meloy, J. R., & Sherman, M., (1995). Detection of malingering in competency to stand trial evaluations. *Law and Human Behavior, 19*, 493-505.

Gothard, S., Rogers, R., & Sewell, K. W. (1995). Feigning incompetency to stand trial. *Law and Human Behavior, 19*, 363-373.

Hoge, S. K., Bonnie, R. J., Poythress, N., Monahan, J., Eisenberg, M., & Feucht-Haviar, T. (1997). The MacArthur adjudicative competence study: Development and validation of a research instrument. *Law and Human Behavior, 21*, 141-179.

Hoge, S. K., Bonnie, R. J., Poythress, N., & Monahan, J. (1999). *The MacArthur Competence Assessment Tool - Criminal Adjudication.* Odessa, FL: Psychological Assessment Resources, Inc.

Jackson v. Indiana, 406 U.S. 715 (1972).

Jacobson, J. W. & Mulick, J. A. (eds.) (1996) *Manual of diagnosis and professional practice in mental retardation.* Washington, DC: American Psychological Association.

Laboratory of Community Psychiatry. (1973). *Competency to stand trial and mental illness. DHEW Publication No. ADM77-103.* Rockville, MD: Department of Health, Education and Welfare.

Ladds, B. & Convit, A. (1994). Involuntary medication of patients who are incompetent to stand trial: A review of empirical studies. *Bulletin of the American Academy of Psychiatry and Law, 22*, 519-532.

Miller, R. D. (1994). Criminal competence. In Rosner, R. (Ed.) *Principles and practice of forensic psychiatry,* (pp. 174-197). New York, NY: Chapman & Hall.

Nestor, P.G., Daggett, D., Haycock, J. & Price, M. (1999) Competence to stand trial: A neuropsychological inquiry. *Law and Human Behavior, 23*, 397-412.

Nicholson, R. A., Briggs, S. R., & Robertson, H. (1988). Instruments for assessing competency to stand trial: How do they work? *Professional Psychology: Research and Practice, 19*, 383-394.

Nobles v. State of Georgia, 168 U.S. 398 (1897).

Ohayon, M. M., Crocker A., St-Onge, B. & Caulet, M. (1998). Fitness, responsibility, and judicially ordered assessments. Canadian *Journal of Psychiatry, 43*, 491-495.

Pate v. Robinson, 383 U.S. 375 (1966).

Perry v. Louisiana, 498 US 38 (1990).

Plotnick, S., Porter, J., & Bagby, M. (1998) Is there bias in the evaluation of fitness to stand trial? *International Journal of Law and Psychiatry. 21*, 291-304.

Phyle v. Duffy, 34 Cal. 2d 144 (1949).

Reich, J., & Tookey, L. (1986). Disagreements between court and psychiatrist on competency to stand trial. *Journal of Clinical Psychiatry, 47*, 616-623.

Riggins v. Nevada, 504 U.S. 127 (1992).

Roesch, R. & Golding, S. L. (1980). *Competency to stand trial.* Urbana, IL: University of Illinois Press.

Skeem, J. L., Golding, S. L., Cohn, N. B., & Berge, G. (1998). Logic and reliability of evaluations of competence to stand trial. *Law and Human Behavior, 22*, 519- 547.

Strafer, G. R. (1983). Volunteering for execution: Competency, voluntariness and the propriety of third party intervention. *Journal of Criminal Law & Criminology, 74*, 860-912.

Ustad, K. L., Rogers, R., Sewell, K. W. & Guarnaccia, C. A. (1996). Restoration of competency to stand trial: Assessment with the Georgia Court Competency Test and the Competency Screening Test. *Law and Human Behavior, 20*, 131-146.

Vernon, M, & Raifman, L.J. (1997). Recognizing and handling problems of incompetent deaf defendants charged with serious offenses. *International Journal of Law and Psychiatry, 20*, 373-387.

Washington v. Harper, 494 U.S. 210 (1990).

Wildman, R. W., II, Batchelor, E. S., Thompson, L., Nelson, F. R., Moore, J. T., Patterson, M.E., & DeLaosa, M. (1978). *The Georgia Court Competency Test: An attempt to develop a rapid, quantitative measure of fitness for trial. Unpublished manuscript,* Forensic Services Division, Central State Hospital, Milledgeville, GA.

Chapter 7

Civil Committment

Kathleen Powers Stafford, Ph.D., ABPP
Psycho-Diagnostic Clinic, Akron, OH

1. INTRODUCTION

Civil commitment, or court-ordered involuntary treatment of people with mental disorders, raises a number of legal, systems, ethical, and clinical issues. The forensic assessment of an individual's appropriateness for civil commitment requires integrated knowledge of these four areas. First, the psychologist must understand the legal history and standards, and the specific psycho-legal questions that need to be addressed. Second, the psychologist must be familiar with specific mental health delivery systems, which determine the available treatment alternatives and their relative effectiveness. Third, knowledge of the clinical and scientific basis for addressing the psycho-legal questions raised by civil commitment law is essential. And finally, the psychologist must carefully weigh the competing ethical and value issues pertaining to the civil commitment of an individual. This chapter summarizes each of these areas in an effort to guide the clinician in making reasoned assessments of an individual's need for involuntary mental health treatment.

2.   LEGAL HISTORY AND STANDARDS

2.1   Commitment in the United States through the Mid-Twentieth Century

In colonial America, individuals considered violent and insane were incarcerated, but those presenting with equally unusual behavior and thinking who appeared harmless were left free, regardless of their ability to care for themselves. In the late eighteenth and early nineteenth centuries, the indigent insane were informally committed to poorhouses, although the first hospitals for the treatment of mental disorders in the United States also opened in Williamsburg, Virginia in 1773, and in Lexington, Kentucky in 1824.

With the mid-nineteenth century came the forerunners of modern civil commitment. Reformers, such as Dorothea Dix, campaigned for the mentally disordered to be considered patients, rather than criminals or paupers. The state began to assume responsibility for the care of the mentally disordered, and more insane asylums, beginning with Worcester State Hospital in Massachusetts in 1833, were built. The existence of state-funded hospitals led to the development of statutes dealing with utilization of these state-funded beds. Early statutes provided for involuntary confinement of individuals based upon the wishes of families and the opinions of physicians.

The common law doctrine of *parens patriae*, the power of the state to act as guardian or in the best interest of minors or incapacitated citizens, has been the rationale underlying the development of commitment laws. From the mid-nineteenth to the mid-twentieth century, the civil commitment system operated without precise statutory criteria, procedural safeguards, or clarity regarding the evidentiary standard of proof. Four different legal standards for civil commitment were widely used. In addition to being mentally ill, individuals had to be considered dangerous to others, dangerous to themselves, unable to care for themselves, or in need of treatment, to be involuntarily hospitalized.

Despite the proliferation of new treatment techniques, professions, and resources during the twentieth century, civil commitment statutes were of little concern to the legal profession until the 1960's. Then, increasing concern about conditions in institutions, development of psychotropic medications effective in treating the symptoms of major mental disorders, and the cost of housing patients in state hospitals led to legislation impacting upon civil commitment (Appelbaum, 1996). In 1963, Congress passed the

Community Mental Health Centers Act, encouraging establishment of a system of outpatient care for formerly hospitalized patients. The 1964 Ervin Act for the District of Columbia limited commitment criteria to mental illness and danger to self or others and added procedural safeguards to the commitment process. In California, the 1967 Lanterman-Petris-Short Act limited commitment for danger to self to 31 days, with recommitment thereafter only if the person qualified for conservatorship. Commitments based on danger to others were renewable after 17 days, but ongoing commitment thereafter required a full hearing every 90 days (Melton, Petrila, Poythress & Slobogin, 1997).

2.2   Case Law Developments

These early legislative reforms were soon overshadowed by the development of a body of case law protecting the rights of individuals subject to commitment proceedings. In 1966, the United States Court of Appeals for the District of Columbia held that a person involuntarily confined in a mental hospital after a finding of not guilty by reason of insanity has a **right to treatment** (*Rouse v. Cameron*). And in *Lake v. Cameron* (1966), the Court remanded the commitment of a woman with apparent dementia to the trial court for consideration of alternative places of treatment, articulating the commitment principle that has come to be known as **least restrictive alternative**.

In 1972, the U.S, District Court case of *Lessard v. Schmidt* struck down Wisconsin's civil commitment statute and effectively challenged commitment statutes in other jurisdictions. The Court labeled a number of Wisconsin's commitment provisions "constitutionally defective." These included detention longer than 48 hours without a probable cause hearing, and longer than two weeks without a full hearing; hearings without adversary counsel; admission of hearsay evidence; presentation of psychiatric evidence obtained from the patient without the benefit of privilege against self-incrimination; failure to consider less restrictive alternatives; and commitment without proof of dangerousness and mental illness beyond a reasonable doubt. As the result of *Lessard v. Schmidt*, every state in the nation modified its commitment statutes by the end of the 1970's, (Appelbaum, 1996).

In 1975, the U.S. Supreme Court held in *O'Connor v. Donaldson* that a state cannot constitutionally confine "without more" a non-dangerous mentally ill person who is capable of surviving safely in the community alone or with the assistance of willing and responsible friends or family.

This case is generally interpreted as constitutionally limiting commitments that are based solely upon grave disability or the need for treatment. It has led to greater emphasis on danger to self or others as prerequisite for commitment.

The Connecticut Supreme Court case of *Fasulo v. Arafeh* (1977), mandated periodic, state-initiated recommitment hearings that included the safeguards of the initial commitment hearings, and it placed the burden on the state to prove that the patient requires continued commitment.

The 1979, Supreme Court case of *Addington v. Texas* set the minimal constitutional level of proof for civil commitment proceedings at clear and convincing evidence. Clear and convincing evidence has been described as about 75% certainty, as compared to preponderance of the evidence (about 51% certainty), the standard of proof required in other civil matters (Stone, 1975). Interestingly, the Court did not require the more rigorous standard of beyond a reasonable doubt (about 95% certainty), which is the standard for criminal proceedings. Instead, the Court noted that the state would have difficulty meeting the rigorous standard of beyond a reasonable doubt because of "the uncertainties of psychiatric diagnosis," and that patients who might benefit from involuntary treatment might therefore not be committed.

The Supreme Court considered due process issues in the commitment of minors in the 1979, case, *Parham v. J.R. and J.L.* The Court ruled that parents or guardians could commit children to hospitals without formal judicial hearings, but that some procedure, entailing periodic review by a neutral fact-finder regarding whether statutory criteria for admission are met, is required.

2.3   Competency to Consent, and the Right to Refuse Treatment

In 1990, the Supreme Court dealt with the issue of *failing to commit* a hospitalized patient when that patient had been incompetent to consent to voluntary admission. The case of *Zinermon v. Burch* was based upon the action of a Florida state hospital in accepting a psychotic patient's written consent for voluntary admission, and his subsequent consent to treatment over a period of months, even though it was documented in treatment records that the patient was confused and believed that he was in heaven. The Court held that, by accepting Mr. Burch's "voluntary" consent to treatment when he was not capable of giving valid, informed consent, instead of initiating an involuntary placement hearing, the state deprived Mr. Burch of his liberty without the benefit of the procedural safeguards against involuntary confinement contained in the Florida commitment statute. This case introduces the concept of competency to consent to treatment to considerations about when to consider involuntary, rather than voluntary, admission of disturbed patients who do not object to treatment.

A related body of case law has developed concerning the issue of patients' rights to **refuse** treatment, particularly medication. In the case of *Rogers v. Commissioner* (1983), the Massachusetts Supreme Judicial Court held that both voluntary and involuntary mental patients, if competent, have the right to refuse treatment with medication, based upon their rights to freedom of speech and to privacy. Patients are presumed to be competent. If a patient's competence is questioned, usually because of his or her refusal to accept treatment, the Court established that a judge would determine whether the patient is incompetent. The Court also articulated a "substituted judgment" model, whereby a judge would make a decision about the involuntary administration of medication based, in part, on whether that incompetent patient, if competent, would have consented to the treatment.

In contrast to the Massachusetts model of judicial review of proposals for involuntary medication, and reliance on substituted judgment for decision-making, an alternative model evolved in New Jersey as the result of another 1983 case. In *Rennie v. Klein*, the U.S. Court of Appeals, Third Circuit affirmed the constitutional right to refuse treatment, but a "professional judgment" model was adopted for making decisions about the involuntary administration of medication. The New Jersey administrative review procedures were considered to satisfy due process requirements for making decisions about whether a mentally ill patient could competently refuse to take prescribed medication or could be administered prescribed medication involuntarily.

The U.S. Supreme Court addressed the right of mentally ill prisoners to refuse treatment in the 1990 case of *Washington v. Harper*. The Court upheld the Washington state procedure, which allowed involuntary medication of prisoners who met the state's dangerousness-based commitment criteria, without requiring a determination of incompetence. Instead, a panel of staff not involved with the prisoner's treatment reviewed each case every two weeks. The Court clarified that the involuntary administration of medication "for no purpose other than treatment" was proper in meeting the state's interest in ensuring the safety of prisoners and prison staff.

In the 1992 case of *Riggins v. Nevada*, the U.S. Supreme Court dealt with the issue of the right of a defendant awaiting trial to refuse to take psychotropic medication. The Court held that involuntary medication of a pretrial detainee must be the least intrusive means of achieving two objectives: 1) protecting the safety of the detainee and others, and 2) ensuring his competency to proceed to trial to resolve the issue of his guilt or innocence. The pretrial detainee has the right to refuse antipsychotic medication absent an "overriding justification and a determination of medical appropriateness."

2.4   Commitment of Persons Found Not Guilty by Reason of Insanity

Individuals who have been found not guilty by reason of insanity of criminal conduct are generally subject to court-ordered treatment by civil commitment standards or some variation, although some jurisdictions provide for automatic commitment of insanity acquittees (Shuman, 1999). The Supreme Court, in *Jones v. United States* (1983), supported the commitment of insanity acquittees under lesser standards than have been imposed for civil commitment. The Court upheld automatic commitment for evaluation after the insanity acquittal. The Court found that any criminal act is indicative of dangerousness, even though the criminal act in the Jones' case was the theft of a jacket, and that "someone whose mental illness was sufficient to lead him to commit a criminal act is likely to remain ill and in need of treatment." It also held that insanity acquittees may be confined until they demonstrate that they no longer require commitment. Therefore, it is constitutional to commit patients found not guilty by reason of insanity for a longer period than they could have been sentenced if they had been found guilty of the criminal charge.

However, the U.S. Supreme Court case of *Foucha v. Louisiana* (1992), clarified that involuntary commitment of an individual must be based on mental illness, not on dangerousness alone, even in the case of an individual acquitted by reason of insanity. Without defining mental illness, the Court concluded that Mr. Foucha's antisocial personality disorder diagnosis was not a mental illness justifying continued hospitalization, regardless of his potential dangerousness.

2.5   Commitment of Sexual Offenders

A growing trend in commitment law is the commitment of offenders who are convicted of sexually violent offenses but who do not have major mental illnesses. Commitment in these cases is based primarily on psycho-sexual disorders with high risk implications for recidivism and potential danger to others. The United States Supreme Court upheld the constitutionality of the Kansas sexual predator commitment law in the 1997 case of *Kansas v. Hendricks*, indicating that the state's overriding interest in protecting its citizens from harm outweighs an individual's constitutionally protected interest in avoiding physical restraint. In this regard, the Court relied on the *police power*, rather than the *parens patriae*, rationale for involuntarily confining individuals for treatment. The Kansas statute requires proof beyond a reasonable doubt, the same level of proof required in criminal proceedings, to commit sexually violent predators, a standard of proof more rigorous than the clear and convincing evidence established as the minimal constitutional standard of proof for civil commitment in *Addington v. Texas*. Aspects of the *Kansas v. Hendricks* decision have some implications for broadening the rationale and the criteria for civil commitment in general. For example, the Supreme Court held that incapacitation is a legitimate goal of civil commitment, as long as treatment programming is adequate to dispel any inference of punitive intent. And, while the Court affirmed that mental disorder is a constitutional predicate for civil commitment, the particular mental dysfunction of "inability to control behavior" was considered sufficient to legitimize the commitment of Mr. Hendricks.

Mental health professionals have expressed concerns about this trend in the commitment of sexual offenders, due to the difficulty in predicting sexual violence and in effectively treating paraphilias. This topic is covered in detail in the chapter on assessment of sexual offenders in this volume.

2.6   Outpatient Commitment

The concept of outpatient commitment was first addressed by the District of Columbia Court of Appeals in a consolidated appeal, *In re Richardson and In re Cade*, in 1984. Both Richardson and Cade had chronic mental illness and were hospitalized on an emergency basis following aggressive behavior. The hospital initiated civil commitment proceedings after an extension of the emergency hospitalization. At that point, both men waived trial and agreed with the recommendation that they be committed to outpatient treatment under the hospital's supervision. The outpatient commitment contained the provision that the patients could be returned to the hospital for up to five days if their conditions deteriorated or if they failed to comply with treatment. The Court of Appeals supported this outpatient commitment arrangement by ruling that this temporary return to the hospital without a hearing was consistent with both the statute and the constitution, as long as an affidavit detailing the reasons for the return was filed with the Court and provided to the patient's counsel within twenty-four hours of return.

Outpatient commitment has the potential to satisfy the calls for both expanded commitment powers and greater use of community services in treating the mentally disordered. Torrey and Kaplan (1995), in a national survey of the use of outpatient commitment, found that 35 states and the District of Columbia had statutes allowing outpatient commitment, and that the majority of other states had other legal provisions to ensure compliance with treatment in the community, such as conservatorship or guardianship, or conditional release from the hospital.

2.7   Implementation of Commitment Law

Case law produced changes in commitment statutes that strengthen due process safeguards and protect the interests of citizens with mental disorders. To be involuntarily committed, virtually all jurisdictions now require that an individual lacks the capacity to recognize the need for treatment of a serious mental disorder, and that the mental disorder creates a danger to self or others. In addition, most jurisdictions provide for commitment when a mental disorder renders one unable to care for his or her basic needs ("grave disability"), and a few states retain the commitment criterion of need for, or potential benefit from, treatment. All states also provide for some means of emergency hospitalization prior to a hearing, but the person so detained is entitled to a full hearing and all of the due process safeguards within days of emergency admission (Melton et al., 1997). Finally, the concept of the least restrictive or intrusive treatment alternative applies not only to decisions about commitment, but also to decisions about involuntary administration of medication in all states.

The actual operation of commitment decision-making varies a good deal from the procedures outlined in the statutes. Turkheimer and Parry (1992), summarized a number of studies that indicate that hearings are not adversarial, particularly when a prior commitment is reviewed. Judges more often than not fail to inform patients of basic rights, such as the right to counsel, the right to seek voluntary commitment status, and the right to appeal. There is a high rate of concordance between clinicians' recommendations about commitment and judicial findings. Patients' attorneys do not have a clear-cut legal adversary to oppose, and statutes generally do not define the role counsel should play in the civil commitment process. A patient's attorney is left to decide which of three basic roles to adopt in representing the patient: 1) a medical decision model in which the attorney ensures procedural safeguards without vigorously challenging expert testimony; 2) a client decision model, driven by representation of the client's liberty interests; or 3) a counsel decision model, in which counsel plays a guardian role in representing what he or she decides are the best interests of the client. Turkheimer and Parry (1992), noted that research indicates that attorneys are reluctant to vigorously advocate for the release of respondents who appear too disorganized to function on their own, and for whom there is a lack of less restrictive alternatives.

It is also clear that the case law, while building in due process safeguards, and insisting that patients be provided reasonable care in hospitals and access to least restrictive alternatives, affirms the value of involuntary treatment, and the importance of balancing individual rights with community safety needs.

3.   SYSTEMS ISSUES

From 1955 to 1965, the number of people confined in public mental hospitals decreased from 558,000 to 475,000, and, by 1975, to 191,000 (Kiesler & Simpkins, 1993). According to Brakel, Parry and Weiner (1985), the decrease in patient census (from 551,390 to 132,000 between 1956 and 1980), has coincided with the doubling of the annual hospital admission rate (from 185,597 to 390,000 during the same period). This trend has been termed the "revolving door," as patients frequently require readmission after brief hospital stays, calling into question the effectiveness of briefer hospitalization. There were probably less than 90,000 patients in public hospitals in the late 1990's (Melton et al, 1997). Winerip (1999), reported that the population of New York state mental hospitals decreased from 93,000 patients in 1953, to 6,000 in 1999, and that one-fourth of current patients have criminal backgrounds.

Despite the tendency to attribute decreased use of hospital-based care to court restrictions on the use of involuntary commitment, the decrease in hospitalization actually predates the case law that increased procedural safeguards for civil commitment. The early decrease in public hospitalization is generally attributed to the post-World War II exposure of poor conditions in these hospitals, the emphasis on less restrictive and more intensive social treatment of patients, and the introduction of chlorpromazine in 1954. The establishment of the National Institute of Mental Health in 1947, and the Community Mental Health Centers Act of 1963 provided further impetus to the decrease in public hospital use. And research indicated that community-based care was associated with more positive outcomes. Kiesler (1982), and Kiesler & Sibulkin (1987), reviewed a total of 14 studies in which patients with severe mental disorders warranting hospital care were randomly assigned to either inpatient care or some form of alternative outpatient care. In each of these studies, outpatients had more positive outcomes, as measured by evaluations and interviews, ability to hold a job, ability to develop more than casual relationships, and subsequent hospital admissions.   Moreover, alternative outpatient care was less expensive.

It is this lower cost of outpatient care that may be the primary factor responsible for the decrease in public hospital utilization.   The Bazelon Center for Mental Health Law in Washington, D.C. indicates that state spending for mental health care, adjusting for population growth and inflation, dropped by nearly one-third between 1955 and 1997 (cited by Winerip, 1999).   States welcomed the passage of the Community Mental Health Centers Act of 1963, with the influx of federal funds for less costly community-based treatment.   More importantly, with coverage under Medicare and Medicaid extended to treatment for mental illness in 1965, and changes in Social Security laws in the 1970's, federal money paid directly to outpatients made it possible for patients from state hospitals to live outside institutions, while receiving some level of continued treatment, at great savings to states.

In 1972, the United States Fifth Circuit Court of Appeals mandated sweeping reforms in the Alabama hospital system in the landmark case of *Wyatt v. Stickney*. These reforms included specifying physical provisions for patient privacy, requiring certain staff/patient ratios, and defining "qualified mental health professionals" at the master degree level in social work and nursing, and the doctoral level in psychiatry and psychology.   These requirements for inpatient treatment were adopted by courts in other jurisdictions as well.   As the result of these court-mandated standards, the quality, but also the cost, of hospital treatment increased dramatically.   Thus, court mandates for better hospital care also provided financial incentive for states to decrease the use of public psychiatric hospitals.

State mental health systems have developed screening procedures and financial contingencies to further decrease public hospital utilization.   For example, in 1989, legislation took effect in Ohio requiring that all civil patients be committed to county mental health boards, and that the county mental health boards assume the cost of their stays in state hospitals. County boards were also mandated to screen emergency admission applications and civil commitment affidavits, and to determine whether patients would be hospitalized and whether the Probate Court would have the opportunity to consider applications for involuntary hospitalization.   Although the intent of the legislation was to encourage development of less restrictive treatment alternatives, there is clearly a financial incentive for boards to set a high threshold for hospitalization and to prevent judicial review of affidavits for commitment filed by treating professionals or by families. Five years after implementation, the average daily resident population in state hospitals had been reduced from over 3,500 to approximately 1,800, with a projected decrease to 1,200 beyond 1999 (Ohio Department of Mental Health, 1994). Similarly, Bongar, Maris, Berman, Litman & Silverman (1998), reported that emergency hospitalization of suicidal patients is complicated in Massachusetts by the requirement for screening by a mental health team in the patient's catchment area, that does not guarantee hospitalization or alternative placement of the suicidal patient.

As the result of fiscal concerns, the site of treatment for the mentally ill has shifted from state psychiatric hospitals to general hospitals, both in and outside of psychiatric units, as well as to nursing homes, and to board and care or other group homes (e.g., Kiesler & Sibulkin, 1987). Housing patients for treatment in these facilities is less costly, particularly since the cost of care is largely borne by federal subsidies to the patient, rather than by state mental health budgets. Standards of living and of care are also less rigorously monitored in some of these facilities. This trend to confine the mentally ill for treatment in facilities other than public psychiatric hospitals has been referred to as **transinstitutionalization** (Turkheimer & Parry, 1992).

3.1 Criminalization of the Mentally Ill

The epitome of transinstitutionalization is the increasing confinement of the mentally ill in prisons and jails. The cost of care and housing of the mentally ill in correctional facilities is generally borne, not by state mental health budgets or federal subsidies to individuals, but by the correctional system itself. This trend has been referred to as criminalization of the mentally ill.

Teplin (1984), reported the first empirical evidence of the shift from hospitalization to incarceration of the mentally ill in a study of over 1,000 police-citizen encounters. She found that suspects exhibiting signs of mental illness had a 20% greater probability of arrest than suspects who did not appear to be mentally ill. The arrest rate for mentally disordered offenders was greater across all categories of offense, with the exception of interpersonal conflict. These differences did not appear to be the result of the failure of police officers to recognize mentally disordered behavior.

Rather, police officers appeared to give themselves the "fall-back" option of arrest when attempts to secure hospitalization failed, or when the officer felt a given suspect was unlikely to be accepted for hospitalization. Teplin noted, "The irony is that it is precisely the requirements for emergency psychiatric detention set forth in most mental health codes ('dangerous to self and others') that render the citizen 'undesirable' by some hospitals and result in his or her arrest . . . Police officers would often make the rounds of the various service agencies - from halfway house to hospital to 'detox' -before resorting to the disposition of arrest" (p. 800). Teplin found that only four of 30 mentally disordered citizens in this study committed crimes serious enough to result in long-term imprisonment. She suggested that the one-third increase in jail populations from 1978 to 1982 may reflect that jails have become the "revolving door" for the chronically mentally ill.

Teplin (1994; Teplin, Abram & McClelland, 1996), also reported that the U.S. jail population has a substantially higher percentage of persons with mental illness than found in the general population. According to the U.S. Department of Justice survey (cited by Gibeaut, 2000), approximately 284,000 inmates, or 16 % of the jail and prison population, were mentally ill in 1998. At the same time, only 61,700 mentally ill patients were being treated in state hospitals.

The popular press has also reported on the criminalization of the mentally ill and the failure to provide the level of care they require, usually in the context of a violent crime committed by a mentally disordered person who had been denied more intensive treatment. One of the most widely publicized of these cases, Andrew Goldstein, has led to criticism and some reform of the New York mental health system (Winerip, 1999). Mr. Goldstein pushed a young woman to her death under a New York City subway train in January of 1999. In the two years preceding this tragic event, he had attacked at least 13 people, including treatment staff at hospitals where he was briefly treated. He had also been voluntarily hospitalized 13 times in 1997 to 1998, but he had often been discharged after just a few days, due to waiting lists for longer-term care at public hospitals. There were also waiting lists for intensive case management in the community, so Andrew Goldstein was discharged to reside in a sub-standard basement apartment with cursory outpatient follow-up. In response to this incident, New York passed an outpatient commitment law, and about a half dozen states have passed new laws allowing commitment of some patients based upon the severity of their conditions and their need for treatment. However, it is difficult to see how an outpatient commitment law would have helped Andrew Goldstein, who voluntarily sought treatment that was not provided to him. As Winerip concluded, "The reason the mental health system behaves so irrationally is usually money" (p. 49). Regarding the relative impact of fiscal concerns versus case law on decreased hospitalization, Winerip noted, "The reality is that commitment is no longer much of a civil liberties threat - state hospitals don't want patients, and the short-term hospitals can't get rid of them fast enough" (p. 70).

The public policy to provide primarily outpatient treatment to the mentally ill who are not considered to be imminently dangerous to themselves or others has impacted not only the nature of jail populations, but also the mix of patients in public psychiatric hospitals. The percentage of patients in these public hospitals who are committed by criminal courts under trial competency and insanity provisions has steadily increased as the number of civil patients has decreased. For example, half of the patients in Missouri's long-term psychiatric hospitals are insanity acquittees whose commitments are based heavily on public safety considerations (Linhorst & Dirks-Linhorst, 1997). These patients are found not guilty by reason of insanity because of a direct relationship between their mental conditions and the offenses they committed. Therefore, the empirical question becomes whether these criminal acts might have been prevented, if the patients been committed for a reasonable time *prior* to their criminal acts, rather than afterwards.

4.   CLINICAL ISSUES

The psychologist who is confronted with the issue of the potential civil commitment of an individual needs to understand the general legal and systems issues outlined above. In addition, the clinician needs to become familiar with the specific legal standard for commitment in the jurisdiction in which he or she practices, and with the less restrictive options provided by local mental health delivery systems. Once the legal and systems framework for the commitment assessment is established, the clinical issues raised by the particular case may be considered.

4.1   Mental Illness

The issue of basic diagnostic assessment is beyond the scope of this chapter. It is essential that any clinician who undertakes a commitment evaluation has the clinical training and experience necessary to conduct a careful diagnostic assessment of major mental disorder. Psychological tests, such as the Minnesota Multiphasic Personality Inventory-Second Edition or the Beck Depression Inventory-II, can be useful in assessing mental disorder in an empirical manner, provided that the person for whom commitment is being considered is not too impaired or uncooperative to be tested. Diagnostic interview schedules, such as the Schedule for Affective Disorder and Schizophrenia (Endicott & Spitzer, 1978), also standardize assessment of major mental disorders.

As noted in the discussion of more recent case law, such as *Foucha v. Louisiana and Kansas v. Hendricks*, mental disorder is not well defined in the law, and there appears to be some latitude built into most legal definitions. The Vermont statute (cited by Melton et al., 1997), is fairly typical: "'Mental illness' means a substantial disorder of thought, mood, perception, orientation or memory, any of which grossly impairs judgment, behavior, capacity to recognize reality, or ability to meet the demands of life, but shall not include mental retardation" (p. 307). Mental disorders that generally have the potential to meet definitions such as this include serious mood disorders, cognitive disorders, and schizophrenia and other psychotic disorders, as described in the Diagnostic and Statistical Manual of Mental Disorders - Fourth Edition (American Psychiatric Association, 1994).

If the threshold for a major mental disorder has been met, three areas of clinical inquiry are generally triggered by commitment laws. These areas deal with risk to others, risk to self, and grave disability or inability to care for oneself. Assessment of each of these three additional criteria for commitment is addressed in the following sections.

4.2   Risk to Others

Serious discussion of the assessment of risk to others in the clinical literature followed closely upon the greater reliance on danger to others for civil commitment engendered by changes in case law and statutes in the late 1970's. This focus on dangerousness in the psychological literature began with Monahan's (1981), monograph, which called for greater reliance upon actuarial assessment and raised cautions about the accuracy of predictions of dangerousness, due to existing research suggesting low base rates of violent behavior, particularly among the mentally ill.

Monahan's monograph triggered interest in more systematic research. Recent studies have dispelled some of the conclusions based on earlier research, as broader populations have been studied over longer follow-up periods, and outcome criteria have moved beyond just records of hospitalizations and arrests. Monahan (1992), masterfully pulled together several lines of this research to dispel the long-held belief among mental health professionals that there is no relationship between mental disorder and violent behavior.

The analysis of the Epidemiologic Catchment Area Study data (Robins & Regier, 1991), by Swanson, Holzer, Ganju & Jono (1990), produced estimated base rates of aggressive behavior across demographic and diagnostic categories in a community sample of 10,000. Swanson et al. (1990), confirmed that violent behavior is more prevalent among the young than the old, males than females, and within the lowest social class. In terms of major mental disorder, they found that prevalence of violence is more than five times higher among people with Axis I diagnoses than among people with no mental disorder; that this increased rate is similar for diagnoses of schizophrenia, major depression and bipolar disorder; and that alcoholism and drug abuse produce a risk of violent behavior 12 and 16 times, respectively, the rate of violent behavior among those with no diagnosis. Well-designed research by Link, Andrews & Cullen (1992), with a community sample indicated that active psychotic symptoms accounted for a greater incidence of violent acts in both patients and in people who had never been treated for mental disorder.

Teplin's work, discussed above in the context of criminalization of the mentally ill, also supports a relatively higher incidence of violent behavior among the mentally ill. She found prevalence rates of schizophrenia three times higher, rates of depression three to four times higher, and rates of mania or bipolar disorder seven to fourteen times higher, in jail and prison samples than in the Epidemiologic Catchment Area general population (Teplin, 1990).

More recent studies of hospitalized patients deemed safe enough to discharge have also dispelled the notion that violent behavior among the mentally ill occurs at such a low base rate that accurate prediction is unlikely. Depending upon the severity of aggression and the number of data sources available, a number of investigators have found rates of aggression of 25-50% within the year following hospital discharge (e.g., Klassen & O'Connor, 1989; Lidz, Mulvey & Gardner, 1993; Steadman, Silver, Monahan, Appelbaum, Robbins, Mulvey, Grisso, Roth & Banks, 1998). Even these findings may underestimate the base rate of violent behavior among the mentally ill, as these studies have been based on patients who have been selected as safe to discharge into the community and who have remained accessible for follow-up study.

McNeil (1994), reviewed the literature on the relationship between violence and hallucinations. Studies of civilly committed and short-term voluntary inpatients have found a significant relationship between the experience of hallucinations and violent behavior during hospitalization. These studies have included patients with diagnoses of schizophrenia, affective disorder, organic psychosis and alcohol dependence who have reported hallucinatory experiences. McNeil noted that many of these studies focused primarily on patients in the acute stage of psychosis, just prior to or just after hospitalization, who displayed other psychotic symptoms as well. These are the patients most likely to be evaluated for civil commitment. Further research could refine knowledge about the relationship between hallucinations and violence, but it is prudent to consider this symptom a risk factor and to inquire about the nature and frequency of hallucinations, as well as the individual's means of coping with hallucinations, as part of a clinical risk assessment.

Link & Stueve (1994), reported a significant relationship between "threat/control-override symptoms" (feelings that one's mind was dominated, that thoughts were inserted in one's head, and that people wished to do one harm, measured by items on the Psychiatric Epidemiology Research Interview), and recent violence (hitting, fighting and use of a weapon in a fight). Treatment status and measures of other psychotic symptoms did not contribute significantly to prediction of violent behavior when threat/control-override symptoms were held constant.

Given the substantial literature supporting the relationship between active symptoms of major mental disorder and increased risk of violence, it is reasonable for clinicians to carefully consider the risk of violence posed by an individual with active symptoms of a major mental disorder who is unwilling or unable to consent to treatment. From an actuarial perspective, substance abuse, youth, lower socioeconomic status, and prior violent behavior all increase the risk of aggression in people with active mental illness. From a clinical perspective, careful consideration of psychotic symptoms, particularly those associated with feeling controlled or threatened by others, is warranted. Focusing upon the areas raised by Monahan's (1981), 14 questions (reprinted in Melton et al., 1997), is a good clinical approach to assessing risk of violence to others. These questions include a careful analysis of the events precipitating the question of the person's potential for violence; focus on the sources of stress in the person's current environment; cognitive and affective factors indicating that the person may be predisposed to cope with stress in a violent, and in a nonviolent, manner; the availability of likely victims and the means to commit violence; and the similarity of the contexts in which the person has been violent in the past to contexts in which the person will function in the future. For both clinical and actuarial risk factors, it is essential that information is gathered from a number of sources, including treatment and legal records, and interviews with significant others.

Traditional psychological testing is not designed to assess short-term predictions of risk to others. Some attempts have been made to develop structured assessment instruments or methodologies that address risk factors in a systematic manner, through self-report and other sources of data. Heilbrun (1991), formulated the Analysis of Aggressive Behavior, which structures the inquiry into incidents of past aggressive behavior to attempt to identify risk factors for the particular individual, as well as strategies to manage or treat these factors. The HCR-20 (Webster, Douglas, Eaves & Hart, 1997), is promising (e.g., Douglas, Ogloff, Nicholls & Grant, 1999). The Iterative Classification Tree (Steadman, Silver, Monahan, Appelbaum, Robbins, Mulvey, Grisso, Roth & Banks, 2000), is in early development stages.

For now, the most accurate approach a psychologist might take in addressing civil commitment based on danger to others is to describe for the Court the clinical and actuarial factors, which both increase and decrease risk for the particular individual. In considering whether to recommend commitment based on risk to others, the clinician needs to keep in mind that the base rate of aggressive behavior in the mentally ill is higher than has been estimated in the past, and that even access to voluntary inpatient care has become overly restricted due to financial concerns. However, it is ultimately the role of the court to weigh the relative social costs of making a false positive error (committing a person who would not have behaved violently if left in the community), or a false negative error (failing to commit a person who then proceeds to commit a violent act in the community.)

4.3   Risk to Self

State statutes vary in terms of how broadly risk to self as a criterion for commitment of a mentally ill person is defined. In states without a grave disability criterion, the risk to self tends to be viewed more broadly than in states with a separate criterion for people unable to care for themselves or in need of treatment. Assessment of grave disability is considered separately in this chapter. This section deals with the assessment of risk to self under statutes requiring narrower justification of such risk for civil commitment.

There is a substantial literature on the base rates and risk factors for suicide attempts and completions (Bongar, 1991; Peruzzi & Bongar, 1999; Maris, Berman & Silverman, 2000). Figures from 1999 indicate an annual rate of suicide of 11.6 per 100,000, based on 30,903 reported deaths by suicide. Older white males are at greatest risk of committing suicide, accounting for 70% of all completed suicides. White females account for approximately 22% of suicides, and suicide is rare among non-whites. The lifetime risk of suicide for patients with untreated depressive or other affective disorders is estimated to be 15-19% (Peruzzi & Bongar, 1999). The prevalence rate among people with schizophrenia is 10% during the first ten years of the disorder, and 15% over the course of their lifetime. Young males with high premorbid functioning are at greatest risk within the first few years after the diagnosis of schizophrenia is made. Sixty to seventy percent of suicide completers succeed on their first known attempt, and an average of 10-15% of people who make non-fatal attempts ultimately kill themselves over the course of their lifetimes (Maris et al., 2000). Although men are four times more likely than women to commit suicide, women make three times as many non-fatal attempts.

Despite generally good consensus in the field about risk factors for suicide, actual prediction of low-rate behaviors such as suicide is poor. The best study, a five-year prospective study of 4,800 psychiatric inpatients by Pokorny (1983), yielded a false positive rate of 30%, and identification of only 55% of the 67 patients who ultimately committed suicide, even in this relatively high risk sample of hospitalized veterans. As with risk to others, the clinician's task is not to predict suicide, but to intervene with patients at high risk to attempt to manage and minimize the risk of death they pose to themselves. Peruzzi & Bongar (1999), reviewed the clinical and empirical literature on risk factors and surveyed practicing psychologists to develop critical risk factors for assessing suicidal risk in people with major depression, who are most likely to be considered for civil commitment due to suicidal risk. They recommend that the following ten factors be carefully assessed: 1) family history of suicide completion; 2) patient history of suicide attempts; 3) medical seriousness of previous patient attempts; 4) hopelessness; 5) attraction to death; 6) anhedonia; 7) psychic anxiety; 8) acute suicidal ideation; 9) acute overuse of alcohol; and 10) losses/ separations. Similarly, Shneidman (1987), developed a "theoretical cubic model of suicide" that posits that maximum suicide threat occurs when "psychache" (pain), "press" (stress), and "perturbation" (agitation) are all at their maximum levels.

It is noteworthy that only one of the ten factors identified by Peruzzi & Bongar (1999), has to do with acute suicidal ideation. Patients who are at high risk for suicide may well deny ideation, intent or plans, while persons with personality disorders may freely threaten suicide and make superficial attempts. Reliance on patient report of suicidal ideation alone in making decisions about hospitalization may miss the highest risk individuals. In this context, it is important to note the common clinical dilemma of managing the crisis-prone individual, often diagnosed with borderline personality disorder, who openly voices suicidal ideation, and who engages in self-mutilating behavior which readily meets the commitment standard in some states of a recent, overt act documenting risk to self.   Linehan (2000), describes this behavior as parasuicide, estimates its prevalence at 300 persons per 100,000 annually, and summarizes the literature on the efficacy of focused, behavioral interventions.

In assessing suicidal ideation, Peruzzi & Bongar (1999), recommend a detailed inquiry regarding passive and active ideation, details, and time spent in planning, scheduling, rehearsing, and experimenting with suicidal behavior.   In assessing hopelessness, the authors recommend the Beck Hopelessness Scale (Beck & Steere, 1988), with a cutoff score of nine or greater.   In assessing anhedonia, they recommend a cutoff score of four or greater on the item measuring anhedonia on the Schedule for Affective Disorders and Schizophrenia (Endicott & Spitzer, 1978).

An additional risk factor for suicide is physical illness, which may partially account for the increased risk among elderly men. As in assessing risk to others, protective factors that decrease risk should also be considered. These include marriage, presence in the home of children under 18, and religious beliefs inconsistent with suicide.

Caution must also be raised about risk to others in the context of serious suicidal ideation. Risk to others is most likely to be a concomitant problem in men with loss of employment or loss of a serious romantic partner, and in mothers with young children who develop psychotic thinking about their children or who feel their children are vulnerable and therefore must die with them (Bongar, Goldberg, Cleary & Brown, 2000).   Individuals in these situations must be handled very carefully as plans for emergency hospitalization are made, in order to prevent a violent incident.

Rothberg & Geer-Williams (1992), reviewed the psychometric properties of a number of suicide prediction scales. In general, these scales have not been subjected to rigorous study, and they function best as structured assessment guides for exploring the domains of suicidal risk. They are generally self-report measures, without measures of response set to determine whether over-reporting or under-reporting of symptoms might be an issue. The Suicide Probability Scale (Cull & Gill, 1982), is one promising measure designed to identify attempters, which it has been found to do with 100% accuracy in one study. However, it does not measure the lethality of the attempt, and it has been found to have only 50% specificity, or accuracy in identifying true negatives (non-attempters). Some measures, such as the Hopelessness Scale, assess discrete variables, which increase the risk of suicide. Other measures incorporate demographic characteristics and information from records or contacts with third parties, ensuring that these factors are routinely considered in making an assessment. Finally, these instruments differ in terms of the populations and the goals for which they were designed; for example, assessing risk of subsequent lethal attempts in hospitalized patients (Neuropsychiatric Hospital Suicide Prediction Schedule) or distinguishing attempters from suicides in a suicide hotline setting (Suicidal Death Prediction Scale). For individuals able to complete a lengthy inventory, the Minnesota Multiphasic Personality Inventory - Second Edition provides empirical measures of response set, and of symptoms and critical items related to suicidal ideation and behavior.

4.4   Inability to Care for Self

This criterion for civil commitment has received the most attention in the context of the homeless mentally ill, but it is also frequently raised by family members, and sometimes by housing authorities when an individual who owns property has become so dysfunctional that the property is not properly maintained and housing code violations arise. It requires a functionally based assessment of capacity to meet basic needs and to protect oneself in one's present situation, as well as in other community settings, which are both available and agreeable to the person. These capacity issues are also relevant in considering conservatorship or guardianship and competency to consent to treatment or to refuse treatment. The clinical literature pertaining to assessment of capacity to manage one's own personal and financial affairs and to make treatment decisions is therefore most helpful in guiding assessments of grave disability, or inability to care for oneself.

Grisso & Appelbaum (1998), have developed a conceptual schema for assessing competency to consent to treatment based on legal standards for judging competency in a number of contexts. Their focus is not the quality of the person's decision itself, but rather, the logic of the decision-making process that the person uses to make important decisions impacting upon his or her well-being. Competence to make decisions is basically dependent upon the ability to: 1) communicate a consistent preference; 2) understand basic information about the available choices; 3) realistically apply information to one's own situation; and 4) reason - consider one's options, assess the likelihood of various outcomes, and weigh the desirability of the consequences in light of one's own values. In assessing competency to consent to treatment, Grisso & Appelbaum (1998), developed the MacArthur Competence Assessment Tool, a semi-structured interview methodology that includes disclosure of information about individuals' own treatment options, and then assessment of their ability to make a choice, understand this information and engage in reasoning processes to make a decision.

Assessment of functional living skills is facilitated by use of instruments or techniques developed for geriatric populations. The Independent Living

Scales (Loeb, 1996), a refinement of the Community Competence Scale, is the most comprehensive and well researched of these, and, like the MacArthur Competence Assessment Tool, it is available from a test publisher. The test was standardized on a non-clinical sample of adults over the age of 65, and a clinical sample of adults 17 and older. It assesses memory/orientation, managing money, managing home and transportation, health and safety issues, and social adjustment, using standardized questions and tasks.

A combination of assessment of the reasoning and decision-making abilities tapped by the MacArthur instrument, and of the basic living skills assessed by the Independent Living Scales, might provide the starting point for a more comprehensive, individualized assessment of ability to care for self. Such an approach would assist the court in making decisions about commitment and other alternatives in a more understandable and value-free manner.

4.5   Least Restrictive Alternative

The concept of least restrictive alternative, first articulated in the 1966 case of *Lake v. Cameron*, prompts the clinician to consider a range of treatment options before recommending involuntary hospitalization, and to consider situational variables in assessing risk to self or others and inability to care for oneself.

In reviewing less restrictive alternatives, the clinician needs to explore community resources for suitable treatment, and to evaluate whether the person is both competent to consent to such treatment and likely to do so. Some communities have developed models of very intensive outpatient treatment, sometimes referred to as Program for Assertive Community Treatment (PACT). These programs include multidisciplinary treatment and outreach designed to engage clients in treatment and meet a variety of their needs (e.g., Drake & Burns, 1995).

The promise of outpatient commitment has not been realized in most jurisdictions for a variety of reasons. The reliance on dangerousness-based criteria for commitment appears inconsistent with commitment to community-based treatment. The lack of intensive outpatient treatment and the lack of provisions for dealing with non-compliance often preclude effective implementation of court-ordered treatment in the community. Issues of competency to consent to treatment and the right to refuse treatment, and difficulties with involuntary administration of medication in the community have not been adequately addressed.

North Carolina modified its commitment law in 1984, to allow a broader, preventive use of outpatient mandated treatment (Hiday & Scheid-Cook, (1987). Criteria for outpatient commitment in North Carolina are presence of serious mental illness, capacity to survive in the community with available supports, clinical history indicative of need for treatment to prevent deterioration predictably leading to dangerousness, and mental status limiting or negating capacity to make informed decisions to seek or comply with treatment. When an outpatient-committed person fails to comply with treatment, the clinician may have law enforcement officers bring the patient to the mental health center, but medication cannot be administered involuntarily through outpatient commitment. Nevertheless, research by Borum, Swartz, Riley, Swanson, Hiday and Wagner (1999), indicates that outpatient-committed persons almost universally believe that the court required them to take medication as prescribed, in addition to keeping appointments, as part of the outpatient commitment order. Keilitz (1990), reviewed studies of outpatient commitment in several jurisdictions that obtained equivocal results, although some studies noted that outpatient commitment compared favorably to hospital outcomes on measures of readmission, program compliance and community functioning. Studies of outpatient commitment in North Carolina (Swartz, Swanson, Wagner, Burns, Hiday & Borum, 1999), have found that outpatient commitment may reduce hospital readmission rates and lengths of stay and reduce the risk of violent behavior in the community. However, the research by Swartz et al. (1999), and research in New York by Policy Research Associates (cited by Gerbasi, Bonnie & Binder, 2000), indicate that outpatient commitment requires high intensity outpatient services to be effective.

Swanson, Borum, Swartz, Hiday, Wagner & Burns (2001), studied a high-risk group of 262 patients with a history of arrest and hospitalization. They found that extended outpatient commitment resulted in a 12% predicted arrest rate, compared to a 44% risk of arrest for patients with briefer commitment, and a 47% rate for those not placed on outpatient commitment. For individual patients, history of prior violence, substance abuse and noncompliance with medication were correlated with subsequent arrest during the one-year follow-up period.

Individuals found not guilty by reason of insanity are committed by courts for community-based treatment, usually termed conditional release, more universally than any other group of mental health clients. Even though these clients have committed criminal acts due to mental illness, they do well on conditional release. Their success may be due to longer hospitalization prior to release, better outpatient follow-up, and ready access to rehospitalization by the court if they develop problems in the community (Wiederanders & Choate, 1994; Stafford & Karpawich, 1997).

Gerbasi et al. (2000), proposed criteria for mandatory outpatient treatment. However, this concept is focused on "preventive" treatment for those patients who do not presently meet criteria for hospitalization but need treatment to prevent exacerbation of chronic mental illness that would lead to meeting criteria for inpatient commitment. The proposal recommends that, if forced medication is a component of mandatory outpatient treatment, it occur only following a court finding that the individual lacks capacity to make an informed decision regarding medication.

In addition to the availability and appropriateness of adequate outpatient treatment, and the individual's willingness to accept it, it is important to consider family, residential, and neighborhood variables in making recommendations about least restrictive alternatives. Silver, Mulvey & Monahan (1999), found that the concentrated poverty of neighborhoods to which hospitalized patients were discharged contributed to their increased risk for violence during a one-year follow-up period, over and above the effects of individual characteristics associated with risk. In addition, poor neighborhoods are likely to have a negative effect on mentally ill persons with compromised abilities to care for themselves. The higher crime rates and more transient populations of these areas may result in increased stress, lack of support, and exploitation or victimization of vulnerable mentally ill persons.

5.   ETHICAL ISSUES

The Ethical Principles of Psychologists and Code of Conduct of the American Psychological Association (1992), and the Specialty Guidelines for Forensic Psychologists (1991), address issues that pertain to psychological assessment in the context of civil commitment. Standard 1.21(a) of the Code, Third-Party Requests for Services, deals with the obligation to clarify at the outset of the evaluation the role of the psychologist, the probable use of the assessment and the information obtained, and the limits of confidentiality. The Specialty Guidelines are more specific, indicating under D2: "When it is necessary to provide both evaluation and treatment services to a party in a legal proceeding . . . the forensic psychologist takes reasonable steps to minimize the potential negative effects of these circumstances on the rights of the party, confidentiality, and the process of treatment and evaluation." (p. 659). These concerns are particularly relevant to commitment evaluations, as the clinician may have some affiliation with the treatment facilities or systems involved in the patient's care, and persons being evaluated for civil commitment may have difficulty understanding the clinician's role in the proceedings.

Standard 7.02, Forensic Assessments, states that assessments, recommendations and reports are based upon sufficient data to substantiate the findings. Again, under Standard 7.04, Truthfulness and Candor, psychologists are reminded to describe fairly the bases for their testimony and to acknowledge the limits of their data and conclusions. As Section F of the Specialty Guidelines concludes: "Forensic psychologists are aware that their essential role as expert to the court is to assist the trier of fact to understand the evidence or to determine a fact in issue. In offering expert evidence, they are aware that their own professional observations, inferences, and conclusions must be distinguished from legal facts, opinions, and conclusions. Forensic psychologists are prepared to explain the relationship between their expert testimony and the legal issues and facts of an instant case." (p. 665)

These standards provide some guidance for the communication of the results of a commitment evaluation to the trier of fact. Both the report and testimony need to lay out in detail the mental status and functioning of the individual, the characteristics of the person, and of the environment, which place him or her and/or the community at risk in specific ways, treatment options, and the advantages and disadvantages of these options. Although the clinician provides an expert recommendation based upon this information, the ultimate decision lies with the court. This approach allows the court to make informed decisions while weighing legal issues and social values that are beyond the expertise of the clinician.

6.   SUMMARY

This chapter has attempted to provide an overview of the scientific and clinical bases for addressing the legal issues raised by civil commitment proceedings. Courts have laid out guidelines for fair procedures and judicial review of involuntary treatment, while recognizing the value of civil commitment. At the same time, fiscal issues and systems changes have made sustained inpatient treatment less available and exposed the mentally ill to the risks of arrest and homelessness. The availability and effectiveness of alternatives to inpatient treatment vary considerably across communities.

Progress has been made in better understanding the relationship between mental disorder and the risk to self or others. Assessment strategies for evaluating competency to make treatment decisions and for identifying mentally ill persons likely to require involuntary treatment continue to be developed. It is in this context that the forensic clinician applies the state of current knowledge to the problem of mentally ill individuals who do not choose to participate in treatment on their own.

7.   REFERENCES

Addington v. Texas, 441 U.S. 418, 99 S Ct. 1804 (1979).

American Academy of Psychiatry and the Law, 28, 127-144.

American Psychiatric Association (1994). *Diagnostic and Statistical Manual of Mental Disorders* - Fourth Edition. Washington, D.C.: Author.

American Psychological Association (1992). Ethical principles of psychologists and code of conduct. *American Psychologist, 47*, 1597-1611.

Appelbaum , P.S. & Kemp, K.N. (1982). The evoluion of commitment law in the nineteenth century. *Law and Human Behavior, 6*, 343-354.

Appelbaum, P.S. (1996). Civil mental health law: Its history and its future. *Mental and Physical Disability Law Reporter, 20* (5), 599-604.

Archives of General Psychiatry, 35, 837-844.

Beck, A.T. & Steer, R.A. (1988). *Beck Hopelessness Scale: Manual*. San Antonio, TX: Psychological Corporation.

Bongar, B. (1991). *The suicidal patient: Clinical and legal standards of care*. Washington, D.C.: American Psychological Association.

Bongar, B., Maris, R., Berman, A., Litman, R. & Silverman, M. (1998). *Inpatient standards of care and the suicidal patient: Part I. General clinical formulations and legal considerations*. In B. Bongar, A. Berman, R. Maris, M.

Bongar, B., Goldberg, L., Cleary, K., & Brown, K. (2000). *Marriage, family, family therapy and suicide*. In R. Maris, A. Berman & M.M. Silverman (Eds.): Comprehensive textbook of suicidology.

Bonta, J., Law, M. & Hanson, K. (1998). The prediction of criminal and violent recidivism among mentally disordered offenders: A meta-analysis. *Psychological Bulletin, 123*, 123-142.

Borum, R., Swartz, M., Riley, S., Swanson, J., Hiday, V., & Wagner, R. (1999). Consumer perceptions of involuntary outpatient commitment. *Psychiatric Services, 50*, 1489-1491.

Brakel, S.J., Parry, J. & Weiner, B. (1985). The mentally disabled and the law, 3rd ed. Chicago: American Bar Foundation.

Committee on Ethical Guidelines for Forensic Psychologists. (1991). Specialty guidelines for forensic psychologists. *Law and Human Behavior, 15*, 655-665.

Cull, J.G. & Gill, W.S. (1982). *Suicide Probability Scale: Manual*. Los Angeles: Western Psychological Services.

Douglas, K., Ogloff, J., Nicholls, T. & Grant, I. (1999). Assessing risk for violence among psychiatric patients: The HCR-20 violence risk assessment scheme: Concurrent validity in a sample of incarcerated offenders. *Criminal Justice and Behavior, 26*, 3-19.

Drake, R.E., & Burns, B.J. (1995). Special section on assertive community treatment: An introduction. *Psychiatric Services, 46*, 667-668.

Endicott, J. & Spitzer, R.L (1978). *A diagnostic interview: The Schedule for Affective Disorders and Schizophrenia*.

Fasulo v. Arafeh, 173 Conn. 473, 378 A.2d. 553 (1977).

Foucha v. Louisiana, 112 S.Ct.1780 (1992).

Gerbasi, J. B., Bonnie, R. J., & Binder, R.L. (2000). Resource document on mandatory outpatient treatment. *Journal of American Academy of Psychiatry and the Law, 28*, 127-144.

Gibeaut, J. (2000). Who knows best? *ABA Journal*, 49-54.

Grann, M., Belfrage, H., & Tengstrom, A. (2000). Actuarial assessment of risk for violence: Predictive validity of the VRAG and historical part of the HCR-20. *Criminal Justice and Behavior, 27*, 97-114.

Grisso, T., & Appelbaum, P. (1998). *Assessing competence to consent to treatment: A guide for physicians and other health professionals.* New York: Oxford University Press.

Heilbrun, K. (1991). *The Analysis of Aggressive Behavior.* Richmond, VA: Medical College of Virginia.

Hiday, V., & Scheid-Cook, T. (1987). The North Carolina experience with outpatient commitment: A critical appraisal. *International Journal of Law and Psychiatry, 10*, 215 - 232.

Jones v. U.S., 463 U.S. 354, 103 S.Ct. 3043 (1983).

Kansas v. Hendricks, 117 S Ct. 2073, 1997.

Kelitz, I. (1990). Empirical studies of involuntary outpatient civil commitment: Is it working? *Mental and Physical Disability Law Reporter, 14*, 368-379.

Kiesler, C.A. (1982). Public and professional myths about mental hospitalization. *American Psychologist, 37*, 1323-1339.

Kiesler, C.A., & Sibulkin, A. (1987). *Mental hospitalization: Myths and facts about a national crisis.* Beverly Hills: Sage Publications.

Kiesler, C.A., & Simpkins, C.G. (1993). *The unnoticed majority in psychiatric inpatient care.* New York: Plenum.

Klassen, D., & O'Connor, W. (1989). Assessing the risk of violence in released mental patients: A cross-validation study. *Psychological Assessment, 1*, 75-81.

Lake v. Cameron, 124 U.S. App. D.C. 264, 364 F2d. 657 (1966).

Lessard v. Schmidt, 349 F.Supp. 1078 (E.D. Wis. 1972).

Lidz, C.W., Mulvey, E.P., & Gardner, W. (1993). The accuracy of predictions of violence to others. *Journal of the American Medical Association, 269*, 1007-1011.

Linehan, M. (2000). Behavioral treatments of suicidal behaviors: Definitional obfuscation and treatment outcomes. In R.W. Maris, S.S. Canetto, J.L McIntosh & M.M. Silverman (Eds): *Review of suicidology*, 2000. New York: Guilford Press.

Linhorst, D. & Dirks-Linhorst, P.A. (1997). The impact of insanity acquittees on Missouri's public mental health system. *Law and Human Behavior, 21*, 327-338.

Link, B.G., Andrews, H.A., & Cullen, F.T. (1992). The violent and illegal behavior of mental patients reconsidered. *American Sociological Review, 57*, 275-292.

Link, B.G., & Stueve, C.A. (1994). Psychotic symptoms and the violent/illegal behavior of mental patients compared to community controls. In J. Monahan & H. Steadman (Eds.): *Violence and mental disorder: Developments in risk assessment.* Chicago: University of Chicago Press.

Maris, R., Berman, A., & Silverman, M.M. (2000). *Comprehensive textbook of suicidology.* New York: The Guilford Press.

McNeil, D. (1994). Hallucinations and violence. In Monahan, J. & Steadman, H.J. (Eds): *Violence and mental disorder: Developments in risk assessment.* Chicago: University of Chicago Press.

Melton, G., Petrila, J., Poythress, N., & Slobogin, C. (1997). *Psychological evaluations for the courts*. 2nd edition. New York: Guilford Press.

Monahan, J. (1981). *The clinical prediction of violent behavior*. National Institute of Mental Health.

Monahan, J. (1992). Mental disorder and violent behavior: Perceptions and evidence. *American Psychologist, 47*(4), 511-521.

Monahan, J. (1993). Limiting therapist exposure to Tarasoff liability: Guidelines for risk containment. *American Psychologist, 48*, 242-250.

O'Connor v. Donaldson, 422 U.S. 563 (1975).

Ohio Department of Mental Health (1994). *Community care and inpatient treatment: Solutions for the next century*. Columbus, OH.

Parham v. JR and JL, 442 U.S. 584, 99 S.Ct. 2493 (1979).

Peruzzi, N. & Bongar, B. (1999). Assessing risk for completed suicide in patients with major depression: Psychologists' views of critical factors. *Professional Psychology: Research and Practice, 30*, 576-580.

Pokorny, A. (1983). Prediction of suicide in psychiatric patients: Report of a prospective study. *Archives of General Psychiatry, 40*, 249-257.

Rennie v. Klein, 720 F.2d 266 (3rd Cir. 1983).

Richardson, In Re, 481 A.2d 473 (D.C. 1984).

Riggins v. Nevada, 112 S.Ct. 1810 (1992).

Robins, L.N. & Regier, D.A. (1991). *Psychiatric disorders in America - The Epidemiologic Catchment Area Study*. New York: The Free Press.

Rogers v. Commissioner, 390 Mass. 489, 458 N.E. 2d 308 (1983).

Rothberg, J.M., & Geer-Williams, C. (1992). A comparison and review of suicide prediction scales. In R.W. Maris, A.L. Berman, J.T. Maltsberger, & R.I. Yufit (Eds.): *Assessment and prediction of suicide*. New York: The Guilford Press.

Rouse v. Cameron, 125 U.S. App. D.C. 366, 373 F.2d 451 (1966).

Shneidman, E. S. (1987). A psychological approach to suicide. In G.R. VandenBos & B.K. Bryant (Eds.): *Cataclysms, crises and catastrophes*. Washington, D.C.: American Psychological Association.

Shuman, D. (1999). *Psychiatric and psychological evidence*. Second edition. West Group.

Silver, E., Mulvey, E., & Monahan, J. (1999). Assessing violence risk among discharged psychiatric patients: Toward an ecological approach. *Law and Human Behavior, 23*, 237-255.

Silverman, E. Harris & W. Packman: *Risk management with suicidal patients*. New York: Guilford Press.

Stafford, K.P., & Karpawich, J.J. (1997). Conditional release: Court-ordered outpatient treatment for insanity acquittees. In M.R. Munetz (Ed.): *Can mandatory treatment be therapeutic?* San Francisco: Jossey-Bass.

Steadman, H.J., Mulvey, E., Monahan, J., Robbins, P., Appelbaum, P., Grisso, T., Roth, L., & Silver, E. (1998). Violence by people discharged from acute psychiatric inpatient facilities and by others in the same neighborhoods. *Archives of General Psychiatry, 55*, 1-9.

Steadman, H.J., Silver, E., Monahan, J., Appelbaum, P., Robbins, P., Mulvey, E., Grisso, T., Roth, L., & Banks, S. (2000). A classification tree approach to the development of actuarial violence risk assessment tools. *Law and Human Behavior, 24*, 83-100.

Stone, A. (1975). *Mental health and the law: A system in transition*. Washington, D.C.: U.S. Government Printing Office.

Swanson, J.W., Holzer, C.E., Ganju, V., & Jono, R. (1990). Violence and psychiatric disorder in the community: Evidence from the Epidemiologic Catchment Area Surveys. *Hospital and Community Psychiatry, 41*, 761-770.

Swanson, J.W., Borum, R., Swartz, M.S., Hiday, V.A., Wagner, H.R., & Burns, B.J. (2001). Can involuntary outpatient commitment reduce arrests among persons with severe mental illness? *Criminal Justice and Behavior, 28*, 156-189.

Swartz, M.S., Swanson, J.W., Wagner, H.R., Burns, B.J., Hiday, V.A., & Borum, R. (1999). *American Journal of Psychiatry, 156*, 1968-1975.

Teplin, L.A. (1984). Criminalizing mental disorder: The comparative arrest rate of the mentally ill. *American Psychologist, 39*, 794-803.

Teplin, L.A. (1990). The prevalence of severe mental disorder among male urban jail detainees: Comparison with the Epidemiologic Catchment Area program. *American Journal of Public Health, 80*, 663-690.

Teplin, L.A. (1994). Psychiatric and substance abuse disorders among male jail detainees. *American Journal of Public Health, 84*, 290-293.

Teplin, L.A., Abram, K.M. & McClelland, G.M. (1996). Prevalence of psychiatric disorders among incarcerated women. *Archives of General Psychiatry, 53*, 505-512.

Torrey, E.F., & Kaplan, R.J. (1995). A national survey of the use of outpatient commitment. *Psychiatric Services, 46*, 778-784.

Turkheimer, E., & Parry, C. (1992). Why the gap? Practice and policy in civil commitment hearings. *American Psychologist, 47*, 646-655.

Washington v. Harper, 494 U.S. 210, 110 S.Ct. 1028 (1990).

Webster, C., Douglas, K., Eaves, D., & Hart, S. (1997). *HCR-20: Assessing risk for violence* (Version 2). Burnaby, British Columbia, Canada: Mental Health, Law and Policy Institute, Simon Fraser University.

Wiederanders, M.R., & Choate, P.A. (1994) Beyond recidivism: Measuring community adjustment of conditionally released insanity acquittees. *Psychological Assessment, 6*, 61-66.

Winerip, M. (1999). *Bedlam on the streets*. The New York Times Magazine, May 23, 42-70.

Wyatt v. Stickney, 344 F.Supp. 387 (M.D. Ala. 1972).

Youngberg v. Romeo, 457 U.S. 307, 102 S.Ct. 2452 (1982).

Zinermon v. Burch, 494 U.S. 113, 110 S.Ct. 975 (1990).

Chapter 8

Child Custody Evaluations

Philip M. Stahl, Ph.D.[104]
Private Practice, Danville, CA

1. INTRODUCTION

In recent years, there has been a steady growth in the use of psychologists and other mental health professionals in child custody evaluations (Ackerman & Ackerman, 1997). These evaluations are used to assist the court in determining custody, visitation, and parenting plans when families divorce. At the same time, there has been an increase in the number of books devoted to child custody evaluations (Stahl, 1994, Ackerman, 1994, Gould, 1997, Galatzer-Levy & Kraus, 1999, Stahl, 1999) and other books devoted to the broader forensic psychology practice.

In considering the necessary ingredients of a child custody evaluation practice, there are many areas in which a psychologist (or other mental health professional) must gain proficiency. At a minimum, these include a fundamental understanding of child development, a comprehensive understanding of the research on divorce, good evaluation skills and techniques, and an understanding of the use and misuse of psychological testing in child custody evaluations. As evaluations have become increasingly more complex (Stahl, 1999), evaluators need a thorough understanding of the issues of the alienation of children, domestic violence,

104 Dr. Stahl is a psychologist in private practice in Dublin, California.

child abuse and sexual abuse, relocation law, and an understanding of family dynamics when conflicts become extreme. Finally, evaluators need to have a thorough understanding of the special ethical issues that surface when undertaking these complex evaluations for families and the courts.

It would be beyond the scope of this chapter to discuss all of these issues. With that in mind, this chapter will focus on four primary areas:
- Considerations for starting a child custody evaluation practice.
- An integration of child development research into the concept of parenting plans.
- A way of understanding the special needs of the high-conflict population.
- Special ethical considerations for mental health professionals who work in the child custody evaluation field.

2.   CONSIDERATIONS IN CONDUCTING CHILD CUSTODY EVALUATIONS

As the field of psychology has moved into the new millennium, many psychologists are frustrated by changes and difficulties with managed care. There is encouragement for psychologists to diversify their work. While many psychologists are returning to a primarily fee-for-service therapy practice, sport psychology practice, or to executive coaching, a more natural transition for many family psychologists is into the field of divorce and child custody work. Most psychologists have been trained in performing evaluations, and most therapists have worked with divorced families. Psychologists are competent to assess family dynamics in order to help the restructured family adjust. It is natural to assume that a transition into the field of child custody evaluations should be easy.

The Ethical Principles of Psychologists, (APA, 1992), clearly state that, when a psychologist moves into a new specialized area of work, the psychologist will get specialized training and consultation upon embarking in the new area. Child custody evaluation work is significantly different than other forms of psychological testing and evaluation. It requires an understanding of the complex issues related to divorce and child custody that the psychological evaluation of adults or children for treatment issues (or neuropsychology or ADHD, for example) doesn't require.

Forensic child custody evaluations are certainly different than therapeutic work. When providing treatment, the treating psychologist's primary task is to assist his/her client, (which may be the family), in understanding individual and family dynamics and improving the life of the individual or system. In non-forensic settings, therapy is largely confidential and one in which a therapist is only likely to make recommendations to the client about that client's functioning and personal (or family) goals. When a therapist provides treatment in a forensic setting, such as with an order of the Juvenile or Family Court, the therapist may be obligated to provide reports to the court. In those circumstances, the limits of confidentiality are usually clear prior to the start of therapy.

In contrast, a child custody evaluation is always non-confidential and requires an analysis of family dynamics in order to make a recommendation to the court about the best interests of the child, according to the laws of one's state. Child custody evaluations and court-connected therapy fall within the specialty guidelines for forensic psychologists. Both the American Psychological Association (APA, 1994), and Association of Family and Conciliation Courts (AFCC, 1994), have published guidelines for child custody evaluations. The practitioner who embarks in this field needs to develop a thorough understanding of child custody evaluation practices, including interviewing adults and children, the forensic use of psychological tests, understanding legal documents and other paperwork, interviewing collateral sources, and writing thorough, concise reports to the court.

Similarly, the child custody evaluator needs to have a thorough understanding of the laws in his/her state pertaining to child custody, child custody evaluations, and family law, as well as local court rules and the legal/psychological "culture" in which the evaluator practices. Many states have specific rules or guidelines about child custody evaluations, such as California Rule of Court 1257.3 (California, 1999), which outline specific procedures and requirements for child custody evaluations. It is important to understand local culture as one embarks on a child custody career.

Child custody evaluators need to be comfortable making specific recommendations to families and the court. Typically, recommendations will fall into several categories, including but not limited to: custody/visitation recommendations; a parenting plan that outlines the time-share between and responsibilities of the parents; how parents might deal with future conflicts; and therapy recommendations for parents and/or children. When special problems exist, such as domestic violence, substance abuse problems, alienation of children, relocation, and others, there will need to be special recommendations focusing on those special issues. New child custody evaluators will need to comprehend each of these complex issues, the research that supports various recommendations, and the developmental or other psychological bases for making such recommendations.

For those just starting to do child custody evaluations, specialized training is needed. There are several good places to acquire training in child custody evaluation work. Division 41 (Psychology and Law) of the American Psychological Association has biennial meetings that often include workshops around child custody work. The annual meeting of the American Psychological Association usually has continuing education workshops on introductory or advanced child custody evaluation issues. The Association of Family and Conciliation Courts (AFCC) (has two meetings per year with workshops or institutes pertaining to child custody evaluations. Approximately every 18-24 months, AFCC has custody evaluation symposia at which training in child custody evaluations is provided. The American Academy of Forensic Psychology (AAFP), (provides ongoing training seminars for a variety of forensic issues, including child custody evaluations. Other child custody evaluation training is usually available in the local community.

In addition to training, there are a number of other resources available to new child custody evaluators. It is important for child custody evaluators to have a firm understanding of the dynamics of divorce, child development, domestic violence, alienation, and a very good understanding of high conflict and custody and visitation issues. A selected bibliography will be included at the end of this chapter. Regardless of the source, ongoing training and consultation in this complex and difficult field is beneficial.

3.   INTEGRATING CHILD DEVELOPMENT RESEARCH INTO THE CONCEPT OF PARENTING PLANS

An important area of recommendation in the child custody evaluation report is the parenting plan. A parenting plan is the blueprint for parents sharing their children. It outlines all of the necessary ingredients for communication, custody and visitation, parenting responsibilities, resolving future differences, and managing necessary change as children get older or circumstances change. A parenting plan can be vague and relatively brief, or extremely detailed and comprehensive. This will be dependent on the nature of the particular evaluation and the parents' ability to share. As a family's level of conflict increases, the parenting plan must become more specific and complete and there should be less room for misinterpretation. Parenting plans must be considered in combination with the developmental needs of children. Here are some considerations.

3.1   Infants and Toddlers (0 - 3 years)

During this stage, the foundations of basic trust and relationships are formed. In the first year of life, children develop initial attachment(s), a necessary precursor for the development of basic trust. By the end of the first year, receptive language skills are developing and the infant's personality is starting to form. Once a predictable, secure relationship with a primary attachment figure has been secured, the infant begins to separate from that primary parent to form his/her own personality. This process is often referred to as "separation-individuation". During the toddler years, children begin developing autonomy and experimenting with separation, starting to assert themselves. Their emotions are quite volatile. By age three, if all goes well, emotions settle down, language skills are intact, and they are likely to be toilet trained. They are ready for a burst of psychological growth, which will take place over the next three years.

Children in this age group require predictability, consistency, and routine. When a divorce occurs during this time, there is a loss, which the child cannot understand (Bray, 1991). This can be pronounced if there is a major disruption in the consistency of the existing primary attachment relationship(s). Symptoms may include regression, problems with feeding, sleeping, self-soothing, and irritability. Some of these children become depressed and withdrawn, especially because they cannot express their loss in words. Separation anxiety for children in this age group can become exaggerated. If one or both parents becomes depressed, which is quite common, basic care may be diminished.

Children at this age are at risk for more serious regression or developmental delays if the basic care giving is lacking due to depressed or disturbed parents (Kelly, 1994; Lamb, 1997a; Lamb et. al., 1997b). It is not uncommon for young, possibly immature adults (aged 18 - 25) to have babies. Sometimes they never lived together, or they may have separated during the first two years of the child's life. The developmental needs of the children may become impacted by the maturity level of the parents. Rather than the idea of "one psychological parent", or a "primary parent", children can have a hierarchy of attachment figures, all of whom have importance for children in their post-divorce adjustment (Kelly and Lamb, 2000; Warshak, 2000). Some children do have one primary parent that has attended to the majority of day-to-day needs. Other children may have two or three adults (two parents and a day-care provider) who have attended to day-to-day needs. Children in this age group need a parenting plan reflecting the following:

1. Children need both of their parents to participate in a wide array of their life functioning. For children of this age, both parents should participate in feeding, toileting, sleeping, soothing, and playing with their child. The child's relationship with both parents is of major importance during these first three years of life.

2. Assuming there is a "primary parent," children can develop within normal limits when separated from the primary parent to be with the other parent. This will be affected by the extent to which each parent has been directly involved in the child's life. However, for many children, there is no "primary parent"; rather, both parents have taken an active role in the child's life.

3. Attachment(s), parenting skills, the child's temperament, and environment are important. Frequent, shorter contacts may be ideal. Overnight visits may need to be limited in the first year of life if there has been one primary parent.

4. With increased capacity for memory and cognition, most children in the group from 18 - 36 months who have had one primary attachment will begin to tolerate and benefit from overnight time with the other parent.

5. It may be difficult to develop a relatively equal parenting plan for children in this age group since there may be too many transitions and disruptions to the primary attachments.

6. With the above in mind, however, the children who do best with relatively equal parenting plans seem to be those children with an easy temperament who have parents that are supportive of one another and exchange their child with little conflict. Children who have disorganized or anxious attachments may need one primary attachment with the psychologically healthier parent.

Other key factors are similar routines in each household, relative stability of the transitions, and parents who can communicate about the child and his/her developmental, medical, and emotional needs. This communication must allow the parents to be sufficiently responsive to the child and his/her needs. These parents need the capacity to help each other understand their infant, work together to develop routines that are familiar to their infant, collaborate on soothing techniques, help each other as language emerges, and reassure each other in their respective parenting techniques. Such parents must be flexible in their response to the child's changing needs. Such a pattern is used in healthy intact families and if it is used in a separated family, the shared parenting plan will be natural for the child and his/her development.

When parents are in significant high-conflict, very young children appear to benefit the most from schedules that resemble their pre-separation patterns of contact with each parent. In such instances, the child needs predictability in his/her environment until the conflict can settle down.

3.2 Preschoolers (3 - 5 years)

During this stage, the child is developing a better ability to understand language, relationships, and feelings. Children of this age are making significant progress in their cognitive skills and peer relationships. Sex role identification is developing. If the separation-individuation process has been healthy, children of this age can be expected to expand their horizons, go to preschool and make friendships. These children are often delightful, learning to manage their feelings and being inquisitive about everything. If attachments and care giving are secure, these children will be ready to venture off to kindergarten with good self-esteem and confidence.

On the other hand, preschoolers are at risk for fairly serious regression when attachments are anxious and they do not understand the conflicts of their parents. They may become easily confused and do not understand what is occurring around them (Bray, 1991, Emery, 1999). Developmental delays and regression in toileting, sleeping, and feeding are common. They may experience irritability and clinging behavior. Some children become depressed and withdrawn. Nightmares may become more pronounced. Self-confidence may suffer and there can be increases in aggressive and anxious behaviors. Many of the children in this age group worry about their parents and may try to act "perfect". They may do this out of fear or they may be unconsciously taking care of their parents. We may be seeing the early signs of parentified behavior, in which they care emotionally for their parents, ignoring their own needs. A certain amount of this behavior is normal during the early stages of divorce, but when such behaviors are many, or extend for more than a year, this could reflect a more serious adjustment problem for the child.

These children need parenting plans consistent with the following:
1. Continued focus on predictability, routine, and structure for the child.
2. Children aged three and older can certainly tolerate overnight contact with each parent.
3. Discipline and routine needs to be consistent in each parent's home.
4. Parents will need to share information about the child and his/her eating, sleeping, toileting, medical, and social / emotional functioning.
5. Children need freedom from direct exposure to parental conflict. If the parents continue to be in conflict, parents might consider using neutral sites (e.g. school or day-care) for transitions and neutral decision-makers.

6. Children in this age group often benefit from longer blocks of time with each parent that enable them to be settled in routines at each home. Many of these children do not do well with frequent transitions.
7. In this age group, parents need to put their needs secondary to the child's. While the non-custodial parent may want longer blocks of time with their younger child, many children of this age still need a primary home. This is dependent on the quality of attachments, whether parents are consistent and relatively free of conflict, and whether the child is experiencing significant vulnerability and stress.
8. There may be situations in which each parent has some pathology or parenting flaws, **but each offers the child something the other does not**. In those cases, it is important to have a parenting plan that maximizes each parent's strengths while minimizing the extent to which the child is exposed to the pathology.

3.3   School - Aged Children (6 - 12 years)

This is an age in which children thrive on structure and routine. Peer relationships are growing, and they are learning to master social rules. Creativity continues to grow and these children are adept at making up games with unique rules. Rules are important as these children focus on fairness in their life. Socialization and being part of a group are important to children of this age. They are learning to better understand and express their feelings and master cognitive and academic skills. They can be quite silly at times and still prefer to play much of the time. They are learning skills in such areas as academics, sports, music, dance, art, etc. Self-esteem grows when they function well in school, on the playground, and in the family. It is not uncommon for children of this age to have different relationships with each parent, preferring mom for some things and dad for others.

Divorce brings many challenges to children of this age (Bray, 1991). Younger school-aged children tend to feel the loss of the family and may experience sadness and crying, often longing for the return of the family unit. Older children in this age-range may be likely to experience anger and use alignment to mobilize self-esteem. Children of this age often feel directly responsible for the divorce, especially if they perceive that conflict focused on them (Kelly, 1994). These children may exhibit multiple symptoms, including tantrums, regression, sleep problems, acting out, behavioral and academic problems in school, withdrawal or aggression with peers, and depression. This is a population that believes in fairness, and wants to please their parents. They feel overwhelmed by their parent's conflict and usually try to fix it, yet they are ill equipped to do so. When a parent is depressed, these children are at risk for parentified behavior in which they emotionally care for that parent.

In extreme high-conflict families, this population may present as asymptomatic on the surface, but feel overwhelmed and vulnerable underneath (Johnston & Roseby, 1997). These children are at risk for emotional splitting in which one parent is "all-good" and the other is "all-bad". They often feel stuck by the loyalty conflicts and may become emotionally constricted, worrying about their parents. Alignments that were natural in the pre-divorce family become highlighted, increasing their risk of alienation. These children have difficulty maintaining a strong internalized self-image as a result of the conflict. They may become overwhelmed and disorganized, struggling with the different emotions and behaviors of each parent.

It is not uncommon for children to hear one parent blame the other or hear different explanations from each parent for things, which they experience. For example, when one parent says, "I don't know why your mother doesn't call you when you're here. She probably doesn't care much for you," and the other parent says, "I called you three times last night, why didn't you call back? Doesn't your dad give you the messages?" this is quite confusing to children, who do not know which parent to believe.

These children need a parenting plan, which encompasses the following concepts:

1. A structured and consistent time-share that assures access to each parent, when indicated. Optimal parenting plans range from 35 - 65 % of time with either parent (and thus a primary home) to 50/50 joint physical custody in which the child is with each parent about half of the time. While children often express a wish for equal time with their parents, this may simply be to keep things fair.

2. While joint physical custody may be best in a given situation, it requires a degree of consistency and willingness for the parents to resolve their conflicts away from the child. It also requires the parents to share all of the tasks of parenting and help the child and each other transfer the child's things (school supplies, athletic equipment, etc.) from one house to the other without conflict.

3. The time-share needs to promote each parent's strengths, while giving each parent time alone to recover from the divorce on his/her own.

4. Exchanges need to minimize the extent to which the child is exposed to the conflict. School or other neutral places are excellent transition places between mom's house and dad's house.

5. The parents need a plan for conflict resolution that keeps the children out of the middle. Children should not be messengers or spies for their

parents. Communication needs to be by and through the parents, with the aid of a neutral professional when required.

6. To the extent the parents can do it, there should be a plan for co-parenting. For those parents in which the conflict is more extreme, a pattern of parallel parenting and detachment from each other will be optimal.

For those families in which the co-parenting relationship is relatively free of conflict, the children have a strong attachment to each parent and are adjusting well and both parents are relatively equal in their attachments, some form of joint physical custody is often ideal.

However, joint physical custody may not be ideal in high-conflict families because school-age children are susceptible to being caught in the middle of the conflict. Instead, when the child is exposed to too much conflict, and when the child is not managing his/her stress very well, or when the routines in each parent's home are significantly different, or when one or both parents struggles to empathize with the child and maintain healthy parent-child boundaries, the child is likely to need a primary home, with blocks of time in the other parent's home to assure continuity and growth of each parent-child relationship.

3.4   Adolescents (13 - 17 years)

The major task of the adolescent is developing greater independence and autonomy from the family. Their separation-individuation process is similar to that of the two-year-old. There can be a tendency to act with oppositional and negative behaviors. Just as with the toddler, adolescents express some resistance and rebelliousness while forming their identity. Healthy adolescents function well in school, have self-confidence, and strong peer relationships. They learn to talk with their parents about life goals and they begin to plan for driving, working, and college or vocational school. As a group, adolescents tend to be somewhat moody and reactive in their emotions. They may feel overwhelmed by pressure from their peers, use poor judgment, and be socially insecure. Their ideas, values, and goals are in a state of turmoil and may change considerably over their junior high and high school years. However, these years can be exciting ones as teens grow into productive and idealistic individuals.

However, with this considerable internal adjustment, this is a population at potential risk. This is true for adolescents of intact families as well as with families of divorce. When a divorce occurs at this age, teens worry about the loss of their family life. They tend to feel a blend of responsibility and guilt, and anger for the way it has affected them. Children of this age tend to be self-centered naturally, and the divorce becomes a disruption to them. They may avoid both their parents, especially if the parents are burdening them with loyalty conflicts and adult problems. When there is a pattern of high-conflict, children in this age group are at risk for persistent academic failure, depression, suicide, delinquency, promiscuity, or substance abuse. With their ability to see things more abstractly, they become much more aware of their parents' flaws. This may lead to a more rapid destruction of their idealized view of their parents, resulting in anxiety and anger. This anger may take a fairly self-righteous stance and adolescents may resist contact with the parent whose flaws have been significantly exposed.

Some adolescents want little or nothing to do with one of his/her parents. This must be understood completely. Sometimes, it is the result of alienation by one parent; sometimes, it is the result of frustration with the conflict; sometimes it relates to the moral indignation of the parent's divorce-related behavior; and sometimes, it is the result of legitimate frustration that has built over a long relationship of pain. When an older adolescent (15 - 17 years old) is adamant about how he/she wants the parenting plan to be, this must be seriously considered. Courts do not want to set up a situation, which may encourage an adolescent to rebel (any more than he/she would anyway).

Adolescents need parenting plans, which reflect the following:

1. A time-share plan, which incorporates a range of possibilities. Many adolescents prefer one primary home, in large part to avoid confusion for their friends. For many of these teens, they will want weekends or evenings with the other parent. Some will prefer a balanced, 50/50 plan with their parents. Much of this will depend on the prior history of the relationships with each parent and the availability of the parents to meet their needs. At times, adolescents use one parent's home to get a break from the other. More than anything, adolescents will often want a say in the parenting plan.
2. Adolescents may require a different schedule than siblings. This can depend on a number of variables, including the adolescent's wishes.
3. A statement about the need for any possible support services such as therapy, substance abuse counseling, tutoring, or other such needs.
4. To the extent this is relevant, statements about the need for the parents to manage their conflicts away from the teen and maintain healthier boundaries with them. To the extent that one or both parents is confiding adult issues to the teen, this should be discouraged.
5. In cases of severe high-conflict, the teen's autonomy and detachment from both parents may be critical. The need to find other appropriate supportive adults may also be indicated. These teens may require someone to monitor and assess the ongoing risks.

The thorough custody evaluator is able to integrate these developmental considerations into the family dynamics when making recommendations on behalf of the children.

4.   THE SPECIAL NEEDS OF THE HIGH-CONFLICT POPULATION

Many families do not fit patterns of domestic violence, yet they experience a high degree of conflict. Many high-conflict families may experience intermittent outbursts of anger or violence. Even when they do not exhibit violent patterns, these families are so conflicted that they routinely go back to court to solve what should be relatively simple problems. They may have problems scheduling holidays and vacations; they may argue during exchanges; they cannot communicate about child-related issues or decide on day-care providers; they disagree on the times and places for exchanging the children and argue about who will attend parent-teacher conferences, arrange and pay for health care, or attend the child's extra-curricular activities; and they may disagree on activities for their children.

In many ways, it appears that the life of the child must stop while the arguments between the parents continue. For many of these families, every issue becomes a potential source of conflict. Sometimes this is related to the history of the relationship and the power dynamics between the parents. Sometimes one parent will not let go of the conflict because this keeps them "together" in their relationship (albeit a destructive one).

It is this author's position that much of this conflict is driven by each parent's respective personality traits, the lack of a system for resolving conflicts, or both. Decisions may get made by the more forceful parent when one parent "gives in" to the other. Sometimes, no rational decision gets made, such as when one parent takes the child to the pediatrician and the other does the same after the exchange because they don't trust each other to communicate medical information to each other. In such situations, children may see two pediatricians when one will do, and no therapist when one is needed. Teachers become frustrated with the lack of cooperation toward the child's schooling. I have seen many instances in which children are enrolled in two different kindergartens because parents cannot plan adequately together for their child's education. Such parents have not learned to implement a system for communication, problem solving, and decision-making. They do things the same way that they have for years. Often one parent does give in. Sadly, this may be the healthier parent.

Research on high-conflict families (Johnston, 1994 and Johnston & Roseby, 1997) reveals a continuum of problems and a variety of factors that contribute to the problems. Some families are mildly entrenched in conflict and can benefit from guidance and structured recommendations. The more difficult of these families may seem to make little progress, even with rather extensive intervention (e.g. therapy and case management). Some parents have personality traits that exacerbate conflicts, perhaps exaggerating or being quite rigid. The next section will focus on the way in which the parent's respective personality traits contribute to the degree and nature of the conflict.

Over the past 20 years, a growing body of literature has developed on personality styles, in particular Narcissistic and Borderline styles. Millon (1996), not only focused on the disorders themselves, but those personality traits and features which impact upon relationships, rather than the individual. He has grouped personality disorders into four types. Many custody evaluators observe that most high-conflict families have one or both parents who exhibit either narcissistic, obsessive-compulsive, histrionic, paranoid, or borderline features. They may have parents who become rigid in their perception of the other and tend to deal with things in their extremes. Many parents are polarized, viewing themselves as all good and the other as all bad. These parents focus on the traits within the other parent that reinforce this perception, and they approach each new conflict as verification of just how difficult the other parent is. These parents experience chronic externalization of blame, possessing little insight into their own role in the conflicts. They usually have little empathy for the impact of this conflict on their children. They routinely feel self-justified, believing that their actions are best for their children. No matter how much the helping professionals try to keep the focus on the child, these parents remain focused on the conflict.

While these parents tend to be motivated by a diverse set of emotions, most of them take this rather rigid position out of fear, often the overwhelming fear that if they let down their defenses, they will be taken advantage of. Many parents say, "If I just give in this one time, she will always take advantage of me," or "if I give him an inch, he'll take a mile." Many parents fear being controlled by the other parent. For the more disturbed of these parents, giving in may represent a fear of annihilation or loss of self. This rigidity assures conflict. Because these families routinely go back to court, they are also afraid that any relaxing of their position might give the other parent an advantage in court. What gets lost in the conflict is the needs of the children. Another source of the fear is that winning or losing is so integrally tied to self-esteem. Narcissistic parents fear losing custody and control, lest they feel abandoned and depressed. Borderline parents must win in order to contain their internal chaos and rage. While losing might mean different things to each parent (e.g. shame, loss, abandonment, rage, etc.) the key ingredient is how **unbearable** such a loss is to each parent. Other difficult parents may be irresponsible, over-reactive, and rigid. Parents with these personality traits often have high-conflict marriages and divorces.

Judges and attorneys express their extreme frustration with these families. Many refer to these families as their "frequent fliers," adding that, even though they may only number ten percent of the families, they require ninety percent of the court's resources. They might come back to court several times a year, and just as it appears that a settlement has been reached, a new issue will arise. Lacking a reasonable dispute resolution mechanism, these parents feel justified in taking the other to court and letting "the judge settle it." Each issue is perceived as a new opportunity for victory, and feared as potential loss. These characterological personality dynamics, along with each parent's righteous self-justification and fear, create the high degree of conflict, and the perpetuation of the court battle.

At the same time, away from the conflict, many of these parents seem concerned for their children's needs and feelings and are capable of good parenting skills. They may be nurturing and set reasonable limits with their children. They are frequently involved in their child's day-to-day activities, participate in schoolwork, and provide encouragement to their children. Many of these parents can be loving, spontaneous, and supportive to their children, even when they are cold, rigid, angry, and fearful toward the other parent. In the abstract, they understand the value of the child's relationship with the other parent, and they may even recognize that the conflict is problematic for their children. Despite this acknowledgment, it is difficult for them to relax their rigid positions and attitudes toward the other parent and extricate their child (and themselves) from the conflict.

For many high-conflict families, it seems that the parents' characterological personality dynamics become manifested in a relationship disorder with the other parent. They may be able to manage some of their chronic traits, including their narcissism, over-reaction, rigidity, and anger, in some of their other relationships. They may be pleasant to co-workers, and show few pathological traits in their work environment. With their children, they may not personalize experiences or show signs of narcissistic injury. In contrast, however, the history of the conflict, the emotions of the divorce, and the fear of letting go are likely to bring out the worst in these parents with each other. In these situations, it appears that the couple's relationship has been unable to withstand the pattern of love, the loss of that love, and the rejection and hurt that have followed. In the newly formed divorce relationship, dysfunctional personality traits flourish, even while healthier personality traits may abound in other relationships, including with the children. For the less disturbed of these parents, the pathological personality traits may only surface in the context of the conflictual relationship between the parents. Each parent's negative individual traits clash and the conflicts continue. Left unchecked, these families return to court year after year to solve what might appear to the neutral observer to be the most minor of issues.

These families require strategies and interventions that assist them in taking care of their children and reducing their conflict. These strategies can include some or all of the following:

5.   NEUTRAL DECISION-MAKING (SPECIAL MASTER)

In a variety of jurisdictions, including Northern California (Special Masters), Maricopa County, Arizona (Family Court Advisors), Boulder, Colorado (Case Managers or Binding Arbitrators), and New Mexico ("Wise Persons"), courts have begun to use attorneys and mental health practitioners as neutral decision-makers to assist families in such day-to-day disputes. While these families frequently return to court, the court system is incapable of handling the types or frequency of problems that these families bring. Instead, they require the assistance of a decision-maker who acts on behalf of the children. This person is empowered by the family and the court to act on behalf of the children and resolve conflicts in an expeditious manner. If neither parent has control, both can relax their fear of being taken advantage of by the other. While each parent may periodically become frustrated with the decisions of the neutral decision-maker, each parent usually trusts that person more than the other parent.

It appears that there are three primary benefits for this role. These include helping families more quickly resolve their differences, unclogging the courts from some of their most difficult families, and helping families with very young children manage the nuances of integrating changing developmental needs of the child into their parenting plan. The major task of the neutral decision-maker is to make decisions that help a family stay out of court and keep their children out of the middle of the conflict. Special Masters need to be decisive. Just as young children often have difficulty sharing, divorced parents often have difficulty sharing their children. While the neutral decision-maker needs to understand the parents' position and feelings, it is more important for the neutral decision-maker to make decisions that are in the child's interest, without taking a lot of time.

There are times when families seek the help of a therapist to assist in decision-making, but without the legal stipulation inherent in the role of neutral decision-maker. While this may be useful for some families, this author urges therapists to exercise caution when asked to participate in such a role. Therapists will need special training to learn how to navigate the ethics and boundaries inherent in this forensic role. While there may be a temptation to make decisions on behalf of the "child" client, therapists are advised to carefully consider these actions and leave "decision-making" or recommendations to the court to the neutral decision-maker. Therapists routinely make therapeutic suggestions to parents based on knowledge of the family and the child's feelings and needs and this can continue. However, if such a therapist makes recommendations to the court or decisions for the family, he/she will be exceeding the therapeutic role and may risk being drawn into the legal dispute and harm the therapeutic process.

6.   PARALLEL PARENTING

A second intervention involves parallel parenting. Psychologists describe young children who play next to each other, but interact very little with each other to be in "parallel play". In the same way, parents who parent their children at different times, but who have little or no direct interaction, are engaged in parallel parenting. This occurs when they engage in the same tasks, as long as they have little or no contact with one another.

While much of the divorce literature focuses on co-parenting, in which parents communicate and work with one another to raise their children in a cooperative fashion, high-conflict families fail miserably at this task. Each parent usually thinks his/her style is the only way to parent and is often quite critical of the other. Interactions stimulate the conflict, reducing benefits to the children.

The goal of parallel parenting is to reduce the level of conflict and make sure that the tasks of parenting are accomplished by one or both parents. It is important for parents, in conjunction with the courts and/or neutral decision-maker to specify which parent is responsible for various parenting tasks. Parents need to develop a plan that identifies how each parent will participate in the child's extracurricular activities, help with school work, or to take care of medical needs. Plans are developed to insure that parents communicate with each other with less conflict. Fax machines and/or e-mail may be used when the conflict is high. Each parent is encouraged to develop his/her separate routine and structure. With such a plan, for example, the child will not be exposed to both parents attending the same field trip and making things miserable with their conflict. It can be helpful for the neutral decision-maker to meet with the parents periodically and develop a schedule of the child's activities and each parent's participation in those activities. The neutral decision-maker can use these sessions to focus on the process of parallel parenting and help parents to disengage from conflict. This is an important step before helping them learn to work together. With the neutral decision-maker's help, they can develop routines for the child and help coordinate a similar routine in each household, schedule times for phone calls between children and the other parent, and assist each parent in doing those tasks that each parent does best. With this process, there are no winners or losers, and the child benefits from separate and parallel interaction with both parents, reducing the extent to which children are exposed to conflict. Once a neutral decision-maker is in place, and the process of parallel parenting is assured, parents can detach from each other and reduce the intensity of their conflict.

7.   STRUCTURED RECOMMENDATIONS

A third important intervention for these families is providing structured recommendations. For high-conflict families, a lack of specificity promotes parental conflict, and conflict breeds insecurity for the children. Attorneys should recommend, and the court needs to adopt, specific and concrete plans to assist parents in fulfilling the tasks of parallel parenting and reducing the likelihood that they remain engaged in conflict. The more specific these plans are, the more parents can understand the structure and avoid conflict.

These parents need a lengthy and detailed parenting plan, giving less room for each parent to manipulate or feel manipulated by the other. The rules are quite clear. In the event of a dispute, it will be relatively easy for the neutral decision-maker to resolve. The recommendation should also include a provision that the neutral decision-maker can make adjustments or modifications in the event of certain situations, such as a family emergency, a special longer vacation, the children's summer schedule, or the needs of one or more family members.

Typically, flexibility is not workable for these high-conflict families without a dispute resolution mechanism such as a neutral decision-maker since flexibility is a breeding ground for new conflict. Parents can feel more comfortable with a structured recommendation if it can be adjusted in the event a specific need arises. For some families, the level of conflict does not get resolved for years, or ever! Neither parent trusts the neutral decision-maker, and the use of a neutral decision-maker only provides one more opportunity for engaging in conflict and battles over power and control. Those families will require a very structured court order that leaves little room for dispute, and potential sanctions from the court in the event that either parent violates the order. Those families will have no room for flexibility, unless mutually agreed-upon. In contrast, many high-conflict parents do trust the neutral decision-maker, benefit from a clear and precise order, and are encouraged by parallel parenting. They neutralize their balance of power and reduce the likelihood for conflict to erupt in front of the children. Because the neutral decision-maker can make decisions (e.g., whether or not the child will participate in Little League and how each parent can participate with the child) in a timely way, the child's life is less likely to be halted or disrupted by the conflict.

By making structured recommendations, the child custody evaluator can help the courts structure a complete court order to help reduce conflict, and the evaluator can help the family understand ways to minimize their conflicts and do a better job parenting their children.

8.   ETHICAL CONSIDERATIONS IN CHILD CUSTODY EVALUATION WORK

Child custody work is considered by many to be the most challenging of all psychological work. The issues are extremely complex, and the tension is usually high. Most psychologists do not like conflict, yet they work with some of the most intense conflicts. An example would be the impact of a divorce between a narcissistic, rigid parent and a histrionic, enmeshed parent. When completing an evaluation, the psychologist is likely to make at least one or both parents angry and may frequently be challenged in court. The situation will be intense as cross-examining attorneys question the evaluator's procedures, data, and conclusions. Evidence in all 50 states suggests that there is an increased risk of lawsuits or licensing complaints, as unhappiness about child custody evaluations and allegations of ethical violations have surpassed all other issues (including sex with a patient) to become the leading cause of licensing board complaints.

When families in conflict are seen in court, a common assumption is that they need a binding answer to help them to resolve their legal dispute. Often times, however, what these families need is not an answer, but rather a process by which they can reach consensus regarding very important parenting decisions. While in some cases, evaluations can provide families with assistance in their decision-making; families may need help with communicating, collaborating, and negotiating in a way that can allow their family to make the transition from a nuclear to bi-nuclear family.

The courts should seek to assist families in a way that will preserve the important relational bonds that must endure for the well being of all concerned. Evaluators and judges must be careful not to impose the values of the evaluator, court, or other professionals on that family unless and until they have first made reasonable efforts to enable the parents to be their own decision-makers. Not only does imposing decisions upon the parents serve as an intrusion upon the integrity of the fragile changing family structure, but it also serves to weaken the parental role, as important decision-making functions have been taken from the parents. Evaluators should keep that principle in mind and be careful to conduct their evaluations in a manner that instills confidence in the impartiality, professionalism, and competence of the evaluator and should strive to produce reports and conclusions, which can be understood and comprehended by all involved.

Evaluators must critically analyze and pay careful attention to all of the research, including child development research, and not just historical theories and philosophies, when formulating recommendations for parenting plans. They need to critically evaluate the ways in which psychological instruments truly enhance their evaluation of a family and to understand the risks and benefits of including these instruments in their assessments. Evaluators need to recognize that they work within a legal system that automatically has multi-faceted approaches and tensions within and between the disciplines. The legal and psychological field needs to pay closer attention to the standards and complex issues inherent in child protection evaluations. The system needs to demand that evaluators approach all evaluations in a careful, ethical, and scientific manner, while being sensitive to the dignity and needs of families and their children. If evaluators and the courts accomplish these goals, all participants will utilize an improved ethical standard in his/her work.

Evaluators can avoid ethical problems by paying attention to the following:

1. *Be court appointed.* By avoiding the temptation to be hired by one side in a custody dispute, the evaluator can reduce the risk of lawsuit or licensing complaint. In most jurisdictions, this neutral court appointment is established by an order from the judge or by stipulation between the attorneys. Such a neutral appointment is the first step in reducing the risk of a complaint about bias. Once a psychologist is identified as an expert in the local jurisdiction, it is not too difficult to get such a neutral appointment.

2. *Obtain informed consent.* By having an informed consent agreement prior to the start of an evaluation, the evaluator can explain the basic principles of an evaluation and help parents understand the role and

procedures of an evaluation. (A Sample Informed Consent Document is presented at the end of this chapter).

3. *Maintain legal and clinical impartiality.* Parents are frequently upset with the results of a child custody evaluation. By maintaining a neutral position throughout the evaluation process, regardless of the allegations of each side, the evaluator can minimize the risk that the court or a licensing board will agree that there was bias in the conclusions. There are several things that the evaluator can do to show evidence of impartiality. The evaluator needs to:

− Spend a relatively equal amount of interview time with each parent.
− Administer any psychological tests or parenting questionnaires to both parents.
− Spend about the same amount of time on observations of the children with each parent.
− Consider the relative strengths and weaknesses of **both** parents.
− Consider the emphasis in the report, making sure that one parent's concerns are not over- or under-emphasized in the report.

4. *Provide appropriate information about confidentiality and disclosure of information.* This is clearly an obligation of the APA Ethical Principles and reduces risk. This is done in both the written informed consent and in verbal discussions with parents at the beginning of the evaluation.

5. *Avoid dual relationships.* The assigned evaluator should not mediate, should not take on therapeutic tasks, and should not make tentative recommendations before finishing the evaluation. The role of evaluator is a clear and impartial one, as an expert for the court and the benefit of the children. Do not compromise that role, and raise the risk of licensing complaint, by engaging in any other role during the time of your evaluation. If, after completing the evaluation, the evaluator is asked to shift to a different role, such as a Special Master or Parenting Coordinator, it may be ethically acceptable, especially in communities in which there are only few qualified psychologists. However, it will be necessary to provide adequate informed consent on the implications of such a role shift. Two particular items would be to inform the participants that the psychologist could not testify in court as an evaluator in the future, since the psychologist is no longer simply an evaluator and has gained new information in the new role. In addition, the psychologist would inform the parties that he/she could never go back to the role of evaluator, in case a new or updated evaluation is needed, once the role shift has taken place.

6. *Obtain specialized training.* As indicated above, when doing forensic work, mental health professionals need specialized training. This chapter is only an introduction into some of the issues for child custody

evaluators. It is necessary to read the forensic psychology literature, the research on divorce and child custody, and learn about the statutory and case law relevant in state where the evaluator works. Do not assume that you're ready to do child custody evaluations by virtue of reading this chapter. It is also necessary to recognize and learn about domestic violence, alienated children, relocation issues, psychological testing, and mediation. Go to the local courthouse and observing judges, parents, and evaluators is quite helpful. Become immersed in this task as you gain the necessary specialized training. Develop inter-disciplinary networks with attorneys, mediators, judges, and other forensic psychologists.

Skilled child custody evaluators are the ones who are thorough, ethical, careful, and get good consultation. Feel gratified and take pride in the fact that the role of the evaluator helps overburdened courts and vulnerable children of the divorcing family by providing valuable input to the long-term resolution of divorce conflict. Enjoy a full and interesting practice including child custody evaluations, therapy, and consultation in your work with families of divorce.

This chapter has focused on the issues that any mental health professional needs to consider when engaging in the practice of child custody evaluations. This includes the ethical issues of a child custody evaluation practice, integrating child development research into one's evaluation practice, and a focus on the special needs of the high-conflict population. However, to be prepared to do thorough child custody evaluations, any potential evaluator would also want to take specialized training related to the effects of divorce on children, the alienation of children in high-conflict divorces, domestic violence, the use of psychological tests with these families and, when indicated, move-away or sexual abuse issues for these families. The families, the courts, and the children need the assistance of these well-trained evaluators, and this chapter has outlined the basic principles that need to be understood by all.

9.   SAMPLE CONSENT FORM

Custody Evaluation Contract and Informed Consent[105]

Thank you for contacting me regarding your child custody evaluation. This contract will explain my procedures for child custody evaluations referred by the court.

I believe that it is in a family's best interests to develop their own post-divorce parenting arrangements, whenever possible. I become part of the process when a family's own attempts to resolve these issues, via mediation or conferences with their attorneys, has reached an impasse. When that occurs, or when the judge orders a child custody evaluation, I am asked to assist the attorneys or the judge in determining the parenting plan which is in your child's best interests. It is my belief, and research shows, that it is best for children when parents can agree on parenting arrangements, and my evaluations are designed to promote resolution of conflicts in this area.

Evaluation Procedures

In order to do a thorough evaluation, I will need to know information about each of you. I will be asking you to fill out a comprehensive form regarding yourself, your perceptions of the other parent, and your children. The evaluation includes appointments with both parents, your children, and perhaps other significant adults in your child's life. The interviews may be individual and/or in any combinations and as often as necessary for the purpose of the evaluation. I might do home visits in your evaluation. In general, I do them when one or more of your children is under the age of six or there are specific issues which can only be answered via the observations of a home visit. In addition to the time that I spend with all of you, I generally administer psychological testing and parenting questionnaires as part of my evaluation. Pursuant to the court order appointing me as your evaluator, I will also ask you to sign a release of information form which will provide me with access to medical, school, legal, and other professional information. These releases will give permission to others to provide necessary information to me. All of these steps are designed to give me a complete understanding of you and your family.

---

105 Prepared by Philip M. Stahl, Ph.D. as a guide for training purposes. This contract should not be construed as a "standard informed
consent contract." Practitioners should modify as needed according to one's state laws, local court culture, and individual practice style.
© Philip M. Stahl, Ph.D.

During the evaluation, it is common for parents to ask me advice or give interim recommendations. My purpose during the evaluation is to evaluate. Until I am done, I cannot give advice or provide interim recommendations since I don't have all of the data regarding your family. On rare occasions I might give a brief, limited, short-term recommendation and then evaluate your ability to follow through with the suggestion, or its impact on the children.

I like to inform parents that you are unlikely to know what I am thinking during the course of the evaluation. I discourage parents from reading into my questions, since they are only designed to give me information, and not to give parents a sense of what I am likely to recommend. While I generally give no clue what I am thinking during the evaluation, I try to be very clear on my recommendations, and I try to explain why I believe those recommendations are in your child's best interests when the evaluation is over.

Collateral Sources

Many parents ask about my policy regarding collateral contacts. I will generally phone those professionals with whom you have worked and who can give me necessary information about you or your children. Generally, these collateral sources might include teachers, childcare providers, law enforcement officers, pediatricians and other medical doctors, and therapists. I can also include others as well. If you have been ordered to participate in drug testing or anger management, I will likely be in contact with those sources. It is rare for me to interview all collateral parties that are suggested. I usually only phone those professional collateral sources who I believe will add information to my evaluation. If you have one or two collateral sources that you believe are crucial to my evaluation, please let me know. Please note that I will inform sources that the content of all interviews may be included in my written evaluation report, and I may be required to testify about these contacts in Court.

It is rare for me to interview friends or relatives, each of whom is often partial to one of the parents. I encourage you to get letters from friends and/or relatives that you believe might have pertinent information. I reserve the right to contact any of those persons if I need clarification of any written information given to me.

Confidentiality

Many parents ask about confidentiality in a child custody evaluation. Quite simply, within the process, there is no confidentiality. I may share information that one parent tells me with the other parent or ask one of you questions about what I hear from a parent, child, or any collateral source. I may ask your children about things that I hear from either of you. I will inform your children that their statements may not be confidential, though I may inform you, your attorneys, and the court if I believe it is in your child's interest to protect that confidentiality. The reason there is no confidentiality within the evaluation is to protect your due process rights and to ensure that I can clarify all issues and gather necessary information for my evaluation and recommendations. In addition, it is understood that I will be providing the Court, Family Court Services, and the attorney(s) with a written report concerning the child custody evaluation.

Please note that California state law requires reporting to the appropriate agencies in cases where there is reasonable suspicion of child abuse, elder abuse, stated intention to injure another person, and/or imminent danger of harming yourself or inability to care for yourself.

Both attorneys and parents are invited to send me any written materials that they think will be useful. Please do not give me originals and please note that I do not make copies of this material for your attorney or the other side. Also please note that the court order appointing me as your evaluator requires that copies of any materials sent to me must also be provided to the other parent or his/her legal representative.

Fees

My fee for conducting this evaluation is $XXXXX. This fee covers all interview time, home visits (if there are any), time spent phoning parents and collateral sources and/or reviewing written material, scoring psychological tests and parenting inventories, writing the evaluation report, and any other time spent in association with the evaluation. All fees are generally to be paid at the first session of the evaluation unless other arrangements have been made. The percentage of the fee paid by each parent is determined by your court order. Payment must be made with cash, check, or credit card. In the event that I have agreed to partial payment at the start of the evaluation, full payment must be made within 4 weeks. In the event that full payment is not received by that time, the evaluation process will be halted and will not be continued until all fees are paid. In the rare event that I spend significantly more time than anticipated, I will inform you of any further charges.

My fee does not include court appearances or depositions. If either party wishes me to testify, I require a subpoena for court testimony or deposition. My fee for court appearances or deposition is $XXXXX per half day (or less) or $XXXXX per full day. This includes my driving time and preparation. I require payment for such appearances at least one week before the court date or deposition. All fees are the responsibility of the party issuing the subpoena. My standard evaluation fee does include being available on phone standby for the court at Recommendation Conferences, provided I can arrange to make the time available.

At least twenty-four hours notice is required to cancel or reschedule an appointment without being charged. Without twenty-four hours notice, the parent who misses the appointment may be billed an additional $XXXXX per appointment hour. If both parents miss a joint appointment, each will be billed for half of the scheduled time. Excessive missed appointments can result in termination of the evaluation with notification to the court of what portion of the evaluation has been completed.

Recommendations

On my custody evaluation form, I will ask each of you how you would suggest settling your dispute with the other parent. It is possible that I might agree with you when I have completed my evaluation. It is also possible that I may disagree with you and recommend something closer to what the other parent wants. Please be aware that whatever I recommend, it will always be based on my analysis of all of the evaluation data and what I believe to be in your children's best interests.

At the end of the evaluation process, I may meet with the parents together to share the findings of my evaluation and my recommendations to the Court. The purpose of this session is to share and explain my observations and recommendations so that you can understand them and hopefully find a way to settle your conflicts. This meeting is not designed to have parents criticize each other or my findings. I do not meet with parents individually to share this information prior to the report being sent. After that meeting, I will then send my written report to the court, to Family Court Services, and to the attorneys. Parents in pro per can make an appointment at Family Court Services to review the complete report.

Settlement Prior to Conclusion or Early Termination of Evaluation

If at any time during the course of the evaluation parents settle their custody or visitation dispute on their own, or jointly agree, with the court's consent to the early termination of the evaluation, it will be discontinued, and the court will be so notified. If I have been paid a fee that exceeds the time I have spent (billed at $XXXXX per hour), I will refund any amount due at the end of the month following my receipt of a written statement that the evaluation has been halted. If at any point in the future either parent wishes to resume the evaluation process, a new evaluation will need to be ordered and new fees will need to be paid.

Consent

By my signature below, I acknowledge that I have read and understand all of the terms within this contract and agree to abide it. I authorize Dr. Smith to complete the evaluation and provide recommendations to the court.

Signed: Date:

Witness: Date:

Please Make a Copy of this Informed Consent Contract for your Own Records!

10.   REFERENCES

Ackerman, M. J. & Ackerman, M. C. (1997). Custody Evaluation Practices: a Survey of Experienced Professionals (Revisited). *Professional Psychology: Research and Practice, 28,* 137-145.

American Psychological Association. (1992). *Ethical Principles of Psychologists and Code of Conduct.* Washington, D.C.

American Psychological Association (1994). Guidelines for Child Custody Evaluations in Divorce Proceedings. *American Psychologist, 49.*

Association of Family & Conciliation Courts (1994). *Model Standards of Practice for Child Custody Evaluations.* Madison, WI: Author.

Bray, J. (1991). Psychosocial factors affecting custodial and visitation agreements. *Behavioral Sciences & the Law. 9,* (4), 419-437.

California, State of (1999). Rule 1257.3. Sacramento, CA: Author.

Emery, R. (1999). *Marriage, Divorce, and Children's Adjustment,* 2nd Edition. Thousand Oaks: Sage Publications.

Galatzer-Levy, R. & Kraus, L. (Eds.). (1999). *The Scientific Basis of Child Custody Decisions.* New York: John Wiley & Sons.

Garrity, C. & Baris, M. (1994). *Caught in the Middle.* New York: Lexington Books.

Gindes, M. (1998). The psychological effects of relocation for children of divorce. *Journal of the American Academy of Matrimonial Lawyers, 15,* (1), 119-148.

Gould, J. (1998*). Conducting Scientifically Crafted Child Custody Evaluations.* Thousand Oaks, CA: Sage Publications.

Gould, J. & Stahl, P. (2000). The Art and Science of Child Custody Evaluations: Integrating Clinical and Forensic Mental Health Models. *Family & Conciliation Courts Review. 38,* (3).

Johnston, J. (1994). High-Conflict Divorce. *The Future of Children, 4,* (1), 165-182.

Johnston, J. & Roseby, V. (1997). *In the Name of the Child.* New York: Free Press.

Kelly, J. (1994). The determination of child custody. *In The Future of Children: Children & Divorce.* The David and Lucille Packard Foundation, 300 Second Street, Los Altos, CA 94022.

Kelly, J. & Lamb, M. (2000). Using child development research to make appropriate custody and access decisions for young children. *Family & Conciliation Courts Review. 38,* (3), 297-311.

Lamb, M. (1997a). *The Role of the Father in Child Development, 3rd Edition.* New York: John Wiley.

Lamb., M., Sternberg, K., & Thompson, R. (1997b). The Effects of Divorce and Custody Arrangements on Children's Behavior, Development, and Adjustment. *Family & Conciliation Courts Review. 35,* (4), 393-404.

Maccoby, E. E., & Mnookin, R. H. (1992). *Dividing The Child: Social And Legal Dimensions of Child Custody.* Cambridge, MA: Harvard University Press.

Melton, G. B., Petrila, J., Poythress, N. G., & Slobogin, C. (1997). *Psychological evaluations for the courts: A handbook for attorneys and mental health professionals* (2nd ed.). New York: Guildford.

Millon, T. (1996). *Disorders of Personality: DSM-IV and Beyond.* New York: Wiley-Interscience.

Otto, R. & Collins, R. (1995). Use of the MMPI-2/MMPI-A in child custody evaluations. In Y. Ben-Porath, J. Graham, G. Hall, R. Hirschman, & M. Zaragoza (Eds.), *Forensic Applications of the MMPI-2.* (pg. 222-252). Thousand Oaks, CA.: Sage Publications.

Otto, R. Edens, J., & Barcus, E. The use of psychological testing in child custody evaluations. *Family & Conciliation Courts Review. 38* (3), 312-340.

Shear, L. (1996). Life Stories, Doctrines, and Decision Making: Three High Courts Confront the Move-away Dilemma. *Family & Conciliation Courts Review. 34,* (4), 439-458.

Stahl, P. (1994). *Conducting Child Custody Evaluations.* Thousand Oaks, CA: Sage Publications.

Stahl, P. (1999). *Complex Issues in Child Custody Evaluations.* Thousand Oaks, CA: Sage Publications.

Stahl, P. (2000). *Parenting After Divorce.* Atascadero, CA: Impact Publishers.

Warshak, R. (1999). *Parental Alienation Syndrome in Court.* Monograph. Author.

Warshak, R. (1999). *Social Science and Children's Best Interests in Relocation Cases: Burgess Revisited.* Monograph. Author.

Warshak, R. (2000). Blanket Restrictions: Overnight Contact Between Parents and Young Children. *Family & Conciliation Courts Review. 38* (4), 422-445.

Chapter 9

Child Abuse

Seth Kalichman, Ph.D.
Department of Psychology, University of Connecticut, Storrs, CT

1.   INTRODUCTION

Each year millions of children in the United States are abused and neglected. There is a long-standing trend toward increased child abuse, although recent years have seen a stabilization in the numbers of child abuse reports (Wang & Daro, 1998). Exhibit 1 summarizes recent statistics regarding the prevalence and characteristics of child abuse. Cases of abuse that were confirmed by child protective service investigations involve neglect, physical abuse, sexual abuse, and emotional maltreatment, with additional cases representing other forms of abuse. Child fatalities resulting from abuse and neglect increased more than 85% between 1985 and 1996 (Wang & Daro, 1992), and the most common cause of death in childhood is trauma; head injuries are the most common cause of trauma-related infant death (Duhaime, Christian, Rorke, & Zimmerman, 1998). The magnitude of even these statistics is dwarfed by estimates of unreported and undocumented cases of child abuse (Maney & Wells, 1988). For example, community-based incidence studies estimate that reported child abuse constitutes only about 40% of all actual cases (U.S. Department of Health and Human Services, 1988). The prevalence of child abuse, along with reductions in child protection services, brought the U.S. Advisory Board on Child Abuse and Neglect (1990), to declare child maltreatment a national emergency. Given the intersection between child abuse and the law, forensic psychologists are likely to encounter abused children and abusive adults. Forensic psychologists often play critical roles in evaluating and assisting in cases of child abuse and neglect. This chapter reviews three primary areas in which forensic psychologists become involved in cases of child abuse: (a) assessing children and adults involved in cases of known abuse and suspected abuse; (b) identifying potentially abused children and abusive adults in forensic practice; and (c) the interaction between forensic psychologists and child protection systems.

2.   ASSESSMENT AND DETECTION OF CHILD ABUSE

Psychological evaluations, such as evaluations conducted in forensic work; offer important information in the assessment of abuse. Subtle indicators of child abuse are easily missed when professionals are unfamiliar with the signs and symptoms of abuse as they present themselves at different periods of child development. Psychologists with limited experience in child abuse and childhood trauma may not recognize emotional responses or child behaviors as signs of abuse. Less than obvious signs of abuse can be confused with trauma unrelated to abuse, such as parental conflict and family strife. Evaluators, who are unfamiliar with the clinical dimensions of child abuse, neglect, and family constellations associated with child abuse, are unlikely to differentiate the sequele of abuse from other sources of child behavior problems. Forensic psychologists with specialized training in child abuse and neglect can therefore make substantial contributions to the evaluation of children and adults involved in abuse cases.

Psychologists need to know what to look for in identifying child abuse, especially when conducting evaluations, and they require specialized training in methods for critically examining their suspicions of abuse. For example, interviewing techniques can guide professionals to follow up on hunches and suspicions within the context of a clinical evaluation. Drawings and interactive play can facilitate young children's expression of trauma and can serve as an important vehicle in evaluating potential abuse (Wiehe, 1992). Techniques for interviewing children, adults, and families must be sensitive to variations in culture, gender, and development. For example, it is not uncommon for normative child rearing practices in unfamiliar cultures such as family boundaries and degrees of physical discipline, to be misinterpreted as abuse (Grey & Crosgrove, 1985).

Clinical evaluations rely more on interpersonal interviews in assessing cases of suspected child abuse than they do standardized tests, perhaps because many instruments lack reliability and validity (Levy, 1989; Mantell, 1988; Walker et al., 1988). One standardized assessment instrument developed for child abuse evaluation is the anatomically detailed doll interview. Although using dolls as an assessment technique is controversial, studies suggest that standardized anatomically detailed doll interviews demonstrate acceptable reliability and validity (Walker, 1988; White, Strom, Santilli, & Halpin, 1986). However, when administered outside of standardized procedures or without sufficient training, the findings from doll interviews are highly suspect. Therefore, evaluators who administer anatomically detailed doll interviews must be competent and experienced, or the practice could be considered unethical. Wolfner, Faust and Dawes (1993), reviewed research on the use of anatomically detailed dolls in assessing child sexual abuse and concluded that: (a) anatomically detailed doll interviews do not elicit a greater base-rate of sexualized play among children who have not been abused; (b) sexualized doll play appears more frequent in abused than non-abused children; (c) it is unknown whether the use of anatomically detailed dolls increases the validity of child sexual abuse assessments or investigations; and (d) there is no scientific evidence to support the use of anatomical doll play for diagnosing sexual abuse. This lack of solid evidence in support of anatomically detailed doll interviews can discredit an entire evaluation under scrutiny and therefore cautions against their use in evaluating cases of sexual abuse.

While there are few valid standardized assessment instruments for children, there are several useful models available for conceptualizing and organizing information gathered from interviews. For example, Walker et al. (1988), developed a framework for organizing potential risk factors associated with physical and sexual abuse based on identifiable characteristics of abusers, victims, family members, and social-situational factors. Similarly, Sgroi, Porter, and Blick (1982), constructed a conceptual framework for validating child sexual abuse. Sgroi et al.'s model incorporates behavioral characteristics of sexually abused children and physical symptoms of sexual abuse, both of which are evaluated within a developmental context. Recognizing child abuse also requires developing a framework for interpreting subtle signs of abuse given that most behaviors and emotional reactions carry different meaning at different developmental periods (Kendall-Tackett, Williams, & Finkelhor, 1993). The value of empirically derived models is that they serve as a structure for professionals to organize their clinical observations.

There are also advances in standardized behavioral checklists for recording information about children and adults. Friedrich et al. (1991, 1992), developed one promising assessment tool for sexual abuse, the Child Sexual Behavior Inventory (CSBI). This assessment instrument consists of

35 items representing a range of child behaviors including sexual self-stimulation, sexual aggression, gender-role behaviors, and personal boundary violations. Each of the behavioral indicators is rated on a 4-point scale by a parent or caregiver. The instrument is modeled after the Child Behavior Checklist (Achenbach & Edelbrock, 1983), and has demonstrated sound measurement properties of reliability and validity. A strength of the CSBI in evaluating child sexual abuse is its empirical basis for identifying behaviors related to child sexual abuse. However, because a caregiver completes the measure it may have limited use in cases of intrafamilial sexual abuse and with parents who minimize or exaggerate child behavior problems.

With respect to assessing adults suspected of abuse, Milner (1989, 1990, 1991; Milner, Gold, & Wimberley, 1986), has developed the Child Abuse Potential Inventory (CAP), a standardized and objective test for screening abusive, or potentially abusive, adults. The CAP consists of 160 items that are responded to on an agree-disagree format. Items are grouped on a number of subscales, including several that serve as indicators of a propensity for child abuse; parental rigidity, unhappiness, distress, and family problems. While the CAP has shown great promise, it was not developed to definitively diagnose abusiveness and should be considered as only one piece of information collected in a more comprehensive assessment battery for evaluating child abuse.

2.1   Interview Techniques

The cornerstone of the forensic evaluation of child abuse is the interview with the child. Although a complete discussion of interviewing children suspected of being abused is beyond the scope of this chapter (see Ceci & Bruck, 1995; Poole & Lamb, 1998), the central issues in conducting child interviews in cases of suspected abuse will be briefly highlighted. Few areas of clinical evaluation are as controversial as the accuracy and reliability of children's recall and accounting of past events. Of particular contention have been questions of how much influence adults may have in shaping children's memories, particularly in terms of memories of abuse. Research shows that detailed clinical interviews and investigative questioning can strongly alter the perceptions and reported memories of young children. Child suggestibility research also shows that young children's memories are somewhat easily manipulated by even the subtlest suggestions (Ceci & Bruck, 1995; Ceci, Loftus, Leichtman, & Bruck, 1994). For example, asking children what happens when a parent is angry may elicit different responses than asking whether a parent gets angry. Even slight changes in wording or alterations in the environment create social pressures that can bias children's memories and descriptions of events (Goodman, Bottoms, Schwartz-Kenny, & Rudy, 1991). Thus, forensic evaluators who lack specialized training in interviewing abused children should be aware that a poorly conducted interview not only yields misinformation, it can also bias responses to later interviews conducted by other interviewers.

Another significant issue in interviewing is the child's developmental level and its implications for a child's ability to interpret questions and provide reliable answers. Cognitive development determines much of what is learned from interviews conducted with children. The quality of information yielded from a child interview depends on the child's cognitive skills, including attention, memory, conversational descriptions of memories, understanding of the distinction between truth and lies, and distinguishing fantasy from reality (Melton et al., 1995; Poole & Lamb, 1998). A factor that influences much of what comes from forensic assessments of child abuse is the family context in which the abuse is suspected. Evaluating potential abuse occurring in the context of a child custody dispute poses some of the greatest challenges. Psychological evaluators must sort through the emotional distress that children experience as part of significant family conflict and separation from at least one parent. There may also be motives for false allegations in custody cases that do not otherwise exist. On the other hand, custody battles can be used as means for abusers to deny allegations of abuse; claiming motives for false allegations. The most complex cases will involve younger children who are more vulnerable to suggestion under circumstances that can manipulate their responses, especially under the duress of a custody dispute.

Walker and Nguyen (1996), discussed guidelines for interviewing child witnesses that may be applied to interviewing abused children. Evaluators should prepare for the interview, create an appropriate environment and climate for the interview, and frame all questions and interview content in developmentally appropriate language and concepts. More specifically, interviewers are suggested to use an active voice to keep the child's attention, avoid negatives, such as "is it not true...", using simple words, and including only one query within a question. Walker and Nguyen also emphasized the importance of establishing rapport, explaining what can be expected in the interview, and engaging the child in the interview process. Without careful attention to the needs and characteristics of children, child interviews may do more harm than good in detecting abuse and protecting children.

3. REPORTING SUSPECTED CHILD ABUSE

Forensic psychologists who, in the course of their work, encounter situations that raise reasonable suspicions of child abuse or neglect are typically required to report their suspicions to child protective services. It is well documented that mental health professionals of all specialties experience conflicts in managing cases of child abuse - particularly with respect to reporting suspected abuse (Brosig, & Kalichman, 1992; Kalichman, Craig, & Follingstad, 1992). Given the nature of forensic work, evaluators of persons prone to violence, and families under significant stress are particularly likely to encounter abusive situations. Forensic psychologists should therefore establish procedures for managing suspicions of abuse and the actions they will perform as mandated reporters.

3.1 The Child Protection System

Child protection is a relatively recent social concept. Until the nineteenth century there was little interest in, and had no policies for protecting children. Although the child welfare movement originated in 1875 with the advent of the New York Society for the Prevention of Cruelty to Children, it was not until the early part of the twentieth century that child protective services were instituted in the United States (Kalichman, 1999; M. Levine & A. Levine, 1992). Child welfare legislation first focused on willful neglect or failure to provide adequate childcare. Since the advent of the child welfare system, any citizen may report known or suspected child abuse to child protection authorities, however, mandatory reporting laws have emerged that require professionals who serve children and families to report suspected child abuse. Psychologists who provide evaluation services are among the numerous human service professionals who are required to report suspected abuse.

Increased public awareness of child abuse and the liberal social climate of the 1960's set child protection policies in motion (National Center on Child Abuse and Neglect, NCCAN, 1979). However, the catalyst for the first child abuse reporting laws was establishing a formal medical profile for abused children. Pediatricians and other physicians published a series of clinical reports describing victims of abuse, and there was an early symposium held by the American Academy of Pediatrics dedicated to describing the ailments of battered children. Indeed, as early as 1946, Caffey described combinations of injuries in infants that suggested abuse. These first clinical reports formed much of the groundwork for defining child abuse as a medical problem (for a review see McCoid, 1965). Kempe, Silverman, Steele, Droegenmueller, and Silver (1962), formally described the battered child syndrome and published the single most influential report on child maltreatment. As a new medical diagnosis, the battered child syndrome was characterized by "injury to soft tissue and skeleton" (p. 105), and accompanied by "evidence of neglect including poor skin hygiene, multiple soft tissue injuries, and malnutrition" (p. 105-106). These authors also provided detailed radiological features and clinical manifestations that were often discrepant with available information from case histories alone. Thus, several specific features, most of which were relevant to the physical and radiological examination of children, objectively defined the battered child syndrome.

In addition to detailed descriptions of the trauma that characterizes the battered child syndrome, Kempe et al. (1962), made reference to the condition being "inadequately handled by the physician because of hesitation to bring the case to the attention of the proper authorities" (p. 105). These authors speculated that reluctance among physicians to report suspicious injuries was due to their unwillingness to consider parents' as the source of such harm. Further, they stated that characteristics of physician "training and personality usually makes it quite difficult for him (her) to assume the role of policeman or district attorney, and start questioning patients as if he (she) were investigating a crime" (p. 107). Kempe et al. noted that some physicians would ignore any suspicions of abuse despite "obvious circumstantial evidence" (p. 107). Therefore, an agenda was put in motion to establish mandatory reporting laws and much of what these pioneering researchers wrote is reflected in contemporary child abuse reporting statutes.

Legislative changes subsequently broadened most aspects of early mandatory reporting statutes, including the range of professionals and types of maltreatment meeting legal standards for required reporting. In the late 1960's and early 1970's, several groups of professionals were added to the list of mandated reporters. Definitions of abuse were also broadened to include emotional and nutritional maltreatment (Giovannoni, 1989), as well as sexual abuse and exploitation. Most states dropped the term 'serious' as a qualifier of the injuries or harm stated in definitions of abuse. The Child Abuse Prevention and Treatment Act of 1974 defined child abuse and neglect and set the standard for state mandatory reporting laws. The Act defined abuse and neglect as: "The physical or mental injury, sexual abuse, negligent treatment, or maltreatment of a child under the age of 18 by a person who is responsible for the child's welfare under circumstances which indicate the child's health or welfare is harmed or threatened thereby as determined in accordance with regulations prescribed..." (Child Abuse

Prevention and Treatment Act of 1974, Section 3). States are required to adopt similar definitions of abuse in order to qualify for federal child protection funds (Daro & McCurdy, 1992; Wells, Stein, Fluke, & Downing, 1989).

States have also broadened and expanded their own reporting laws, with California amending its reporting statute more than 15 times in the 20 years following its passage (Meriwether, 1986). The expansion of reporting laws has not, unfortunately, taken into account the diversity of professionals who were added to the roster of mandated reporters. Because the battered child syndrome originally described cases that were most likely seen by emergency room physicians, radiologists, and pediatricians, first generation reporting statutes understandably targeted medical professionals. When reporting laws were expanded to include non-medical professionals, there was also an expansion of definitions of abuse and conditions under which reporting was required. But reporting laws do not differentiate between mandated reporters who differ in their professional training, circumstances of practice, and conditions under which suspicions of maltreatment arise.

Because reporting laws are blind to particular circumstances, their uniform application has often been criticized (Ansell & Ross, 1990; Berlin, Main, & Dean, 1991; Bollas & Sundelson, 1995). With few exceptions, reporting statutes place limits on confidentiality and privileged communications. Forensic psychologists hired by attorneys must be aware of any limits that attorney-client privileges place on their requirements to report suspected abuse. Professional discretion and judgment are rarely given consideration in reporting requirements. As a result, laws that require reporting suspected child abuse and neglect in professional contexts often conflict with basic professional values and ethical principles. Professional conflicts in turn interfere with adherence to mandatory reporting laws, creating situations where professionals do not follow the law and therefore, by definition, breach professional ethics.

Mandatory reporting laws hold professionals responsible for alerting authorities about potential abuse on the premise that maltreated children are too young, too frightened, and too vulnerable to seek their own assistance. There are three objectives that reporting laws assert to achieve: (a) expedite the identification of abused children by the child protection system; (b) designate agencies to receive, investigate, and manage cases of child maltreatment; and (c) provide protective services to prevent further abuse and to help preserve family unity and welfare (NCCAN, 1979). These objectives are consistent with the spirit of all human services, including the duties and activities of forensic psychologists.

4.   CHILD ABUSE INVESTIGATIONS

Forensic psychologists may interface with child protective investigations in their roles as evaluators in child abuse cases as well as their roles as reporters of suspected abuse. Reports that are accepted by child protection agencies proceed through the child protection system, usually involving a series of actions required by state law. Specific interventions vary with local agencies. The roles of law enforcement agencies in child abuse investigations also vary across community standards. Some states require law enforcement officers be notified upon receipt of a report, while others require law enforcement involvement only when reported abuse is substantiated. Still other states immediately involve police only in certain types or conditions of abuse. For example, states can require immediate law enforcement notification and a joint investigation with child protection workers for reports of sexual abuse only. When law enforcement officers are involved, it is the child protection agency's responsibility to make these collateral contacts.

Child protection investigations typically involve home visits by caseworkers who interview the parents, child, and alleged perpetrator. Individuals included in the report, such as children, parents, and siblings are also usually interviewed. Not obtaining interviews from persons included in the report is often officially acceptable assuming repeated failed attempts to contact these persons. In addition, teachers, school administrators, family members, neighbors, and others may be interviewed as a part of the investigation. Child abuse investigative interviews usually solicit information to answer specific questions regarding the alleged abuse. Investigation procedures are typically idiosyncratic to the circumstances of the report, the local agency procedures, and the individual style of the assigned worker. Investigations are conducted to determine the child's condition and potential risk for injury or harm. The purpose of the investigation is therefore one of fact-finding for evidence of maltreatment to determine a child's risk for abuse. However, child abuse investigations do have common purposes and goals that can serve as frameworks for procedures.

Child abuse investigations serve two purposes: (a) criminal investigation - to evaluate the extent of harm and danger posed to a child; and (b) social service - to protect children and predict whether or not a child will be maltreated in the future. Risk assessments involve comprehensive examinations of the child's well being, family resources, and living conditions (Pecora, 1991). Although a brief assessment of risk for abuse is conducted during an initial intake, risk assessments are considered an ongoing process and involve more elaborate methods introduced during the course of the investigation. One common method used by investigation agencies involves rating child and family characteristics along several dimensions of potential risk. Factors assessed in a risk assessment include parenting skills, frequency and severity of abuse, the perpetrator's accessibility to the child, the child's ability for self-protection, and the recency of abuse. Each factor may be rated as low, moderate, or high level of risk (Pecora, 1991; Wisconsin Department of Health and Social Services, 1985). A matrix is constructed to comprehensively represent levels of risk for each assessed factor. Risk factors included in the risk assessment may consist of constellations of associated factors or may emphasize empirically defined predictors of child abuse (Pecora, 1991).

In addition to assessments that tabulate risk factors, matrices have been developed to assess family strengths and resources. Family assets and strengths provide valuable information for long-term predictions of abuse that may not be readily apparent to field workers who might otherwise be focused on identifying problems. In addition, family resiliency can be overlooked when working with families from unfamiliar cultural backgrounds (Caldwell et al., 1992). Family strengths and resiliency can form a context within which risk factors are embedded, allowing for more comprehensive determinations of abuse and service needs. The majority of state child protection agencies have adopted an instrument to facilitate systematic evaluations of children and families (Berkowitz, 1991).

The goals of child protection investigations are to assess children's risks and to determine the occurrence or non-occurrence of child abuse. Local child protection agencies vary in their definitions and criteria for substantiating child abuse. In almost all systems there are, however, three potential outcomes from a child abuse investigation: (a) *Not able to substantiate/inconclusive*: Maltreatment is not determined given the availability of factual information, as is the case when the child or parents cannot be located for investigative interview; (b) *Unsubstantiated*: insufficient information exists to pursue charges of child abuse (Weissman, 1991). Here, abuse and neglect are not found and the family is not in need of protective services. However, children, adults, and families may be experiencing problems uncovered in the investigation and are therefore referred to outside services; (c) *Substantiated*: abuse or neglect is confirmed and activating child protective services may be appropriate. Investigation may also have found that individuals or families require intervention. Assuming adequate resources, substantiated abuse triggers some form of intervention - ranging from a referral for services to placing the child in protective care.

Almost half of all reports of child abuse are substantiated upon investigation. Substantiation rates for reports filed by mandated reporters are, however, as much as 23% higher for physical abuse and 13% higher for sexual abuse when compared to reports filed by non-mandated reporters (Eckenrode, Powers, et al., 1988; Eckenrode, Munsch, Powers, & Doris, 1988). Not all families with substantiated abuse, however, receive services. In fact, resources for social services have decreased at the same time that reports have increased. Some studies show that nearly half of confirmed cases of child abuse receive social service intervention (Meddin & Hansen, 1985; Salovitz & Keys, 1988). Nationally, about 30% of confirmed cases of child abuse are receiving some type of services (Wang and Daro, 1997). Although over 1 million children were being served in 1994, this number shrank from 1.8 million in 1977. Similar reductions in services are observed for children receiving in-home services, foster care, and other types of child welfare. For families that do receive services, the most common assistance involves preventive, protective, and support services (Wang & Daro, 1997).

Unsubstantiated reports filed by professionals may reflect the narrowing of standards between criteria for reporting suspected child abuse and criteria for substantiating abuse. For example, definitions of abuse are far narrower for substantiating abuse than the reasonable suspicion of abuse required for reporting (Giovannoni, 1989). The intent of mandatory reporting laws is to detect a maximum number of cases of child abuse. Therefore greater sensitivity to detect abuse is invoked in reporting (e.g., reasonable suspicion), compared with the increased burden of proof for substantiation (e.g., preponderance of evidence), which is less restrictive than the standard for convicting in a criminal case (e.g., beyond reasonable doubt).

Incomplete information and vagueness often characterize unsubstantiated reports of abuse. Reports with less detailed information are less likely to proceed through each step of the child protection system (Wells, et al., 1989). Unsubstantiated cases do not necessarily mean that abuse has not occurred, but rather that the preponderance of evidence resulting from the investigation does not meet the standards required for substantiation. Criteria set by the child protection system, therefore, result in a higher threshold for intervention, accepting that some cases of abuse will go undetected. The logic behind the system as a whole follows that the reporting system accepts higher rates of *false positives* - cases where abuse may not be occurring, in balance against higher rates of *false negatives* - cases where abuse is occurring but not substantiated. The result is that there will invariably be more reports made by professionals than there are investigations and more investigations of abuse than there are substantiated cases (Kalichman, 1999).

One reason for higher substantiation rates among reports filed by mandated reporters is that human service professionals obtain detailed and specific information regarding child abuse. Medical professionals, for example, are likely to observe symptoms consistent with non-accidental injuries and these observations are expected to raise suspicions of child abuse. Likewise, mental health professionals frequently observe emotional and behavioral changes in children that raise suspicions of child abuse. Psychologists, guidance counselors, schoolteachers, and other professionals who develop trusting relationships with children are also likely to learn about the lives of children, which can include abuse. However, every instance of suspected child abuse does not constitute a *reasonable suspicion*, and therefore may not warrant reporting. To help resolve ambiguous cases, mandated reporters, including psychologists, should consult their colleagues for an outside perspective. Professionals may also contact child protection workers to informally ask questions about specific cases. Child protection workers will often share their impressions of whether or not the circumstances warrant reporting. Taking such steps can help professionals report cases with greater confidence as well as avoid reporting cases that child protective services deems as inappropriate at initial glance and therefore avoid cluttering an already over-burdened system.

5.   SUMMARY

   Forensic psychology intersects with the sources and sequele of many social problems, including child abuse and neglect. Forensic psychologists are likely called upon to assist in the determination of child abuse, the examination of abusive adults, and the formulation of interventions to stop abuse. Forensic work will also expose psychologists to cases in which they suspect abuse, triggering their role as mandated reporters. Although some forensic psychologists will specialize in child abuse, most will merely encounter abuse in the course of their larger practice. Kalichman (1999), provides guidelines for managing clinical decisions in cases of child abuse. The six guidelines presented below are adapted for forensic practice.

1. **Psychologists should have current and accurate knowledge of their state mandatory reporting laws**. Forensic psychologists should be familiar with how their state defines child abuse and neglect, the conditions under which reporting is required, time constraints, and procedures for filing verbal and written reports. Managing reporting requirements as an evaluator in criminal and civil cases, including the implications of attorney-client privilege, will vary from state-to-state and requires reference to current state laws.

2. **Informed consent procedures should be used to clearly demarcate the conditions under which confidentiality is limited.** Clients should be provided with informed consent that includes the limits of confidentiality at the outset of a professional relationship. Procedures for informing persons of limited confidentiality can be delivered in writing, verbally, or preferably both.

3. **Parents and guardians should be informed before reporting, unless doing so endangers children.** The negative effects that reporting can have on professional relationships are minimized when the report is placed in the context of a therapeutic relationship. Professionals who believe that informing parents of a report could endanger children should definitely include these concerns in their report.

4. **When reporting, always document information released in a report.** Records of oral reports as well as copies of written reports are an essential part of reporting. In addition, subsequent contact with the child protection system, the police, or anyone else regarding the reported abuse should be documented.

5. **Professionals should follow up reports with the child protection system.** Information about the screening, outcome, investigation, and status of a report can be requested from child protection workers. Contact with case workers can occur from the time the report is filed until the case is closed.

6. **Suspected child abuse that psychologists are unsure about reporting should be discussed with a colleague or a child protection worker.** Professionals who state that they consistently report suspected child abuse are also the most likely to discuss cases of suspected child abuse with colleagues. Discussing dilemmas and ambiguities of cases is a recommended ethical practice and can be among the most effective safe guards in clinical practice.

Exhibit 1

Summary of Recent Child Abuse Prevalence and Characteristics of Abuse

Characteristics of Victims

Victims of maltreatment are defined as children who are found to have experienced or be at risk of experiencing a substantiated or indicated maltreatment.

There were an estimated 903,000 victims of maltreatment nationwide*. The 1998 rate of victimization was 12.9 per 1,000 children, a decrease from the 1997 rate of 13.9 per 1,000.

More than half of all victims (53.5%) suffered neglect, while almost a quarter (22.7%) suffered physical abuse. Nearly 12 percent of the victims (11.5%) were sexually abused. Victims of psychological abuse and medical neglect accounted for 6 percent or fewer each. In addition, a quarter of victims (25.3%) were reported to be victims of more than one type of maltreatment.

The highest victimization{ XE "victimization-child abuse" } rates were for the 0-3 age group (14.8 maltreatments per 1,000 children of this age in the population), and rates declined as age increased.

Victimization rates by race/ethnicity ranged from a low of 3.8 Asian/Pacific Islander victims per 1,000 children of the same race in the population to 20.7 African-American victims per 1,000 children of the same race in the population. The victimization rate for American Indians/Alaska Natives was 19.8, for Hispanics 10.6 and for Caucasian 8.5.

Exhibit 1 Continued

**Summary of Recent Child Abuse Prevalence and Characteristics
of Abuse**

Characteristics of Perpetrators.

A perpetrator of child abuse and/or neglect is a person who has
maltreated a child while in a care taking relationship to the child.
Three-fifths (60.4%) of perpetrators were female. Female perpetrators
were typically younger than their male counterparts, as reflected by
the difference in their respective median ages, 31 and 34.

More than four-fifths (87.1%) of all victims were maltreated by one or
both parents. The most common pattern of maltreatment was a child
neglected by a female parent with no other perpetrators identified
(44.7%).
Victims of physical and sexual abuse, compared to victims of neglect
and medical neglect, were more likely to be maltreated by a male
parent acting alone. In cases of sexual abuse, more than half of
victims (55.9%) were abused by male parents, male relatives, or other
males.

Exhibit 1 Continued

Summary of Recent Child Abuse Prevalence and Characteristics
of Abuse

Child Abuse Fatalities

Child fatality estimates are based primarily on fatalities of abuse and neglect victims known to CPS agencies and fatalities not previously reported as abused or neglected.

An estimated 1,100 children died of abuse and neglect, a rate of approximately 1.6 deaths per 100,000 children in the general populations.*

Children not yet a year old accounted for 37.9 percent of the fatalities, and 77.5 percent were not yet 5 years of age.

Perpetrators of fatalities were considerably younger than perpetrators in
general. Nearly two-thirds (62.3%) were younger than 30 years of age, compared to the percentage of all perpetrators who were younger than 30 (38.7%).

Source: U.S. Department of Health and Human Services. Child Maltreatment 1998: Reports from the States to t
The National Child Abuse and Neglect Data System. (Washington, DC: U.S. Government Printing Office, 2000).

6.   REFERENCES

Achenbach, T.M., & Edelbrock, C. (1983). *Manual for the Child Behavior Checklist and revised Child Behavior Profile.* Burlington, VT: University of Vermont.

Ansell, C., & Ross, H. (1990). Reply to Pope and Bajt. *American Psychologist, 45,* 399.

Berkowitz, S. (1991). *Key findings from the state survey component of the study of high risk child abuse and neglect groups.* Rockville, MD: Westat.

Berlin, F., Malin, H., & Dean, S. (1991). Effects of statutes requiring psychiatrists to report suspected sexual abuse of children. American Journal of Psychiatry, 148, 449-453.

Bollas, C. & Sundelson, D. (1995). *The new informants: The betrayal of confidentiality in psychoanalysis and psychotherapy.* Northvale, NJ: Aronson.

Brosig, C.L., & Kalichman, S. (1992). Clinicians' reporting of suspected child abuse: A review of the empirical literature. *Clinical Psychology Review, 12*, 155-168.

Caffey, J. (1946). Multiple fractures in the long bones of infants suffering from chronic subdural hematoma. *American Journal of Roentgenology, 56*, 163-173.

Caldwell, S., English, D., Foote, A., Hodges, V., Nguyen, Q., Pecora, P.J., Pien, D., Stallings, Z., Tong, C., et al. (1992). *An approach to strength and risk assessment with multicultural guidelines.* Available from Peter J. Pecora, School of Social Work, JH-30, University of Washington, 4101 15th Street NE, Seattle, WA 98195.

Ceci, S. L. & Buck, M. (1995). *Jeopardy in the court: A scientific analysis of children's testimony.* Washington, D.C.: American Psychological Association.

Ceci, S.J., Loftus, E.F., Leicvhtman, M., & Buck, M. (1994). The role of source misattributions in the creation of false beliefs among preschoolers. *International Journal of Clinical and Experimental Hypnosis, 62*, 304-320.

Child Abuse Prevention and Treatment Act of 1974, 42 U.S.C., Supp. III 1985.

Daro, D., & McCurdy, K. (1992). *Current Trends in Child Abuse Reporting and Fatalities: The Results of the 1991 Annual Fifty State Survey.* Available from the National Committee for the Prevention of Child Abuse, 332 S. Michigan Ave., Suite 1600, Chicago, IL, 60604.

Duhaime, A.C., Christian, C.W., Rorke, L.B., & Zimmerman, R.A. (1998). Nonaccidental head injury in infants: The "shaken-baby syndrome". *New England Journal of Medicine, 338*, 1822-1829.

Eckenrode, J., Munsch, J., Powers, J., & Doris, J. (1988). The nature and substantiation of official sexual abuse reports. *Child Abuse and Neglect, 12*, 311-319.

Eckenrode, J., Powers, J., Doris, J., Munsch, J., & Bolger, N. (1988). Substantiation of child abuse and neglect reports. *Journal of Consulting and Clinical Psychology, 56*, 9-16.

Friedrich, W.N., Grambsch, P., Broughton, D., Kuiper, J., & Beilke, R.L. (1991). Normative sexual behavior in children. *Pediatrics, 88*, 456-464.

Friedrich, W.N., Grambsch, P., Damon, L., Hewitt, S., Koverola, C., Lang, R.A., Wolfe, V., & Broughton, D. (1992). Child Sexual Abuse Inventory: Normative and Clinical Comparisons. *Psychological Assessment, 4*, 303-311.

Giovannoni, J. (1989b). Definitional issues in child maltreatment. In D. Ciccetti & V. Carlson (Eds.), *Child Maltreatment.* New York: Cambridge University Press.

Goodman, , G.S., Bottoms, B.L., Schwartz-Kenny, B.M., & Rudy, L. (1991). Children's testimony about a stressful event: Improving children's reports. *Journal of Narrative and Life History, 1*, 69-99.

Grey, E., & Crosgrove, J. (1985). Ethnocentric perception of child rearing practices in protective services. *Child Abuse and Neglect, 9*, 389-396.

Kalichman, S.C. (1999). Mandated Reporting of Suspected Child Abuse: *Ethics, Law, and Policy* [2nd Ed.]. Washington, D.C.: American Psychological Association.

Kalichman, S.C., Craig, M.E., & Follingstad, D. (1992). Mental health professionals' treatment of child abuse: Why professionals may not report. In E. Viano (Ed.) *Critical issues in victimology.* New York: Springer.

Kempe, C., Silverman, F., Steele, B., Droegemueller, W., & Silver, H. (1962). The battered child syndrome. *Journal of the American Medical Association, 181*, 4-11.

Kendall-Tackett, K.A., Williams, L.M., & Finkelhor, D. (1993). Impact of sexual abuse on children: A review and synthesis of recent empirical studies. *Psychological Bulletin, 113*, 164-180.

Levine, A., & Levine, M. (1992). *Helping Children: A Social History.* New York: Oxford Press.

Levy, R.J. (1989). Using "scientific" testimony to prove child sexual abuse. *Family Law Quarterly, 23*, 383-409.

Maney, A., & Wells, S.(Eds.). (1988). *Professional responsibilities in protecting children: A public health approach to child sexual abuse.* New York: Praeger.

Mantell, D.M. (1988). Clarifying erroneous child sexual abuse allegations. *American Journal of Orthopsychiatry, 58*, 618-621.

McCoid, A.H. (1965). The battered child and other assaults upon the family: Part one. *Minnesota Law Review, 50*, 1-59.

Meddin, J., & Hansen, I. (1985). The services provided during a child abuse and or neglect case investigation and the barriers that exist to service provision. *Child Abuse and Neglect, 9*, 175-182.

Melton, G.B., Goodman, G.S., Kalichman, S.C., Levine, M., Saywitz, K.J., & Koocher, G.P. (1995). Empirical Research on Child Maltreatment and the Law. *Journal of Child Clinical Psychology, 24* (Suppl), 47-77.

Meriwether, M.H. (1986). Child abuse reporting laws: Time for a change. *Family Law Quarterly, 20*, 141-171.

Milner, J.S. (1989). Additional cross-validation of the Child Abuse Potential Inventory. Psychological Assessment: *A Journal of Consulting and Clinical Psychology. 1*, 219-233.

Milner, J.S. (1990). *An interpretive manual for the Child Abuse Potential Inventory.* Webster, NC: Psytec Corporation

Milner, J.S. (1991). Medical conditions and Child Abuse Potential Inventory specificity. *Psychological Assessment, 3*, 208-212.

Milner, J.S., Gold, R.G., & Wimberley, R.C. (1986). Prediction and explanation of child abuse: Cross-validation of the Child Abuse Potential Inventory. *Journal of Consulting and Clinical Psychology, 54*, 865-866.

National Center on Child Abuse and Neglect. (1989). *State statutes related to child abuse and neglect*: 1988. Available from the Clearinghouse on Child Abuse and Neglect Information, P.O. Box 1182, Washington, DC, 20013.

Newberger, E.H. (1983). The helping hand strikes again: Unintended consequences of child abuse reporting. *Journal of Clinical Child Psychology, 12*, 307-311.

Parker, J.F. (1995). Age differences in source monitoring of performed and imagined actions on immediate and delayed tests. *Journal of Experimental Child Psychology. 60*, 84-101.

Pecora, P.J. (1991). Investigating allegations of child maltreatment: The strengths and limitations of current risk assessment systems. *Child and Youth Services, 15*, 73-92.

Poole, D.A. & Lamb, M.E. (1998). *Investigative interviews of children: A guide for helping professionals.* Washington, D.C.: American Psychological Association.

Salovitz, B., & Keys, D. (1988). Is the child protective service still a service? *Protecting Children, 5*(2), 17-23.

Sgroi, S., Porter, F., & Blick, L. (1982). Validation of child sexual abuse. In S. Sgroi (Ed.) *Handbook of clinical intervention in child sexual abuse.* Lexington, MA: Lexington.

Wang, C.T., & Daro, D. (1998). *Current Trends in Child Abuse Reporting and Fatalities: The Results of the 1997 Annual Fifty State Survey.* Chicago, IL: National Committee to Prevent Child Abuse.

U.S. Advisory Board on Child Abuse and Neglect. (1990). *Child Abuse and Neglect: Critical First Steps in Response to a National Emergency.* Available from the author, Switzer Building, Room 2070C, 200 Independence Avenue, S.W., Washington, DC 20201.

U.S. Department of Health and Human Services. (1988). *Study findings: Study of National Incidence and Prevalence of Child Abuse and Neglect.* Bethesda, MD: Westat.

Walker, L.E. (1988). *Handbook on sexual abuse of children.* New York: Springer.

Walker, C.E., Bonner, B., & Kaufman, K. (1988). *The physically and sexually abused child: Evaluation and treatment.* New York: Pergamon Press.

Walker, N.E., & Nguyen, M. (1996). Interviewing the child witness: The do's and the dont's, the how's and the why's. *Creighton Law Review, 29*,1587-1617.

Wells, S., Stein, T., Fluke, J. & Downing, J. (1989). Screening in child protective services. *Social Work, 34*, 45-48.

White, S., Strom, G.A., Santilli, G.A., & Halpin, B.M. (1986). Interviewing young sexual abuse victims with anatomically correct dolls. *Child Abuse and Neglect, 19*, 519-529.

Wiehe, V.R. (1992). Working with child abuse and neglect. Itasca, IL: F.E. Peacock.

Wilcoxon, S.A. (1991). Clarifying expectations in therapy relationships: Suggestions for written guidelines. *Journal of Independent Social Work, 5*, 65-71.

Wisconsin Department of Health and Social Services. (1985). *Investigation handbook for child protective service workers.* Madison, WI: Author.

Wolfner, G., Faust, D., & Dawes, R.W. (1993). The use of anatomically detailed dolls in sexual abuse evaluations: The state of the science. *Applied and Preventive Medicine, 2*, 1-11.

Chapter 10

Assessment of Sexual Offenders

Mary Alice Conroy, Ph.D.
Department of Psychology, Sam Houston State University, Huntsville, TX

1. INTRODUCTION

Recent legal developments have increased the demand for forensic mental health professionals willing to provide assessments of persons with a history of committing sexual offenses. This is due in part to the 1996 passage of "Megan's Law," a federal statute requiring states to enact community registration and notification procedures when a known sex offender is released. However, greater impetus came from the U. S. Supreme Court decision in *Kansas v. Hendricks* (1997). By a five to four vote, the justices upheld Kansas' Sexually Violent Predator Act, which established procedures for civilly committing sexual predators who had completed prison term, but who were still found to be at risk for future sexual violence due to some mental abnormality. Subsequent to the Court's ruling, a number of states passed similar legislation, and others are in the process of following suit. At the time of this writing, more than 30 court cases have been published, generally upholding the constitutionality of specific procedures outlined in such statutes. Jurisdictions not using civil commitment have established other procedures for tracking and restricting known sex offenders. Arizona, for instance, utilizes a program of lifetime probation.

In deciding cases relative to Sexually Violent Predators (SVPs), courts have increasingly turned to mental health professionals for assistance in predicting whether a given offender is apt to engage in future acts of predatory sexual violence. Courts also request information regarding treatment approaches, which can be proven to prevent or reduce the probability of sexually violent recidivism.

The discussion, which follows, will hopefully aid forensic psychologists tasked with providing expertise in this endeavor in adult courts. Since the great majority of offenders are men and little research has been done regarding female sex offenders, consideration will be limited to the evaluation and treatment of males. The first section will be devoted to risk assessment techniques, specifically applied to sex offender recidivism. This will include an enumeration of individual factors, which are (and are not) predictive of re-offending, as well as familiarizing the reader with state-of-the-art instruments designed for prediction. Next, current data on treatment efficacy will be presented, and its usefulness in risk management discussed. The final section will consider the principle roles available to the forensic psychologist in this arena, including independent expert, trial consultant, and policy maker.

2.   RISK ASSESSMENT

Throughout much of the twentieth century, mental health professionals in the United States were called to testify in courts as to the likelihood that specific individuals would engage in acts of future violence. In many instances, this was not the profession's finest hour. Data from early field studies yielded high rates of false positive predictions. That is, large numbers of individuals were predicted to be violent who, when actually released, were not. In 1983, the U. S. Supreme Court considered whether mental health professionals should be allowed to present testimony concerning a defendant's future dangerousness. Despite an *amicus curiae* brief filed by the American Psychiatric Association, estimating that psychiatric predictions of long-term future dangerousness were wrong two out of three times, the Court ruled that such testimony could continue. In their final opinion, the justices offer the rather remarkable observation that the practice should continue because the experts were not always wrong; they were only wrong most of the time (*Barefoot v. Estelle*, 1983).

For the 15 years that followed the *Barefoot* case, an entire second generation of "dangerousness prediction" research emerged. It gradually evolved into what we now term "risk assessment" and further into "risk management." A very large body of literature has now been published providing actuarial data for the assessment of future risk. Of that literature, the single topic having the most extensive database is sex offender recidivism.

2.1 Actuarial Versus Clinical Prediction

A primary reason for the gross inaccuracy of early risk assessments was the almost exclusive reliance on clinical prediction. Evaluators typically looked to their clinical training and experience, sometimes supplemented by standardized tests designed to measure psychopathology, rather than examining hard data relative to recidivism. As early as 1954, Meehl pointed to the superiority of the actuarial approach to prediction, and recent studies, including broad-based meta-analyses, have continued to demonstrate it (Grove & Meehl, 1996; Hanson & Bussiere, 1998; Mossman, 1994). Given the relative inaccuracy of clinical prediction, its use as a primary tool for risk assessment would likely constitute poor professional practice.

In using actuarial prediction it is essential to recognize and acknowledge its limitations. Predictive data are most often correlational. Correlations may be significant, yet quite small. The highest correlation coefficients on single risk factors represented in the risk assessment data fall between 0.30 and 0.40. Another statistical device used to describe the accuracy of a given predictive instrument is the receiver-operating characteristic (ROC) (Mossman, 1994). Put simply, the ROC of a specific predictor may range from 0.50 (indicating equivalent to chance) to 1.00 (indicating perfect prediction). The ROCs of the most respectable instruments currently available are in the 0.70 range. Clearly then, use of available scientific data can facilitate predictions of risk significantly above the chance level, yet be far from perfect. An important task for the forensic psychologist comes in educating the judicial constituency as to the appropriate use of risk assessment data.

Up to the present time, research on sex offender risk assessment has concentrated primarily on static variables (Bonta & Hanson, 1998; Quinsey, Lalumiere, Rice, & Harris, 1995). These are variables generally not subject to change over time and not under the control of the parties involved. Typically included are factors such as history of offenses, types and number of victims, marital history, and age at first offense. While these factors have proven very valuable in making long-term predictions regarding recidivism, they are not designed to measure change or to predict risk, which is transient. So, for example, they would not be appropriate for use in evaluating treatment outcome or to alert caregivers to situational risk factors. Some research on more dynamic variables has been conducted, but is still in its infancy (Hanson & Harris, 1998). More studies need to be done on issues such as deviant sexual preferences and the role of active substance abuse.

2.2   Establishing Base Rates

Risk assessments ordinarily begin with an examination of the expected base rates in the general population for the target behavior. If one can establish a base rate for a specific type of recidivism, it then becomes possible to examine the risk factors relative to a specific defendant and estimate that person's risk as high, moderate, or low by comparison. However, base rates for sexual re-offending are particularly difficult to establish (Prentky & Burgess, 2000).

The public generally believes the recidivism for sex offenders is extremely high - that almost all sex offenders will re-offend. However, some published data would challenge this assumption. For example, Hanson and Bussiere (1998), reviewed studies with a total of over 23,000 subjects and found the sex offender recidivism rate over the first five-year period to be 13.4%. Heilbrun, Nezu, Keeney, Chung, and Wasserman (1998), examined Bureau of Justice parole statistics for 1992, 1993, and 1995, and found sex offenders' rate of violation was no higher than that of other offenders.

Given available data, establishing an accurate base rate for recidivism in this area is a daunting task. There is general agreement that sexual offenses are significantly under reported. It is much more likely, for instance, to have unreported child molestations than unreported bank robberies. In studies in which offenders have been guaranteed confidentiality, they have admitted multiple offenses with many victims for which they have not been apprehended (Abel, Becker, Mittelman, Cunningham-Rathner, Rouleau, & Murphy, 1987; Doren, 1998).

Probably the most solid, conservative measure of an individual's offense behavior is the number of convictions for sexual misconduct. However, this measure not only ignores undetected offenses, but also charges, which were dropped or reduced by plea bargain to something, not labeled a sexual offense. When base rates are calculated using less official sources, the rate often more than doubles (Barbaree & Marshall, 1998). In an effort to obtain accurate data, statisticians often go beyond the number of convictions. Some base rates are calculated on charges, arrests, hospital admissions, and/or parole violations, leading to widely varying results. Methods of data analysis differ, with some researchers averaging the number of offenses over a specified time period, while others utilize survival analysis (number of non-recidivists at a given point in time).

The majority of studies of sex offender recidivism are relatively short-term, covering periods of less than five years (Dwyer & Myers, 1990). However, some sex offenders have been found to re-offend for the first time as long as 20 years after the original offense (Hanson, Steffey, & Gauthier, 1993). Rice and Harris (1997), note that the slope of the curve describing sex offender recidivism over time tapers more slowly than for other violent offenders. Therefore, short-term studies may seriously underestimate the problem.

Base rates will also differ depending on the exact type of offense being measured. If only sex offenses (and not violent offenses in general) are of concern, the rate is apt to be lower, particularly for rapists (Hanson, 1998). Incest offenders generally evidence lower rates of recidivism than rapists or extrafamilial child molesters (Doren, 1998). If relatively short-term reconviction is being predicted, rapists are apt to have higher base rates than child molesters (Quinsey, et al., 1995). However, if one projects up to a 25-year period, Doren (1998), calculated the reverse would be true, with child molester recidivism estimated as high as 52%.

Depending upon many of the factors discussed above, Furby, Weinrott, & Blackshaw (1989), found base rates ranging from 0 to 50%. Very few studies provide data, which is actually comparable, leaving the forensic psychologist to utilize them only with great caution and explanation. In many cases it may be wise not to attempt base rate comparisons.

2.3 General Indicators of Sex Offender Recidivism

Research has revealed a number of factors, which appear to be predictive of recidivism and are resilient across studies and meta-analyses. Hanson (1998), described a general pattern of sexual deviance as predictive. This included having a broad range of victims, perpetrating on males, and having victims outside of the immediate family. Persons who commit both sexual and non-sexual offenses are also at higher risk. Offenders in younger age groups are more apt to recidivate (Harris, Rice, & Quinsey, 1998), as are those who begin offending at a younger age (Hanson & Bussiere, 1998). Persons who have maintained stable marriages are less prone to re-offending than those who have not (Hanson & Bussiere, 1998; Prentky, Knight, & Lee, 1997). Deviant sexual preferences appear to be predictive particularly for child molesters (Hanson & Bussiere, 1998).

With one exception, variables of personality and psychopathology have not been very helpful in the effort to predict recidivism. Major mental disorders are rare among sex offenders (Barbaree & Marshall, 1998). One prominent research group did find schizophrenia to be negatively correlated with violent recidivism in general (Quinsey, Harris, Rice, & Cormier, 1998). The *DSM-IV-TR* (2000), diagnosis of Antisocial Personality Disorder is applied to many who have committed numerous crimes. However, this diagnosis has been given liberally to anyone with a criminal history. Depending upon whose research one examines, between 50% and 80% of those incarcerated are so diagnosed. This leaves the diagnosis with little discriminant validity as a predictor.

The one personality factor, which has demonstrated value as a recidivism predictor, is psychopathy, as conceptualized by Hervey Cleckley (1941), and more recently by Robert Hare (1996). Although the vast majority of psychopaths would also qualify for the diagnosis of Antisocial Personality Disorder, the reverse is not the case. True psychopaths constitute a much smaller group. In addition to significant antisocial behavioral patterns, these individuals tend to be superficially charming, grandiose, stimulation seeking, impulsive, and engage in pathological lying. They are often characterized as callous, manipulative, and shallow in relationships with other people and rarely take responsibility for the havoc they wreak on those around them. Psychopathy, as measured by the Hare Psychopathy Checklist-Revised (PCL-R), has been demonstrated to have solid predictive validity in the area of sex offender recidivism (Hanson & Bussiere, 1998; Prentky et al., 1997). For example, in a recent study of 409 sex offenders, Hanson (1998), reported that 21% of recidivists met Hare's criteria for psychopathy, compared to only 8% of non-recidivists. However, Rice and Harris (1997), report psychopathy is a much stronger predictor for rapists than for child molesters. Thus, a heavy reliance on psychopathy in making assessments of those who exclusively offend against children may artificially deflate the level of risk.

Although research remains sparse, there is some evidence addressing dynamic factors, which may be predictive of re-offending. The most general conclusion is that lower risk is related to a higher level of cooperation with supervision and treatment (Epperson, Kaul, & Hesselton, 1998; Hanson & Bussiere, 1998; Hanson & Harris, 1998). Although symptoms of psychopathology and poor coping skills under stress have not been associated with long-term recidivism risk, they may function as immediate predictors, evident just before violation occurs (Bonta, Law, & Hanson, 1998). Some dynamic variables have been shown to be predictive in the area of non-sexual re-offending (Gendreau, Little, & Goggin, 1996). Research currently available suggests that both intimacy deficits (Seidman,

Marshall, Hudson, & Robertson, 1994), and attitudes tolerant of sexual offenses (Hanson & Harris, 1998), merit further exploration.

Perhaps a word of caution is in order regarding variables, which have not been found to be predictive of sexual re-offending. Purported experts who confuse their personal opinions and experiences with the science of the discipline have frequently misled courts. Unfortunately, the judiciary has been known to uphold the appropriateness of testimony on clinical predictions even when provided with data on their inaccuracy. It thus becomes incumbent upon forensic psychologists to police themselves by taking great care that what is presented to the courts is truly science, accurately portrayed. Hanson (1998), strongly advocates against referring to variables that in broader analyses correlate close to zero with future risk. Among those most frequently used are low self-esteem, a history of abuse in childhood, and continued denial of one's offense. Although Pithers and Gray (1998), and others indicate many sex offenders have a history of abuse, they also agree most victims of abuse do not become sex offenders, let alone repeat sex offenders. In their very large 1998 meta-analysis (N=28,972), Hanson & Bussiere found a negligible correlation between a history of sexual abuse as a child and sexual offense recidivism (average r = -.01). The same meta-analysis revealed an average correlation of 0.02 between denial of offense and recidivism. A study recently reported by Seto and Barbaree (1999), found that offenders, who are judged to be among the best program participants, but have high PCL-R scores, are at very high risk once released to the community.

It should be clear at this point that to best serve the courts in the area of sex offender risk assessment the expert's knowledge must be broad based and current. Risk assessment research is, and always will be, a work in progress. New discoveries are rapidly emerging which change what factors one should use to measure risk and how best to apply them.

2.4   Should an Instrument Be Used

A number of actuarial instruments have been developed and researched in recent years to assist the mental health professional in making accurate appraisals of risk. Several of them specifically target those at risk for sexual re-offending. They offer a number of distinct advantages. Although criminal history (particularly a history of committing sex offenses) is one of the most well established predictors of future behavior, using a validated instrument which includes other factors can significantly enhance the accuracy of a prediction (Quinsey, Harris, et al., 1998).

Use of an instrument which provides an overall score can make evaluations comparable and provide jurisdictions a basis on which to rank order offenders. This can be particularly valuable in jurisdictions, which allow for commitment of only a small number of the highest risk offenders. For example, Wisconsin commits approximately 12% of eligible offenders following incarceration, while Washington commits less than one percent. A scorable instrument allows cutoff points to be established by social policy and not on the judgment of the expert (Lieb, Quinsey, & Berliner, 1998). The higher the cutoff score is set, the fewer false positives are likely. A validated instrument provides a justification for the variables, which were utilized, and demonstrates the evaluation was conducted within the current standards of the field. It also provides the expert witness with answers to questions raised in the often-mentioned *Daubert* challenge (*Daubert v. Merrell Dow Pharmaceuticals*, 1993). Instrument manuals include validity and reliability data, as well as established error rates.

The primary difficulty in relying on an established instrument involves finding one, which closely fits each individual and/or situation involved. As will be seen from the following review of available instruments, the majority were developed in Canada and validated on a Canadian offender sample. Few studies have been done with African Americans, Hispanics, or other cultural groups not common to Canada. Serious ethical concerns regarding the adequate validity of any instrument must be addressed before adopting it for court use (Campbell, 2000).

One additional concern for those scoring an instrument is the availability of reliable records. Although accurate information is essential to any risk assessment, it is even more so when a specific score will be calculated. With the exception of phallometric devices, test instruments require a considerable amount of historical information, which has been appropriately verified. To report such a score based upon an inadequate database could seriously mislead.

3.   AVAILABLE INSTRUMENTS

3.1   The Plethysmograph

The penile plethysmograph is a phallometric device designed to measure penile tumescence in order to assess patterns of sexual arousal. More complete descriptions of its use can be found elsewhere (Lalumiere &

Harris, 1998). For purposes of this discussion, its utility in sex offender recidivism assessments will be addressed. Available research indicates that this mechanism can identify pedophiles that are at particularly high risk to reoffend (Barbaree & Marshall, 1988; Freund & Blanchard, 1989). However, it appears to have little utility in assessing risk in rapists (Hanson & Bussiere, 1998). Harris, Rice, and Quinsey (1998), look favorably on phallometric assessment and believe it is particularly effective when used in combination with measures of psychopathy. However, critics of the plethysmograph point to the lack of standardization of stimuli and procedures, the lack of uniform training requirements for plethysmographers, the variability in data interpretation, and the lack of norms for subgroups of sexual offenders (Prentky & Burgess, 2000).

An important question regarding the plethysmograph is whether results can be faked. As early as 1978, Quinsey and Carrigan found research subjects could successfully fake responses when so instructed. However, successful faking could be reduced through the addition of a semantic tracking task. This is designed to insure that participants' attention is focused by having them indicate what they observe by pushing appropriate buttons. Recent research by Harris, Rice, and Quinsey (1998), indicates greater potential for faking develops after the initial session. The concern, generally, is over the potential for false negatives, as there would be little incentive to fake sexually deviant responses. However, Becker and Murphy (1998), point out false positives can occur, with potentially devastating effects for the offender. In 1989, Freund and Blanchard found the plethysmograph to have 55% sensitivity among offenders who continued to deny their offense. Phallometric techniques require both equipment and specially trained evaluators.

3.2 The Hare Psychopathy Checklist-Revised (PCL-R)

Developed by Robert Hare (1991), and his colleagues, this instrument is used to assess the psychopathic personality as characterized by Hervey Cleckley (1941), and not the Antisocial Personality Disorder described in the *DSM-IV-TR* (2000). This is one of the few commercially available instruments with very promising predictive validity in regard to violence. In the specific area of sexual recidivism, its greatest utility has been shown with rapists, who also have a history of non-sexual offenses. It is least effective with exclusive pedophiles. It is composed almost entirely of static variables and users are cautioned not to view it as a measure of change. Research about its use with ethnic minorities remains sparse.

Administering the PCL-R involves both a structured interview and an extensive review of collateral information. If sufficient verified collateral information is available, it is possible to obtain a score without benefit of an interview and without the cooperation of the evaluee. However, scores obtained in this manner may underestimate the true level of psychopathy. Either way, the instrument commonly requires several hours to complete. A screening version, the PCL-SV, is also available. The author recommends rather extensive training before using the PCL-R and cautions against the use of untrained evaluators. The published reliability data is quite impressive; however, the research was conducted with thoroughly trained evaluators.

3.3   The Violence Risk Appraisal Guide (VRAG)

This instrument was developed by Vernon Quinsey and his colleagues and validated primarily on populations of violent offenders in Canada (Quinsey, Harris et al., 1998). The inventory, originally published as the Violence Prediction Scheme (Webster, Harris, Rice Cormier, & Quinsey, 1994), contains a list of 12 static factors, which must be assessed and scored. These include: results of the PCL-R, living with biological parents until age 16, elementary school maladjustment, history of alcohol problems, marital status, non-violent criminal history, conditional release failures, age at index offense (scored negatively), victim injury (scored negatively), sex of victim, personality disorder, and schizophrenia (scored negatively).

Research has found the VRAG to perform better in predicting general violent recidivism than in predicting sexual re-offending specifically. The developers report an ROC of 0.76 for violent recidivism and an ROC of 0.62 for sexual re-offending in a study spanning seven years (Quinsey, Harris, et al., 1998). However, Rice and Harris (1997), report data suggesting the VRAG may be very helpful with sex offender risk assessment if the jurisdiction is attempting in some way to compare risk levels and identify those having the highest probability of re-offending. When VRAG scores of sex offenders were divided into nine equally spaced risk levels, no one in the lowest category re-offended violently, while everyone in the highest category did. Barbaree (1999), recently reported the results of a prospective study comparing various methods of risk assessment in a sex offender population. He found the VRAG to be the most accurate measure.

3.4   The Sex Offender Risk Appraisal Guide (SORAG)

This instrument was designed by the developers of the VRAG in an effort to produce an instrument, which would be more sensitive to sexual re-offending. It outlines 14 specific factors to be assessed and scored, including both results of the PCL-R and the results of a penile plethysmograph. Given the predictive power of the latter two factors alone, it seemed it would be a very promising approach. However, actual validation results have been somewhat disappointing, as it was found to perform no better than the VRAG (Rice & Harris, 1997).

3.5   The Minnesota Sex Offender Screening Tool - Revised (MnSOST-R)

This is a 16-item inventory developed for use by the Minnesota Department of Corrections (Epperson, et al., 1998). In its revised form, it is based upon actuarial data and is very different from the original MnSOST protocol developed in 1991, which was primarily based on clinical observations. The revised instrument includes 12 static and four dynamic variables. It is designed for completion by persons such as case managers from data readily available in most prison files. Suggested cutoff scores are provided and matched with expected rates of recidivism. Given this is a very new instrument, research to date has been limited and conducted primarily by the developers.

3.6   The Rapid Risk Assessment for Sexual Offender Recidivism (RRASOR)

Developed by Karl Hanson in 1997, the RRASOR is currently one of the most common post-detention risk assessment procedures used in the United States and Canada. The four-item scale was constructed from variables identified through meta-analytic techniques as predictive of sexual re-offending. These include prior arrests for sexual misconduct (most heavily weighted), age, targeting of male victims, and targeting of unrelated victims. At the lowest level of risk is the incest offender with no prior offense record, while at the highest is the person who perpetrates on unrelated males and has an extensive prior record. Hanson (1998), reported an ROC of 0.71 for this instrument.

3.7   The Structured Anchored Clinical Judgment (SACJ-Min)

.This instrument was designed and tested in the United Kingdom to assess the risk of sex offender recidivism based upon a three-stage approach (Grubin, 1998). Stage One considers official convictions, Stage Two potentially aggravating factors, and Stage Three treatment variables (usually only available on those who have been in a sex offender treatment program.) Available research is limited and conducted primarily by the developer.

3.8   The Static-99

Developed through the combined efforts of Karl Hanson and David Thornton in 1999, this instrument utilizes items from the RRASOR and the SACJ-Min. Studies thus far indicate its predictive accuracy exceeds that of either of the previous instruments used alone. The authors report an ROC of 0.71 for prediction of sexual recidivism and an ROC of 0.69 for predicting violent recidivism. In initial validity studies, the instrument was able to identify a substantial population of offenders (approximately 12%) whose long-term recidivism rate exceeded 50% (Hanson & Thornton, 2000).

True to its name, the Static-99 is based completely on static variables including prior sex offenses, unrelated victims, stranger victims, male victims, age, never married, non-contact sex offenses, prior sentences, current non-sexual violence, and prior non-sexual violence. It is designed to measure long-term risk potential and can be completed by case management personnel based on file data. It is considered by its developers to be a work in progress with much research yet to be done.

3.9   The Sexual/Violence/Risk Instrument (SVR-20)

The risk assessment researchers at Simon Fraser University in British Columbia (Boer, Wilson, Gauther, & Hart, 1997), developed this inventory.

studies of higher quality have failed to find positive treatment effects. He strongly discourages the use of clinical assessments of treatment outcome or progress in assessing future risk. Quinsey, Khanna, and Malcolm (1998), while investigating sex offenders who had completed a cognitive-behavioral treatment program, found clinicians' assessments of treatment progress to be unrelated to recidivism. Overall outcome for the treated offenders (as measured using recidivism data) was poor, yet clinicians reported very significant improvement between pre- and post-treatment measures.

In the absence of definitive outcome data, it would be inappropriate to assure the judicial system that a particular treatment is known to be effective or that offenders must be required to participate in a treatment program to reduce their level of risk. However, the methodological quagmire has not shown treatments to be universally ineffective nor given us reason to abandon the effort entirely. While striving to improve and refine data collection, mental health professionals must still be knowledgeable regarding what is known about the various treatments currently in use.

4.1   Organic Approaches to Treatment

Various medical interventions have been proposed in an effort to control the repeat sex offender. Although proposed approaches have gone so far as to include psychosurgery and physical castration, it is unlikely these drastic interventions will ever be widely adopted. This discussion will therefore, focus on medications.

Treatments using progesterone derivatives, which control serum levels of testosterone, have been utilized in an effort to reduce the sexual drives of offenders. Although such therapies have been labeled "chemical castration," this is a misnomer. Appropriate clinical use is directed toward the reduction of sexual drives and fantasies, not the production of impotence. The two most widely used drugs for this purpose are cyproterone acetate (CPA) and medroxyprogesterone (MPA). CPA is used in Europe and Canada and has never gained FDA approval for use in the United States. Dr. John Money and his colleagues at Johns Hopkins University pioneered early research using MPA treating sex offenders in this country. Some degree of success with MPA has been documented in the literature. These drugs have been found to be effective in suppressing overall sexual behaviors (Bradford, 1990; Marshall, 1993; Kravitz, Haywood, Kelly, Wahlstrom, Liles, & Cavanaugh, 1995). Re-offense rates for some child molesters willing to continue the treatment have been reduced (Harris et al. 1998). The data, however, is sparse and difficult to interpret. It is possible that the medications provide assistance to those offenders who are truly motivated to change their behavior. Some research has also suggested hormonal treatment may be useful as an adjunct to other therapies (Hall, 1995). However, only a small percentage of sex offenders evidence exaggerated sexual drives (Barbaree & Marshall, 1998; Rosler & Witztum, 2000), and medications such as these do nothing to change the object of their attraction. MPA is generally contraindicated for use with juveniles due to issues of sexual maturity (Barbaree & Marshall, 1988).

MPA comes in injectible form, and, therefore, its administration can be closely monitored. This has made it attractive to a number of criminal justice agencies. In 1997, California became the first state to require its use by sex offenders as a condition of probation and several other states have since passed similar legislation. Agreeing voluntarily to remain on this medication is relatively rare, given its unpleasant side effects. These may include weight gain, fatigue, headaches, depression, gastrointestinal difficulties, irregular gallbladder function, sweats, leg cramps, hypertension, diverticulitis, nightmares, thrombosis, hot/cold flashes, dyspnea, malaise, insomnia, infertility, feminization, and irregular responses to glucose (Bradford, 1985; Emory, Cole, & Meyer, 1992; Miller, 1998). All side effects are reported to be reversible, but the process may take up to six months. The reduction in sexual arousal produced by this medication can also be counteracted by the ingestion of additional testosterone or anabolic steroids.

Some research has suggested that serotonin levels may impact sex offenders and the Selective Serotonin Reuptake Inhibitors (SSRIs) may hold some promise for treatment (Fedoroff, 1993; Kafka, 1991). Serotonin is a neurotransmitter of which lower levels appear to be associated with depression, aggression, and obsessive compulsive thinking. In treating sex offenders, serotonin is thought to reduce sexual arousal, perhaps by reducing fantasies, similar to its mechanism in controlling obsessions (Miller, 1998). If successful, the SSRIs could have the possible advantage of reducing deviant interests, while not affecting healthy ones. However, research on the effectiveness of such treatment is still in its infancy.

The Gonadotropin-Releasing Hormone (GnRH) has recently received some attention in the treatment literature. Potential side effects have elicited concern because in rare cases it can induce severe hypogonadism and some reduction in normal sex drive is often noted. It is considered promising by some, but is still in the early research phase (Rosler & Witztum, 2000).

4.2   The Plethysmograph

In addition to reported utility in assessment, phallometric devices have found their place in the treatment arena. Those who advocate the use of the plethysmograph as an adjunct to psychotherapy explain that sex offenders notoriously under report behaviors indicative of re-offending and, therefore, the therapist needs an objective measure. Dutton and Emerick (1996), suggest data from phallometric testing be used in treatment to challenge the offender's denial and defensive justifications and to establish a realistic relapse prevention plan. They also believe the technique is useful in identifying preferences and measuring change over time. The Association for the Treatment of Sexual Abusers (ATSA), the largest national organization to establish standards for sex offender treatment professionals, incorporated the use of plethysmographs in their protocol in 1993. A recent national survey of over 700 sex offender treatment programs found 22% of the juvenile programs and 31% of the adult programs were using the plethysmograph (Knopp, Freeman-Longo, & Stevenson, 1992). At the present time, however, data as to the efficacy of this approach remains primarily anecdotal.

Any practitioner considering the use of phallometric techniques should carefully examine the relevant ethical guidelines (ATSA, 1993), as well as the laws in their jurisdiction. The use of the plethysmograph with juveniles has generated great controversy, particularly if visual stimuli are being employed. One jurisdiction (Texas) has completely banned plethysmography with juveniles and requires a physician's prescription before it can be used with adults (Dutton & Emerick, 1996).

4.3   The Polygraph

When employed as an adjunct to sex offender treatment, polygraphs are used for much the same reason as phallometric devices. Offenders are deemed to be unreliable sources of information and it is thought to be essential for the therapist to have accurate information in order to confront denial and distortion (Wilcox, 2001). The ATSA (1993), specifically recommends using polygraph examinations to establish an accurate sexual history, and in conjunction with other measures, to monitor on-going behavior.

Research on both sides of the raging debate surrounding the validity of polygraph results can be found elsewhere (Saxe, Dougherty, & Cross, 1985).

Proponents of the use of polygraphs in sex offender treatment would argue polygraph results are surely more reliable than the offender's self-report (English, Pullen, & Jones, 1996). However, other issues remain to be resolved. Programs using the polygraph ordinarily advocate complete open communication among the therapist, the polygraph examiner, and the case managers or probation officers assigned to the case. Thus, patient-therapist confidentiality is non- existent. Polygraph assessment may be inappropriate for persons with certain serious medical problems (e.g., cardiac conditions), the mentally ill offender, persons with borderline intelligence or who are mentally retarded, or for individuals who are intoxicated, sleep deprived, or pregnant (English, 1998).

The issue of Fifth Amendment rights must be resolved before incorporating polygraphs into sex offender programs. It is not difficult to imagine additional crimes being disclosed during this phase of treatment. Communities have resolved this dilemma in various ways. While some have provided for limited immunity agreements, prosecutors often oppose such arrangements. Other jurisdictions seriously restrict the questions, which are allowable during the examinations.

A 1992 survey found approximately one quarter of adult sex offender treatment programs nationally made some use of the polygraph (Knopp et al., 1992). Results of a 1994 study found 11% of probation and parole offices charged with supervising sex offenders used them (English et al., 1996). The literature is replete with anecdotal information on the polygraph's value, as well as compelling testimonials (English et al., 1996; English, 1998). However, there are no actual scientific data demonstrating the polygraph's effectiveness as a treatment tool to date. One of the difficulties in gathering appropriate data is the instrument's role as an adjunct. When used, it is almost invariably part of a multi- faceted approach designed to use every available method to reduce the likelihood of re-offense. As such, it becomes extremely difficult to assess its specific contribution to any outcome.

4.4   Cognitive-Behavioral Therapy

One point on which most researchers and practitioners concur is the complete lack of evidence supporting the use of humanistic or psychodynamic approaches in treating sex offenders (Harris et al., 1998). Data also suggest behavioral techniques alone yield poor results (Hall, 1995). The most significant conclusion from Hall's 1995 meta-analysis was that Cognitive-Behavioral Therapy (CBT) had a small, but statistically significant effect, particularly when used in conjunction with hormonal interventions. Programs using a CBT model generally includes cognitive restructuring, empathy building, problem solving, social skills training, affective management techniques, and the development of self control strategies. Inclusion of a relapse prevention component is thought to be essential (Marques & Nelson, 1992; Pithers, 1990).

Early evaluations of CBT programs were generally positive and led to considerable optimism (Freeman-Longo & Knopp, 1992; Hall, 1995; Hildebran & Pithers, 1992; Marques, et al., 1994; Marshall, Jones, Ward, Johnson, & Barbaree, 1991). However, much of this research has since been challenged on methodological grounds (Quinsey, Harris, Rice, & Lalumiere, 1993; Barbaree, 1999), and other data collection has yielded conflicting results. For example, data initially gathered on sex offenders treated at the Oak Ridge Mental Health Centre in Ontario showed significant improvement in sexual preferences and social competence. However, long-term follow-up failed to demonstrate any reduction in recidivism (Rice, Harris, & Quinsey, 1991). A more recent study compared offenders who completed a CBT sex offender treatment program with those who had refused or had been deemed inappropriate or not in need of such treatment. Results indicated treated offenders were the most frequently rearrested for sex offenses (Quinsey, Khanna, et al., 1998). Following a review of the available outcome literature, Marshall and Anderson (1996), failed to find positive benefits demonstrated by the addition of a relapse prevention component to the CBT model.

Given the conflicting data and serious methodological problems in refining the data, it remains impossible for the forensic psychologist to testify to the specific efficacy of any current treatment modality. However, of those available, the cognitive-behavioral remains the most promising. Janice Marques and her colleagues are continuing research on the Sex Offender Treatment and Evaluation Project (SOTEP) at Atascadero State Hospital in California, which may provide valuable answers (Marques, 1999).

4.5   Psychopathy: The Intervening Variable

The construct of psychopathy as conceptualized by Cleckley and Hare has proven central to understanding the chronic sex offender and to assessing the level of risk presented. As currently described, psychopathy is characterized by a total lack of remorse for one's misdeeds, an inability to empathize with one's victims, a glib superficiality in dealing with others, a grandiose sense of self, a propensity for shallow manipulation of one's peers, and a tendency to behave in reckless and impulsive fashion. The literature suggests the true psychopath constitutes a relatively small percentage of people who engage in anti-social conduct, but a much larger proportion of those prone to violent recidivism (Hare & McPherson, 1984). One current theory even postulates that psychopathy may represent a taxon - that is, a separate entity, a class unto itself (Harris, Rice, & Quinsey, 1994).

To date, no treatment modality has been demonstrated to effectively address the psychopathic personality (Hare, 1993). In fact, a Canadian study evaluating the efficacy of a therapeutic community in treating violent offenders, uncovered data suggesting treatment may have the potential to actually increase the probability of violent recidivism. Matching offenders who participated in treatment with those who were simply sent to prison, researchers found a surprising interaction: the treated psychopaths had a higher rate of violent recidivism than their untreated counterparts, with the reverse being true for those offenders not evidencing psychopathy (Rice, 1997). This could mean that raising the psychopath's self-esteem increases their potential for aggression. It could also mean that psychopaths use their enhanced knowledge of interpersonal psychology simply to improve their manipulative skills.

None of the research conducted to evaluate sex offender treatment has separated results for the psychopathic offender from the non-psychopathic offender. If psychopathic offenders are truly untreatable by currently known methods, their presence in a treatment sample could seriously skew the outcome results. If their response to treatment is actually paradoxical, as suggested by Rice, their presence could totally mask any treatment gains for others in the sample. Therefore, it could be very informative for future researchers to analyze outcome data separately for psychopathic and non-psychopathic segments of their populations.

4.6   The Containment Approach

In *Kansas v. Hendricks* (1997), the U. S. Supreme Court opined that the availability of effective treatment was not a prerequisite to civilly committing those who present a danger to the community. The justices argued it was of primary importance to contain the problem and protect the public. Kim English (1998), makes a similar argument in proposing what she terms "the Containment Approach" for treating sex offenders. Under this system, the paramount goal is public safety rather than rehabilitation of the offender. Traditional treatment takes a back seat to a multi-disciplinary effort to prevent the offender from engaging in additional sex offenses by whatever means necessary. Interventions range from geographic restrictions to random, unannounced search and seizures. Programs of this type are in place in a number of jurisdictions, including Maricopa County, AZ; Jackson County, OR; and Boulder County, CO. Civil commitment statutes are being drafted allowing for interventions, which mental health professionals do not usually classify as treatment. For example, in Texas, a sex offender who has been committed by the court may be required to reside in a certain location, to wear a tracking device, or be prohibited from associating with certain individuals or classes of individuals. It behooves any mental health professional participating in sex offender assessment or treatment in a jurisdiction focusing on containment to fully understand what the court is defining as treatment. While a forensic psychologist may have considerable expertise regarding psychotherapy outcome, they may have little to offer on what have been traditionally considered law enforcement techniques. Before one agrees to be a treatment provider under such a rubric, it is critical to know the limits of confidentiality, the exact reporting requirements, and how the court expects the provider to assess treatment progress.

A number of jurisdictions currently using the containment model are collecting outcome data on substantial numbers of offenders. However, such data collection will need to be longitudinal to have validity with this population. Even when results are analyzed it will be difficult to determine which containment strategies are actually responsible for any positive results.

5. ROLES OF THE FORENSIC PSYCHOLOGIST

When one visualizes a forensic psychologist, one often pictures an expert witness testifying from the witness stand. While this is a key function, two other roles for the forensic psychologist will be considered: trial consultant and policy maker.

5.1 Expert Witness

A psychologist may be called to court to provide expert testimony either because they have personally evaluated a particular offender or because they have specialized knowledge of the discipline, which the court requires. In either case, their primary purpose is to be of assistance to the trier of fact. To be of maximum assistance in the case of a sex offender assessment, an expert must have broad knowledge of the primary areas of concern, be current in that knowledge, understand the limits of one's expertise, and be prepared to function as an educator.

The literature on sex offender assessment is vast, and this chapter provides only a brief summary. To be competent as an expert in this area, it is essential to have a thorough understanding of aberrant sexual behavior, its etiology, and available treatments. Second, one must be thoroughly familiar with the risk assessment literature, including how risk assessment schemes are developed and what instruments are available and valid for the task at hand. Finally, one cannot be proffered as an expert in assessing sex offenders without a thorough understanding of the construct of psychopathy, its consequences, and how it is best measured.

The most current scientific data available will be of greatest assistance to the trier of fact. The earth is constantly shifting under our feet and new findings are coming to light almost daily. Errors in older research are being uncovered, and the most prominent experts in the field are radically changing earlier views based upon the new realizations. For example, a 1991 quotation from Howard Barbaree regarding the unequivocal evidence of treatment effectiveness would be unfortunate in light of his most recent statements that we have no conclusive evidence demonstrating significantly positive outcomes. What is published, as hard copy, is often outdated before the presses are cold. To feel secure in one's expertise, it is wise to visit the Internet and bookmark key sites. For instance, the web site of the Canadian Solicitor General (www.sgc.gc.ca) often contains the latest reports from Karl Hanson and his colleagues regarding new instruments and meta-analyses. Establishing correspondence with prominent researchers may also be advantageous.

Knowing the limits of one's science is critical in the courtroom. The expert witness is not tasked with defending psychology as a discipline nor the absolute validity of even the most rigorous risk assessments. Rather, the expert witness should report accurately the scientific knowledge currently available and apply it as fairly as possible to a given situation. Experts may become too helpful to the trier of fact by going beyond the hard science into the realm of personal speculation. Recently a judge asked an expert witness in a sex offender case: "Doctor, are you 95% certain Mr. X is going to re-offend if I release him?" Unfortunately, the witness responded: "Yes." The witness undoubtedly felt pressured by the court's demands. Yet, given the current state of knowledge, there is no means by which anyone could proffer a risk assessment with 95% certainty.

Finally, it is important that the expert witness remember the forensic psychologist's role as educator. As this chapter demonstrates, the data in this field is highly complex. To be of assistance, the expert must present it in such a way that it would be clear to the non-professional.

5.2   Trial Consultant

The role of trial consultant varies from that of expert witness in that one is no longer independent and unbiased. Rather one is tasked with assisting one side or the other in presenting the best case possible. Played well, this is the role of educator.

In the case of a sex offender assessment, the first task would often be assisting the attorney in seeking appropriate records. No risk assessment can be done - or challenged - without a very complete, verified body of information regarding the offender's history. Many attorneys assume when a psychologist asks for records, this means psychological treatment records. Attorneys may be unaware of the emphasis a good forensic psychologist would place on family, social, and especially criminal history. Victim statements and police reports may provide significant information.

It is important to begin trial consultation well in advance. The most ineffective way to consult with an attorney is to sit beside him or her in the courtroom and suggest questions on the spot. The discipline is complicated, and the expert needs to explain the key concepts until the lawyer is comfortable with them and able to formulate his or her own questions. Areas central to sex offender assessments, but often new to the legal arena, may include statistical issues such as correlation, statistical significance, and positive predictive power. If psychometric instruments were used (or should have been used), the attorney will need an intimate familiarity with them. Critical areas for emphasis are the limits of psychological expertise.

5.3   Policy Maker

In closing, a brief word will be said about the forensic psychologist in the policy arena. If the professional is truly an expert regarding the areas most pertinent to assessing sex offenders, that person is probably at least somewhat dismayed by the state of laws, policies, and procedures used to deal with persons who commit sex offenses in their jurisdiction. That expert probably has knowledge and experience, which could contribute to better solutions. One way of sharing this knowledge is by testifying in courts before judges who apply those laws. Another is participation in the construction of *amicus curiae* briefs in appropriate cases. However, even the most activist jurists on the bench are limited by actions of the legislature and executive.

An alternate avenue is becoming involved while policy is in the making. This means lending one's expertise to legislators and administrators. It may mean testifying before legislative committees rather than in courtrooms. It may mean assuming a more activist role in state and local professional organizations and encouraging others to do likewise. Contributing to the formation of good law, however, may in the end be the most effective therapeutic jurisprudence.

6.   REFERENCES

Abel, G. G., Becker, J. V., Mittelman, M. S., Cunningham-Rathner, J., Rouleau, J. L., and Murphy, W. D. (1987). Self-reported sex crimes of nonincarcerated paraphiliacs. *Journal of Interpersonal Violence, 2*, 3-25.

American Psychiatric Association. (2000). *Diagnostic and statistical manual of mental disorders - Text revision* (4th ed.). Washington, DC: Author.

Association for the Treatment of Sexual Abusers (1993). *The ATSA practitioner's handbook.* Lake Oswego, OR: ATSA.

Barbaree, H. E. (1999). The effect of treatment on risk for recidivism in sex offenders. In American Psychological Association, *Psychological expertise and criminal justice: A conference for psychologists and lawyers* (pp. 217-220). Washington, DC: American Psychological Association.

Barbaree, H. E., & Marshall, W. L. (1988). Deviant sexual arousal, demographic features, and offense history variables as predictors of reoffense among untreated child molesters and incest offenders. *Behavioral Sciences and the Law, 6*, 257-280.

Barbaree, H. E., & Marshall, W. L. (1998). Treatment of the sexual offender. In R. M. Wettstein (Ed.), *Treatment of offenders with mental disorders* (pp. 265-328).   New York: Guilford.

Barefoot v. Estelle, 463 U. S. 880, 103 S. Ct. 3383, 77 L.Ed. 2d 1090 (1983).

Becker, J. V., & Murphy, W. D. (1998). What we know and do not know about assessing and treating sex offenders. *Psychology, Public Policy, and Law, 4*, 116-137.

Boer, D. P., Wilson, R. J., Gauthier, C. M., & Hart, S. (1997). Assessing risk of sexual violence: Guidelines for clinical practice. In C. D. Webster & M. A. Jackson (Eds.), *Impulsivity: Theory, assessment, and treatment* (pp. 326-342). New York: Guilford.

Bonta, J., Law, M., & Hanson, R. K. (1998). The prediction of criminal and violent recidivism among mentally disordered offenders: A meta-analysis. *Psychological Bulletin, 123*, 123-142.

Bradford, J. M. W. (1985). Organic treatments for the male sexual offender. *Behavioral Sciences and the Law, 3,* 355-375.

Bradford, J. M. W. (1990). The antiandrogen and hormonal treatment of sex offenders. In W. L. Marshall, D R. Laws, & H. E. Barbaree (Eds.), *Handbook of sexual assault: Issues, theory, and treatment of the offender* (pp. 297-310). New York: Plenum.

Campbell, T. (2000). Sexual predator evaluations and phrenology: Considering issues of evidentiary reliability. *Behavioral Sciences and the Law, 18,* 111-130.

Cleckley, H. (1941). *The mask of sanity.* St. Louis, MO: Mosby.

Daubert v. Merrell Dow Pharmaceuticals, Inc. 113 S. Ct. 2786 (1993).

Doren, D. M. (1998). Recidivism base rates, predictions of sex offender recidivism, and the "sexual predator" commitment laws. *Behavioral Sciences and the Law, 16,* 97-114.

Dutton, W. A., & Emerick, R. L. (1996). Plethysmorgraph assessment. In K. English, S. Pullen, & L. Jones (Eds.), *Managing adult sex offenders: A containment approach* (pp. 14-1-14-13). Lexington, KY: American Probation and Parole Association.

Dwyer, S. M., & Myers, S. (1990). Sex offender treatment: A six-month to ten-year follow-up study. *Annals of Sex Research, 3,* 305-318.

Emory, L. E., Cole, C. M., & Meyer, W. J. (1992). The Texas experience with depoprovera: 1980-1990. *Journal of Offender Rehabilitation, 18,* 89-108.

English, K. (1998). The containment approach: An aggressive strategy for the community management of adult sex offenders. *Psychology, Public Policy, and Law, 4,* 218-235.

English, K., Pullen, S., & Jones, L. (Eds.). (1996). *Managing adult sex offenders: A containment approach.* Lexington, KY: American Probation and Parole Association.

Epperson, D. L., Kaul, J. D., & Hasselton, D. (1998, October). *Final report of the development of the Minnesota Sex Offender Screening Tool-Revised (MnSOST-R).* Presentation at the 17th Annual Research and Treatment Conference of the Association for the Treatment of Sexual Abusers, Vancouver, British Columbia, Canada.

Federoff, J. P. (1993). Serotonergic drug treatment of deviant sexual interests. *Annals of Sex Research, 6,* 105-121.

Freeman-Longo, R. E., & Knopp, F. H. (1992). State-of-the-art sex offender treatment: Outcomes and issues. *Annals of Sex Research, 5,* 141-160.

Freund, K., & Blanchard, R. (1989). Phallometric diagnosis of pedophilia. *Journal of Consulting and Clinical Psychology, 57,* 100-105.

Furby, L., Weinrott, M. R., & Blackshaw, L. (1989). Sex offender recidivism: A review. *Psychological Bulletin, 105,* 3-30.

Gendreau, P., Little, T., & Goggin, C. (1996). A meta-analysis of the predictors of adult offender recidivism: What works! *Criminology, 34,* 575-607.

Grove, W. M., & Meehl, P. E. (1996). Comparative efficiency of informal (subjective impressionistic) and formal (mechanical, algorithmic) prediction procedures: The clinical-statistical controversy. *Psychology, Public Policy, and Law, 2,* 293-323.

Grubin, D. (1998). Sex offending against children: Understanding the risk. *Police Research Series Paper London:* Home Office.

Hall, G. C. N. (1995). Sexual offender recidivism revisited: A meta-analysis of recent treatment studies. *Journal of Consulting and Clinical Psychology, 63,* 802-809.

Hanson, R. K. (1997). *The development of a brief actuarial risk scale for sex offender recidivism.* (User Report 97-04). Ottawa: Department of the Solicitor General of Canada.

Hanson, R. K. (1998). What do we know about sex offender risk assessment? *Psychology, Public Policy, and Law, 4,* 50-72.

Hanson, R. K., & Bussiere, M. T. (1998). Predicting relapse: A meta-analysis of sexual offender recidivism studies. *Journal of Consulting and Clinical Psychology, 66,* 348-362.

Hanson, R. K., & Harris, A. J. R. (1998). *Dynamic predictors of sexual recidivism (User Report No. 8-01).* Ottawa: Department of the Solicitor General of Canada.

Hanson, R. K., & Harris A. H. (2000). The Sex Offender Need Assessment Rating (SONAR): *A method for measuring change in risk levels. (User Report 2000-1).* Ottawa: Department of Solicitor General of Canada.

Hanson, R. K., Steffey, R. A., & Gauthier, R. (1993). Long-term recidivism of child molesters. *Journal of Consulting and Clinical Psychology, 61*, 646-652.

Hanson, R. K., & Thornton, D. (2000). Improving risk assessments for sex offenders: A comparison of three actuarial scales. *Law and Human Behavior, 24*, 119-136.

Hare, R. D. (1991). *The Hare Psychopathy Checklist-Revised.* Toronto, Ontario: Multi Health Systems.

Hare, R. D. (1993). *Without conscience: The disturbing world of the psychopaths among us.* New York: Pocket Books.

Hare, R. D., & McPherson, L. M. (1984). Violent aggressive behavior by criminal psychopaths. *International Journal of Law and Psychiatry, 7*, 35-50.

Harris, G. T., Rice, M. E., & Quinsey, V. L. (1994). Psychopathy as a taxon: Evidence that psychopaths are a discrete class. *Journal of Consulting and Clinical Psychology, 62*, 387-397.

Harris, G. T., Rice, M. E., & Quinsey, V. L. (1998). Appraisal and management of risk in sexual aggressors: Implications for criminal justice policy. *Psychology, Public Policy, and Law, 4*, 73-115.

Heilbrun, K., Nezu, C. M., Keeney, M., Chung, S., & Wasserman, A. L. (1998). Sexual offending: Linking assessment, intervention, and decision making. *Psychology, Public Policy, and Law, 4*, 138-174.

Hildebran, D. D., & Pithers, W. D. (1992). Relapse prevention: Application and outcome. In W. O'Donohue & J. H. Greer (Eds.)., *The sexual abuse of children: Clinical issues (Vol. 2, pp. 365-393).* Hillsdale, N J: Erlbaum.

Kafka, M. P. (1991). Successful antidepressant treatment of nonparaphilic sexual addictions and paraphilics in men. *Journal of Clinical Psychiatry, 52*, 60-65.

Kansas v. Hendricks, 117 S. Ct. 2072 (1997).

Knopp, F. H., Freeman-Longo, R., & Stevenson, W. F. (1992). *Nationwide survey of juvenile and adult sex offender treatment programs and models.* Orwell, VT: The Safer Society Press.

Kravitz, H. M., Haywood, T. W., Kelly, J., Wahlstrom, C., Liles, S., & Cavanaugh, J. L., Jr. (1995). Medroxyprogesterone treatment for paraphilics. *Bulletin of the American Academy of Psychiatry and the Law, 23*, 19-33.

Lalumiere, M. L., & Harris, G. T. (1998). Common questions regarding the use of phallometric testing with sexual offenders. Sexual Abuse: *A Journal of Research and Treatment, 10*, 227-237.

Lieb, R., Quinsey, V. L., & Berliner, L. (1998). Sexual predators and social policy. *Crime and Justice: A Review of Research, 23*, 43-114.

Marques, J. K. (1999). How to answer the question: "Does sex offender treatment work?" *Journal of Interpersonal Violence, 14*, 437-451.

Marques, J. K., & Nelson, C. (1992). The relapse prevention model: Can it work with sex offenders? In R. D. Peters, R. J. McMahon, & V. L. Quinsey (Eds.), *Aggression and violence throughout the lifespan* (pp. 222-243). Newbury Park, CA: Sage.

Marques, J. K., Day, D. M., Nelson, C., & West, M. A. (1994). Effects of cognitive-behavioral treatment on sex offender recidivism: Preliminary results of a longitudinal study. *Criminal Justice and Behavior, 21*, 28-54.

Marshall, W. L. (1993). A revised approach to the treatment of men who sexually assault adult females. In G. C. Hall, R. Hirschman, J. R. Graham, & M. S. Zaragoza (Eds.), Sexual aggression: *Issues in etiology, assessment, and treatment* (pp. 143-165). Washington, DC: Taylor & Francis.

Marshall, W. L., & Anderson, D. (1996). An evaluation of the benefits of relapse prevention programs with sexual offenders. Sexual Abuse: *A Journal of Research and Treatment, 3*, 209-221.

Marshall, W. L., & Barbaree, H. E. (1988). The long-term evaluation of a cognitive-behavioral treatment program for child molesters. *Behavior Research and Therapy, 26*, 499-511.

Marshall, W. L., Jones, R., Ward, T., Johnston, P., & Barbaree, H. E. (1991). Treatment outcome with sex offenders. *Clinical Psychology Review, 11*, 465-485.

McConaghy, N. (1999). Methodological issues concerning evaluation of treatment for sexual offenders: Randomization, treatment dropouts, untreated controls, and within-treatment studies. Sexual Abuse: *A Journal of Research and Treatment, 11*, 183-194.

Meehl, P. E. (1954). *Clinical versus statistical prediction: A theoretical analysis and a review of the evidence.* Minneapolis, MN: University of Minnesota Press.

Miller, R. D. (1998). Forced administration of sex drive reducing medications to sex offenders: Treatment or punishment? *Psychology, Public Policy, and Law, 4*, 175-199.

Mossman, D. (1994). Assessing predictions of violence: Being accurate about accuracy. *Journal of Consulting and Clinical Psychology, 62*, 783-792.

Pithers, W. D. (1990). Relapse prevention with sexual aggressors: A method for maintaining therapeutic gain and enhancing external supervision. In W. L. Marshall, D. R. Laws, & H. E. Barbaree (Eds.), *Handbook of sexual assault: Issues, theories, and treatment of the offender* (pp. 343-361). New York: Plenum.

Pithers, W. D., & Gray, A. (1998). The other half of the story: Children with sexual behavior problems. *Psychology, Public Policy, and Law, 4*, 200-217.

Prentky, R. A., & Burgess, A. W. (2000). *Forensic management of sexual offenders.* NY: Kluwer Academic/Plenum Publishers.

Prentky, R. A., Knight, R. A., & Lee, A. F. S. (1997). Risk factors associated with recidivism among extrafamilial child molesters. *Journal of Consulting and Clinical Psychology, 65*, 141-149.

Quinsey, V. L., & Carrigan, W. F. (1978). Penile responses to visual stimuli: Instructional control with and without auditory sexual fantasy correlates. *Criminal Justice and Behavior, 5*, 333-342.

Quinsey, V. L., Harris, G. T., Rice, M. E., & Cormier, C. A. (1998). *Violent offenders: Appraising and managing risk.* Washington, DC: American Psychological Association.

Quinsey, V. L., Harris, G. T., Rice, M. E., & Lalumiere, M. L. (1993). Assessing treatment efficacy in outcome studies of sex offenders. *Journal of Interpersonal Violence, 8*, 512-523.

Quinsey, V. L., Lalumiere, M. L., Rice, M. E., & Harris, G. T. (1995). Predicting sexual offenses. In J. C. Campbell (Ed.), *Assessing dangerousness: Violence by sexual offenders, batterers, and child abusers* (pp. 114-137). Thousand Oaks, CA: Sage.

Quinsey, V. L., Khanna, A., & Malcolm, B. (1998). A retrospective evaluation of the Regional Treatment Centre Sex Offender Treatment Program. *Journal of Interpersonal Violence, 13*, 621-644.

Rice, M. E. (1997). Violent offender research and implications for the criminal justice system. *American Psychologist, 52*, 414-423.

Rice, M. E., & Harris, G. T. (1997). Cross validation and extension of the Violence Risk Appraisal Guide for child molesters and rapists. *Law and Human Behavior, 21*, 231-241.

Rice, M. E., Harris, G. T., & Quinsey, V. L. (1991). Sexual recidivism among child molesters released from a maximum security psychiatric institution. *Journal of Consulting and Clinical Psychology, 59*, 381-386.

Rosler, A., & Witztum, E. (2000). Pharmacology of paraphilias in the next millennium. *Behavioral Sciences and the Law, 18*, 43-56.

Saxe, L., Dougherty, D., & Cross, T. (1985). The validity of polygraph testing: Scientific analysis and public controversy. *American Psychologist, 40*, 355-366.

Seidman, B. T., Marshall, W. L., Hudson, S. M., & Robertson, P. J. (1994). An examination of intimacy and loneliness in sex offenders. *Journal of Interpersonal Violence, 9*, 415-534.

Seto, M. C., & Barbaree, H. E. (1999). Psychopathy, treatment behavior, and sex offender recidivism. *Journal of Interpersonal Violence, 14*, 1235-1248.

Webster, C. D., Harris, G. T., Rice, M. E., Cormier, C., & Quinsey, V. L. (1994). *The Violence Prediction Scheme: Assessing dangerousness in high risk men.* Toronto, Canada: University of Toronto, Centre of Criminology.

Wilcox, D. T. (2001). Application of clinical polygraph examination to the assessment, treatment, and monitoring of sex offenders. *Journal of Sexual Aggression, 5*, 134-152.

Chapter 11

Forensic Medical Psychology
Personal Injury Litigation

Brent Van Dorsten, Ph.D.[1] and Laurence B. James, Ph.D., J.D.[2]
Department of Rehabilitation Medicine, University of Colorado Health Sciences Center, Denver, CO[1]:Ewing & Ewing, P.C., Englewood, CO[2]

1.   INTRODUCTION

Personal injury cases account for a significant portion of modern civil lawsuits, and is an area where psychologists are frequently retained to provide expert testimony. Though there is no precise definition, personal injury law deals with persons who have been injured by the wrongs of others, and constitutes a large sub-category of law known as "torts." While most practicing psychologists are likely unfamiliar with the term, torts is one of the major areas of law, and describes conduct that is considered legally improper and causes harm to another (Dobbs, 2000). Thus the law of torts is concerned with civil compensation for wrongful conduct.

Personal injury law involves the sub-category of torts that is devoted to physical or emotional harm to the individual. Personal injury cases evolve from a wide variety of precipitating circumstances, such as motor vehicle accidents, injuries sustained on another's property, violence, defective products, professional malpractice, or environmental contamination. Similarly, the types of claims can be as varied as the circumstances which produce them and can include physical and emotional damages, exacerbation of pre-existing conditions, and actual and perceived disability claims. A brief mention of work-related injuries is indicated as they are managed by an operationally different system from tort proceedings. Prior to the development of the modern worker's compensation system, compensation for work-related personal injuries was directed through the tort law system (Melton, Petrila, Poythress, & Slobogin, 1997). This often lengthy and cumbersome process proved insufficient, and was refined to the current system with both employers and employees having made certain sacrifices. Specifically, employers have necessarily provided insurance for job-related injuries which does not specifically provide a damage "award," but rather regularly provides a portion of the worker's lost salary. In return for this income guarantee, workers have sacrificed the potentially unlimited compensations awards that might have been granted via tort proceedings.

In order to prevail in a personal injury claim, the plaintiff (or the party bringing the suit) must prove three basic elements: fault, damages, and causation. Assume that a defendant (i.e., the person accused of producing the harm) was driving down the street one day, tuning his radio and failing to notice that traffic in front of him had stopped. As a result, he rear-ended a car driven by the plaintiff, who was subsequently taken to a hospital with complaints of back pain. In order to win a personal injury lawsuit in this circumstance, the plaintiff would have to prove the three basic elements against the defendant. First, it must be proven that the defendant was at fault (i.e., that the defendant operated his vehicle in a negligent manner). Second, it must be proven that the plaintiff was injured. Third, it must be proven that the defendant's negligent driving caused the plaintiff's injuries.

In this chapter, we will discuss each of the elements of a personal injury claim and the psychologist's various roles and challenges within those elements. It is not our intent to approach this discussion from either a plaintiff or defense standpoint, but to address the professional issues as objectively as possible. We will emphasize the inherent difficulties in establishing expert opinions in what might seem to some to be even "straight-forward" cases. In personal injury cases, expert witnesses and independent psychological evaluators are inevitably at times called upon to assess the impact of specific *evidence* of injury (i.e., fractures, disfigurement, or loss of limb), and at other times to assess and quantify a plaintiff's *perception* of injury (i.e., impaired self-esteem, body image, "suffering", or perceived disability). A variety of assessment methods may be used to formulate one's forensic impressions including comprehensive record reviews, consultation with other professionals, structured clinical interviews with the individual and available collateral sources (i.e., employers, family, or teachers), psychometric testing inventories, or even clinical observation. One might assume at the conclusion of such a comprehensive effort, that the "real truth" may confidently be known concerning what "really happened" during the precipitating event. We might also assume that we would know the precise extent of physical injury, emotional damage, and even the potential that a plaintiff may be embellishing or exaggerating their complaints for an identifiable purpose (i.e., compensation). However, as is clear to most experienced expert witnesses, perhaps the most solid platform that any investigator might hope for is a reasonable approximation of this presumed real value or truth. Accepting this humbling proposition, one author has somewhat facetiously adopted the concept of the "Van Dorsten Law of Thirds" to maintain objectivity, and to remain vigilant that several important facts may elude even the most ardent investigator. This self-developed guiding perception assumes that about one third of the information necessary to make an objective determination of a plaintiff's current physical and emotional status, functional capacity, subjectively perceived inabilities, and potential for embellishment, might be obtained via a comprehensive review of records. Another third of the critical information is likely to be obtained during comprehensive interviews and psychometric assessment of the individual, and interviews with appropriate corroborating resources. The final third is considered likely never to be objectively known. While this "law-of-thirds" philosophy is empirically untested, it might at least serve as a reminder of the limitations incumbent in most assessment modalities, and unknown motivations of some plaintiffs, so that practitioners might maintain reasonable borders with scientific testimony.

2. FAULT

In order to recover compensation for injuries sustained, a plaintiff must prove that a defendant was legally at fault. Negligence, intentional torts, and strict liability are the three basic categories of fault found in personal injury cases. Additionally, reckless misconduct, negligence per se, and contributory negligence will be briefly described.

2.1 Negligence

Negligence is the most common fault used in personal injury cases. In general, a defendant is negligent when they have a duty of reasonable care relative to the plaintiff, and when the defendant's conduct falls below the standard of reasonable care (Dobbs, 2000). In order to be liable to a particular plaintiff, the defendant must have a legal duty of reasonable care relative to the plaintiff. The concept of duty is one way of attempting to define, and limit, the scope of a citizen's responsibilities. For example, a person operating a motor vehicle is under a duty to all persons who could foreseeably be injured by its negligent operation (*Hatcher v. Mewborn*, 1970). Conversely, a landowner may have differing levels of duty to people on his property, depending on the reason for the visit. That is, in many jurisdictions the duty of care owed to an uninvited trespasser may be low or non-existent, while the duty of care owed to an invited guest, such as a retail customer, may be high (*Cain v. Johnson*, 2000; *Lyle v. Mladnich*, 1991).

The issue of duty can be important in malpractice suits against psychologists. For example, a psychologist conducting an independent psychological evaluation for the defendant in a lawsuit may have no duty to the plaintiff being evaluated, and therefore cannot be sued in malpractice by the plaintiff (*Hafner v. Beck*, 1995). A psychologist may also have no duty to third parties, such as family members, for negligently diagnosing a client (*Bird v. W.C.W.*, 1994), yet may have a duty to victims of their clients' violence in other circumstances (*Perreira v. State*, 1989).

The concept of negligence does not rely on the defendant's *intent*, but rather on the defendant's *conduct* (Kionka, 1977). The law applies an objective standard of reasonableness, such as what a "reasonable and prudent" person would have done in the same circumstances (American Law Institute, 1965). This is sometimes referred to as "ordinary care," "due care," or "reasonable care" (Kionka, 1977).

If the defendant was engaged in a situation requiring special skills, then the standard of care will be based on a specialized reference group. For example, if the defendant is the plaintiff's treating psychologist, the standard of care will be based on what a reasonable and prudent psychologist would have done in that situation (*Doe v. Board. of Education, Montgomery County*, 1981). As a general rule, the standard of care for a professional must be determined by expert testimony of peers from that profession (*Mitchell v. United States*, 1998).

2.2   Intentional Torts

Proof of fault as to an intentional tort involves the defendant's state of mind and the consequences that were intended (Keeton, 19840). That is, a tort is intentional when the defendant desired to cause the consequences that resulted, or believed that the consequences were substantially certain to result (American Law Institute, 1965). The focus is on the consequences of the defendant's act, not the act itself. For example, assume a defendant fired a gun while target shooting in the forest. Unknown to the defendant, the plaintiff was camping nearby and was struck by the bullet. Even though the defendant intentionally fired the gun, they did not intend for this specific result to occur or believe that such a result was substantially certain. Thus, it would be insufficient to maintain an intentional tort claim. However, intent is not limited only to consequences that the defendant desired to produce. Intent may be determined if the defendant knew that certain consequences were substantially certain to result from their actions. For example, assume a defendant threw a bomb into a lawyer's office in an attempt to harm the lawyer. The defendant knew that the lawyer's secretary was also in the office and would likely be injured. Even though the defendant had no particular desire to injure the secretary, the defendant would be liable in intentional tort for the secretary's injury as this was a consequence that was substantially certain to result (American Law Institute, 1965). Primary examples of intentional torts most common in personal injury litigation include battery, assault, false imprisonment, and intentional infliction of emotional distress - outrageous conduct.

Battery describes the intentional and unpermitted physical contact with a plaintiff's person (Kionka, 1977). There are two basic types of actionable contact including physical harm and those acts which do not produce physical harm, but are considered hostile, offensive or insulting. Physical harm can range from severe (e.g., gun shot wound) to relatively minor (e.g., abrasion or bruise). The contact can be actionable, even if the plaintiff benefits from it, such as surgery without proper consent (*Gragg v. Calandra*, 1998). Types of contact considered offensive or insulting include bodily contact that would offend a reasonable person's sense of dignity (American Law Institute, 1965). Examples of such contact might include unwanted sexual advances (*Skousen v. Nidy*, 1962).

Assault is an act by the defendant that intentionally creates in the plaintiff an apprehension of imminent battery (Shapo, 1999). Words alone are not sufficient to establish a cause of action for assault; there must be accompanying actions. As an example, pointing of one's finger at another and making threats of violence have been determined sufficient to establish a claim of assault (*Allen v. Walker*, 1990).

False imprisonment is the intentional and unlawful confinement of another (Dobbs, 2000). The actual confinement used can vary, and might include locking the plaintiff in a room, using physical restraints, alleging legal authority to detain someone, or holding one by threatening to use physical restraint. A mental health professional, who improperly initiates or continues an involuntary hold, can be liable for false imprisonment (*Sassali v. DeFauw*, 1998; *Jillson v. Caprio*, 1950).

Intentional infliction of emotional distress may be determined if it is proven that a defendant's conduct was (a) extreme and outrageous, (b) with the intent to cause severe emotional distress or a reckless disregard for such harm, and (c) did cause the plaintiff severe emotional harm (*Ahlers v. Schebil*, 1999; *Stuto v. Fleishman*, 1999). The claim is sometimes called an "outrageous conduct" claim. In order to be sufficiently outrageous to be actionable, the conduct must be "extreme...atrocious...and utterly intolerable to civilized society" (*Fusaro v. First Family Mortgage Corp.*, 1995).

2.3   Strict Liability

There are some situations where it is not necessary to prove the defendant's conduct was wrongful in order to hold the defendant liable. When a defendant is involved in abnormally dangerous activities, they can be held liable for a plaintiff's injuries without a showing of wrongful conduct. This kind of strict liability has been applied to such commercial activities as storing dynamite, oil drilling, fumigation, commercial fuel handling, the use of explosives, and crop dusting (Nolan & Ursin, 1987). Additionally, manufacturers of products are commonly held strictly liable if a defective product causes harm (American Law Institute, 1965).

2.4   Willful, Wanton or Reckless Misconduct

In some cases the defendant's conduct may not have been intentional, but it was beyond mere negligence. There can be additional claims, such as claims for punitive damages, or a broader imposed duty, when it is determined that a defendant's conduct was willful, wanton or reckless (Keeton, 1984). The terms, frequently used interchangeably, are generally intended to mean aggravated negligence. Many courts have found that driving while intoxicated rises to the level willful, wanton or reckless conduct (Keeton, 1988).

2.5   Negligence Per se

In some situations a defendant's actual conduct might have been a violation of law. For example, many courts will apply the rule of negligence per se in situations such as failing to yield right-of-way by turning in front of a plaintiff who has a traffic right-of-way (*Kesmarki v. Kisling*, 1968). That is, a defendant would be held negligent if their conduct violated a statute that was intended to protect people like the plaintiff.

2.6   Contributory Negligence and Comparative Fault

A plaintiff's injuries may be caused, in full or part, by his or her own negligent conduct. Traditionally in these cases, the courts follow the rule of contributory negligence (*McIntyre v. Balentine*, 1992). If a plaintiff's own negligence contributed to their harm, a defendant may be completely excused from liability. However, after developing many exceptions to this rule, the majority of jurisdictions now favor a comparative fault model. Under a comparative fault model, the plaintiff is not compensated for that portion of the damages caused by their own negligence. Various jurisdictions have adopted differing models of comparative fault, with some using a "pure" comparative fault model. That is, the plaintiff's and the defendant's fault are apportioned, and the plaintiff is awarded only the portion attributed to the defendant. So if a plaintiff were found to be 90% at fault and a defendant found to be 10% at fault, the defendant would pay 10% of the damages. A majority of jurisdictions use a "modified" model in which the defendant must be found to be at least 50% or 51% at fault before the defendant would be required to pay anything (Shapo, 1999, Dobbs, 2000).

3.   DAMAGES

A primary area of psychologist involvement in personal injury cases is in determining the type and extent of a plaintiff's damages. The intended purpose of a damage award is to "make the plaintiff whole" by providing financial compensation for injuries received (*Snow v. Villacci*, 2000). In general, two areas of damages are allowed in personal injury claims - economic and non-economic losses, and a plaintiff may be compensated for both past and future losses in both categories. In each case, the trier of fact must subjectively determine a dollar value for these losses, as no legal guidelines exist for such decisions (*Hilao v. Estate of Marcos*, 1996). This unenviable task forms perhaps the greatest controversy in personal injury cases - determining the amount of money one is "entitled to" after sustaining an injury due to the "negligence" of another. According to the National Safety Council (1998; cited from Szautner, 2001), the gross total compensation for unintentional injuries in the United States, including work, automobile, home, and public non-motor-vehicle injuries (e.g., falls in public, fire damage) reached nearly one-half trillion dollars. This amount constitutes nearly 60% of all monies spent on food in the country in this same period. Publication of these unfathomable expenditures have, over time, created a pejorative "general public" impression that people claiming injury routinely overstate complaints or outright "fake." Whether explicitly stated or not, the suspicion of malingering or exaggeration of symptoms for the purpose of obtaining money is a matter for consideration in the majority of forensic personal injury cases. It need be remembered that published data assessing the influence of financial compensation on physical complaints and treatment outcome has long been equivocal, with many studies showing little effect and others showing considerable impact (Cassidy, Carroll, Cote, Lemstra, Berglund, & Nygren, 2000; Rohling, Binder, & Langhinrichsen-Rohling, 1995). Indeed, the very perception by a plaintiff that others disbelieve their symptom report is likely to increase emotional distress and in some cases, increase symptom report to "verify" the severity of one's suffering. It creates an unfortunate "lose-lose" situation for many plaintiffs who feel they must amplify complaints to obtain adequate treatment, yet risk being considered an "exaggerator."

3.1   Economic Damages

Economic damages are losses the plaintiff has sustained that have an actual dollar value in the market place. Two commonly debated damages are lost earnings and medical costs.

Lost earnings can often be the most significant damage compensation in a personal injury case. Lost earnings can include past and future lost earnings (*Glasscock v. Armstrong Cork Co.*, 1991), and are calculated by deducting what the plaintiff will now be able to earn from the amount they would have been able to earn had they not been injured (*Reed v. Union Pacific Railroad Co.*, 1999). The calculation of lost earnings commonly requires the testimony of experts from such areas as health care, economics, and vocational rehabilitation, and can range from fairly simple to extremely complex. For example, assume a plaintiff worked at an hourly factory job, and because of an injury, missed work for two months prior to returning full time. The calculation of lost income would consider the amount of compensation they would have received during those months had the injury not occurred. To add complexity, consider this same case had treating experts testified that the plaintiff were now permanently limited to working only thirty hours per week. An expert economist would be consulted to determine the difference in income the plaintiff would receive over a lifetime, given the thirty-hour limitation. Consideration of such factors as cost of living raises, inflation, and the average working life of a person like the plaintiff would all be required. The obvious difficulty in assessing a person's capacity for return to work on even a modified basis is not in determining the hourly rate of pay or the job performance demands, but in attempting to specify their exact ability and motivation to consistently perform each of the necessary behaviors.

The plaintiff discussed thus far had a non-skilled hourly job and a simple employment situation. The considerations become much more complex as we deviate from these facts. For example, if the plaintiff had made plans to leave this hourly unskilled job and start a personal business, this would constitute a legitimate area of compensation so long as verifiable evidence of this plan existed (*Reed v. Union Pacific Railroad Co.*, 1999). If the plaintiff were a doctoral student in psychology, and because of injuries sustained was no longer able to continue, experts would be called upon to differentiate the plaintiff's pre- and post-accident career potential. Needless to say, expert opinions differ greatly on the complex issues of determining the plaintiff's actual career potential, potential embellishment of the purported disabilities, recovery prognosis, and the extent to which injuries might limit the plaintiff's future work performance.

A plaintiff is also entitled to be compensated for reasonable and necessary past and future medical costs resulting from an injury (*Monsanto Co. v. Johnson*, 1984), with the most complex determination being that of future medical costs. These estimates require both an assessment of the types of care needed as well as the future cost of that care, and expert testimony from several disciplines is typically necessary to prove future medical costs (*Lamont v. Independent School Dist. No. 395*, 1967). While it is not necessary to establish future costs with precise mathematical certainty, experts must hold their opinions within a reasonable probability, and the information offered must be sufficiently definite to allow the trier of fact to make a determination (*Renne v. Moser*, 1992).

Finally, a plaintiff may be awarded any other economic damages that result from the defendant's negligence. For example, an award may be made for past and future household services damages if were determined that the plaintiff was no longer able to complete home care duties and must hire others for this purpose (*Schultz v. Harrison Radiator Div. General Motors Corp.*, 1997).

3.2   Non-Economic Damages

A plaintiff is entitled to compensation for the physical and emotional pain and suffering that is the result of the defendant's wrongful conduct. This is a highly contentious area of expert input because of the difficulty in defining and quantifying such subjective complaints. Compensation in personal injury cases is awarded in the form of money, and the trier of fact must decide how much money the plaintiff should receive in order to be compensated for the misery suffered in the past and the anticipated misery in the future. In non-economic damages, a variety of factors are assessed to determine the impact of one's injuries on the present and future functioning and quality of life. These factors include pain and suffering, loss of enjoyment of life, physical impairment, disfigurement, bereavement, loss of consortium, and other punitive damages. A brief discussion of each follows.

Pain and suffering is the most common non-economic damage awarded in personal injury cases. This highly controversial and non-specific label encompasses both the past and future physical and emotional misery the plaintiff might experience, including the actual sensation of pain, inconvenience related to the injuries, loss of bodily function, emotional distress, and associated psychological issues (Dobbs, 2000). "Emotional distress" is a subcategory of pain and suffering that is also broadly and vaguely defined as the following:

> "[E]motional distress" means mental distress, mental pain and suffering, or mental anguish. It includes all highly unpleasant mental reactions, such as fright, horror, grief, humiliation, embarrassment, anger, chagrin, disappointment, and worry. (Oklahoma Uniform Jury Instr. - Civil, sec. 20.3)

While perhaps tightly intertwined from a legal standpoint, the forensic psychologist may separate pain and suffering for subjective evaluation. In a commonly accepted definition, Loeser (1989) has differentiated *pain* as a nociceptive stimulus representing tissue damage; and *suffering* as the negative emotional consequences produced by pain perception. Like pain, which is considered an exclusively subjective phenomenon in most avenues of medicine, an objective assessment of "suffering" may seem literally impossible. No valid and reliable measures exist to assist the forensic examiner in the quantifying this specific construct. Accordingly, no empirical analysis has identified "sub-components" of suffering, which might allow some cumulative quantification of each sub-component into an overall "suffering index." Much like the intangible constructs of "belief" or "desire," it is a considerable challenge for a forensic investigator to provide an estimate of how much suffering a plaintiff might have experienced to date, or will continue to experience in the future. Suffering is most commonly expressed in courts as a subjective combination of verbal pain report, depression, suicidal ideation, anxiety, or impaired cognitive functioning or efficiency. For an expert to deduce that a plaintiff has experienced an increase in this construct over time would obviate the necessity to quantify the levels of each factor the plaintiff might have experienced pre-injury. While one may be tempted to believe that litigants easily receive compensation for suffering, one must recall that it is the responsibility of the plaintiff to "prove" that they have experienced "suffering" due to the injuries caused by another. The nebulous foothold upon which experts might base their opinion has made proof of this claim somewhat difficult in cases without accompanying levels of severe pain or prolonged disability. Interestingly, an investigation of a system-wide elimination of payments for pain and suffering has recently shown to produced a rapid decrease in the incidence of claims for whiplash and improved prognosis for treatment of whiplash injury (Cassidy, Carroll, Cote, Lemstra, Berglund, & Nygren, 2000).

Loss of enjoyment of life damages, a sub-category of pain and suffering, is allowed by many courts to compensate an injured party for undue restrictions placed upon their ability to enjoy certain previous pleasures because of injuries sustained. Thus, a plaintiff could be awarded damages for the loss of ability to play golf, dance, bowl, see the sunset, hear music, or engage in sexual activity (*Fantozzi v. Sandusky Cement Prod. Co., 1992; Dobbs, 2000*).

"Physical impairment" and "disfigurement" are additional categories for which a plaintiff may receive damages following injury (*Herrera v. Gene's Towing*, 1992). Physical impairment usually refers to the objective physical limitations that a plaintiff experiences as a result of their injuries, as opposed to any loss of income or resulting emotional disorders (Kionka, 1977). Thus, a plaintiff may be compensated for no longer being able to walk, talk, hear, see, or perform some other basic function of life. This use of "physical impairment" in the tort system need be differentiated from the more detailed use of the term "physical impairment" in the worker's compensation system. Some jurisdictions also allow for compensation for any disfigurement the plaintiff has experienced. One court has defined "disfigurement" as:

[T] hat which impairs the beauty, symmetry, or appearance of a person . .
. that which renders unsightly, misshaped, or imperfect, or deforms in
some manner. (*Terry v. Garcia*, 1990, p. 858).

Assessing the impact of disfigurement is central in cases in which a
plaintiff has sustained changes in the physical appearance of their body from
burn injuries, violence, loss of limb, or unintended radical surgical alteration.
An individual's subjective response to these physical changes has been
empirically shown to adversely affect one's self-perception, the perception of
others towards the individual with altered appearance, interactions with the
general public, and to place some individuals at greater risk for emotional
degeneration (Baur, Hardy, & Van Dorsten, 1998; Rybarczyk, Nyenhuis,
Nicholas, Cash, & Kaiser, 1995; Rybarczyk, Nyenhuis, Nicholas, Schulz,
Alioto, & Blair, 1992; Van Dorsten, 2000). Only very rarely might a case be
brought regarding an individual whose disfigurement is not visually apparent
to others, but rather a personal perception (e.g., body dysmorphic disorder).
  Quantification of total body impairment is commonly achieved in
medicine via impairment ratings conducted by specially training physicians.
These ratings are, in turn, used to determine the extent of residual permanent
impairment once the person is determined to have reached maximum
medical improvement - or the stage at which continued treatment efforts are
unlikely to substantially alter their functional ability. Objective findings of
physical impairment are combined via structured rating formulas to calculate
the percentage of permanent total body impairment (American Medical
Association, 1993). Less objective, yet contributing to this rating of whole
person impairment, is a quantification of the contribution of "mental and
behavioral" factors influencing the patient's ability to function. These
ratings constitute a subjective estimate by providers as to the extent that
emotional or behavioral factors independently limit the person's ability for
activities of daily living, social functioning, concentration, persistence and
pace, and their ability to adapt to stressful circumstances. In most cases,
mental and behavioral ratings are quite small (i.e., 0-5% permanent
impairment), given the criterion requiring at least episodic supervision for
daily activities at higher levels.
  Bereavement damages may be awarded to family members when a
person dies as the result of a defendant's wrongful conduct. In addition to
applicable economic damages, such as loss of financial support, family
members are usually entitled to damages for their bereavement and
emotional distress resulting from the decedent's death (Shapo, 1999).
  Loss of consortium damages may be awarded as compensation in
response to negative consequences encountered by the injured party's
spouse. These losses may be compensable, and generally include loss of

affection, solace, comfort, companionship, society, assistance, and sexual relations (*Whittlesey v. Miller*, 1978).

Punitive damages, sometimes called "exemplary damages," are not for the purpose of compensating the plaintiff, but rather for the purpose of punishing the defendant. In order to obtain an award of punitive damages it is usually necessary to show that the defendant's wrongful conduct was intentional, or willful, wanton and reckless (Kionka, 1977).

4.   CAUSATION

In order to prevail in a personal injury case, the plaintiff must prove that the defendant's conduct was a cause of the plaintiff's harm. It is somewhat difficult to analyze causation issues, because courts often use the terms and concepts of causation in inconsistent and contradictory ways.

There are generally two levels of causation a plaintiff must prove - cause in fact and proximate or "legal" cause (*Hagan v. Texaco Refining and Marketing, Inc.*, 1995; Dobbs, 2000). Along with these two levels, the more complicated issue of apportioning partial liability in the event of multiple causation will be addressed in the following section.

4.1   Cause in Fact

A plaintiff must prove that a defendant's conduct was an actual cause of the plaintiff's injuries. In some cases this can be a straightforward issue. If a defendant negligently rear-ended the plaintiff's car and the plaintiff was taken to the hospital with a broken arm, it might be easy to conclude that the plaintiff's emergent need for a cast on the arm that day was caused by the defendant's conduct. However, causation issues can quickly become very complex, and two other principles, the but-for test and the substantial factor rule, may be used in the determination.

In order to establish causation, the plaintiff must first satisfy the "but-for" test. That is, the plaintiff must prove that, *but for* the defendant's conduct, the plaintiff's injuries would not have occurred (*Callahan v. Cardinal Glennon Hospital*, 1993; Keeton, 1984). In some cases the but-for test can be overly broad. For example, if a driver was speeding through town, and a tree fell onto their car, it could be argued that, but for the excess speed, the automobile would not have arrived at that particular spot in time for the tree to fall on it. While this may seem true from a purely logical sense, it would likely offend our sense of justice to find that the driver's speeding was determined to be the cause of that accident. Conversely, the but-for test can be too narrow when multiple potential causes of the plaintiff's injury exist. For example, consider a case in which a plaintiff worked in a refinery for thirty years, and developed asbestosis as a result of prolonged exposure to asbestos at work. Over the years, there were multiple suppliers of the toxic insulation, allowing each individual supplier to argue that the plaintiff could not prove they would be healthy, *but for* the presence of their specific product in the refinery. In this example of multiple causes, a court held that the plaintiff need only show that the defendant's product was a substantial factor in the cause of his condition (*Lineaweaver v. Plant Insulation Co.*, 1995).

As the but-for test is comparatively simplistic and insufficient in many cases, courts have adopted the "substantial factor rule" as an alternative or additional consideration. The substantial factor rule has been interpreted as meaning the defendant's conduct is a substantial factor in bringing about the harm (*Parks v. AlliedSignal, Inc.*, 1997), and applies not only to the predominate cause, but to any other cause which constitutes a "substantial factor" in bringing about the injury (*Peer v. City of Newark*, 1961). Thus, it does not apply to acts that are considered merely negligible causes (*Acands v. Asner*, 1966).

4.2   Proximate or Legal Cause

The term "proximate cause" is used in a variety of contradictory and confusing ways in legal writing and is probably most usefully described as "legal cause." That is, once it has been determined that a defendant's conduct is a cause in fact of a plaintiff's harm, there is still a question of whether, from a legal policy perspective, the defendant should be held liable. Proximate cause considerations frequently involve the issues of remoteness and foreseeability (*Oregon Laborers-Employers Health & Welfare Trust Fund v. Philip Morris, Inc.*, 1998), with the general rule being that the defendant is only liable for the kinds of harms they foreseeably risked by their conduct and to the class of people specifically put at risk by that conduct (Dobbs, 2000).

4.3 Multiple Causation

Issues of causation are most challenging when there are multiple causes of the plaintiff's injuries. In order to be liable, the defendant's conduct need not be the sole cause of the injury, the closest in time, or the nearest (Kionka, 1977). Three concepts - apportionment, the eggshell skull rule, and joint and several liability - may be considered when determining the contribution of multiple sources of causation.

In some cases, a plaintiff's injuries may be differentially apportioned to more than one contributing cause. For example, consider a case in which a plaintiff with chronic shoulder problems was involved in an accident which worsened the condition of their shoulder. Two years after the accident, this same plaintiff required surgery. Testifying experts disagreed and it was deemed by the court that the plaintiff's need for surgery was caused by both chronic degeneration and by the accident. In this case, the court found that the defendant was only liable for a certain percentage of the plaintiff's shoulder problems (*Browning v. Ringel*, 2000).

It is important to distinguish apportionment from the "eggshell skull rule." Using the classic law school hypothetical, assume two men were having a verbal disagreement in a bar, and one struck the other on the head. Though the defendant's blow was such that it would have caused only a swollen bump on most heads, the victim fell dead. It was subsequently discovered that where the victim was struck, their skull was "thin as an eggshell." Thus, the reason for this peculiar death was an unknown birth defect. The fact that the victim had a pre-existing vulnerability would not reduce the defendant's liability for the victim's death (Dobbs. 2000). This "eggshell skull" rule is cited throughout the cases in America, standing for the principle that "the defendant must take the plaintiff as [they were found]" (*Callan v. Hackett*, 2000). After apportionment, the defendant would be liable only for the additional damages their conduct caused.

Finally, in some cases multiple defendants might be jointly liable for the plaintiff's injuries. There are three situations where this is likely to occur. First, a plaintiff's injuries may be caused by defendants who act in concert (Dobbs, 2000). For example, if two friends were riding down the road, heavily drinking together, and the driver crashed into the plaintiff because of his inebriation, the friend who was not driving may be liable because he was involved in a "joint concerted tortious activity" (*Price v. Halstead*, 1987). Second, an uninvolved defendant may be vicariously liable for the acts of the wrongdoer, as when an employer could be liable for the conduct of an employee, or that partners and persons engaged in joint enterprises are often liable for each others' conduct (Dobbs, 2000). Finally, if the damages cannot be apportioned between multiple wrongdoers, the wrongdoers may be jointly liable for all damages (Kionka, 1977).

5.   FORENSIC PSYCHOLOGY AND PERSONAL INJURY LITIGATION

In the introductory chapter, Van Dorsten identified several historical challenges to the use of mental health professionals as expert witnesses in forensic cases. These issues included the limited scientific validity of certain measures, vast heterogeneity of both practitioners and specific behavioral responses, limited diagnostic agreement and predictive accuracy among providers, and high reliance upon verbal measures for both diagnosis and assessment of change. It has been discussed that multiple behavioral and emotional responses might be anticipated in any given population of people in response to a common event (e.g., tornado, loss of job, or car accident). A person's behavioral history, exposure to trauma, coping repertoire, abilities for resource utilization, and personal motivations may all drastically impact the number and severity of complaints that follow a given event. Certainly the interplay of these factors, along with the symptoms of physical injury, provides a considerable challenge for the forensic psychologist in the area of personal injury litigation.

Psychological or emotional issues are routinely considered by those in law to be less "clean" or precise in diagnosis and treatment than common medical conditions. For example, few controversial theories exist regarding the reliable detection of high blood pressure, x-ray interpretation, appendix removal, or measuring body weight. However, one needn't wander far in considering some of the most commonly debated medico-legal conditions to debunk this argument. For example, many of the medical conditions routinely compensated in personal injury cases have few, if any, "gold-standard" or confirmatory measures of presence/absence. An exemplary list might include repetitive motion syndrome, vertigo, TMJ, low back pain, fibromyalgia, mild brain injury, headache, or whiplash. Diagnosis of these medical conditions is also primarily verbal in nature, with potential insidious waxing and waning of symptoms. These conditions may be greatly affected by "non-physical" factors including specific cognitions or emotions, and can produce periods of disability greatly in excess of that expected by their associated physical findings. Further, the *severity* of these conditions is verbally and behaviorally dependent, and literally impossible to empirically verify (e.g., slight versus severe headache, slight versus severe dizziness).

There is little documented scientific relationship between the amount of tissue damage experienced in an injury and the extent or duration of pain or disability that a person might experience. For example, the loss of a little finger may have minimal impact on a person who operates a jackhammer for employment, and yet be completely disabling for a concert pianist. Further, in the absence of actual observation of a person performing a task they have labeled as impossible, it is very difficult to quantify a plaintiff's actual versus reported ability to drive, provide child-care, complete self-care activities, participate with home care, or to engage in work or recreational activities (e.g., skiing, jogging, sewing, playing a piano, exercise, or attending church or social events). Only observed inconsistencies in reported inabilities and actual behaviors might provide information to challenge a person's perceptions of their abilities.

5.1   Personal Injury Assessments

Considering the scientific challenges inherent in assessing and quantifying a given individual's emotional or behavioral response to physical injury, the forensic psychologist must begin with a comprehensive knowledge of the empirical assessment and treatment literature. This knowledge must necessarily include an understanding of the prevalence of common emotional conditions following injury, the most valid and reliable means of assessing these phenomena, frequent co-morbid conditions, accepted treatment algorithms, prognosis for resolution, and extraneous factors which might adversely effect timely resolution. It is also the forensic psychologist's responsibility to be familiar with gaps or "unknowns" in the available literature, populations or circumstances which might pose exceptions to prevalent findings, and corresponding areas of literature from which one might "borrow" clinical impressions to reasonably generalize to the specific case or population in question. As each and every individual assessed in a forensic circumstance constitutes a single case design study, the relative applicability of the available literature to each specific circumstance is of issue. Finally, the forensic psychologist must be aware of the inherent limitations in tools of their practice including the current literature base, available assessment strategies, normative populations, reliability of certain measures to predict outcome, and factors influencing prognosis. While obviously not asked to provide medical opinions regarding a plaintiff's condition, a forensic psychologist may benefit greatly from at least a modicum of medical knowledge, including an understanding of common treatment algorithms for specific physical conditions, "normative" courses of recovery, reasonably expected time frames for symptom resolution, medical or behavioral factors affecting prognosis, and the patient's responsibilities in their treatment.

As per the preceding discussion regarding the lack of definitive measures to verify the actual presence or severity of many medical and psychological complaints, the need to compare individual circumstances with reasonable normative data to discern the probability that available clinical information accurately represents a person's actual abilities is obviated. Forensic psychologists are asked to determine extent of emotional and behavioral inabilities, and to estimate future abilities and prognosis from a relatively limited behavioral sample. For example, even in the ideal clinical environment, a daunting ratio of 167:1 hours exists. Specifically, even if a provider were to spend one full hour per week with each of their patients, there would still be 167 hours per week that they had no contact. As such, it is quite a task to accurately quantify or predict a patient's abilities across time and setting from this limited exposure. Obviously, the amount of contact in forensic examinations is markedly less than this "ideal" standard. To meet their considerable obligation to the court, and to ensure reliability and validity of impressions to whatever extent possible, forensic psychologists must perform multi-modal assessments involving archival record review, clinical observations of behavior in office, clinical interviews, and appropriate psychometric testing inventories to expand their behavioral sample and develop clinical impressions that might most accurately represent the patient's actual emotional and behavioral status at any given time. As the commonly used assessment strategies have been thoroughly discussed elsewhere in this book, only brief discussion of their specific applications in personal injury cases will be attempted. To further exemplify assessment and prognostic challenges, the application of forensic psychology principles in two common personal injury circumstances, low back pain and mild traumatic brain injury, will be discussed. These discussions are not meant to overly simplify these complex medical issues, and only select topics will be raised to exemplify psychologist activity.

5.2   Archival Record Review

Review of archival records is critical in understanding the circumstances of injury at the time that they unfolded. As time progresses following the date of injury, patient reports of acute accident issues can become increasingly inaccurate. As opposed to immediately assuming diabolical intent for these inaccuracies, many potential explanatory factors need be considered including acute loss of consciousness or change in sensorium at the scene of the event, anxiety interference, intoxication or substance use, or provision of information by others over time after the event. If each of these factors could reasonably be ruled out, then consideration of intentional misreporting might be indicated. Reviews of accident reports often shed light on potentially important diagnostic issues including speed of impact, personal or automobile damage recorded at the scene, observations of the person's acute state of consciousness and/or sensorium, post-accident medical observations, descriptions, diagnosis, or care offered by others at the scene. This information "snapshot" usually constitutes the most reliable post-accident baseline information with which to compare symptom development or resolution in the weeks or months following the event. Review of available ongoing treatment records offers insights as to medical or psychological assessment and treatment efforts, changes in conditions over time, the individual's cooperation with treatment, and changes in independent daily functioning.

5.3   Behavioral Interviews

Behavioral interviews are conducted for the purpose of obtaining the individual's depiction of their subjective historical (i.e., pre-morbid) physical and emotional functioning with which to contrast their current status. Examiners may often find that descriptions of pre-injury status are comparatively glorified and again, review of medical history and pre-morbid emotional symptoms similar to those experienced post-accident are necessary. Examinees may often minimize pre-morbid health or emotional issues in comparison with the myriad of concerns harbored post injury. Interviews also allow the examiner to obtain relevant family, occupational, educational, or military history information. A comprehensive assessment of the person's daily personal, marital, family, occupational, or recreational activities need be conducted. Efforts to obtain interval or ordinal estimates of frequency, intensity and duration of changes in activities should be conducted to quantify gradients of change following injury however possible.   A solid functional behavioral analysis approach to the quantification of both pre- and post-injury abilities is likely to be more helpful to a court than any clinical description offered by an examiner. Accordingly, Likert ratings of emotional distress pre- and post-injury may assist the examiner in documenting the individual's subjective impressions of changes in emotional status.   This strategy may assume paramount importance in a forensic psychologist's attempts to assist the court with apportioning the effects of an injury.

Comprehensive interviews allow the examiner to obtain information regarding the person's goals for current or future treatment, and perceived abilities to resume of vocational, educational, or avocational activities. Interviews with spouses or family members may offer corroborating or conflicting views of the person's individual impressions, but this information is often subject to the same inaccuracies, interpretations, and potential distortions as the report of the patient. A comprehensive interview allows the examiner to obtain data regarding abilities which the person has retained, those which are lost or limited, and to deduce the relative consistencies of these limitations across time (e.g., day-to-day or time of day), setting (e.g., home, work, doctor's office), and circumstance (e.g., work, recreation). This information may be critical to the forensic examiner in determining an impression regarding the validity of complaints.

5.4   Psychological Testing

A wide variety of psychometric inventories exist to assist in forensic examinations. Simplistically, the data obtained from psychometric testing provides the best vehicle with which to compare the reported symptoms and opinions of the person under examination with comparable normative patient populations. Obviously, no individual inventory possesses the power of diagnostic exclusivity (e.g., surpassing a criterion score confirms a specific diagnosis), but the vast psychological literature supporting the use of psychometric inventories to determine presence or severity of psychopathology, coping strategies, intellectual abilities, or one's perceived abilities or inabilities is a critical supplement to clinical information. Many inventories offer at least moderate predictive ability regarding prognosis (i.e., persons producing this profile, or achieving this level of severity frequently benefit less from treatment). There is no standardized battery of tests that has consistently been recommended for use with personal injury cases, and thus each examiner assumes responsibility for the validity, reliability and applicability of the specific instruments they choose for use.

Given the repeated cautions regarding the lack of a reliable "truth-o-meter" to measure the accuracy of verbal report, no forensic examination should be conducted without obtaining response style or validity testing information. Appreciating the relative discomfort of many professionals regarding assessment of malingering, this recommendation is not made to insinuate that all plaintiff report is suspicious or embellished. It need be remembered that the process for identifying evidence to *support* the conclusion of malingering is exactly the same as the process used to determine the *absence of evidence* of malingering. It is often unnatural for mental health practitioners to suspect malingering when recording a person's symptoms, and many may be reluctant to report malingering even with supporting data, given concerns over legal liability for the claim, or fears of violence or revenge by the individual being assessed (Resnick, 1997). However, in the absence of validity testing, one cannot offer forensic conclusions with any sense of relative confidence. Validity impressions can be obtained by conducting forced choice testing as part of a neuropsychological test battery, or administering the Minnesota Multiphasic Personality Inventory- Revised (MMPI-2: Butcher, Dahlstrom Graham, Tellegen, & Kaemmer, 1989). Please see Butcher, Chapter Four of this book for information regarding the properties and utility of the MMPI-2 in forensic assessments, and Goodyear (1998), for a thorough discussion of validity testing strategies associated with forensic neuropsychological testing.

While the specific prevalence of malingering of psychological symptoms following medical injury is unknown (Resnick, 1997), the rate of malingering in forensic cases overall has been estimated at 15-17% (Rogers, Sewell, and Goldstein, 1994). To supplement validity testing data, the forensic examiner is obligated to comprehensively assess the consistency of a plaintiff's reports and abilities across time and setting as previously mentioned. Rogers (1997) has suggested a characteristic pattern in those who falsely embellish or malinger symptoms to include demonstrating inconsistent behavioral abilities across settings, or producing symptoms that are highly improbable in light of one's injury. Only structured efforts at behavioral analysis and quantification are likely to consistently detect such patterns. Physical disabilities should present consistent obstacles across similar tasks at work, recreation, and in the completion of routine daily activities. For example, a person who claims an inability to walk more than one block, but ambulates several blocks without assistance to appointments might seem suspect. Likewise, a person who suggests that they are incapable of sitting over thirty minutes which would allow them to work, but routinely drives over sixty minutes to and from therapy appointments should raise an objective eyebrow. In some personal injury cases, the strategy of insurance surveillance may be employed in an apparent attempt to "catch" a person performing activities which have been deemed beyond their capacity. While most experienced forensic examiners have seen blatant cases of malingering caught on film, this is rare and this strategy can equally create anger, anxiety and resentment in an injured person who might have been specifically instructed by treating physicians to perform all physical activities possible to expedite recovery. In the following sections, the challenges of assessing psychological and behavioral changes in response to common medical conditions will be exemplified.

5.5   Low Back Pain

Low back pain is a common condition which afflicts millions of people over the course of their lifetime, and one of the most commonly debated medical conditions in personal injury litigation cases. It has been estimated that up to 80% of people in the United States will experience low back pain at some time in their life (Robertson, 1993), and that up to 80-90% of those with back pain will experience a remission of their symptoms within six weeks without regard for the type of treatment attempted, if any (Waddell, 1987). Whether back pain appears insidiously, or following an accident or injury, there will be no objective diagnostic findings to substantiate the complaint in up to 80% of cases (Deyo, 1986).

Despite this high population base rate, low back pain is frequently considered an "abnormal" condition, and diagnostic testing (e.g., x-ray, CT, MRI) may be exhaustively conducted in an effort to "find the problem." In cases such as motor vehicle accidents in which back pain is a residual symptom, multiple diagnostic procedures are commonly conducted to rule out structural damage. Given the likely absence of diagnostic findings, most low back pain cases carry the diagnosis of musculo-ligamentous pain or "soft tissue" injury, and an accompanying expectation for resolution with conservative care within weeks to months. Should a patient evidence an identifiable lesion on diagnostic testing, it is often considered that the pain "generator" has been found and can be corrected either surgically or non-surgically. However, recent studies have found that the relationship between any specific precipitating event, back pain, and diagnostic findings may not be so clear. In a study of healthy, asymptomatic adults (i.e., no current or historical back problems), only 36% had normal lumbar disks on MRI (Jensen, Brant-Zawadski, Obuchowski, Modic, Malkansian, & Ross, 1994). These authors concluded that disk abnormalities are not uncommon in the general healthy public and may be coincidental to the development of pain. Similarly, Bowden, Davis, Dina, Patronas, & Wiesel (1990) reported that one-third of lumbar scans were abnormal in healthy, asymptomatic adults, including the finding that some 35% of young adults between the ages of 20-39 showed evidence of disk degeneration or bulging. Such data provides contestation of the facile conclusion that objective findings of disk injury provides compensable "evidence" of injury related to any one specific event.

Back pain accounts for nearly one quarter of all disability claims and over 40% of all disability expenditures. Within these staggering numbers rests the ominous fact that less than 10% of claimants account for nearly 75% of these expenditures (Spengler, Bigos, Martin, Zeh, Fisher, & Nachemson, 1986). Such dramatic compensation for back pain is a relatively new phenomenon, with expenditures increasing nearly 2,700% from 1960-80, despite no change in the incidence of disorder (Fordyce, 1985). This number can be compared with a 400% in compensation for lung disease, the second highest prevalence increase, over this same time period. The amount of compensation for a disorder so difficult to empirically verify presents ripe opportunity for frequent litigation.

Persistent back pain is commonly associated with elevated rates of depression (Atkinson, Ingram, Kremer, & Saccuzo, 1986; Sullivan, Reesor, Mikail, & Fisher, 1992); and legal claims of post-traumatic stress disorder (PTSD) stemming from circumstances of injury have skyrocketed in the past two decades. Depression is currently believed to be a rapidly independent contributing factor to disability in the United States, and PTSD claims have burgeoned in the personal injury arena since the introduction of the diagnosis in 1980. In fact, the number of claims for PTSD, and the difficulty in proving or disproving the clinical diagnosis, has led some authors to declare it a "growth industry" for U.S. courts (Simon, 1995). Others have opined that PTSD may have the greatest effect on the legal system of any emotional diagnosis in American history (Stone, 1993).

In a book on pre-surgical psychological assessments, Block (1996) detailed the most common non-medical reasons that a patient with prolonged pain might be referred to a psychologist for behavioral evaluation of factors potentially affecting treatment outcome. Included among these criteria are: (a) extended disability (e.g., over six months) without improvement or with functional decline; (b) behavioral limitations determined to be in excess of those expected by the relative physical findings; (c) clinical symptoms of depression or anxiety; (d) unreasonable expectations about future improvement or anticipated deterioration of function; (e) work dissatisfaction or nebulous return to work goals; and (f) evidence of financial gain or involvement in litigation. Interestingly, these same issues form the foundation for the vast majority of requests for forensic behavioral assessment in personal injury cases.

In light of the data discussed above - that few with low back pain might have explanatory diagnostic findings to account for their complaints, and that findings may have little or no functional relationship to complaints - subjective factors affecting disability become the primary issues of debate in most cases. Despite the expectation for swift resolution of low back pain in most cases, there seems a common public mentality that "once you have it, you're always going to have it." The conflicting nature of these two opinions creates the controversy in law. The fundamental legal debate in many personal injury cases often centers on exploration of the potential reasons that remission failed to occur in a timely fashion in a given case. Once the medical aspects of the case are verified, the potential emotional, behavioral, or motivational reasons that this particular person has not achieved the remission that would have been expected is the issue for debate. It is comparatively easy to litigate cases with ample evidence of physical damage from assault or injury, but a much more contentious issue when little objective evidence of injury exists. Many cases involve competing experts who embrace either side of the "can't prove they have it, can't prove they don't" contest, and except in rare blatant cases, these debates typically continue into the "can't prove they're faking, can't prove they're not" conundrum. Forensic psychologists must anticipate and prepare their arguments for these challenges, and enlisting the variety of assessment strategies previously discussed, should provide adequate foundation for their opinions. In the legal arena, having a clinical opinion is analogous to having eyebrows. Forensic experts who base their opinions on scientific literature, clinical interviews, archival records, behavioral observations, and psychometric responses compared with appropriate norms, have the greatest likelihood of providing valid information to the trier of fact. It is the ethical responsibility of the examiner to report whether an empirical, multi-modal evaluation reveals either presence or absence of support for any extraneous factors potentially affecting recovery.

Many of the criteria for psychological exploration listed above are weakly defined and subjective to the treating health care specialist. For example, the perception of pain or disability "in excess of findings" primarily provides information about the treating professional's subjective impression versus very gross norms for recovery for patients with low back pain. This is not to say that *relative* normative time periods for recovery do not exist in medicine, just that this normative range is very broad and may not adequately account for the complexities of any given case. Similarly, the criterion of potential financial gain or involvement in active litigation is a mute point by the time the forensic assessment is requested. Forensic psychologists are advised to withhold suspicions based upon this criteria and to routinely proceed with validity testing. A thorough forensic psychological evaluation will investigate many subjective factors potentially affecting clinical recovery including unreasonable treatment expectations, cognitive impairment, poor adherence with treatments, maladaptive emotional repertoires (i.e., "catastrophizing" regarding one's circumstance, prominent depressive or anxiety symptoms), or excessive perceived disability (e.g., "...nothing I can do to make this better").

A mammoth literature regarding the correlation of depression and pain exists and merits only brief mention here. Depression is one of the most common co-morbid states accompanying persistent pain, with estimates ranging as high as one-third or more of all patients meeting the diagnosis (Turner & Romano, 1984). If depression inventories are used as part of a psychometric battery, one need be mindful of data suggesting that paper-and-pencil inventories might over-diagnose by two to three fold the actual prevalence of depression given high concordance of behavioral and emotional symptoms between the two disorders (Boyd & Weisman, 1982). Mindful awareness of this type of data will minimize the introduction of a "false positive" diagnosis which might redirect the legal debate.

Finally, a brief discussion of the issues affecting a plaintiff's likelihood of returning to work following personal injury is merited. Return to work is commonly held as the bellwether of successful medical treatment and formal recovery from injuries. Both forensic medical and psychological examiners are routinely asked to comment on whether they believe a person has the "capacity" to return to work. In some cases, it may be determined that a plaintiff's severe physical injuries preclude their ability to return to a labor-oriented position, and retraining for modified employment might be considered. Similarly, a person may sustain severe brain damage which prohibits return to certain jobs, and in extreme cases, depression or anxiety may be the prohibitive disabling factor. Burton, Conti, Chen, Schultz, & Edington (1999), reported that mental health disorders were the number one cause of absence from work and the number three cause of lower workplace productivity. As such, the appropriate debate regarding return to work in these circumstance is not *whether* a plaintiff might ever return to work, but rather defining the *circumstances* under which one could attempt even graded reintroduction into the work environment. In many cases, the return to the structure of work and social reward of returning to co-workers might provide a positive influence to control emotional symptoms.

For the purpose of determining economic damages as lost wages, one must consider both the ability and *desire* of the individual to return to their usual and customary employment. This is a particularly important distinction, because job dissatisfaction, or anger at an employer are not specific criteria for disability, yet may have significant impact on one's willingness to return to employment. Previous studies have shown that psychosocial and personality variables are stronger predictors than medical variables as to who might file an injury claim at work, and in the prediction of work-related disability (Battie & Bigos, 1991; Bigos, Battie, Spengler, Fisher, Fordyce, Hansson, Nachemson, & Wortley, 1991; Ormel, VonDorff, Ustun, Pini, Forten, & Oldehinkel, 1994). This data, much like the MRI and lumbar disk data earlier discussed, suggests that determination of one's capacity to return to work following injury may have little association with physical injury and again fall into the realm of the forensic psychologist.

5.6   Mild Traumatic Brain Injury

Millions of people in the United States sustain undiagnosed and untreated injuries to their brain each year. In fact, Hartlage (1990) estimated that the average adult is likely to have sustained two significant injuries to their brain by age 60, but less that 5% might ever be hospitalized for such event. In any given audience of the general public, the vast majority may indeed report at some time having been rendered briefly unconscious, or experienced brief periods of time after the injury in which they could "hardly remember what [they] were doing." Further, surveys of any public audience will likely find that most acknowledge having experienced an event which left them "dazed," "confused," or having "seen stars" as the result of a fall, sports injury, or otherwise having been "conked on the head." Interestingly, virtually all of these common claims would likely meet a frequently used medical diagnosis of mild traumatic brain injury (American Congress of Rehabilitation Medicine Head Injury Special Interest Group, 1993). This liberal definition often eradicates the debate as to whether or not it is believed that any given plaintiff sustained a diagnostic brain injury, and directs most forensic psychological and neuropsychological assessments towards those factors which might be contributing to delayed recovery or excessive disability compared to what might be expected given the initial evidence of injury. In fact, to meet this particular diagnosis for brain injury, neither loss of consciousness nor any period of post-traumatic amnesia is required. A plaintiff's report of change in sensorium or feeling "dazed, disoriented or confused" (p. 86) satisfies the criteria, and is likely to prompt emergency room or other primary medical personnel to offer precautions regarding observation for symptoms "associated with brain injury." To be sure, most individuals would not be expected to be certain of brief loss of consciousness, or short-term amnesia. Thus, without supporting impressions and documentation from others available in the acute post-injury phase, it is likely to never be known what the exact presence, or duration of any symptoms were. Another tough spot for a litigant in light of an often-suspicious public, and an area ripe for misuse for those who would intentionally produce false symptoms. Consequently, many forensic practitioners actually accept that the client's initial complaints fulfilled the diagnosis of mild traumatic brain injury at the time of the event, and concentrate their assessment on the prognostic expectation that up to 85-90%

of patients will fully recover from similar events within six to nine months (Alexander, 1985, Binder & Rolling, 1996). As with low back pain, most patients would be expected to have few, if any, confirming medical diagnostic findings to support a claim of mild brain injury, and again the cognitive, emotional and behavioral sequelae of the event are likely to be the most hotly debated issues.

Despite the apparent frequency of minor injuries to the head in the general population, the term "brain injury" often conjures up a much more ominous image in the layperson. Conceptualizations of this as a "normal" event, and expectations of swift resolution of symptoms cease. This "common sense" generalization is important because it very likely shapes the expectations of the average person once they sustain a similar injury. Hyper-vigilant observation for symptoms suggestive of injury by the individual, family, or treatment providers typically produce a myriad of complaints believed to provide "evidence" of brain injury. Any of a broad spectrum of complaints may surface including headache, impaired memory, decreased attention or concentration, anxiety, depression, sleeping problems, fatigue, irritability or confusion. Each of these complaints may again be compared with the person's recall of any similar symptoms pre-injury. Some combination of "indirect" physical symptoms following "brain injury" (i.e., headache, cervical problems, jaw alignment issues, vision changes, imbalance) and emotional changes (e.g., cognition, depression, anxiety, anger) form the typical basis of a personal injury claim following an event which has allegedly damaged a person. Resnick (1997) estimated that approximately 30% of all personal injury claimants report both physical and emotional damages, while roughly only half this number present claims for emotional damage only. As per the discussion of base-rates of low back pain, the difficulty in establishing valid base-rate estimates of cognitive or emotional functioning exists in mild brain injury as well. Injured patients frequently deny having experienced any persistent pre-morbid attention, concentration, memory, or physical problems (e.g., headaches, fatigue). This phenomenon of glorification of pre-morbid abilities is one which consistently challenges the ability to establish an objective base rate of a person's functioning in the absence of other available documentation. Even if prior documentation exists, it is likely to be available only for persistent somatic symptoms for which the person sought treatment (i.e., frequent headache, neck pain, dizziness) and less available for transient or low-grade cognitive complaints. In a survey to determine the heterogeneity of cognitive and neuropsychological complaints across different populations of personal injury litigants *with no injury to the brain*, Lees-Haley & Brown (1993), reported that 50-90% of those surveyed identified experiencing the symptoms listed above in the first two years after their specific health events.

Consequently, these authors held that the mere report of any subset of these symptoms after an injury did not constitute specific evidence of injury to the brain. These results are consistent with those of other authors who have concluded that involvement in litigation alone might adversely affect the accuracy of neuropsychological results by creating increased false-positives (Lees-Haley & Fox, 1990; Price, 1990). Similar findings were reported by Gouvier, Uddo-Crane, and Brown (1988), who used questionnaires to determine the base rates of somatic, psychological, and neuropsychological symptoms in both brain injured and healthy (i.e., non-injured) populations. These authors found no significant differences between groups, and concluded that several symptoms associated with traumatic brain injury also readily occur in the general population. Dikman, McLean, & Temkin (1986) reported essentially the same results in a study with mild brain injury patients.

Concerns regarding intentional symptom production or malingering also equally exist in the area of mild brain injury and validity testing is mandatory in assessing these cases as well. Actual rates of malingering symptoms of brain injury are difficult to attain with published opinions ranging from most cases to few (Goodyear, 1998). More specifically, Binder & Rohling (1996) reported that nearly one quarter were considered to embellish symptoms in traumatic brain injury, while Youngjohn, Burrows & Erdal (1995) concluded malingering in nearly half of patients with symptoms of post-concussive symptoms.

Given the relative frequency of emotional compromise in patients following alleged brain injury, forensic psychologists are often asked to pass judgment on the effect of certain emotional states on neuropsychological testing results. Neuropsychological testing reports often contain the qualification that depression "may have exerted some impact on profiles produced." However little empirical evidence exists to support an adverse effect of mild or moderate depression symptoms on neuropsychological testing outcome. Even at the level of major depressive disorder, controversy exists with some authors suggesting an influence on scores (Kalska, Punamaeki, Maekinen, & Saarinen, 1999; Veiel, 1997), and others suggesting no effect (Reitan, & Wolfson, 1997).

To determine the deviation from one's pre-morbid status, post-injury cognitive functioning must be contrasted with information believed to best represent the person's pre-morbid abilities. Pre-injury estimates of intellectual and cognitive abilities may be obtained via history taking with the patient and family, assessing educational history and academic achievements, technical work duties, specific military skills, or intellectually based hobbies. Investigating the typical neuropsychological performance of normal, healthy populations also provides some interesting information. For example, Heaton, Grant & Matthews (1991), demonstrated that healthy individuals (i.e., no evidence of brain injury) were found to score below the normative or "expected" level on 10% of neuropsychological tests on a given day, and concluded that deviations in some neuropsychological abilities are normal, and should not be automatically considered evidence of brain injury. Consequently, the most commonly reported symptoms following brain injury, and subtle deficits commonly found on neuropsychological testing, may have little relevant value in determining the effects of a specific precipitating event on a plaintiff's specific deficits or complaints. Pervasive neuropsychological deficits might be more directly suggestive of damage in relation to injury, but would be rare in mild brain injuries, and a very rare finding in the absence of corroborating evidence of significant physical damage. Neuropsychological testing may provide information regarding focal deficits and helpful treatment insights to compensate for deficits so as to minimize their impact on independent functioning. Unfortunately, little consensus appears in the neuropsychological literature to relate specific neuropsychological testing findings with specific correlating behavioral abilities or inabilities. For example, little predictive relationship exists between a given level of neuropsychological impairment and the very activities commonly at issue in litigation cases such as ability to perform self or child-care behaviors, drive safely, complete modest home-care, participate in social activities, or to participate in even unskilled employment. A more comprehensive discussion of neuropsychological contributions in personal injury cases can be found in Chapter 12 of this book.

A review of the common clinical reasons for referral for psychological assessment following even mild injury to one's head might seem uncannily similar to those discussed in the previous section on back pain, and again nearly identical to the most commonly debated issues in personal injury matters. For example, any of the following clinical issues may form the foundation for clinical referral: (a) markedly delayed onset of physical, emotional, or cognitive symptoms; (b) extended disability (i.e., over 9-12 months) without improvement or with increased symptoms; (c) behavioral limitations in excess of physical findings, (d) inconsistent cognitive functioning across settings; (e) suspected contribution of depression or anxiety symptoms; (f) unfounded expectations about future improvement or deterioration; (g) poor return to work attitude or excessive pessimism about return to work abilities; or (h) financial gain or litigation related to illness/injury.

Considering the similar issues of diagnostic uncertainty, high population base rates of symptoms, and inherent limitations of psychological and neuropsychological conclusions, the forensic psychologist ironically faces many of the same challenges in brain injury as in back pain. The need to investigate those factors potentially impacting the timely resolution of symptoms, potential contributions of pre- or post-morbid emotional conditions, potential for intentional production of symptoms, patient adherence with treatments, personality issues or unfounded beliefs about recovery which are impeding progress, relevance of neuropsychological findings to reported deficits, prognosis for symptom resolution versus permanence, and/or an estimate of the person's capacity to return to work all remain.   Considering that limited work has been completed in the occupational sciences to empirically specify the cognitive abilities necessary to complete different jobs, assessment of potential for return to work following head injury would presumably entail assessment of the same factors discussed in the back pain section. The forensic psychologist would again consider that return to work following mild brain injury may in part be influenced by factors which have little relevance to any physical injury.

6.   SUMMARY

This chapter has detailed the anatomy of personal injury law, and identified the considerable challenges and responsibilities of the forensic psychologist in providing personal injury assessments.   From the philosophical underpinnings of behavioral sciences to the limits in the current literature and available technology, few psychological opinions are beyond contest in the legal arena. This is a far cry however from accepting that behavioral opinions are of no value, futilely random, or inherently scientifically unfounded.   Forensic applications of behavioral findings remain embryonic and can only be improved with continued scientific study in *forensic* settings. Forensic psychologists must provide adequate scientific defense in support of their opinions and openly recognize the limitations inherent in the data collection strategies. They should avoid being enticed into making statements of scientific certainty which lie beyond the reaches of the science of human behavior. Far more important than clinical opinion, behavioral analysis estimates of pre-morbid qualities contrasted with physical and emotional abilities post-injury will offer unique and valuable assistance to the trier of fact. While differing clinical impressions might be formed by professionals of different theoretical training when observing the same literature or data base, each bears the responsibility to testify to the preponderance of the scientific data, and use single case or small group data only when it can be directly related to the case at hand. Introducing such data for the sole purpose to suggest that the occurrence of a phenomenon is "possible" might be considered an irresponsible professional act. Assuming the limited diagnostic capacity of medical science in the areas of low back pain and mild brain injury as discussed in this chapter, the vast majority of factors influencing recovery, prognosis, and return to work are likely to fall into the forensic psychology arena. This responsibility is not to be taken lightly, and structured efforts to improve the validity of predictor variables must be made. With persistent clinical and empirical efforts, the predictive ability of psychological and behavioral measures can be improved, and will strengthen the contribution of forensic psychology in the both legal and clinical arenas. Finally, the issue of suspected malingering is unlikely to ever be eradicated in the field of personal injury, and should be routinely assessed in a multi-modal fashion and reported in forensic psychology records. This practice will help to eliminate the suspicion that all litigants are "faking for money," when in fact, available literature suggests that only a minority of litigants might intentionally produce false symptoms. The development and inclusion of structured observation strategies to assess consistency in behavioral deficits across time, setting, and circumstance further strengthens these impressions.

Forensic psychologists might less frequently be asked to assist the trier of fact as to the determination of fault, than to assist in the determination of damages or causation. However, certain information obtained during forensic interviews may prove helpful in attributing fault, such as should a defendant report the specific intent of their actions in question (e.g., specifically intended to harm another). Further, one may obtain information applicable to fault determination should an assessment of a plaintiff identify the specific source they hold responsible for creating emotional distress (e.g., unwanted sexual advances by a superior which causes employment distress). Forensic assessments may be valuable in identifying indirect causal relationships such as vicarious development of PTSD symptoms in those who observe an event. Without actually physically harming a plaintiff, perpetrators of violence might be held liable for perceived threat of loss of life or limb. Multiple recent disheartening reminders exist to typify the incredible impact of civil disasters or large-scale violence on passive observers or unintended victims.

The bulk of the information in this chapter is largely applicable in allowing a forensic psychologist to provide specialized information to the court regarding the presence or absence of damages. Behavior analysis strategies may enhance the quantification of the specific duties or portions of duties that a plaintiff feels unable to perform, and may be applied in the determination of lost wages. Similarly, the unique abilities of forensic psychology to collect valid impressions of psychological functioning, cognition, motivations, perceived suffering, loss of lifestyle activities, or subjective impact of disfiguring injuries are all valuable in the determination of whether a plaintiff might receive compensation for damages sustained.

Moreover, a psychologist's ability to provide pre-injury estimates of a plaintiff's cognitive, emotional, and behavioral functioning can help to form the foundation upon which the determination of relative causation is made. For example, if a comprehensive assessment finds that a plaintiff had little pre-morbid history of emotional impairment, and a consistent history of independently performing self, home, family and employment activities, then any changes following injury might reasonably be attributed to the event in question. In cases involving prior injury, or cumulative work injuries, only clear behavioral differentiation of pre-morbid abilities, those which remained following an initial injury, and those present following a second injury might assist the court in apportioning cause to the third party. Quantification of events unrelated to an accident (e.g., depression related to divorce proceedings which have no relationship to a plaintiff's involvement in motor vehicle accident) might seem nearly impossible to differentiate without forensic psychological input.

Finally, to return to the proposed Van Dorsten Law of Thirds, it must remain in the forefront of investigative awareness that the limitations of behavioral science and available technology obviate that many necessary "facts" in all cases will be unknown. Therefore, it is the explicit responsibility of the forensic examiner to build the best "empirically probable" opinion that they might uphold the scientific integrity of this field until science advances our domain.

7.   REFERENCES

Abenheim, L. & Suissa, S. (1987). Importance and economic burden of occupational low back pain: A study of 2,500 cases representative of Quebec. *Journal of Occupational Medicine*, 29, 670-674.

Acands v. Asner, 686 A.2d 250, 260 (Md. 1966).

Ahlers v. Schebil, 188 F.3d 365, 374 (6th Cir. 1999).

Alexander, M.P. (1995). Mild traumatic brain injury: Pathophysiology, natural history, and clinical management. *Neurology*, 45, 1253-1260.

Allen v. Walker, 569 So.2d 350 (Ala. 1990).

American Medical Association (1990). *Guides to the Evaluation of Permanent Impairment*, (4th ed. rev. 1993).

Atkinson, J.H., Ingram, R.E., Kremer, E.F. & Saccuzo, D.P. (1986). MMPI subgroups and affective disorder in chronic pain patients. *Journal of Nervous and Mental Disorders*, 174, 408-413.

Battie, M.C., & Bigos, S.J. (1991). Industrial back pain complaints: A broader perspective. *Orthopedic Clinics of North America*, 22, 2, 273-282.

Baur, K.M., Hardy, P.E., & Van Dorsten, B. (1998). Post-traumatic stress disorder in burn populations: A critical review. *Journal of Burn Care and Rehabilitation*, 19, 3, 230-240.

Bigos, S.J., Battie, M.C., Spengler, D.M., Fisher, L.D., Fordyce, W.E., Hansson, T.H., Nachemson, A.L., & Wortley, M.D. (1991). A prospective study of work perceptions and psychosocial factors affecting the report of back injury. *Spine*, 16, 1, 1-6.

Binder, L.M. & Rohling, M.L. (1996). Money matters: A meta-analytic review of the effects of financial incentive on recovery after closed head injury. *American Journal of Psychiatry*, 153, 1, 7-10.

Bird v. W.C.W., 868 S.W.2d 767 (Tex. 1994).

Block, A.R. (1996). *Pre-Surgical Psychological Screening in Chronic Pain Syndromes: A Guide for the Behavioral Health Practitioner. Lawrence Erlbaum Associates*: Mahwah, NJ.

Boyd, J.H., & Weisman, M.M. (1982). Epidemiology. In E.S. Payke (Ed.), *Handbook of Affective Disorders*. Guilford Press: New York.

Bowden, S.D., Davis, D.O., Dina, T.S., Patronas, N.J., & Wiesel, S.W. (1990). Abnormal magnetic resonance scans of the lumbar spine in asymptomatic subjects. *The Journal of Bone and Joint Surgery*, 72, 3, 403-408.

Browning v. Ringel, 995 P.2d 351 (Ida. 2000).

Burton, W., Conti, D., Chen, C., Schultz, A., & Edington, D. (1999). The role of health risk factors and disease on worker productivity. *Journal of Occupational and Environmental Medicine*, 41, 10, 863-877.

Butcher, J.N., Dahlstrom, W.G., Graham, J.R., Tellegen, A. & Kaemmer, B. (1989). *Manual for administration and scoring the Minnesota Multiphasic Personality Inventory*. University of Minnesota Press: Minneapolis, MN.

Butcher, J.N. & Miller, K.B. (1998). Personality assessment in personal injury litigation. In A.K. Hess & I.B. Weiner (Eds.), *The Handbook of Forensic Psychology*. John Wiley & Sons: New York.

Cain v. Johnson, 755 A.2d 156 (R.I. 2000).

Callahan v. Cardinal Glennon Hospital, 863 S.W.2d 852, 860-861 (Mo. 1993).

Callan v. Hackett, 749 A.2d 626, 629 (Vt. 2000).

Cassidy, J.D., Carroll, L.J., Cote, P., Lemstra, M., Berglund, A., & Nygren, A. (2000). Effect of eliminating compensation for pain and suffering on the outcome of insurance claims for whiplash injury. *The New England Journal of Medicine*, 342, 16, 1179-1186.

Cullum, C.M., & Thompson, L.L. (1999). Evaluation of neuropsychological status following mild traumatic brain injury. In M.J. Raymond, T.L. Bennett, L.C. Hartlage, & C.M. Cullum (Eds.), *Mild Traumatic Brain Injury: A Clinician's Guide*. Pro-Ed: Austin, TX.

Dikmen, S., McLean, A., & Temkin, N. (1986). Neuropsychological and psychosocial consequences of minor head injury. *Mild Head Injury*. Oxford Press: New York.

Dobbs D. B. (2000). *The law of torts*. St. Paul: West Group.

Doe v. Bd. of Education, Montgomery County, 453 A.2d 814 (Md. App. 1981).

Fantozzi v. Sandusky Cement Prod. Co., 597 N.E.2d 474, 485 (Ohio 1992).

Fonseca, C.A. (2001). Pain and suffering and the expert witness. *The Forensic Examiner*, May/June.

Fordyce, W.E. (1985). Back pain, compensation, and public policy. In J.C. Rosen & L.J. Solomon (Eds.), *Prevention in Health Psychology*, University Press of New England: Hanover, N.H. (pp. 390-400).

Fusaro v. First Family Mortgage Corp. 897 P.2d 123, 131 (Kan. 1995).

Glasscock v. Armstrong Cork Co., 946 F.2d 1085, 1090-1091 (Fifth Cir. 1991).

Goodyear, B. (1998). Neuropsychological evaluation of mild traumatic brain injury: Detection of malingering and other functional disorders. *The Forensic Examiner*, November/December.

Gouvier, W.D., Uddo-Crane, M. & Brown, L.M. (1988). Base rates of post-concussional symptoms. *Archives of Clinical Neuropsychology*, 3, 273-278.

Gragg v. Calandra, 696 N.E.2d 1282 (Colo. App. 1998).

Hafner v. Beck, 916 P.2d 1105 (Ariz. App. 1995).

Hagan v. Texaco Refining and Marketing, Inc., 526 N.W.2d 531, 537 (Iowa 1995).

Hartlage, R.C. (1990). *Neuropsychological Evaluation of Head Injury*. Professional Resource Exchange, Inc: Sarasota, FL.

Hatcher v. Mewborn, 457 S.W.2d 151 (Tex. App. 1970).

Heaton, R.K., Grant, I., & Matthews, C.G. (1991). *Comprehensive Norms for an Expanded Halstead-Reitan Battery*.

Psychological Assessment Resources, Inc.: Odessa, FL.

Herrera v. Gene's Towing, 827 P.2d 619, 620-621 (Colo. App. 1992).

Hilao v. Estate of Marcos, 103 F.3d 789, 793 fn3 (9th Cir. 1996).

Jensen, M.C., Brant-Zawadski, M.N., Obuchowski, N., Modic, M.T., Malkansian, D., & Ross, J. (1994). Magnetic resonant imaging of the lumbar spine in people without back pain. *The New England Journal of Medicine*, 331, 2, 69-73.

Jillson v. Caprio, 181 F.2d 523 (D.C. Cir. 1950).

Kalska, H.O., Punamaeki, R., Maekinen, T., & Saarinen, M. (1999). Memory and metamemory functioning among depressed patients. *Applied Neuropsychology*, 6, 2, 96-107.

Keeton, W.P. (1984). *Prosser and Keeton on the law of torts* (5th ed.). West Publishing: St. Paul, MN.

Kesmarki v. Kisling, 400 F.2d 97 (6th Cir. 1968).

Kionka, E. J. (1977). *Torts: injuries to persons and property*. West Group: St. Paul, MN.

Lamont v. Independent School Dist. No. 395, 154 N.W.2d 188, 192 (Minn. 1967).

Lees-Haley, P. R., & Brown, R.S. (1993). Neuropsychological complaint base rates of 170 personal injury claimants. *Archives of Clinical Neuropsychology*, 8, 203-209.

Lees-Haley, P.R., & Fox, D. (1990). Neurological false positives in litigation: Trail making test findings. *Perceptual and Motor Skills*, 90, 1379-1382.

Lineaweaver v. Plant Insulation Co., 37 Cal. Rptr. 2d 902, 905-906 (Cal. App. 1995).

Lyle v. Mladnich, 584 So.2d 397, 399 (Miss. 1991).

McIntyre v. Balentine, 833 S.W.2d 52, 54 (Tenn. 1992).

Melton, G., Petrilla, J., Poythress, N.G., & Slobogin, C. (1997). *Psychological Evaluations for the Courts*. The Guilford Press: New York.

Mild Traumatic Brain Injury Committee. (1993). Definition of mild traumatic brain injury. *Journal of Head Trauma Rehabilitation*, 8, 3, 86-87.

Mitchell v. United States, 141 F.3d 8, 13 (1st Cir. 1998).

Monsanto Co. v. Johnson, 675 S.W.2d 305, 312 (Tex. App. 1984).

Nolan, V., & Ursin E. (1987). The revitalization of hazardous activity strict liability. North Carolina Law Review, 65, 257.

Oklahoma Uniform Jury Instr. (Civil), 20.3.

Oregon Laborers-Employers Health & Welfare Trust Fund v. Philip Morris, Inc., 17 F. Supp.2d 1170, 1175 (D. Ore. 1998).

Ormel, J., VonDorff, M., Ustun, T.B., Pini, S. Doiren, A., & Oldehinkel , T. (1994). Common mental disorders and disability across cultures. *Journal of the American Medical Association*, 272, 22, 1741-1748.

Parks v. Allied Signal, Inc., 113 F.2d 1327, 1332 (3rd Cir. 1997).

Peer v. City of Newark, 176 A.2d 249, 257 (N.J. Super. 1961).

Perreira v. State, 768 P.2d 1198 (Colo. 1989).

Price, D. (1990). *Compendium on Malingering*. Psychological Seminars: Tampa, FL.

Price v. Halstead, 355 S.E.2d 380, 386 (W.Va. 1987).

Reed v. Union Pacific Railroad Co., 185 F.3d 712, 719 (7th Cir. 1999).

Reitan, R. & Wolfson, D. (1997). Emotional disturbances and their interaction with neuropsychological deficits. *Neuropsychology Review*, 7, 1, 3-9.

Renne v. Moser, 490 WN.W.2d 193, 200-201 (Neb. 1992).

Resnick, P.J. (1997). Malingering of posttraumatic disorders. In R. Rogers (Ed.), *Clinical Assessment of Malingering and Deception* (2nd ed.). The Guilford Press: New York.

Resnick, P.J. (1997). *Clinical Assessment of Malingering and Deception*. Denver: CO: Specialized Training Services, Inc.

Reynolds, C. R. (1998). Common sense, clinicians, and actuarialism in the detection of malingering during head injury litigation. In C.R. Reynolds (Ed.), *Detection of Malingering in Head Injury Litigation*. Plenum Press: New York

Rogers, R. (1997). Current status of clinical methods. In R. Rogers (Ed.), *Clinical Assessment of Malingering and Deception* (2nd ed.). The Guilford Press: New York.

Rogers, R., Sewell, K.W., & Goldstein, A. (1994). Explanatory models of malingering: A prototypical analysis. *Law and Human Behavior*, 18, 543-522.

Rohling, M.L., Binder, L.M., & Langhinrichsen-Rohling, J. (1995). Money matters: Review of the association between financial compensation and the experience and treatment of chronic pain. *Health Psychology*, 14, 6, 537-547.

Rybarczyk, B.D., Nyenhuis, D.L., Nicholas, J.J., Cash, S., & Kaiser, J. (1995). Body image, perceived social stigma, and the prediction of psychosocial adjustment to leg amputation. *Rehabilitation Psychology*, 40, 95-110.

Rybarczyk, B.D., Nyenhuis, D.L., Nicholas, J.J., Schulz, R., Alioto, R.J., & Blair, C. (1992). Social discomfort and depression in a sample of adults with leg amputations. *Archives of Physical Medicine and Rehabilitation*, 73, 1169-1173.

Sassali v. DeFauw, 696 N.E.2d 1217 (Ill. App. 1998).

Schultz v. Harrison Radiator Div. General Motors Corp., 683 N.E.2d 307, 307 (NY 1997).

Shapo, M. S. (1999). *Basic principles of tort law*. West Group: St. Paul, MN.

Simon, R.I. (1995). *Posttraumatic Stress Disorder in Litigation: Guidelines for Forensic Assessment*. American Psychiatric Press: Washington DC.

Skousen v. Nidy, 367 P.2d 248 (Ariz. 1962).

Snow v. Villacci, 754 A.2d 360, 363 (Me. 2000).

Spengler, D.M., Bigos, SJ., Martin, N.A., Zeh, J., Fisher, L, & Nachemson, A. (1986). Back injuries in industry: A retrospective study. I. Overview and cost analysis. *Spine*, 11, 241-245.

Stone, A.A. (1993). Post-traumatic stress disorder and the law: Critical review of the new frontier. *Bulletin of the American Academy of Psychiatry and Law*, 21, 23-26.

Stuto v. Fleishman, 164 F.3d 820, 827 (2nd Cir. 1999).

Sullivan, M.J.L., Reesor, K., Mikail, S., & Fisher, R. (1992). The treatment of depression in chronic low back pain: Review and recommendations. *Pain*, 50, 5-13.

Szautner, J.R. (2001). Personal injury as a systems failure: Systems analysis. *The Forensic Examiner*, November/December.

Terry v. Garcia, 800 S.W.2d 854, 858 (Tex. App. 1990).

Turner, J.A., & Romano, J.M. (1984). Self-report screening measures for depression in chronic pain. *Journal of Clinical Psychology*, 40, 909-913.

Van Dorsten, B. (2000). Amputation. In Radnitz, C.L. (Ed.), *Cognitive-Behavioral Therapy for Persons with Disabilities*. Jason Aronson, Inc.: Northvale, NJ.

Veiel, H. (1997). A preliminary profile of neuropsychological deficits associated with major depression. *Journal of Clinical and Experimental Neuropsychology*, 19, 4, 587-603.

Waddell, G. (1986). A new clinical model for the treatment of low back pain. *Spine*, 12, 632-644.

Whittlesey v. Miller, 572 S.W.2d 665 (Tex. 1978).

Youngjohn, J.R., Burrows, L., & Erdal, K. (1995). Brain damage or compensation neurosis: The controversial post-concussion syndrome. *The Clinical Neuropsychologist*, 9, 112-123.

Appellate case quotations were reprinted with written authorization of the West Group, St. Paul, MN.

Chapter 12

Selected Issues in Forensic Neuropsychology

Brian Goodyear, Ph.D.[1] and Douglas Umetsu, Ph.D., ABPP[2]
Private Practice, Aiea, HI[1]:Tripler Army MC, Honolulu, HI[2]

1.   INTRODUCTION

The past two decades have seen rapid growth in the field of forensic neuropsychology. For example, Taylor (1999), reviewed a major online computerized database of reported court decisions to April 1997, and found that 98% of all cases mentioning the word "neuropsychologist" had been published since 1980. During this time frame, neuropsychological evidence and testimony have become widely utilized in a variety of forensic settings.

Some clinicians may tend to think of forensic neuropsychology in rather narrow terms, encompassing only those cases that are directly involved in courtroom litigation. However, forensic neuropsychology can be defined much more broadly, to also include cases involved in quasi-legal settings such as state or federal Workers' Compensation systems, as well as in disability determinations for both private disability insurance programs and government-sponsored entitlement programs such as Social Security. Thus, a wide variety of opportunities exist for neuropsychologists to become involved in some form of forensic practice. The forensic arena in general can be subdivided into two somewhat more specific branches: criminal and civil.

Although the role of clinical psychology has been quite well established in the criminal arena for some time, the role of neuropsychology has been less prominent.   While some writers have addressed the potential contributions of neuropsychology (Denney & Wynkoop, 2000; Martell, 1992; Rehkopf & Fisher, 1997), a relative paucity of literature still exists on the role of neuropsychology in the criminal arena as compared to the civil arena.   Nevertheless, neuropsychological evidence may be of relevance in criminal competency issues such as insanity determination or fitness to stand trial.   Criminal competence is an area in which there is significant potential for the further involvement of neuropsychologists in the future.

In the civil arena, the role of neuropsychology is quite well established. Neuropsychologists are frequently called upon to evaluate individuals involved in legal and administrative proceedings related to issues such as personal injury claims, determination of testamentary capacity, and other civil competency issues.   The single most prominent area of involvement for neuropsychologists is personal injury claims for brain injury resulting from events such as motor vehicle accidents, assaults, slip and fall injuries, and neurotoxic exposure.   This chapter will primarily focus upon issues related to personal injury, with particular emphasis on the evaluation of mild traumatic brain injury.

As in other areas of forensic psychology, the forensic neuropsychologist may function as treating clinician, independent examiner, consultant, or expert witness.   In fact, due to the nature of the cases with which many clinical neuropsychologists typically work, one may assume that the majority of clinicians will sometimes be drawn into the forensic arena in the role of treating clinician, even if they do not choose to make forensic neuropsychology a major career focus.   Therefore, it is useful for every neuropsychologist to have some familiarity with issues related to forensic practice.

This chapter provides a brief overview of a number of selected issues of particular relevance to forensic neuropsychology: the content and purpose of the forensic neuropsychological evaluation; mild traumatic brain injury; malingering; test selection; estimation of premorbid functioning; and, admissibility of expert testimony.

2.   CONTENT AND PURPOSE OF THE FORENSIC NEUROPSYCHOLOGICAL EVALUATION

The content of a comprehensive neuropsychological evaluation should always include data from a variety of different sources.   In the forensic arena, it is particularly critical for the neuropsychologist to examine data from all relevant sources before arriving at any conclusions. Unfortunately, it is not unusual to see reports of evaluations that reach conclusions based only upon a brief history taken from the patient, and a simplistic interpretation of the results of standard neuropsychological tests, without regard for critical factors such as test validity or the details of the case history beyond the patient's subjective account. A thorough neuropsychological evaluation always involves more than just testing (Rankin & Adams, 1999). A detailed history of the injury should be taken from the patient, and corroborated with interviews of significant others, witnesses, co-workers, or other relevant third parties. In addition, all relevant records should be carefully reviewed. These records may include current and prior medical histories, academic records, employment records, military records, and any other relevant documentation. In the case of traumatic brain injury, ambulance reports and emergency room reports may be particularly important in assessing the initial severity of the injury. Validity testing, for the purpose of assessing effort and motivation, should routinely be embedded in the administration of standard neuropsychological tests in forensic cases. Conclusions should then be based on an integration of all the available data. The relative weight given to data derived from any given source, including test results may vary considerably from case to case. For example, it is quite reasonable to place considerable weight on standard neuropsychological test results if the records clearly document a significant brain injury, there are no inconsistencies in the history, and validity testing is within acceptable limits. On the other hand, if there are significant inconsistencies between the claimant's account of the injury and the medical records, the claimant has been observed performing activities that he or she denies being able to perform, or validity indicators suggest a lack of complete effort, then the test results should be interpreted with an appropriate degree of caution.

The purpose of neuropsychological evaluation may vary considerably depending on the nature of the specific case. One purpose is to determine the extent of impairment in cognitive functioning resulting from a particular injury. This issue tends to be especially important in cases involving moderate and severe brain injuries. In such cases, the presence of brain injury is usually not in question, as this has already been confirmed by imaging studies and other objective indicators. In other instances, such as uncomplicated mild TBI or neurotoxic exposure cases, the neuropsychological evaluation may play a critical role in determining the presence or absence of cognitive impairment, since the results of structural imaging studies are typically negative. Usually, the purpose of an evaluation is specified by the referring party. For example, a typical letter from an attorney or insurance adjuster requesting a neuropsychological evaluation of a claimant might include the following questions:

1. *What is your diagnosis of the claimant's condition?* This question relates to the critical issue of whether or not any diagnosable neuropsychological impairment is present.
2. *If any diagnosable condition is present, what is the etiology?* This question relates to the issue of causation of the impairment, which is obviously critical in establishing liability and compensability in many forensic cases.
3. *What is the prognosis?* This question relates to the expected course and outcome of the condition in question.
4. *Is the condition permanent and stationary?* This question relates to the issue of whether or not the condition has reached a level of maximum improvement.
5. *If the condition is permanent and stationary, what is the extent of any permanent impairment that is present?* This question relates to the issue of whether or not there is any permanent impairment resulting from the injury. The question may contain the request that any impairment be rated according to guidelines contained in Guides to the Evaluation of Permanent Impairment, Fifth Edition (AMA, 2001). This rating may be used in determining the basis for a settlement of the claim. In some cases, total impairment must be apportioned between the injury in question and pre-existing or intervening conditions.
6. *What are your recommendations for further treatment, if any?* This question relates to the issue of whether or not additional treatment is expected to markedly improve the patient's condition. In cases where apportionment is an issue, there may also be a question as to what extent treatment is related to the injury in question.

In the event that the purpose of the evaluation is not completely clear, the neuropsychologist should not hesitate to contact the referring party to request any clarification that may be required. Similarly, additional records or other relevant documentation should be requested as determined to be necessary in order to complete the evaluation. If additional information becomes available after a report has been submitted, it may be necessary to provide an addendum, particularly if opinions are changed in any way by the additional information.

3.   MILD TRAUMATIC BRAIN INJURY

The assessment of traumatic brain injury (TBI) constitutes the single largest component in the workloads of clinical neuropsychologists (Putnam & DeLuca, 1990). Both epidemiological (Torner & Schootman, 1996) and clinical (Tsushima, 1996) studies suggest that the great majority of TBI cases are mild in severity. Studies typically suggest that about 70 to 80 % of hospital admissions for TBI fall in the mild range (Kraus & Nourjah, 1989). Furthermore, it appears that at least 30% of all mild TBI cases (Sosin, Sniezek, & Thurman, 1996) are not seen in hospital settings. Thus, it seems likely that as many as 90% or more of all TBI cases fall within the mild range. It is evident that the assessment of mild TBI is an area of critical importance to any neuropsychologist working in the forensic field.

3.1   Definitional Issues

A number of still evolving definitional issues with regard to mild TBI are evident in the literature. Three definitional issues will be discussed, including the distinction between the terms "head injury" and "brain injury," the parameters and application of the definition of mild traumatic brain injury, and the definition of postconcussion syndrome.

3.2   Head injury versus brain injury

The terms "head injury" and "brain injury" are often used interchangeably in the literature. However, it is important to distinguish between these two terms. It is obviously possible to suffer some type of head injury, such as a scalp laceration, without necessarily suffering injury to the brain. Even a direct blow to the head may not cause a brain injury if the force of the blow is below a certain threshold. Conversely, it is possible for a person to suffer a brain injury without a direct blow to the head, as may occur in the case of a severe whiplash injury. To avoid confusion, the term "traumatic brain injury" should be reserved for those cases in which there is clear evidence of a physiological disruption of brain function, documented by an unequivocal disturbance in mental status following the injury. A subjective report of feeling "dazed" for a few seconds should not automatically be considered evidence of a brain injury, as the patient may be using "dazed" as a synonym for "startled" or "shocked." In those questionable cases in which it is not completely clear whether or not a physiological disturbance of brain function occurred, the terms "possible" or "probable" should be utilized to qualify the term "traumatic brain injury."

3.3   Definition of mild traumatic brain injury

Although relatively well-defined parameters have been proposed for mild TBI, there are often practical problems in the application of any specific definition to the individual case. The American Congress of Rehabilitation Medicine (ACRM) has defined mild TBI as a traumatically induced physiological disruption of brain function, as manifested by at least one of the following: (1) any period of loss of consciousness; (2) any loss of memory for events immediately before or after the accident; (3) any alteration in mental state at the time of the accident (e.g., feeling dazed, disoriented, or confused); and (4) focal neurological deficit(s) that may or may not be transient. In addition, the severity of the injury does not exceed the following: loss of consciousness of 30 minutes or less; after 30 minutes, an initial Glasgow Coma Scale (GCS: Teasdale & Jennett, 1974) of 13-15; and post-traumatic amnesia (PTA) not greater than 24 hours (Mild Traumatic Brain Injury Committee, 1993).

This definition, or relatively minor variations thereof, has achieved fairly wide recognition, but it is not without certain problems. First, when adequate documentation of the circumstances of the injury is lacking, there is an inherent difficulty in making an accurate, retrospective assessment of the duration of both loss of consciousness and post-traumatic amnesia. Second, the ACRM definition lacks a clearly defined lower limit (Kibby & Long, 1999). It is not unusual to encounter cases in which there is, at most, only very questionable evidence of any physiological disruption of brain function. In such cases, it is not at all clear whether a brain injury has actually occurred. Third, the ACRM definition encompasses a rather wide range of injury severity. It can include, at the lower extreme, individuals who experience only being dazed or disoriented for a few seconds, with neither loss of consciousness nor post-traumatic amnesia, and, at the upper extreme, individuals who experience a quite lengthy period of disruption of consciousness. Thus, it has been suggested that there is a need for subtyping of mild TBI. Kibby and Long (1999) have offered a proposal for such subtyping, as have Ruff & Richardson (1999). The sports neuropsychology literature may also be helpful in this regard, as there is a fairly well established history of assessing three or more grades of concussion in sports-related injuries (Erlanger, Kutner, Barth & Barnes, 1999).

3.4   Postconcussion syndrome

A third definitional issue relates to another commonly used, but also rather ill defined term, namely "postconcussion syndrome" (PCS). Typically, this term has been used to describe a range of symptoms that may occur following a mild TBI, including headache, dizziness, irritability, fatigue, insomnia, anxiety, depression, and subjective complaints of memory and concentration problems.   Both the International Classification of Diseases, Ninth Revision, Clinical Modification (ICD-9-CM; American Medical Association, 1999) and the Diagnostic and Statistical Manual of Mental Disorders, Fourth Edition (DSM-IV; American Psychiatric Association, 1994) attempt to provide more specific definitions, but neither definition has yet achieved general acceptance, and both are open to considerable criticism.   Nevertheless, these attempts to specify diagnostic criteria for the sequelae of mild TBI certainly represent steps in the right direction.

In ICD-9-CM, the category of Postconcussion Syndrome is defined in terms of behavioral manifestations and subjective complaints occurring after "generalized contusion of the brain." The definition notes that symptoms are more common in persons who have previously suffered from neurotic or personality disorders, or when there is a possibility of compensation.   A definition of Postconcussion Syndrome is also included in the International Classification of Diseases, Tenth Revision (ICD-10; World Health Organization, 1992).   ICD-10 is not yet in widespread clinical use in the United States, although the Clinical Modification will be phased in over the next few years.   As in ICD-9-CM, the ICD-10 definition focuses on subjective complaints, and specifically indicates that these complaints occur without neuropsychological evidence of marked impairment.   Among the symptom categories included in the ICD-10 definition is a preoccupation with symptoms and fear of brain damage, with hypochondriacal concern and adoption of the sick role.

In DSM-IV, no formal category is included in the current diagnostic system, but a proposal was included for the experimental category of Postconcussional Disorder. In addition to the presence of certain subjective complaints lasting in excess of three months, research criteria for this condition also include evidence from neuropsychological testing of difficulty in attention or memory. The inclusion in the DSM-IV criteria of both subjective complaints and neuropsychological test findings is probably a step forward, but a clearer distinction needs to be made between the two, as they may not always be highly correlated.

A clearer distinction also needs to be made between the acute and chronic manifestations of PCS. Acute PCS symptoms are an expectable outcome of injuries involving a clear-cut physiological disruption of brain function, and probably have an organic basis. It is reasonable to expect that a diagnostic system should include a category for these acute symptoms. It has been noted that in the majority of mild TBI cases, PCS symptoms typically resolve within a matter of weeks or months (Alexander, 1997). It is probably reasonable to say that the exact duration of time tends to vary as a function of initial injury severity, although the correlation is by no means perfect. In a minority of cases, however, PCS symptoms seem to persist on a more long-term basis, evolving into what has been called persistent post-concussion syndrome (PPCS; Alexander, 1995). Estimates of the incidence of PPCS following mild TBI have typically been in the area of 10% (Alexander, 1995; Binder, 1997). The status of PPCS remains somewhat controversial, but it seems reasonable to expect that a comprehensive diagnostic system should make some type of distinction between acute and chronic manifestations of PCS. There is clearly an organic basis to acute PCS symptoms, but this is not at all clear in the case of PPCS. It has been suggested that there may sometimes be an organic basis to PPCS (Wrightson & Gronwall, 1999). Logically, this would seem more likely in those cases falling toward the upper limit of the range of mild TBI. However, many observers believe that PPCS is attributable primarily to nonorganic, psychosocial factors such as reactive emotional distress, fears and expectations regarding injury severity and symptom persistence, and symptom preoccupation (Alexander, 1997; Gasquoine, 1997; Mittenberg & Strauman, 2000; Putnam & Millis, 1994), or motivational factors (Youngjohn, Burrows & Erdal, 1995). This would logically seem to be more likely if the initial injury falls toward the lower end of the range of mild TBI. It thus seems likely that psychosocial factors may be more salient than organic factors in many cases of PPCS. More specifically, Putnam and Millis (1994) have suggested that some cases of PPCS may be thought of as being a form of somatoform disorder. Similarly, Mittenberg and Strauman (2000) note that PPCS shares numerous features with anxiety, depressive, and somatoform disorders.

3.5 Expected outcomes in mild TBI

In order to understand potential outcomes in mild TBI cases, it is advisable for the forensic neuropsychologist to have at least a rudimentary knowledge of the complex neuropathology of TBI. Gennarelli and Graham (1998) have recently provided a good summary of findings in this area. Recent studies have shown that it is possible for mild TBI to result in some degree of structural damage to the brain, even in the absence of objective findings on structural imaging studies such as CT and MRI scans. This typically takes the form of diffuse axonal injury (DAI), which is hypothesized to result from compression or stretching of axons (Povlishock, 1993), particularly in long white matter tracts or around white and gray matter junctions. Disruption of the neuronal membrane appears to trigger a number of changes in axonal function that may lead to eventual neuronal death. Some of the initial changes include biochemical cascades involving sharp transient increases in the release of neurotransmitters such as glutamate, and increased ionic flux resulting in disruptions of normal intra-cellular and extra-cellular concentrations of substances such as potassium, sodium, and calcium. This in turn produces a state of decreased neuronal metabolism and regional cerebral blood flow. The extent to which affected neurons are able to recover from these changes appears dependent on numerous factors. It would seem reasonable that the severity of the initial injury, based on indicators such as duration of loss of consciousness and post-traumatic amnesia, might be a contributing variable. Thus, DAI would seem to be more likely to occur in cases falling toward the upper end of the range of mild TBI, and relatively unlikely in cases falling toward the lower end of the range.

Although the possibility of DAI should be kept in mind when evaluating mild TBI cases, one should not assume that mild TBI necessarily produces clinically significant DAI. However, it is not uncommon to see references in neuropsychological reports to DAI as a putative mechanism of injury, even when evidence for it is minimal. The first author recently reviewed a case involving a relatively trivial blow to the head, with no evidence of any loss of consciousness, nor of any post-traumatic amnesia. Imaging studies of the brain were completely negative. The neuropsychologist who initially evaluated this individual reported test scores as much as five standard deviations below the mean on certain measures, and went on to conclude that the individual had suffered significant brain damage resulting from diffuse axonal injury. This type of reasoning seems to depend on the logically flawed proposition that if mild TBI is capable of producing DAI, then any impairment found in test performance after a mild TBI must be due to DAI.

It is also particularly important for the neuropsychologist involved in the evaluation of mild TBI to be familiar with expected outcomes with regard to test performance (Ruff & Richardson, 1999). A number of important methodological issues in the study of outcome in mild TBI have previously been identified, including classification of injury severity, biases in selection of patients, attrition rates, duration of time since injury, and use of controls (Dikmen & Levin, 1993). Further refinements in the design of outcome research have recently been proposed by Satz and his associates (Satz, Alfano, Light, Morgenstern, Zaucha, Asarnow, & Newton, 1999), emphasizing the need to compare a mild head injury group with both normal and other injury control groups. Their proposed study should throw additional light on expected outcomes in mild TBI. The available evidence to date from a number of well-designed outcome studies seems to indicate relatively good long-term neuropsychological recovery for the majority of cases of mild TBI (Dikmen, Machamer, Winn, & Temkin, 1995; Levin, Mattis, Ruff, Eisenberg, Marshall, Tabaddor, & Frankowski, 1987). A recent meta-analytic review of outcome studies seems to confirm this finding (Binder, Rohling, & Larrabee, 1997). There also appears to be a clear dose-response relationship between initial injury severity and later cognitive impairment across a broad range of severity of TBI (Dikmen, et al., 1995). In the case of mild TBI, cognitive deficits, if present, are likely to be relatively subtle in the absence of complicating psychosocial factors, and are most likely to affect areas such as cognitive processing speed and capacity, and attention and concentration abilities. A conservative interpretation of the evidence to date suggests that subtle neuropsychological deficits may persist beyond typical time limits in a minority of cases, but severe neuropsychological impairment is not an expected outcome of mild TBI. In fact, it has been observed that significant neuropsychological impairment at one year follow-up in mild TBI is as unlikely as escaping such impairment in severe TBI (Dikmen, et al., 1995). Thus, a finding of severe impairment in neuropsychological test performance a year or more after a mild TBI must inevitably raise questions about the possible presence of complicating psychosocial and motivational factors, such as conversion/somatization tendencies or the potential influence of secondary gain factors.

3.6   Base Rate Issues

The assessment of mild TBI and PCS symptomatology is complicated also by a number of base rate issues. Gouvier (1999) has recently noted that the clinical utility of any diagnostic indicator varies as a function of the base rate of the condition being diagnosed, and that the effect size for base rates may sometimes be much larger than the effect size for positive test findings. This presents a particular problem in the diagnosis of neuropsychological impairment in mild TBI. For example, it has been noted that base rates for many PCS symptoms are quite high in a variety of non-brain injured populations (Dikmen, McLean, & Temkin, 1986; Gouvier, Uddo-Crane, & Brown, 1988; Lees-Haley & Brown, 1993). Similarly, a significant number of "normal" individuals obtain impaired scores on at least one or more measures when a comprehensive neuropsychological battery is administered (Heaton, Grant & Matthews, 1991). Conversely, in the population of all mild TBI cases, the base rates for both persistent PCS symptoms and persistent deficits on neuropsychological testing are relatively low (Alexander, 1997; Dikmen, et al., 1995). As Binder (1997) has noted, this combination of base rate phenomena tends to increase the likelihood of false positives (i.e., diagnosing brain injury when none is present). Obviously, this is likely to become a particularly thorny problem in those cases in which presence versus absence of brain injury is a critical issue.

4.   MALINGERING

Malingering is never a pleasant issue to address. Psychologists are basically trained to provide help to people who are assumed to be honestly seeking help. It is disturbing to think that our patients may sometimes exaggerate or even fake symptoms. Nevertheless, malingering is an issue that inevitably must be taken into consideration in forensic neuropsychological evaluations. These evaluations frequently occur in a context in which financial compensation or other secondary gain is a significant issue. This possibility of gain must be taken into account as a potential motivational factor that can affect test performance. Although the degree of impairment may sometimes be exaggerated in cases involving more severe brain injury, malingering tends to be less of an issue in such cases, since objective findings from imaging and other diagnostic studies leave no doubt that a significant insult to the brain has occurred. Malingering tends to become a more critical issue when there are no objective findings of brain injury other than neuropsychological test results. This often includes cases involving conditions such as mild TBI and toxic exposure. It behooves us all as neuropsychologists to remember that our tests are not completely objective measures, and that the validity of any particular score depends entirely on the assumption that the examinee has performed to the best of his or her ability on that task. Unfortunately, in certain forensic cases, this may be an untenable assumption.

4.1   Definition and Prevalence of Malingering

Malingering is defined in DSM-IV as the intentional production of false or grossly exaggerated physical or psychological symptoms, motivated by external incentives.   Slick, Sherman and Iverson (1999) have recently proposed more specific criteria for the diagnosis of possible, probable, and definite malingering of neurocognitive dysfunction, including psychometric, behavioral, and collateral data.   It has been noted that it is very difficult to conclusively confirm a diagnosis of malingering, in the absence of a confession (Brandt, 1988), or perhaps an unequivocal observation that the individual is actually able to perform an activity that he or she denies being able to perform.   In neuropsychological settings, potential differential diagnoses may include factitious disorder, or, more commonly, conversion disorder and other somatoform disorders.

The prevalence of malingering probably varies considerably from one setting to another, depending on a variety of factors involving both patient and system variables.   With regard to mild TBI, Wrightson and Gronwall (1999) have recently noted that frank malingering appears to be relatively rare in New Zealand, perhaps because of the structure of their legal system. On the other hand, a number of recent studies have suggested that, in certain areas of the United States, malingering is a fairly common finding in forensic neuropsychological evaluations of mild TBI (Binder, 1993; Griffenstein, Baker & Gola, 1994; Youngjohn, et al., 1995).   There are probably a number of social factors that contribute to this phenomenon. The increasingly litigious nature of the general social environment may be a factor that has led to an increased frequency of claims for damages as the result of TBI (Glass, 1991).   The possibility of "brain damage" and the potential for large awards of compensation may make mild TBI an area of injury that is particularly likely to elicit malingering (Binder & Rohling, 1996), especially in individuals who feel that they have been egregiously wronged and/or whose options in life are relatively limited.

The prevalence of malingering may depend not only on the geographical setting, but also on how the population of interest is defined. For example, it has recently been noted that persons involved in litigation may represent a unique subpopulation (Berent & Swartz, 1999). This is probably due, at least in part, to the increased significance of secondary gain factors as compared to other clinical settings. It seems likely that malingering may be more common within this subpopulation than within the population of brain-injured individuals as a whole.

4.2   Testing for Malingering

It is clear that forensic neuropsychological evaluations must routinely include assessment for the possible presence of malingering. To accomplish this, forensic neuropsychologists must be willing to look beyond simplistic interpretations of the data obtained from standard neuropsychological tests. Excessive reliance by some clinicians on simplistic interpretations that routinely equate poor neuropsychological test performance with brain damage has led to what a number of observers have identified as an increasing problem of over-diagnosis of neuropsychological deficits in legal settings (Faust, Ziskin, & Hiers, 1991; Larrabee, 1997).   In addition, criticism has been leveled at neuropsychologists regarding their inability to detect malingering, and the lack of an adequate scientific basis of neuropsychological data (Faust, et al., 1991).

Many neuropsychological tests are quite sensitive to the presence of cognitive impairment, but also tend to lack a high degree of specificity relative to mild TBI (Millis & Putnam, 1996; Taylor, Cox & Mailis, 1996). In fact, our most sensitive tests may also be our least specific tests, as performance may be affected by a range of extraneous variables. There are many possible explanations other than "brain damage" for apparently impaired test scores, including acute anxiety, severe depressive symptoms, pain, fatigue, medication effects, and submaximal effort. Lack of effort is certainly not synonymous with malingering, but when lack of effort appears to be a factor, some consideration must be given to the possibility that the individual is malingering.

The testing phase of the neuropsychological evaluation should always include the administration of tests aimed specifically at the detection of incomplete effort, as well as a critical analysis of both the level of scores and qualitative aspects of performance on standard neuropsychological tests. A number of tests designed specifically for validity assessment purposes are now available; however, a detailed review of all of these tests is beyond the scope of this chapter. Iverson and Binder (2000) have recently provided an excellent, detailed review of the assessment of malingering. Briefly, tests of malingering tend to fall into two somewhat overlapping categories. The first category includes simple tasks that are presented as being more difficult than they are in reality, such as Rey's 15 Item Memory Test and Dot Counting procedures (Lezak, 1995).   The second category includes forced choice procedures such as the Portland Digit Recognition Test (Binder & Willis, 1991), the Computerized Assessment of Response Bias (Conder, Allen & Cox, 1992), and the Victoria Symptom Validity Test (Slick, Hopp, Strauss, & Thompson, 1997), all of which involve number recognition. The Victoria Symptom Validity Test also includes measures of reaction time, which may be helpful in the detection of incomplete effort. Other forced choice procedures include the Word Memory Test (Green, Allen & Astner, 1996), which involves word recognition, and the Test of Memory Malingering (Tombaugh, 1996), which involves picture recognition. The Word Memory Test may be a particularly useful instrument in the detection of malingering. Gervais, Green and Allen (1999) have reported evidence that a symptom validity test based on verbal memory, such as the Word Memory Test, may be more sensitive to incomplete effort than procedures based on digit recognition or visual memory. They hypothesize that this may be because the layman typically associates impaired cognitive function with deficits in verbal memory. Another potentially useful tool is the Validity Indicator Profile (Frederick, 1997). This also employs forced choice methodology, but it is not a memory-based instrument. It includes verbal and non-verbal subtests, and also compares the pattern of actual performance against expected performance on tasks involving items of varying degrees of difficulty. In addition to these instruments, there are a number of other tests not designed specifically for the detection of malingering, but which also involve a dichotomous choice of response, such as the Recognition Memory Test (Warrington, 1984) and the Seashore Rhythm Test (Seashore, Lewis & Saetveit, 1960).

A performance at or below the level of chance on a forced choice test is usually considered virtually pathognomonic of malingering in cases involving mild injury. Larrabee (2000) has commented that such performances may be considered "tantamount to a confession." While a number of studies have tended to show that most suspected malingerers do not perform below chance (Binder, 1993; Green, et al., 1996; Tombaugh 1996), their scores are often relatively poor in comparison to controls, even severely brain injured controls (Allen & Green, 1999; Green, et al., 1996; Millis & Putnam, 1996; Tombaugh, 1996). In general, depending on the specific test, performances below 80% to 90% correct on the more simple forced choice procedures should be regarded as suspicious (Green, et al., 1996; Guilmette, Hart & Giuliano, 1993; Martin, Bolter, Todd, Gouvier & Niccolls, 1993; Tombaugh, 1996). A strict adherence to a worse than chance criterion may render forced choice tests relatively insensitive to more sophisticated attempts at symptom exaggeration. Iverson and Binder (2000) comment that any forced choice test that relies on binomial significance but does not have an empirically-based cutoff score is not sensitive enough for routine clinical use.

In addition to the administration of tests specifically designed for validity assessment, a careful analysis of the level and pattern of performance on all standard neuropsychological tests is essential. Scores that appear grossly out of proportion to the severity of the injury must raise questions about potential malingering, even if validity testing appears relatively clean. In addition, patterns of performance that are inconsistent in some way, or that are at odds with accepted neuropsychological principles, must be viewed with an appropriate degree of scientific skepticism. A number of studies have reported cutoff scores for potential malingering on certain common tests, based on comparisons with the performances of more severely brain injured subjects who are believed to be responding with an optimal level of effort. For example, cutoff scores have recently been developed for the California Verbal Learning Test (Millis, Putnam, Adams & Ricker, 1995). In addition, statistical procedures such as discriminant function analysis have allowed the use of linear combinations of scores from a number of tests in order to differentiate malingerers from non-malingerers (Millis et al., 1995; Mittenberg, Azrin, Millsaps & Heilbronner, 1993). One major limitation of the cutoff score approach involves the extent to which such scores can be generalized from the normative sample to particular forensic cases. In addition, when relatively conservative cutoff scores are utilized, a rigid adherence to such scores may result in a tendency to produce false negatives, and a consequent failure to detect more sophisticated malingerers.

Repeated testing may also be helpful in identifying inconsistent patterns of responding that may be associated with symptom exaggeration. For example, Reitan and Wolfson (1997) have proposed a test-retest method as a way of identifying potential malingerers. They have developed a set of measures including the Retest Consistency Index, the Response Consistency Index and the Dissimulation Index. This offers considerable promise as a way of quantifying inconsistencies in performance. However, a potential limitation is that the examiner may not always have the opportunity to administer a second testing. Further, as with other cutoff score approaches, it is not clear that their algorithms would necessarily be applicable to a particular individual case, as they were developed from a relatively limited sample. Theoretically, malingering may involve a virtually limitless variety of patterns of inconsistency. Consequently, patterns of inconsistency across test administrations might vary greatly from one case to another.

Personality testing may be helpful in the detection of exaggerated subjective complaints. The Minnesota Multiphasic Personality Inventory - 2 (MMPI-2: Butcher, Dahlstrom, Graham, Tellegen, & Kaemmer, 1989) is the most widely researched instrument in this regard. Youngjohn, Davis, &

Wolf (1997) reported paradoxical effects of head injury severity on MMPI-2 profile elevation in a sample of head injury patients. Contrary to expectations, higher elevations were associated with less severe injuries. Similarly, Hoffman, Scott, Emick, & Adams, (1999) reported that MMPI-2 scale elevations did not appear to be directly related to injury severity in another sample of head injury patients. Both groups of researchers noted that litigation status was a significant moderating factor in determining item endorsement on the MMPI-2. Berry, Wetter, Baer, Youngjohn, Gass, Lamb, Franzen, MacInnes, & Buchholz, (1995) have also reported that higher scores on traditional MMPI-2 overreporting scales (F, FB, F-K, Ds2, and Fp) were obtained by compensation-seeking relative to non-compensation seeking CHI patients. However, Larrabee (1997) warned that these traditional validity indicators may be relatively insensitive to symptom overreporting in TBI, and that the Fake Bad Scale (FBS: Lees-Haley, English, & Glenn, 1991) may be more useful in the detection of "somatic malingering." In general, some degree of elevation on MMPI-2 scales 1, 2, 3, 7 and 8 may reasonably be expected in TBI patients (Cripe, 1999). However, marked elevations on these scales in chronic mild TBI may suggest a tendency to over-report symptoms, even in the absence of elevations on traditional validity indicators such as the F scale. More specifically, Larrabee (1997) has suggested that malingering should be considered in mild TBI whenever elevations on scales 1 and 3 exceed a T-score of 80, and the FBS is elevated. A recent study by Tsushima & Tsushima (2001) also supports the utility of the FBS in the detection of symptom magnification in personal injury plaintiffs. In this study, among five MMPI-2 validity scales, only the FBS significantly differentiated litigation patients and clinical patients.

4.3 Inconsistency Analysis

Despite the obvious importance of testing, it must be kept in mind that testing is only one component of a comprehensive neuropsychological evaluation. The assessment of possible malingering is a process that should be ongoing throughout every stage of a forensic evaluation. Although signs that are virtually pathognomonic of malingering may sometimes be found in any given component of the evaluation, a clinical diagnosis of malingering will typically not be based on any one specific finding or even a set of findings from only one component of the evaluation. This is particularly true in the case of more sophisticated malingerers. Rather, the diagnosis will be based on an accumulation of inconsistencies or "red flags" throughout the different stages of the evaluation. Test results are certainly an important component in this process, but a certain cutoff score on a particular neuropsychological test, or even a pattern of scores on a set of tests, will probably never constitute a general definition of malingering.

The hallmark of malingering is inconsistency (Larrabee, 1997; Tombaugh, 1996), and the diagnosis will usually be based on an accumulation of inconsistencies that may be found in any and all phases of the evaluation. Virtually all of the clinical signs of malingering can be described in terms of some form of inconsistency. Larrabee (1997; 2000) has proposed a four-part approach to analyzing the consistency/inconsistency of neuropsychological data. He suggests that the following questions should be asked:

1. *Are the data consistent within and between neuropsychological domains?*
2. *Is the neuropsychological profile consistent with the suspected etiologic condition?*
3. *Are the neuropsychological data consistent with the documented severity of the injury?*
4. *Are the neuropsychological data consistent with the client's behavioral presentation?*

In forensic evaluations, this type of detailed analysis of consistency should be applied not only to the test data but to all aspects of the evaluation, including data obtained from interviews, record reviews and other relevant sources.

4.4   Differential Diagnosis of Other Functional Disorders

If an accumulation of inconsistencies from various components of the examination raises suspicion of malingering, there is an important issue that should be considered before concluding that malingering is present. This is the issue of differential diagnosis of other functional disorders, particularly those potentially involving motivational factors, such as factitious disorders and conversion or other somatoform disorders (Cullum, Heaton & Grant, 1991). A recent study by Boone and Lu (1999) suggests that symptom fabrication associated with somatization/conversion orientations, as reflected by 1-3/3-1 MMPI-2 code types, can extend to noncredible cognitive complaints in additional to the typical physical manifestations. It should be noted, however, that these code types do not necessarily preclude a diagnosis of malingering. Furthermore, Putnam and Millis (1994) have specifically suggested that some cases of PPCS may be conceptualized as a type of somatoform disorder. At the heart of this particular issue of differential diagnosis is the critical question of the extent to which the motives for, and the mechanisms of, symptom production are judged to be conscious and intentional (Kathol, 1996). There are rarely any easy answers to this question. Although DSM-IV categories tend to represent it as such, consciousness is perhaps best not viewed as a dichotomous variable. It has been suggested that psychologically determined physical symptoms may have both volitional and nonvolitional elements (Cullum, et al., 1991; Lezak, 1995). It has also been noted that in clinical practice the boundaries between conversion and other hysterical disorders, factitious disorders and malingering are often quite blurred (Ford, 1995; Merskey, 1995). One observer has specifically suggested that a mixture of conversion disorder and malingering may sometimes be found (Weintraub, 1996). Similar views have been expressed by Williams (1998) in his discussion of types of factitious responding, as well as by Bieliauskas (1999) in his consideration of the utility of the term "compensation neurosis."

At the very least, neuropsychologists should be alert to the possible role that unconscious factors may play in symptom production, rather than simply assuming that inconsistencies are entirely attributable to a conscious and intentional process of deception. In some mild TBI cases, for example, the patient may genuinely experience some acute PCS symptoms, become anxious and preoccupied with the symptoms, and then develop the belief that he or she has been seriously injured. Well-meaning clinicians may sometimes unwittingly reinforce that belief, and even promote the proliferation of symptoms. This process may be further reinforced by the presence of significant potential secondary gain factors. Over a period of time, the patient becomes increasingly entrenched in the role of the disabled patient, presenting symptoms in accordance with his or her beliefs about the nature and severity of the injury. In the process, life prior to the injury tends to be idealized, and the injury in question becomes a convenient focus for the attribution of responsibility for all problems and symptoms experienced by the patient. The extent to which this process is conscious or unconscious is not at all clear, and thus open to interpretation.

5.   TEST SELECTION

Appropriate test selection is important in any neuropsychological evaluation. Within this general area, a number of specific issues are of relevance to forensic practice. In particular, the issue of fixed versus flexible batteries has received a good deal of attention in the literature in the recent past. General guidelines for test selection and length of test battery are also briefly reviewed. In addition, some suggestions for future directions are offered.

5.1 Fixed versus Flexible Batteries

For some years there has been considerable debate in the neuropsychological literature about the relative merits of fixed versus flexible test batteries (Lezak, 1995). Recently, this debate has also entered the forensic arena. Several chapters in a recently published book (Williams, 1997a; 1997b; Laing & Fisher, 1997) argue strongly for the use of a fixed battery in forensic settings. The writers propose a battery composed specifically of the Halstead-Reitan Neuropsychological Test Battery, the Wechsler Intelligence Scales, the Memory Assessment Scales, the Western Aphasia Battery, and the Minnesota Multiphasic Personality Inventory. In addition, Williams (1997a) sharply criticizes the flexible battery approach, noting a primary concern that the various tests have been normed on different samples, so that z scores on different tests cannot be directly compared. Furthermore, patterns of performance across tests cannot be determined, as there are virtually no studies on how well any given flexible battery measures any particular disorder. The essential implication of this position is that only a fixed battery meets the standard of scientific acceptability.

On the other hand, Ruff and Richardson (1999) have countered that the tests included in the Halstead-Reitan battery were developed prior to recent advances in the cognitive neurosciences, and are not particularly sensitive to the attentional and memory deficits which tend to be most pronounced in mild TBI. Similarly, Hartman (1999) has commented on weaknesses of the Halstead-Reitan battery with regard to evaluation of neurotoxic exposure cases. Moreover, Ruff and Richardson (1999) assert that the Halstead-Reitan battery as a whole has no empirically proven advantages in the evaluation of mild TBI, and that no impairment index has been designed for the specific deficits caused by mild TBI.

The issue of the admissibility of fixed versus flexible batteries has already been addressed at the federal district court level in the case of *Chapple v. Ganger* (1994). The court's decision essentially favored the fixed battery approach embodied in the Halstead-Reitan battery. Reed (1996) has noted that if federal courts continue to follow the holding in this case, fixed batteries are more likely than flexible batteries to pass the Daubert standard for the admissibility of expert testimony.

Regarding test interpretation, it must be admitted that there are some advantages to using a fixed battery in which all of the tests have been co-normed. In particular, a fixed battery does faciliate the analysis of patterns of performance on different tasks. However, the use of certain tests that have not been co-normed does not completely preclude pattern analysis. For example, a comparison of performances on the California Verbal Learning Test and the Rey Complex Figure Test may yield useful information about the relative strengths of verbal and visual memory abilities. Moreover, it does not seem reasonable to insist that in order to be scientific, all diagnostic procedures administered to a patient must be co-normed. If one were to adhere rigidly to such a position, it would not be scientific, for example, for a neurologist to concurrently order MRI, EEG and laboratory studies for a patient, as these procedures have not been normed on the same sample. There is nothing inherently wrong with administering a number of individually normed diagnostic procedures, provided that each of those procedures has been shown to be psychometrically sound and relevant to the clinical issue at hand. Parenthetically, it is worth noting that even the battery proposed by Williams (1997a) contains components that have not been co-normed.

5.2   Guidelines for Test Selection

Some specific guidelines for psychometric test selection have been proposed by Heilbrun (1992). In general, these guidelines include the need to use well-standardized, commercially available tests with sound psychometric properties, supported in particular by positive reviews in publications such as the Mental Measurements Yearbook. If one follows these guidelines, one can be relatively confident that the instruments are of a standard that would be generally acceptable to the profession. In forensic settings, it would seem prudent to use a relatively comprehensive battery of such tests in order to evaluate all of the major areas of cognitive functioning typically included in the field of neuropsychology. Careful adherence to standardized administration procedures and data recording are also usually recommended. The chosen battery should certainly include tests with demonstrated sensitivity to the condition in question, as well as tests of abilities that are typically known to remain relatively intact, so that observed patterns of performance can be compared to expectations. A recently published volume of meta-analytic studies (Zakzanis, Leach, & Kaplan, 1999) provides some information on the relative sensitivities of various tests to a number of conditions that are commonly encountered by clinical and forensic neuropsychologists. Unfortunately, in the case of mild TBI, many of the effect sizes appear to be derived from only a single study, so the conclusions must be regarded as tentative at best.

It is also important to keep in mind that the tests most sensitive to conditions such as mild TBI and neurotoxic exposure may also be the least specific. For any given test, one would ideally have access to information regarding not only reliability, validity, sensitivity and specificity, but also the positive and negative predictive values with regard to the condition and population in question. Unfortunately, despite the huge number of neuropsychological tests now available, there are still relatively few, fixed battery or otherwise, that ever clearly meet these criteria. As a general rule, the most prudent course of action is to rely primarily on well-developed, psychometrically sound instruments and actuarial methods of interpretation. However, in certain exceptional circumstances it may be necessary to supplement standardized tests with less formal procedures, for example if testing a patient that is vision or hearing impaired.

5.3 Length of test battery

Another issue in test selection is the appropriate length of the test battery. In some respects, this is closely related to the fixed versus flexible battery issue, although it has not received as much attention in the literature. Neuropsychological batteries tend to be quite time-consuming. Sometimes, perhaps, they are excessively so. A balance needs to be maintained between comprehensiveness and economy of time and cost. Time and cost may not be considered as important as limiting factors in forensic settings as they may be in other clinical settings, but they should not be ignored in any context. Comprehensiveness is certainly a desirable goal, but exactly how comprehensive does a battery need to be? The critical issue related to battery length has to do with incremental validity. For example, it is reasonable and appropriate to ask how much more relevant information will be gained from an eight-hour battery as opposed to a four-hour battery.

Complete comprehensiveness is probably an impossible goal in neuropsychology, as the range of potential cognitive tasks that might be given is virtually limitless. Moreover, an excessive focus on comprehensiveness may, to at least some degree, be counterproductive. A particular problem is that the longer the battery, the more likely it is that impaired scores will occur by chance. This may be one reason for the common finding of at least a few impaired scores among normals on a comprehensive test battery (Heaton, et al., 1991). In forensic practice, it is usually prudent to select tests that survey all of the main areas of cognitive functioning. In some cases, more detailed probing of certain areas may be appropriate. However, the administration of excessively long batteries of tests simply for the sake of comprehensiveness is neither desirable nor necessary.

5.4   Future Directions in Test Selection

Despite the enormous number of tests now available, there remains a great need for the development of a state of the art, comprehensive neuropsychological test battery for use in the forensic arena, with particular emphasis on the assessment of mild TBI and neurotoxic exposure. The construction and content of the battery should be based on current developments in cognitive neuroscience, so that it could potentially serve as a core battery for the evaluation of a wide variety of neuropsychological conditions. Such a core battery would be capable of standing alone, although it could certainly be supplemented with other tests, as necessary, in order to further clarify the nature and extent of impairment in cognitive processes.

Basic normative data for the battery would optimally be obtained from a large national sample, stratified by variables such as age, education, gender, and, if possible, ethnicity. In addition, the results of a number of relevant clinical comparison group studies should be included with the normative data. In particular, these should include groups of confirmed non-malingering mild, moderate and severe TBI patients. This would permit the inclusion of information regarding the sensitivity, specificity, and positive and negative predictive values with regard to these specific groups. Built-in validity indicators should be included throughout the battery. At least part of the battery should make use of computer technology so that measures of response latency could be built into certain tasks, and sophisticated actuarial analyses easily conducted for interpretation purposes. It should attempt to balance comprehensiveness with economy of time and cost. We believe that it is possible to construct a relatively comprehensive battery, covering all major areas of neuropsychological functioning, with the exception of general intelligence and personality that could normally be administered in its entirety in no more than four hours. An abbreviated version would also be helpful, so that the battery could be used in non-forensic clinical settings in which time and cost considerations resulting from factors such as managed care restrictions need to be taken into account.

6.   ESTIMATION OF PREMORBID FUNCTIONING

The accurate estimation of premorbid functioning is a critical element in determining the degree of impairment sustained in both severe and mild injuries. For example, a particular test score may be considered normal or impaired, depending on the individual's level of premorbid functioning. This issue has recently been reviewed in some detail (Putnam, Ricker, Ross & Kurtz, 1999). Subjective reports of premorbid functioning by the patient or significant others may not always be reliable, and in some cases may be significantly biased. Although subjective reports should not be completely discounted, they should routinely be corroborated with more objective data. Actuarial approaches have been used to estimate premorbid IQ from demographic variables, performance variables, or a combination of both. Performance is typically based on tests thought to be relatively resistant to the effects of brain injury, such as the North American Adult Reading Test (NAART; Blair & Spreen, 1989), the Reading subtest of various versions the Wide Range Achievement Test, and the Vocabulary subtest of the Wechsler intelligence scales. A recent comparison of methods found no differences in classification accuracy among five such prediction methods (Axelrod, Vanderploeg & Schinka, 1999).

In addition to actuarial methods focused on predicting premorbid performance on specific measures such as Wechsler Scales IQ, a detailed, qualitative review of the individual's psychosocial history may be extremely helpful in assessing premorbid functioning more generally. Particular attention should be paid to medical, psychological, academic, employment and military records, when available. Interviews with collateral sources such as significant others may also sometimes be very helpful, although the possibility of some form of bias must be considered, depending on the source. Finally, the results of any previous standardized testing such as psychological assessments and SAT scores may also be very useful, if and when available.

7.   ADMISSIBILITY OF EXPERT NEUROPSYCHOLOGICAL TESTIMONY

A good deal of attention in the neuropsychological literature has recently been devoted to the implications of the recent U.S. Supreme Court decision in the case of *Daubert v. Merrell Dow Pharmaceuticals* (1993) regarding the admissibility of expert neuropsychological testimony in forensic settings. Briefly, the general purpose of the Daubert decision has been to clarify Federal Rules of Evidence 702 and 703, which refer more generally to testimony by experts. In essence, the Daubert decision attempts to provide guidelines to ensure that expert testimony, particularly on matters of opinion, is reliably grounded in an appropriate degree of professional rigor. An additional decision in the case of *General Electric Co. v. Joiner* (1997) appears to extend Daubert by giving judges significant discretion in determining the admissibility of expert testimony (Reed, 1999).

There has been considerable speculation in the recent literature regarding the implications of the Daubert decision for the admissibility of neuropsychological testimony. At the time of this writing, the full implications of this decision are still not entirely clear. Reed (1999) recently provided an excellent review of the relevant issues and related developments in a number of jurisdictions, and noted two significant unresolved issues related to the legal status of neuropsychological testimony. The first issue involved an unresolved split within the Federal Circuit Courts of Appeals as to whether the Daubert standard should narrowly apply only to scientific expert testimony, or more broadly to expert testimony based on technical or other specialized knowledge in addition to scientific knowledge. The second issue involved the question of whether neuropsychological testimony, particularly clinical opinion related to a specific individual case, constitutes "scientific" as opposed to "technical or other specialized" knowledge. The Supreme Court has subsequently issued a decision in the case of *Kumho Tire Co. v. Carmichael* (1999) that seems to make clear that the Daubert standard is generally applicable to all forms of expert testimony. However, it also appears likely that the specific criteria used for determining admissibility may vary considerably from case to case, depending on the discipline of the expert, as well as the discretion of the particular trial judge.

It now seems clear that the Daubert standard will apply to neuropsychological testimony in those jurisdictions where it is used, regardless of whether the testimony is based on "scientific" or "technical or other specialized" forms of knowledge. Nevertheless, the issue of whether or not clinical knowledge should be considered a form of scientific knowledge remains an important one for neuropsychology, and indeed for psychology in general. In a now classic paper, Thorne (1947) emphasized the importance of the scientific method in clinical work, while also noting that clinical practice usually represents a compromise between what is scientifically ideal and what is practically desirable. Similarly, the scientist-practitioner model that forms the basis for training in clinical psychology and neuropsychology emphasizes the need for a scientific basis to clinical practice. Nevertheless, it can be argued that clinical work is basically technical in nature, akin to a discipline such as engineering, in that its primary function is not to generate scientific knowledge, but to apply scientific knowledge to the individual case. It is conceivable that a neuropsychologist testifying in regard to a specific case might present a combination of both "scientific" and "technical or other specialized" forms of knowledge during the course of testimony. For example, reference to specific research findings relevant to a particular case might be considered the presentation of scientific knowledge, whereas clinical diagnostic opinion about that same case might be considered a form of technical or other specialized knowledge. Although the Daubert standard would be expected to generally apply to both forms of knowledge, the specific standards applied to each by the court might differ considerably. Thus, it seems likely that there will be a need for additional clarification by the courts regarding the status and admissibility of clinical knowledge.

8. SUMMARY

Despite its rapid growth in recent years, in many respects the field of forensic neuropsychology is still in its infancy. Numerous opportunities remain for neuropsychologists who wish to include some form of forensic work in their scope of practice. A good deal more research needs to be done in specific areas of interest to forensic neuropsychologists, such as malingering, mild TBI and toxic exposure. In addition, despite the proliferation of tests in recent years, there remains a need for the development of a state of the art, psychometrically sophisticated, comprehensive test battery that will permit neuropsychologists to be optimally rigorous and scientific in their work. The forensic role of neuropsychology, along with many other disciplines, is still being clarified by the courts. The full implications of the Daubert decision are not yet clear, but it would seem that the utility of neuropsychological testimony is sufficiently established in the forensic arena that its complete exclusion is highly unlikely. Regardless of whether neuropsychological testimony is ultimately defined as scientific knowledge or as some form of technical knowledge, it is incumbent on neuropsychologists to demonstrate that forensic neuropsychology is conducted in a rigorous, unbiased, professional manner so that opinions and conclusions can truly be offered with a reasonable degree of neuropsychological probability.

9.   REFERENCES

Allen, L., & Green, P. (1999). *CARB and WMT effort scores in 57 patients with severe traumatic brain injury.* Poster presented at the annual meeting of the National Academy of Neuropsychology, San Antonio, TX.

Alexander, M.P. (1995). Mild traumatic brain injury: Pathophysiology, natural history, and clinical management. *Neurology, 45,* 1253-1260.

Alexander, M.P. (1997). Minor traumatic brain injury: A review of physiogenesis and psychogenesis. *Seminars in Clinical Neuropsychiatry, 2,* 177-187.

American Medical Association (2001). *Guides to the evaluation of permanent impairment* (5th ed.). Chicago: Author.

American Medical Association (1999). International classification of diseases, 9th rev., clinical modification. Chicago: Author.

American Psychiatric Association (1994). *Diagnostic and statistical manual of mental disorders* (4th ed.). Washington, DC: Author.

Axelrod, B.N., Vanderploeg, R.D., & Schinka, J.A. (1999). Comparing methods for estimating premorbid intellectual functioning. *Archives of Clinical Neuropsychology, 14,* 341-346.

Berent, S. & Swartz, C.L. (1999). Essential psychometrics. In J.J. Sweet (Ed.), *Forensic neuropsychology: Fundamentals and practice* (pp. 1-26). Lisse, The Netherlands: Swets & Zeitlinger.

Berry, D.T.R., Wetter, M.W., Baer, R.A., Youngjohn, J.R., Gass, C.S., Lamb, D.G., Franzen, M.D., MacInnes, W.D., & Buchholz, D. (1995). Overreporting of closed-head injury symptoms on the MMPI-2. *Psychological Assessment, 7,* 517-523.

Bieliauskas, L. (1999). The measurement of personality and emotional functioning. In J.J. Sweet (Ed.), *Forensic neuropsychology: Fundamentals and practice* (pp. 121-143). Lisse, The Netherlands: Swets & Zeitlinger.

Binder, L.M. & Willis, S.C. (1991). Assessment of motivation after financially compensable minor head injury. *Psychological Assessment, 3,* 175-181.

Binder, L.M. (1993). Assessment of malingering after mild head trauma with the Portland Digit Recognition Test. *Journal of Clinical and Experimental Neuropsychology, 15,* 170-182.

Binder, L.M., & Rohling, M.L. (1996). Money matters: A meta-analytic review of the effects of financial incentives on recovery after closed-head injury. *American Journal of Psychiatry, 153,* 7-10.

Binder, L.M. (1997). A review of mild head trauma. Part II: Clinical implications. *Journal of Clinical and Experimental Neuropsychology, 19,* 432-457.

Binder, L.M., Rohling, M.L., & Larrabee, G.J. (1997). A review of mild head trauma. Part I: Meta-analytic review of neuropsychological studies. *Journal of Clinical and Experimental Neuropsychology, 19,* 421-431.

Blair, J.R., & Spreen, O. (1989). Predicting premorbid IQ: A revision of the National Adult Reading Test. *The Clinical Neuropsychologist, 3,* 129-136.

Boone, K.B., & Lu, P.H. (1999). Impact of somatoform symptomatology on credibility of cognitive performance. *The Clinical Neuropsychologist, 13,* 414-419.

Brandt, J. (1988). Malingered amnesia. In R. Rogers (Ed.), *Clinical assessment of malingering and deception* (pp.65-83). New York: Guilford Press.

Butcher, J.N., Dahlstrom, W.G., Graham, J.R., Tellegen, A. & Kaemmer, B. (1989). *Manual for administration and scoring the Minnesota Multiphasic Personality Inventory - 2.* Minneapolis: University of Minnesota Press.

Chapple v. Ganger. 851 F.Supp. 1481 (E.D. Wash, 1994).

Conder, R., Allen, L., & Cox, D. (1992). *Computerized Assessment of Response Bias test manual.* Durham, NC: CogniSyst.

Cripe, L.I. (1999). The use of the MMPI with closed head injury. In N.R. Varney & R.J. Roberts (Eds.), *The evaluation and treatment of mild traumatic brain injury.* Mahwah, NJ: Lawrence Erlbaum Associates.

Cullum, C.M., Heaton, R.K., & Grant, I. (1991). Psychogenic factors influencing neuropsychological performance: Somatoform disorders, factitious disorders and malingering. In H.O. Doerr & A.S. Carlin (Eds.), *Forensic neuropsychology: Legal and scientific bases.* New York: Guilford.

Daubert v. Merrell Dow Pharmaceuticals, Inc. 113 S.Ct. 2786 (1993).

Dikmen, S.S., McLean, A., & Temkin, N. (1986). Neuropsychological and psychosocial consequences of mild head injury. *Journal of Neurology, Neurosurgery, and Psychiatry, 49,* 1227-1232.

Dikmen, S.S., & Levin, H.S. (1993). Methodological issues in the study of mild head injury. *Journal of Head Trauma Rehabilitation, 8*(3), 30-37.

Dikmen, S.S., Machamer, J.E., Winn, H.R., & Temkin, N.R. (1995). Neuropsychological outcome at 1-year post head injury. *Neuropsychology, 9,* 80-90.

Erlanger, D.M., Kutner, K.C., Barth, J.T., & Barnes, R. (1999). Neuropsychology of sports-related head injury: Dementia pugilistica to post concussion syndrome. *The Clinical Neuropsychologist, 13,* 193-209.

Faust, D., Ziskin, J., & Hiers, J.B. (1991). *Brain damage claims: Coping with neuropsychological evidence.* Los Angeles: Law and Psychology Press.

Ford, C.V. (1995). Conversion disorder and somatoform disorder not otherwise specifed. In G.O. Gabbard (Ed.), *Treatments of psychiatric disorders* (2nd ed., Vol. 2, pp. 1735-1753). Washington, DC: American Psychiatric Press.

Frederick, R.I. (1997). *Validity Indicator Profile: Manual.* Minnetonka: NCS Assessments.

Gasquoine, P.G. (1997). Postconcussion symptoms. *Neuropsychology Review, 7,* 77-85.

General Electric Co. v. Joiner. 117 S. Ct. 1243 (1997).

Gennarelli, T.A., & Graham, D.I. (1998). Neuropathology of the head injuries. *Seminars in Clinical Neuropsychiatry, 3,* 160-175.

Gervais, R., Green, P., & Allen, L. (1999). *Differential sensitivity to symptom exaggeration of verbal, visual, and numerical symptom validity tests.* Poster presented at the annual meeting of the National Academy of Neuropsychology, San Antonio, TX.

Glass, L.S. (1991). The legal base in forensic neuropsychology. In H.O. Doerr & A.S. Carlin(Eds.), *Forensic neuropsychology: legal and scientific bases.* New York: Guilford.

Gouvier, W., Uddo-Crane, M., & Brown, L. (1988). Base rates of post-concussional symptoms. *Archives of Clinical Neuropsychology, 3,* 273-278.

Gouvier, W.D. (1999). Base rates and clinical decision making in neuropsychology. In J.J. Sweet (Ed.), *Forensic neuropsychology: Fundamentals and practice* (pp. 27-37). Lisse, The Netherlands: Swets & Zeitlinger.

Green, W.P., Allen, L.M., & Astner, K. (1996). *The Word Memory Test: A user's guide to the oral and computer-administered forms.* Durham, NC: CogniSyst.

Griffenstein, M.F., Baker, W.J., & Gola, T. (1994). Validation of malingered amnesia measures with a large clinical sample. *Psychological Assessment, 6,* 218-224.

Guilmette, T.J., Hart, K.J., & Giuliano, A.J. (1993). Malingering detection: The use of a forced-choice method in identifying organic versus simulated memory impairment. *The Clinical Neuropsychologist, 7*, 59-69.

Hartman, D.E. (1999). Neuropsychology and the (neuro)toxic tort. In J.J. Sweet (Ed.), *Forensic neuropsychology: Fundamentals and practice* (pp. 339-367). Lisse, The Netherlands: Swets & Zeitlinger.

Hathaway, S.R., & McKinley, J.C. (1951). *The Minnesota Multiphasic Personality Inventory manual*. New York: Psychological Corporation.

Heaton, R., Grant, I., & Matthews, C. (1991). Comprehensive norms for an expanded Halstead-Reitan battery. Odessa, FL: Psychological Assessment Resources.

Heilbrun, K. (1992). The role of psychological testing in forensic assessment. *Law and Human Behavior, 16*, 257-272.

Hoffman, R.G., Scott, J.G., Emick, M.A., & Adams, R.L. (1999). The MMPI-2 and closed-head injury: Effects of litigation and head injury severity. *Journal of Forensic Neuropsychology, 1*(2), 3-13.

Iverson, G.L., & Binder, L.M. (2000). Detecting exaggeration and malingering in neuropsychological assessment. *Journal of Head Trauma Rehabilitation, 15*, 829-858.

Kathol, R. (1996). Unexplained neurologic complaints. In M. Rizzo & D. Tranel (Eds.), *Head injury and postconcussive syndrome* (pp. 321-332). New York: Churchill Livingstone.

Kibby, M., & Long, C.J. (1999). Effective treatment of mild traumatic brain injury and understanding its neurological consequences. In M.J. Raymond, T.L. Bennett, L.C. Hartlage, & C.M. Cullum (Eds.), *Mild traumatic brain injury: A clinician's guide*. Austin, TX: Pro-Ed.

Kraus, J.F., & Nourjah, P. (1989). The epidemiology of mild head injury. In H.S. Levin, H.M. Eisenberg, & A.L. Benton (Eds.), *Mild head injury* (pp. 8-22).

Kumho Tire Co. v. Carmichael. 119 S. Ct. 1167 (1999).

Laing, L.C., & Fisher, J.M. (1997). Neuropsychology in civil proceedings. In R.J. McCaffrey, A.D. Williams, J.M Fisher, & L.C. Laing (Eds.), *The practice of forensic neuropsychology: Meeting challenges in the courtroom* (pp. 117-133). New York: Plenum Press.

Larrabee, G. (1997). Neuropsychological outcome, post concussion symptoms, and forensic considerations in mild closed head trauma. *Seminars in Clinical Neuropsychiatry, 2*, 196-206.

Larrabee, G. (2000). Forensic neuropsychological assessment. In R.D. Vanderploeg (Ed.), *Clinician's guide to neuropsychological assessment* (2nd ed.). Mahwah, NJ: Lawrence Erlbaum Associates.

Lees-Haley, P.R., English, L.T., & Glenn, W.J. (1991). A fake bad scale on the MMPI-2 for personal injury claimants. *Psychological Reports, 68*, 203-210.

Lees-Haley, P.R., & Brown, R.S. (1993). Neuropsychological complaint base rates of 170 personal injury claimants. *Archives of Clinical Neuropsychology, 8*, 203-209.

Lees-Haley, P.R., & Dunn, J.T. (1996). Forensic issues in the neuropsychological assessment of patients with postconcussive syndrome. In M. Rizzo & D. Tranel (Eds.), *Head injury and postconcussive syndrome* (pp.481-498). New York: Churchill Livingstone.

Levin, H., Mattis, S., Ruff, R., Eisenberg, H., Marshall, L., Tabaddor, K., High, W., & Frankowski, R., (1987). Neurobehavioral outcome following minor head injury: A three-center study. *Journal of Neurosurgery, 66*, 234-243.

Lezak, M.D. (1995). *Neuropsychological assessment* (3rd ed.). New York: Oxford University Press.

Martell, D.A. (1992). Forensic neuropsychology and the criminal law. *Law and human behavior*, 16, 313-336.

Martin, R.C., Bolter, J.F., Todd, M.E., Gouvier, W.D., & Niccolls, R. (1993). Effects of sophistication and motivation on the detection of malingered memory performance using a computerized forced-choice task. *Journal of Clinical and Experimental Neuropsychology*, 15, 867-880.

Merskey, H. (1995). *The analysis of hysteria: Understanding conversion and dissociation* (2nd ed.). London: Gaskell.

Mild Traumatic Brain Injury Committee of the Head Injury Interdisciplinary Special Interest Group of the American Congress of Rehabilitation Medicine. (1993). Definition of mild traumatic brain injury. *Journal of Head Trauma Rehabilitation, 8*, 86-87.

Millis, S.R., Putnam, S.H., Adams, K.M., & Ricker, J.H. (1995). The California Verbal Learning Test in the detection of incomplete effort in neuropsychological evaluation. *Psychological Assessment*, 7, 463-471.

Millis, S.R. & Putnam, S.H. (1996). Detection of malingering in postconcussive syndrome. In M. Rizzo & D. Tranel (Eds.), *Head injury and postconcussive syndrome* (pp.481-498). New York: Churchill Livingstone.

Mittenberg, W., Azrin, R., Millsaps, C., & Heilbronner, R. (1993). Identification of malingered head injury on the Wechsler Memory Scale - Revised. *Psychological Assessment, 5*, 34-40.

Mittenberg, W., & Strauman, S. (2000). Diagnosis of mild head injury and the postconcussion syndrome. *Journal of Head Trauma Rehabilitation, 15*, 783-791.

Povlishock, J. (1993). Pathobiology of traumatically induced axonal injury in animals and man. *Annals of Emergency Medicine, 22*, 41-47.

Putnam, S.H., & DeLuca, J.W. (1990). The TCN professional practice survey: Part 1: General practices of neuropsychologists in primary employment and private practice settings. *The Clinical Neuropsychologist, 4*, 199-243.

Putnam, S.H., & Millis, S.R. (1994). Psychosocial factors in the development and maintenance of chronic somatic and functional symptoms following mild traumatic brain injury. *Advances in Medical Psychotherapy, 7*, 1-22.

Putnam, S.H., Ricker, J.H., Ross, S.R., & Kurtz, J.E. (1999). Considering premorbid functioning: Beyond cognition to a conceptualization of personality in postinjury functioning. In J.J. Sweet (Ed.), *Forensic neuropsychology: Fundamentals and practice* (pp. 83-119). Lisse, The Netherlands: Swets & Zeitlinger.

Rankin, E.J., & Adams, R.L. (1999). The neuropsychological evaluation: Clinical and scientific foundations. In J.J. Sweet (Ed.), *Forensic neuropsychology: Fundamentals and practice* (pp. 83-119). Lisse, The Netherlands: Swets & Zeitlinger.

Reed, J. (1996). Fixed vs. flexible neuropsychological test batteries under the Daubert standard for the admissibility of scientific evidence. *Behavioral Sciences and the Law, 14*, 315-322.

Reed, J. (1999). Current status of the admissibility of expert testimony after Daubert and Joiner. *Journal of Forensic Neuropsychology, 1*(1), 49-71.

Rehkopf, D.G., & Fisher, J.M. (1997). Neuropsychology in criminal proceedings. In R.J. McCaffrey, A.D. Williams, J.M Fisher, & L.C. Laing (Eds.), *The practice of forensic neuropsychology: Meeting challenges in the courtroom* (pp. 135-151). New York: Plenum Press.

Reitan, R., & Wolfson, D. (1997a). Emotional disturbances and their interaction with neuropsychological deficits. *Neuropsychology Review, 7*, 3-19.

Reitan, R., & Wolfson, D. (1997b). Consistency of neuropsychological test scores of head-injured subjects involved in litigation compared with head-injured subjects not involved in litigation: Development of the Retest Consistency Index. *The Clinical Neuropsychologist*, 11, 69-76.

Rizzo, M. & Tranel, D. (1996). Overview of head injury and postconcussive syndrome. In M. Rizzo & D.Tranel (Eds.), *Head injury and postconcussive syndrome* (pp.1-18). New York: Churchill Livingstone.

Ruff, R.M., & Richardson, A.M. (1999). Mild traumatic brain injury. In J.J. Sweet (Ed.), *Forensic neuropsychology: Fundamentals and practice* (pp. 313-338). Lisse, The Netherlands: Swets & Zeitlinger.

Satz, P., Alfano, M.S., Light, R., Morgenstern, H., Zaucha, K., Asarnow, R.F., & Newton, S. (1999). Persistent post-concussive syndrome: A proposed methodology and literature review to determine the effects, if any, of mild head and other bodily injury. *Journal of Clinical and Experimental Neuropsychology, 21*, 620-628.

Seashore, C.E., Lewis, D. & Saetveit, D.L. (1960). *Seashore measures of musical talent* (rev. ed.). New York: The Psychological Corporation.

Slick, D., Hopp, G., Strauss, E., & Thompson, G. (1997). *Victoria Symptom Validity Test*. Odessa, FL: Psychological Assessment Resources.

Slick, D.J., Sherman, E.M.S., & Iverson, G.L. (1999). Diagnostic criteria for malingered neurocognitive dysfunction: Proposed standards for clinical practice and research. *The Clinical Neuropsychological, 13*, 545-561.

Sosin, D.M., Sniezek, J.E., & Thurman, D.J. (1996). Incidence of mild and moderate brain injury in the United States, 1991. *Brain Injury, 10*, 47-54.

Taylor, A.E., Cox, C.A., & Mailis, A. (1996). Persistent neuropsychological deficits following whiplash: Evidence for chronic mild traumatic brain injury? *Archives of Physical Medicine and Rehabilitation, 77*, 529-535.

Taylor, J.S. (1999). The legal environment pertaining to clinical neuropsychology. In J.J. Sweet (Ed.), *Forensic neuropsychology: Fundamentals and practice* (pp. 419-442). Lisse, The Netherlands: Swets & Zeitlinger.

Teasdale, G., & Jennett, B. (1974). Assessment of coma and impaired consciousness: A practical scale. *Lancet, 2*, 81-83.

Thorne, F.C. (1947). The clinical method in science. *American Psychologist, 2*, 159-166.

Tombaugh, T. (1996). *Test of Memory Malingering*. North Tonawanda, NY: Multi-Health Systems.

Torner, J.C., & Schootman, M. (1996). Epidemiology of closed head injury. In M. Rizzo & D. Tranel (Eds.), *Head injury and postconcussive syndrome* (pp. 19-46). New York: Churchill Livingstone.

Tsushima, W.T. (1996). MMPI measures of malingering and neuropsychological test performance among head injury patients. *The Forensic Examiner, 5*(5&6), 34-35.

Tsushima, W.T., & Tsushima, V.G. (2001). Comparison of the Fake Bad Scale and other MMPI-2 validity scales with personal injury litigants. *Assessment, 8*, 205-212.

Warrington, E.K. (1984). *Recognition Memory Test: Manual*. Windsor, U.K.: NFER-Nelson.

Weintraub, M.I. (1996). Chronic pain, soft-tissue injury, and litigation law. In M. Rizzo & D. Tranel (Eds.), *Head injury and postconcussive syndrome* (pp. 499-506). New York: Churchill Livingstone.

Williams, A.D. (1997a). Fixed versus flexible batteries. In R.J. McCaffrey, A.D. Williams, J.M Fisher, & L.C. Laing (Eds.), *The practice of forensic neuropsychology: Meeting challenges in the courtroom* (pp. 57-70). New York: Plenum Press.

Williams, A.D. (1997b). Special issues in the evaluation of mild traumatic brain injury. In R.J. McCaffrey, A.D. Williams, J.M Fisher, & L.C. Laing (Eds.), *The practice of forensic neuropsychology: Meeting challenges in the courtroom* (pp. 71-89). New York: Plenum Press.

Williams, J.M. (1998). The malingering of memory disorder. In C.R. Reynolds (Ed.), *Detection of malingering during head injury litigation.* New York: Plenum.

World Health Organization (1992). *International statistical classification of diseases and related health problems* (10th ed.). Geneva, Switzerland: Author.

Wrightson, P., & Gronwall, D. (1999). *Mild head injury: A guide to management.* New York: Oxford University Press.

Youngjohn, J.R. (1995). Confirmed attorney coaching prior to neuropsychological evaluation. *Assessment, 2,* 279-283.

Youngjohn, J.R., Burrows, L. & Erdal, K. (1995). Brain damage or compensation neurosis? The controversial post-concussion syndrome. *The Clinical Neuropsychologist, 9,* 112-123.

Youngjohn, J.R., Davis, D., & Wolf, I. (1997). Head injury and the MMPI-2: Paradoxical severity effects and the influence of litigation. *Psychological Assessment, 9,* 177-184.

Zakzanis, K.K., Leach, L., & Kaplan, E. (1999). *Neuropsychological differential diagnosis.* Lisse, The Netherlands: Swets & Zeitlinger.

Index